simple, delicious recipes for a long, healthy life

eat to beat
high blood pressure

lower your blood pressure 10% or more without drugs!
featuring the **DASH-Plus Plan**

edited by
ROBYN WEBB, M.S. and **JAMY D. ARD, M.D.**

Reader's Digest

The Reader's Digest Association, Inc.
New York, New York • Montreal

PROJECT STAFF

Recipe Editor	Robyn Webb, M.S.
Writer	Debra L. Gordon
Medical Advisor	Jamy D. Ard, M.D.
Nutrition Analyst	William Demott
Editor	Neil Wertheimer
Copy Editors	Jeanette Gingold and Jane Sherman
Indexer	Nanette Bendyna
Cover Photography	David Bishop
Book Design	Amy Tromat Elizabeth Tunnicliffe Michele Laseau
Cover Design	George McKeon
Page Layout	Leslie Ann Caraballo

READER'S DIGEST HEALTH PUBLISHING

Editor in Chief and Publishing Director	Neil Wertheimer
Managing Editor	Suzanne G. Beason
Art Director	Michele Laseau
Production Technology Manager	Douglas A. Croll
Manufacturing Manager	John L. Cassidy
Marketing Director	Dawn Nelson
Vice President and General Manager	Keira Krausz

READER'S DIGEST ASSOCIATION, INC.

President, North America Global Editor-in-Chief	Eric W. Schrier

Photographers
Sang An, Sue Atkinson, Martin Brigdale, Beatriz DaCosta, Mark Ferri, Gus Filgate, Michael Grand, Amanda Heywood, Martin Jacobs, Graham Kirk, Lisa Koening, William Lingwood, David Murray, Sean Myers, Simon Smith, Jules Selmes, Elizabeth Watt

Additional images courtesy of Photodisc

The recipes in *Eat to Beat High Blood Pressure* were adapted from the Reader's Digest *Eat Well, Live Well* and *Cooking Smart for a Healthy Heart* series and *Vegetables for Vitality*.

First printing in paperback 2008

Copyright © 2004 The Reader's Digest Association, Inc.

Reader's Digest and the Pegasus logo are registered trademarks of The Reader's Digest Association, Inc.

Library of Congress Cataloging-in-Publication Data
Eat to beat high blood pressure / edited by Robyn Webb.
     p. cm.
   Includes index.
   ISBN 0-7621-0508-9 (hardcover)
   ISBN 978-7621-0898-5 (paperback)
   1. Hypertension—Diet therapy—Popular works. 2. Hypertension—Diet therapy—Recipes—Popular works. 3. Hypertension—Nutritional aspects—Popular works. I. Webb, Robin.
   RC685.H8E28 2004
   616.1'320654—dc22

          2004003556

We are committed to both the quality of our products and the service we provide to our customers. We value your comments, so please feel free to contact us.
   The Reader's Digest Association, Inc.
   Adult Trade Publishing
   44 S. Broadway
   White Plains, NY 10601

For more Reader's Digest products and information, visit our website:
www. rd.com (in the United States)
www. readersdigest.ca (in Canada)

Printed in the United States of America

1 3 5 7 9 10 8 6 4 2 (hardcover)
5 7 9 10 8 6 (paperback)

Note to Readers
The information in this book should not be substituted for, or used to alter, any medical treatment or therapy without your doctor's advice.

Introduction

Working on *Eat to Beat High Blood Pressure* caused some dizziness among us editors and designers. One moment we'd be lost in scrumptious food photos and recipes, all abuzz about the success of one of the dishes we made the previous night. The next moment we'd be arguing about the healing potential of potassium, searching the Internet for the latest study results. That is the challenge—and pleasure—of putting together a cookbook with two goals: to offer the most wonderful meals possible, and to provide a plan to defeat one of the most serious health concerns of our times.

We hope you agree that we have delivered on both. The recipes in *Eat to Beat High Blood Pressure* were chosen for their taste, easiness, and accessible ingredients. We bypassed the esoteric and exotic recipes, but we didn't hold back on creativity. Thumb through the pages and we are certain your mouth will water at what you see. This is great everyday food—popular dishes with a fresh twist, fun and easy to prepare, and oh-so-delicious. Even if you completely ignore the health parts of the book, we're certain you will still find this one of the freshest and most useful cookbooks in your kitchen!

But as much as we love great food, we are passionate about health too. And in that regard, we believe we have put together the most powerful, all-natural plan for beating high blood pressure yet to be created. Thanks to Dr. Jamy Ard, our extraordinary medical advisor, we have taken the gold standard eating plan—DASH, or Dietary Approaches to Stop Hypertension—and made it platinum by expanding it to include a lifestyle program that factors in many other daily actions that research has proven can significantly reduce blood pressure.

Based on the science now available, it is fair to assume you will cut your blood pressure by 10 percent—and quickly—by following our DASH-Plus Plan. But that's not all. People who follow the tenets of the DASH-Plus Plan have achieved not only significantly lower blood pressure, but lower weight, lower cholesterol, and greater energy as well. And imagine the improvement in your attitude when you achieve such important health goals!

High blood pressure has become a major threat to America's health. But unlike other serious diseases, it is mostly caused—and controlled—through diet and basic life choices. With *Eat to Beat High Blood Pressure*, we've tried to make the right choices as easy and delectable to make as possible. Try these recipes, follow the DASH-Plus Plan, and you, too, can join the ranks of those who have beaten the silent but deadly disease of high blood pressure. And what a pleasure it will have been!

Neil Wertheimer

EDITOR IN CHIEF, HOME & HEALTH BOOKS, READER'S DIGEST

contents

the recipes

THE RECIPES

THE RECIPES

the Recipes

It's good-eating time!

In front of you are hundreds of recipes that feature fresh ingredients and wonderful flavors, and that are easy and fun to prepare. Just as importantly, each recipe is filled with good health, and in particular, nutrients that are of greatest importance to healthy blood pressure.

So cook well, eat well, and be well.

breakfast

High-Vitality Milk Shake

This satisfying "breakfast in a glass" makes a great energizing start to the day. It is ideal for people in a hurry or those who aren't keen on eating in the morning.

Preparation time **5 minutes**   *Serves 2*

1 1/2 cups fat-free milk, chilled
1 cup plain nonfat yogurt
Juice of 1 large orange
1 large banana, sliced
1 teaspoon honey
1 tablespoon wheat germ

1 Place all the ingredients in a blender or food processor and process for a couple of minutes until smooth and creamy.

2 Pour into 2 tall glasses and enjoy immediately, while the milk shake is still frothy.

(Some More Ideas)

Berry shake: Use 1/2 cup strawberries instead of banana. Raspberries are good too, or try the chopped flesh of 1 mango.

• Replace the wheat germ with 1 tablespoon ground sunflower seeds (grind them in a coffee grinder or with a pestle and mortar).

• Use nonfat vanilla frozen yogurt instead of plain yogurt.

Health Points

• The addition of wheat germ boosts the content of vitamin E and B vitamins in this recipe, and orange juice provides vitamin C, so this is truly a "high vitality" drink.

Each serving provides

Key Nutrients 220 Calories, 10 Calories from Fat, 1g Fat, 0g Saturated Fat, 0g Trans Fat, 13g Protein, 44g Carb, 29g Fiber, 160mg Sodium
Blood Pressure Nutrients 36mg Vitamin C, 53mg Magnesium, 694mg Potassium, 386mg Calcium

Banana and Apricot Smoothie

Milk shakes used to be dense in calories and low in nutrition. Today fruity smoothies have reinvented how we use the blender. "Shakes" are now fresher and lighter, made with fruit and yogurt, or fruit juice and milk, and bursting with nutrients.

Preparation time **10 minutes**   *Serves 4*

2 large bananas, thickly sliced
1 can (15 ounces) apricot halves in natural juice
1 cup plain low-fat yogurt
4 teaspoons chopped fresh mint
1 tablespoon honey
1 cup orange juice
Sprigs of fresh mint (*garnish*)

1 Put the bananas, apricots, and their juice, yogurt, mint, and honey into a food processor or blender and blend to a smooth puree, scraping down the sides of the container once or twice. If you like your smoothies cold, add a few ice cubes to the mix. The blending will take longer as the blades pulverize the ice. Add the orange juice and blend briefly until mixed.

2 Pour the smoothie into tall glasses and decorate with sprigs of mint. Serve immediately.

(Some More Ideas)

Strawberry and banana smoothie: Instead of apricots use 8 ounces strawberries. Reserve 4 strawberries and blend the remainder with the bananas and yogurt (there is no need to add honey or mint). Mix in apple juice in place of the orange juice. Stir in the grated zest and juice of 1 lime. Pour into glasses and decorate each one with a reserved strawberry skewered on a cocktail stick and placed across the top of the glass.

Peach and cinnamon smoothie: Blend 1 can (15 ounces) peaches in natural juice, with 1 tablespoon sugar, 1/4 teaspoon ground cinnamon, and the bananas and yogurt. Add fat-free milk in place of the orange juice. Sprinkle each glass with a little extra cinnamon.

Health Points

• These drinks are completely additive-free, unlike their commercial versions.

Each serving provides

Key Nutrients 180 Calories, 15 Calories from Fat, 2g Fat, 1g Saturated Fat, 0g Trans Fat, 5g Protein, 39g Carb, 3g Fiber, 45mg Sodium
Blood Pressure Nutrients 10mg Vitamin C, 38mg Magnesium, 623mg Potassium, 126mg Calcium

Banana and Mango Shake

A thick banana-flavored milk shake with a tropical touch, this will certainly appeal to children and adults alike. It is filling, nourishing, and quick—as appropriate for dessert as it is for breakfast.

Preparation time **5 minutes**   *Serves 2*

1/2 ripe mango
1 small ripe banana, sliced
1/2 cup fat-free milk
1/2 cup orange juice
2 teaspoons lime juice
1 teaspoon sugar
2 heaping tablespoons vanilla frozen yogurt
Sprigs of mint *(garnish)*

1 Peel the skin from the mango and cut the flesh away from the pit. Chop the flesh roughly. Put into a blender with the banana.

2 Add the milk, orange juice, lime juice, sugar, and frozen yogurt and blend on maximum speed until mixed and frothy, about 30 seconds.

3 Pour into glasses and serve immediately, decorated with sprigs of mint.

(Some More Ideas)

• Use soy milk for the cow's milk, and omit the frozen yogurt or use soy ice cream.

• Use a ripe peach instead of the mango half.

• For a shake rich in fiber, use 4 ounces pitted prunes instead of the mango, and lemon juice instead of lime juice.

Health Points

• Milk is an excellent source of several important nutrients— protein, calcium, and phosphorus (important for strong bones and teeth), and many of the B vitamins, particularly B1, B2, B6, and B12.

• Bananas are a good source of potassium, which helps regulate blood pressure as well as being vital for muscle and nerve function. They are also naturally sweet.

• Mangoes are rich in carotenoid compounds and vitamin C, both antioxidants that protect the body against damage by free radicals.

Each serving provides

Key Nutrients 70 Calories, 0 Calories from Fat, 0g Fat, 0g Saturated Fat, 0g Trans Fat, 2g Protein, 16g Carb, 1g Fiber, 20mg Sodium
Blood Pressure Nutrients 5mg Vitamin C, 14mg Magnesium, 185mg Potassium, 62mg Calcium

Strawberry-Yogurt Smoothie

This refreshing drink is perfect for summer, when strawberries are plentiful and full of flavor and vitamins. It takes only a few minutes to prepare, so it is ideal as a nourishing start to the day or as a snack-in-a-glass at any time.

Preparation time **5 minutes**   *Serves 4*

1 pound ripe strawberries, hulled

Grated zest and juice of 1 large orange

1 cup plain low-fat yogurt

1 tablespoon sugar, or to taste (optional)

4 small strawberries (garnish)

4 small slices of orange (garnish)

1 Add the strawberries to a food processor or blender and add the grated orange zest, orange juice, and yogurt. Blend to a smooth puree, scraping down the sides of the container once or twice. Taste the mixture and sweeten with the sugar, if necessary.

2 For a really smooth consistency, press through a sieve to remove the strawberry seeds.

3 Pour into glasses. Garnish with small strawberries and slices of orange, both split so they sit on the rim of the glass.

(Some More Ideas)

Apricot-yogurt smoothie:
Use dried apricots to make a smoothie with an extra charge of beta-carotene and fiber. Gently simmer 7 ounces dried apricots in 3 cups strained Earl Grey tea until tender, about 30 minutes. Cool and then pour the apricots and liquid into a blender. Add the orange zest, juice, and yogurt and blend until smooth. Taste and sweeten with sugar if required.

• Add a sliced banana to the strawberries. This will thicken the texture of the smoothie and will also add natural sweetness, so be sure to taste before adding sugar. You may not need any.

Health Points

• Strawberries contain higher levels of vitamin C than any other berries. And despite their sweetness, 4 ounces of strawberries contain less than 32 calories!

photo, page 15

Each serving provides

Key Nutrients 80 Calories, 15 Calories from Fat, 2g Fat, 1g Saturated Fat, 0g Trans Fat, 4g Protein, 15g Carb, 3g Fiber, 45mg Sodium
Blood Pressure Nutrients 78mg Vitamin C, 24mg Magnesium, 378mg Potassium, 133mg Calcium

Fruity Muesli

This breakfast cereal was invented over a century ago by Dr. Bircher-Benner at his clinic in Zurich to improve children's diet. Soaking the cereal, here using milk, makes it easier to eat and digest.

Preparation time **10 minutes, plus overnight soaking**   *Serves 4*

1 cup rolled oats
1/2 cup raisins
1 1/2 cups fat-free milk
1 apple
2 teaspoons lemon juice
1 ounce hazelnuts, roughly chopped
1/2 ounce pumpkin seeds
1 tablespoon sesame seeds
1/2 cup chopped strawberries
4 tablespoons plain nonfat yogurt
4 teaspoons honey

1 Place the oats and raisins in a large bowl and add the milk. Stir to mix evenly, then cover and place in the refrigerator. Leave to soak overnight.

2 The next day, just before eating, grate the apple, discarding the core. Toss the apple with the lemon juice to prevent browning.

3 Stir the hazelnuts, pumpkin seeds, and sesame seeds into the oat mixture, then stir in the grated apple and strawberries.

4 To serve, divide the muesli among 4 cereal bowls, and top each with a spoonful of yogurt and honey.

(Some More Ideas)

Mango muesli: Soak the rolled oats in 1 1/2 cups low-fat buttermilk. Just before eating, stir in 1/2 cup roughly chopped almonds and 1/3 cup sunflower seeds, then add 1 roughly mashed banana and 1 chopped mango. Serve topped with plain nonfat yogurt.

Health Points

• Hazelnuts are a particularly good source of vitamin E and most of the B vitamins, apart from B12. Like most other nuts, they have a high fat content; however, this is mostly the more beneficial monounsaturated fat.

• By making your own cereal, you know exactly what's in it and what's not! High levels of sodium, fat, and sugar are missing from this nutritious cereal recipe.

Each serving provides

Key Nutrients 330 Calories, 80 Calories from Fat, 9g Fat, 1g Saturated Fat, 0g Trans Fat, 11g Protein, 57g Carb, 7g Fiber, 65mg Sodium
Blood Pressure Nutrients 19mg Vitamin C, 54mg Magnesium, 577mg Potassium, 166mg Calcium

Fruity Muesli *p14*

Strawberry-Yogurt Smoothie *p13*

Sweet Couscous *p16*

Denver Omelet *p17*

Sweet Couscous

Couscous isn't just a dinner side dish. It can be used for both savory dishes and for sweet ones, such as this quickly made, delicious hot cereal that uses both dried and fresh fruit.

Preparation and cooking time **about 20 minutes**   *Serves 4*

Couscous

1 cup couscous

1/2 cup raisins

1/2 cup chopped, pitted prunes

Finely grated zest of 1 small orange

2 cups fat-free milk

To Serve

2 nectarines, sliced

8 tablespoons plain nonfat yogurt

1 Put the couscous in a bowl with the raisins, prunes, and orange zest, and stir to mix thoroughly.

2 Pour the milk into a saucepan and bring just to the boil. Pour the hot milk over the couscous mixture, stirring well, then cover with foil. Leave to soak for about 10 minutes or until the couscous is plumped up and all the milk has been absorbed.

3 Spoon the couscous into bowls and top with sliced nectarines and yogurt. Serve immediately.

(Some More Ideas)

• Instead of raisins and prunes, use other dried fruit such as dried pears or peaches.

• Use the finely grated zest of 1 small pink grapefruit or 1 lemon rather than orange zest.

Health Points

• Prunes, or dried plums, are a great source of fiber, vitamins, minerals, and phytochemicals. They are also known to have a laxative effect.

photo, page 15

Each serving provides

Key Nutrients 370 Calories, 10 Calories from Fat, 1g Fat, 0g Saturated Fat, 0g Trans Fat, 13g Protein, 80g Carb, 6g Fiber, 90mg Sodium
Blood Pressure Nutrients 10mg Vitamin C, 55mg Magnesium, 736mg Potassium, 225mg Calcium

Denver Omelet

Whip up an omelet the Denver way, but in a more healthful fashion. We use the same peppers and onions as in the original, but egg whites replace some of the whole eggs, and potatoes stand in for the ham.

Preparation time **10 minutes**   Cooking time **18 minutes**   *Serves 2*

1 medium red-skinned potato, chopped (about 3/4 cup)

1 medium onion, chopped

1/2 cup chopped green bell pepper

1/2 cup chopped red bell pepper

2 large eggs

3 large egg whites

1/2 teaspoon hot red pepper sauce

Salt to taste

2 slices whole-wheat bread, toasted

1 Preheat oven to 400°F. Coat 8-inch ovenproof nonstick skillet with nonstick cooking spray and set over medium heat. Sauté potato until soft, about 5 minutes.

2 Stir in onion and green and red peppers. Sauté until soft, about 5 minutes. Remove skillet from heat. Transfer vegetables to plate. Coat skillet again with cooking spray and return to heat.

3 Meanwhile, whisk eggs, egg whites, red pepper sauce, and salt in medium bowl. Pour into hot skillet. Cook until set on bottom, lifting up edge with heatproof rubber spatula to let uncooked portion flow underneath.

4 Spoon vegetables over half of omelet and fold omelet over filling. Transfer skillet to oven and bake until eggs are completely set, about 3 minutes. Cut omelet in half and serve with toast.

(Some More Ideas)

• Add 1/2 cup finely diced skinless, boneless chicken breast to the recipe. Sauté it along with the onions and peppers in Step 2.

• Make a puffy omelet. Whip the egg whites until stiff and fold them into the eggs and hot sauce in Step 3. The omelet will seem much bigger, but there is no change in calories!

Health Points

• This omelet is a wonderful way for you to get a serving of vegetables at breakfast. When part of a recipe, even finicky eaters get their healthy share of produce.

photo, page 15

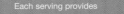
Each serving provides

Key Nutrients 290 Calories, 60 Calories from Fat, 7g Fat, 2g Saturated Fat, 0g Trans Fat, 18g Protein, 42g Carb, 6g Fiber, 340mg Sodium
Blood Pressure Nutrients 117mg Vitamin C, 72mg Magnesium, 884mg Potassium, 78mg Calcium

Mushroom and Herb Omelet

An omelet is the ultimate impromptu meal, prepared quickly and easily from a few simple ingredients. This classic version is made more delicious with garlicky mushrooms. Serve as a lunch or dinner with a green salad and warm, crusty bread.

Preparation time **5 minutes**   Cooking time **10 minutes**   *Serves 1*

2 large eggs
1 teaspoon chopped fresh chervil
1 teaspoon chopped fresh tarragon
1 teaspoon snipped fresh chives
1/4 cup sliced mushrooms
1 garlic clove, crushed
2 teaspoons unsalted butter
Salt and pepper to taste

1 Crack the eggs into a bowl, then add the chervil, tarragon, chives, 1 tablespoon water, and salt and pepper to taste. Beat just enough to break up the eggs. Take care not to over-beat, as this will spoil the texture of the omelet. Set aside while preparing the mushrooms.

2 Heat a 7-inch omelet or nonstick skillet. Add the sliced mushrooms and garlic, and cook gently until the mushrooms have softened and released their juices, 3–4 minutes. Turn up the heat a little and continue cooking until the mushroom juices have evaporated, about 1 minute. Tip the mushrooms into a small bowl and set aside. Wipe the pan clean with a paper towel.

3 Heat the pan over a high heat for a few seconds until hot. Add the butter and melt it, tilting the pan to coat the bottom. Pour in the egg and herb mixture. Cook for about 1 minute, stirring gently with a wooden spatula and pulling the cooked egg from the edge toward the center to let the liquid egg flow onto the pan.

4 When the omelet holds together, stop stirring and cook until the underside is golden brown, about 30 seconds. The top surface should be just setting.

5 Scatter the mushrooms along the middle third of the omelet. Using the spatula, fold an outside third of the omelet into the center, over the mushrooms, then fold the opposite third over that. Quickly slide the folded omelet onto a warmed plate and serve immediately.

(Some More Ideas)

Tomato and basil soufflé omelet: Separate the eggs and beat the yolks with 1 teaspoon water, 4 seeded and chopped plum tomatoes, 2 tablespoons torn fresh basil leaves, and salt and pepper to taste. Whisk the egg whites until stiff. Stir a spoonful into the egg yolk and tomato mixture, then carefully fold in the rest of the whites with a metal spoon. Preheat the grill to moderate. Melt 2 teaspoons butter in the omelet pan and pour in the egg and tomato mixture. Cook over a low heat until the underside of the omelet is lightly browned, 2–3 minutes. Place the pan under the grill and cook until the top is golden brown and puffed up, another 2–3 minutes. Carefully fold the omelet in half, then slide onto a warmed plate and serve immediately.

Health Points

• Chives are mild-flavored miniature versions of the onion, but only the green shoots are used in cooking. They are believed to stimulate the appetite.

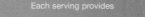
Each serving provides

Key Nutrients 200 Calories, 130 Calories from Fat, 14g Fat, 6g Saturated Fat, 0g Trans Fat, 14g Protein, 4g Carb, 0g Fiber, 130mg Sodium
Blood Pressure Nutrients 3mg Vitamin C, 19mg Magnesium, 278mg Potassium, 83mg Calcium

Mushroom and Herb Omelet *p18*

Potato, Corn, and Pepper Frittata *p20*

Zesty Cheddar-Asparagus Quiche *p21*

Breakfast Sausage Patties *p22*

Potato, Corn, and Pepper Frittata

Known in Italy as a frittata, or in Spain as a tortilla, a flat omelet can be served hot or at room temperature at any meal (including picnics). This delicious version can be kept for a day in the refrigerator before serving.

Preparation time **10 minutes**   Cooking time **about 20 minutes**   *Serves 4*

1 1/2 pounds potatoes, peeled, quartered lengthwise, and thinly sliced across

1 red, yellow, or orange bell pepper, seeded and chopped

2 tablespoons olive oil

1 onion, halved and thinly sliced

1 cup frozen corn, thawed

3 eggs

4 tablespoons finely chopped parsley

Salt and pepper to taste

1 Put the potatoes in a saucepan, cover with boiling water, and bring back to the boil. Reduce the heat, then add the chopped peppers and simmer until the potatoes are just starting to cook, about 3 minutes. Drain well, cover, and keep hot.

2 Heat a 10-inch nonstick frying pan over a high heat. Add the oil to the pan and swirl it around. When the oil is hot, reduce the heat to medium, add the onion, and sauté, stirring often, until softened, about 3 minutes.

3 Add the potatoes, chopped pepper, and sweet corn and continue sautéing, stirring and turning the vegetables, until the potatoes are tender, about 8 minutes. Remove from the heat.

4 In a large bowl, beat the eggs with the parsley and seasoning to taste. Use a slotted spoon to add the vegetables to the eggs, stirring them in thoroughly. (If any vegetables have stuck to the bottom of the pan, thoroughly clean and dry the pan before heating it with an additional 1 tablespoon oil; however, this should not be necessary with a reliable nonstick pan.)

5 Replace the skillet, with the oil remaining from cooking the vegetables, over a moderate heat. When the pan is hot, pour in the egg mixture, spreading out the vegetables evenly. Cook the omelet, shaking the pan frequently, until the edges are set and the top is beginning to look set, 3–4 minutes.

6 Meanwhile, preheat the grill to the hottest setting. Place the frittata under the grill until the eggs are just set, about 2 minutes. Pierce the top of the mixture with a knife to check that the omelet is cooked through.

7 Remove the pan from under the grill and leave the frittata to set for 2 minutes, then slide it onto a serving plate. Serve hot or at room temperature, cut into wedges.

(Some More Ideas)

Fennel and zucchini frittata: Replace the pepper, onion, and corn with 1 bulb of fennel, thinly sliced; 1/2 cup sliced mushrooms; and 1 zucchini, cut in half lengthwise and thinly sliced across. Sauté these vegetables in the hot oil for 3 minutes before adding the partly cooked potatoes.

Pepper and potato frittata: Take a tip from Spanish tapas bars and serve a frittata at room temperature, cut into bite-size pieces, as an alternative to salty or high-fat fried snacks with drinks.

• Use 3 peppers (any color) and 2 onions, and omit the corn.

Health Points

• Corn is a useful source of dietary fiber and vitamins A, C and folate. Although some vitamins are lost in canned corn, they are retained in the frozen vegetable.

• Potatoes and peppers contribute vitamin C to this dish.

photo, page 19

Each serving provides

Key Nutrients 190 Calories, 100 Calories from Fat, 11g Fat, 2g Saturated Fat, 0g Trans Fat, 7g Protein, 18g Carb, 3g Fiber, 190mg Sodium
Blood Pressure Nutrients 87mg Vitamin C, 24mg Magnesium, 281mg Potassium, 37mg Calcium

Zesty Cheddar-Asparagus Quiche

How do you get the rich taste of a classic quiche with a fraction of the fat? One technique: Make the crust with thinly sliced potatoes. It's a heart-smart substitute for traditional piecrust!

Preparation time **30 minutes**   Cooking time **45 minutes**   *Serves 6*

1 tablespoon plain dry bread crumbs

8 ounces small all-purpose potatoes, peeled and very thinly sliced

1 pound asparagus, trimmed

Salt to taste

3/4 cup shredded reduced-fat sharp cheddar cheese

3 scallions, sliced

1 can (12 ounces) evaporated fat-free milk

1/2 cup fat-free egg substitute

1 large egg

2 teaspoons margarine, melted

1 teaspoon dry mustard

1/4 teaspoon freshly ground black pepper

1 Preheat oven to 400°F. Coat 9-inch pie plate with nonstick cooking spray and sprinkle with bread crumbs. Beginning in center, arrange potato slices in slightly overlapping circles up to rim. Lightly coat with nonstick cooking spray and press down gently. Bake 10 minutes.

2 Set 8 to 12 asparagus spears aside. Cut remaining spears into 1-inch pieces.

3 Sprinkle crust with 1/4 teaspoon salt and 1/4 cup cheddar. Cover with asparagus pieces, then sprinkle with scallions and another 1/4 cup cheese. Arrange whole asparagus spears on top.

4 Beat evaporated milk, egg substitute, egg, margarine, mustard, pepper, and remaining salt in medium bowl. Pour into pie plate and sprinkle with remaining cheddar. Bake until knife inserted in center comes out clean, about 35 minutes.

(Some More Ideas)

• This versatile recipe tastes great with broccoli spears and chopped broccoli in place of the asparagus.

• You can change the cheese to low-fat Swiss or mozzarella.

Health Points

• Egg substitute is not an all-or-nothing ingredient. By combining it with the whole egg, you reduce the fat and cholesterol in the quiche, but retain the rich flavor and texture that only the egg yolks provide.

• One large egg has 6 grams of protein as well as riboflavin, vitamin E, folate, B vitamins, and iron.

photo, page 19

Each serving provides

Key Nutrients 240 Calories, 80 Calories from Fat, 9g Fat, 5g Saturated Fat, 0g Trans Fat, 17g Protein, 21g Carb, 2g Fiber, 390mg Sodium
Blood Pressure Nutrients 16mg Vitamin C, 28mg Magnesium, 699mg Potassium, 384mg Calcium

Breakfast Sausage Patties

For a satisfying Sunday breakfast, you can't beat savory homemade sausage. By making these patties with turkey breast and some secret ingredients, the fat content falls to just 1 gram a piece!

Preparation time **10 minutes**   Cooking time **6 minutes**   *Serves 12 (12 patties)*

1 pound skinless, boneless turkey breast

3/4 cup cooked brown or basmati rice

1/4 cup pureed prunes

1 tablespoon Dijon mustard

Salt to taste

1/2 teaspoon rubbed sage

1/2 teaspoon dried rosemary, minced

1 Cut turkey breast into large chunks. Place in food processor and pulse until coarsely ground.

2 Transfer ground turkey to medium bowl. Add rice, prune butter, mustard, salt, sage, and rosemary, and stir to just combine.

3 Shape mixture into twelve 2-inch patties. Spray a broiler pan with nonstick cooking spray. Preheat broiler.

4 Place patties on pan and broil 4 inches from heat, turning once, until cooked through, about 3 minutes per side.

(Some More Ideas)

• For easier mornings, make the sausage patties the night before. Store them on a platter covered with plastic wrap in the refrigerator. Add an extra 30 seconds or so per side to the cooking time to compensate for the fact that the meat is chilled.

• You can substitute ground white-meat chicken breast or lean ground pork for the turkey.

Health Points

• Pureed prunes, also known and sold as prune butter, are great for healthy cooking. They replace the fat in this recipe, and can also be used as a fat substitute in baking.

photo, page 19

Each serving (1 patty) provides

Key Nutrients 100 Calories, 5 Calories from Fat, 1g Fat, 0g Saturated Fat, 0g Trans Fat, 10g Protein, 12g Carb, 1g Fiber, 35mg Sodium
Blood Pressure Nutrients 0mg Vitamin C, 28mg Magnesium, 184mg Potassium, 11mg Calcium

Whole-Grain Pancakes with Fresh Fruit and Yogurt

Wheat germ, rolled oats, and whole-wheat flour make these delicious pancakes high in fiber as well as iron and B vitamins. Raspberries or blueberries bring vitamin C to the nutritional party.

Preparation time **10 minutes**   Cooking time **15 minutes**   *Makes 12 pancakes*

1 cup whole-wheat flour
1/4 cup rolled oats
1 tablespoon toasted wheat germ
2 tablespoons brown sugar
2 teaspoons baking powder
Salt to taste
1 cup 1% low-fat milk
1 1/4 cups plain nonfat yogurt
2 egg whites
2 cups raspberries or blueberries

1 In large bowl, mix flour, oats, wheat germ, sugar, baking powder, and salt. In another bowl, beat milk and 1/2 cup yogurt with egg whites. Add to flour mixture and stir quickly just to moisten dry ingredients.

2 Spray nonstick skillet with cooking spray and heat until hot. Do not use cooking spray near flame. Measure 1/4 cup of batter for each pancake and pour into hot skillet, making 3 or 4 pancakes at a time.

3 When bubbles show on top, lift pancakes with a spatula. If browned underneath, turn over and cook until other side is golden brown.

4 Transfer pancakes to heated platter. Serve with raspberries and remaining yogurt. If not serving at once, cover and keep warm in low oven.

(Some More Ideas)

• Try buckwheat flour for a nutty flavor in place of whole-wheat flour.

• For a corn flavor, use 1/3 cup cornmeal in place of some of the whole-wheat flour.

Health Points

• Buttermilk and yogurt replace vegetable oil or butter in these pancakes, making them significantly lower in fat.

• Keeping pancakes in the freezer allows for a nice, healthy change from morning cereal.

Each serving provides

Key Nutrients 160 Calories, 10 Calories from Fat, 2g Fat, 0g Saturated Fat, 0g Trans Fat, 8g Protein, 34g Carb, 6g Fiber, 200mg Sodium
Blood Pressure Nutrients 14mg Vitamin C, 46mg Magnesium, 264mg Potassium, 214mg Calcium

Pecan Waffles with Maple, Pear, and Blackberry Sauce

Crisp, crunchy waffles are as popular around the world come Sunday morning as they are in Iowa, Arkansas, or Oregon. This version sounds fancy, but it's actually quite simple and delicious.

Preparation time **20 minutes**   Cooking time **10–15 minutes**   *Makes 4 waffles*

Waffles
2/3 cup flour
1/2 teaspoon ground cinnamon
1 teaspoon baking powder
1 tablespoon sugar
1 large egg, separated
1 cup fat-free milk
2 tablespoons margarine, melted
1/2 ounce pecans, finely chopped

Sauce
1 large, ripe dessert pear
4 tablespoons maple syrup
2 ounces pecan nut halves
1/2 cup blackberries

1 First make the maple and fruit sauce. Cut the pear lengthwise into quarters and cut out the core, then cut the pear into fine dice. Put into a small heavy saucepan and add the maple syrup. Warm gently, then remove the pan from the heat. Stir in the pecan nut halves and the blackberries. Set aside while making the waffles.

2 Heat and lightly grease the waffle iron or maker according to the manufacturer's instructions.

3 Meanwhile, make the waffle batter. Sift the flour, cinnamon, baking powder, and sugar into a medium mixing bowl. Make a well in the center, and add the egg yolk and milk to the well. Gently whisk the egg yolk and milk together, then gradually whisk in the flour to make a thick, smooth batter. Whisk in the melted margarine, then stir in the finely chopped pecans.

4 Whisk the egg white in a separate bowl until stiff. Pile it on top of the batter and, using a large metal spoon, fold it in gently.

5 Spoon a small ladleful (3–4 tablespoons) of batter into the center of the hot waffle iron or maker, then close the lid tightly. After about 2–3 minutes, open the waffle iron: The waffle should be golden brown on both sides and should come away easily from the iron.

6 Lift the cooked waffle from the iron using a butter knife, and keep warm while cooking the rest of the waffles.

7 Just before all the waffles are ready, gently warm the fruit sauce, then pour into a sauceboat or serving bowl. Serve with the warm waffles.

(Some More Ideas)

Parmesan waffles: Omit the cinnamon, sugar, and pecans from the batter. Instead, sift the flour with a good pinch each of black pepper and cayenne pepper, and salt to taste. Add 2 tablespoons freshly grated Parmesan cheese before folding in the egg white. Omit the fruit sauce.

• To keep waffles warm, spread them in a single layer on a rack in an oven set to its lowest temperature.

• Use walnuts instead of pecans, and either maple syrup or clear honey in the sauce.

Health Points

• The pectin in pears is a good source of soluble fiber, which helps to lower blood cholesterol levels.

• Authentic maple syrup contains healthy amounts of zinc.

photo, page 27

Each serving (1 waffle) provides

Key Nutrients 360 Calories, 140 Calories from Fat, 15g Fat, 2g Saturated Fat, 0g Trans Fat, 8g Protein, 51g Carb, 4g Fiber, 180mg Sodium
Blood Pressure Nutrients 6mg Vitamin C, 43mg Magnesium, 341mg Potassium, 184mg Calcium

Multi-Grain Waffles with Apple-Raspberry Sauce

Nothing gets people to the breakfast table like the smell of waffles. The robust flavor of these waffles, made with whole-wheat and buckwheat flours and flaxseed, is complemented by a sweet, tangy fruit sauce.

Preparation time **10 minutes**　　Cooking time **15 minutes**　　*Makes 8 waffles*

Waffles

1/4 cup flaxseeds
1/4 cup whole-wheat flour
1/4 cup buckwheat flour
1/4 cup all-purpose flour
2 teaspoons brown sugar
2 teaspoons baking powder
Salt to taste
1 large egg, separated, plus 2 large egg whites
1 cup buttermilk

Sauce

3/4 cup apple cider
2 red or green apples, cut into 1/2-inch chunks
1/2 teaspoon vanilla
1 cup fresh raspberries

1 Bring apple cider to a boil in medium skillet over high heat and cook 1 minute. Add apples and simmer until firm-tender, about 4 minutes. Remove from heat and let cool to room temperature. Stir in vanilla and raspberries.

2 Place flaxseeds in a spice grinder or mini food processor and grind to the consistency of coarse flour. Transfer to large bowl and add whole-wheat flour, buckwheat flour, all-purpose flour, brown sugar, baking powder, and salt. Stir to mix well.

3 Combine egg yolk and buttermilk in small bowl. Beat 3 egg whites in large bowl until stiff peaks form. Make a well in center of dry ingredients and stir in egg yolk mixture. Gently fold in egg whites.

4 Spray a nonstick waffle iron (with two 4- to 4 1/2-inch squares) with nonstick cooking spray. Preheat iron. Spoon batter into iron, 1/2 cup per waffle. Cook until golden brown and crisp, about 2 minutes. Repeat with remaining batter. Serve warm with apple-raspberry sauce.

(Some More Ideas)

• You can make the waffles partially or completely in advance. For the former, mix the dry ingredients and freeze in a ziplock bag. When it's waffle time, add the eggs and buttermilk as directed. Or prepare and cook the waffles, then cool them and wrap in foil. Refrigerate or freeze. At serving time, toast in a toaster or toaster oven. You can also make the sauce in advance.

• Use fresh blueberries in place of raspberries.

Health Points

• Flaxseed oil is a rich source of omega-3 fatty acids, which help reduce the risk of heart disease and stroke. To make flaxseeds' oil and fiber available to the body, the seeds need to be ground.

photo, page 27

Each serving (1 waffle) provides

Key Nutrients 150 Calories, 30 Calories from Fat, 3g Fat, 1g Saturated Fat, 0g Trans Fat, 5g Protein, 26g Carb, 5g Fiber, 160mg Sodium
Blood Pressure Nutrients 7mg Vitamin C, 31mg Magnesium, 182mg Potassium, 114mg Calcium

Blueberry Swirl Coffee Cake

This moist and tender cake is bursting with juicy berries. Brown sugar and cinnamon make it so melt-in-your-mouth delicious you won't believe it's lower in calories, fat, and cholesterol than traditional coffee cake.

Preparation time **20 minutes**   Cooking time **40 minutes**   *Serves 16*

2 1/2 cups fresh or frozen blueberries
1/3 cup packed light brown sugar
1 teaspoon cinnamon
1/2 cup (1 stick) margarine
1 cup granulated sugar
1 large egg
1 large egg white
1 tablespoon grated lemon zest
2 1/2 cups self-rising flour
1 1/4 cups reduced-fat (2%) milk

1 Preheat oven to 350°F. Grease and flour 13 x 9-inch baking pan. Toss 2 cups blueberries, brown sugar, and cinnamon in small bowl until berries are coated.

2 Cream margarine and granulated sugar in large bowl with electric mixer at high speed until light and fluffy, about 4 minutes. Add egg and egg white and beat 2 minutes. Beat in lemon zest. Reduce speed to low. Add flour alternately with milk, one-third at a time, stopping mixer occasionally to scrape bowl with rubber spatula. Do not overbeat.

3 Spread half of batter into pan and sprinkle with blueberry mixture. Spoon remaining batter on top, spreading evenly. Swirl through batter several times with knife, then top with remaining blueberries.

4 Bake until toothpick inserted in center comes out with moist crumbs clinging, 40–45 minutes. Cool in pan on wire rack 15 minutes. Cut into 16 equal pieces. Serve warm or at room temperature.

(Some More Ideas)

• Fresh raspberries or sliced strawberries work equally well in this recipe.

• Add orange zest in place of lemon zest and add 2 tablespoons fresh orange juice to the batter for more citrus flavor.

Health Points

• Blueberries are very low in calories and high in vitamin C. They also have high antioxidant properties.

Each serving provides

Key Nutrients 210 Calories, 60 Calories from Fat, 7g Fat, 2g Saturated Fat, 1g Trans Fat, 3g Protein, 36g Carb, 1g Fiber, 340mg Sodium
Blood Pressure Nutrients 4mg Vitamin C, 7mg Magnesium, 127mg Potassium, 97mg Calcium

Blueberry Swirl Coffee Cake *p26*

Pecan Waffles with Maple, Pear, and Blackberry Sauce *p24*

Multi-Grain Waffles with Apple-Raspberry Sauce *p25*

Orange Coffee Cake Braid *p28*

Orange Coffee Cake Braid

This beautiful Danish-inspired pastry is sure to become a breakfast favorite (and no one will suspect it's low in fat and low in cholesterol!). It's also wonderful with afternoon coffee or as a weekend treat.

Preparation time **30 minutes**   Cooking time **20 minutes**   *Serves 16*

3 1/2 cups all-purpose flour
1/3 cup plus 1/2 cup granulated sugar
1 package (1/4 ounce) rapid-rise dry yeast
Salt to taste
1 1/4 cups reduced-fat (2%) milk
6 tablespoons margarine
1 large egg, beaten
1/2 cup finely chopped toasted walnuts
1/4 cup golden raisins
1 1/2 tablespoons grated orange zest
1 cup confectioners' sugar, sifted
3 tablespoons fresh orange juice

1 Mix 2 cups flour, 1/3 cup granulated sugar, yeast, and salt in large bowl. Heat milk and 4 tablespoons margarine in small saucepan until warm (120°F–130°F). Stir into flour mixture. Stir in egg. Add 1 cup flour and stir vigorously until dough pulls away from side of bowl, 2 to 3 minutes.

2 Dust work surface with remaining flour. Turn out dough and knead until smooth and elastic, about 10 minutes, working in enough flour to keep it from sticking. Coat large bowl with nonstick cooking spray and put dough in bowl; turn to coat. Cover with damp towel and let rest 10 minutes.

3 Meanwhile, line baking sheet with parchment paper. Toss walnuts, raisins, remaining granulated sugar, and 1 tablespoon orange zest; set aside. Melt remaining margarine; set aside. Place dough on parchment; pat into 14 x 9-inch oval.

4 Brush dough with melted margarine. Score dough lengthwise into three equal sections; do not cut through dough. Cut outer sections into 3-inch-long and 1-inch-wide strips. Spread walnut filling down center. Fold strips over filling and seal ends. Cover with towel. Let rise in warm place until almost doubled, for 45 minutes.

5 Meanwhile, preheat oven to 375°F. Bake bread until golden, about 20 minutes. Cool on wire rack 15 minutes. Stir confectioners' sugar, remaining orange zest, and orange juice in small bowl until smooth. Drizzle over warm bread. Serve warm or at room temperature.

(Some More Ideas)

• Substitute 1 3/4 cups whole-wheat flour for some of the all-purpose flour for more fiber.

• Add dried cherries or cranberries in place of the raisins.

Health Points

• Who doesn't like coffee cake–style breads? By making them yourself, you can control the amount of fat, sodium, and sugar they contain.

• Baking from scratch is a great opportunity to add fiber-rich ingredients such as wheat germ and nuts and seeds to most cake and bread batters.

photo, page 27

Each serving provides

Key Nutrients 250 Calories, 60 Calories from Fat, 7g Fat, 1g Saturated Fat, 1g Trans Fat, 5g Protein, 43g Carb, 1g Fiber, 70mg Sodium
Blood Pressure Nutrients 1mg Vitamin C, 18mg Magnesium, 117mg Potassium, 36mg Calcium

Pop-Up Scallion Popovers

Twelve towering popovers—as easy as 1, 2, 3! Just measure, mix, and bake. A sprinkling of Parmesan adds a big boost of flavor, so no one will ever guess you've cut back on the fat!

Preparation time **15 minutes**   Cooking time **25 minutes**   *Serves 12*

1 cup sifted all-purpose flour
3 tablespoons Parmesan cheese
Salt to taste
1/4 teaspoon pepper
2 large eggs
1 egg white
1 cup reduced-fat (2%) milk
1 tablespoon margarine, melted
2 scallions, minced

1 Preheat oven to 425°F. Lightly coat a 12-cup popover pan or muffin pan with nonstick cooking spray and put in oven to preheat. Whisk flour, Parmesan, salt, and pepper in medium bowl. Make well in center of flour mixture.

2 Whisk eggs, egg white, milk, and margarine until frothy. Pour into well in flour mixture and stir just until smooth. Stir in scallions.

3 When a drop of water dances and sizzles in the pan, it's hot enough. Spoon in batter, dividing it evenly among 12 cups. Bake 15 minutes. Reduce oven temperature to 350°F and bake until golden and puffed, about 10 minutes longer. Immediately remove popovers from pan and quickly make a small slit in the side of each to release steam.

(Some More Ideas)

• To make these popovers stronger in taste, use Romano cheese instead of Parmesan.

• Add a few dried herbs such as dried thyme or oregano into the batter.

Health Points

• By using cheeses in small amounts, you can bolster the flavor of meals, while still keeping the fat and sodium to a minimum.

• Scallions are a member of the onion family. Allium compounds in the onion family may help relieve high blood pressure.

photo, page 31

Each serving provides

Key Nutrients 80 Calories, 20 Calories from Fat, 3g Fat, 1g Saturated Fat, 0g Trans Fat, 3g Protein, 9g Carb, 0g Fiber, 50mg Sodium
Blood Pressure Nutrients 1mg Vitamin C, 4mg Magnesium, 34mg Potassium, 36mg Calcium

Blueberry Muffins with Lemon Glaze

What makes these muffins extra special is the abundance of berries and the sweet lemon glaze drizzled on top.
You can freeze some for up to a month. Take them out of the freezer the night before for a perfect breakfast.

Preparation time **20 minutes**   Cooking time **20 minutes plus cooling**   *Serves 12*

Muffins

2 cups self-rising flour
1/2 cup granulated sugar
1 cup reduced-fat (2%) milk
1/2 cup fat-free egg substitute
4 tablespoons margarine, melted
1/3 cup reduced-fat sour cream
2 teaspoons vanilla
1 1/2 cups fresh blueberries

Glaze

1 cup sifted confectioners' sugar
1 tablespoon grated lemon zest
2 tablespoons reduced-fat (2%) milk

1 Preheat oven to 400°F. Line 12-cup muffin pan with paper liners. Whisk flour and sugar in large bowl. Whisk milk, egg substitute, margarine, sour cream, and vanilla in medium bowl until blended.

2 Make well in center of the flour mixture. Pour in milk mixture and stir with fork just until blended. Fold in 1 cup blueberries.

3 Spoon batter into muffin cups and sprinkle evenly with remaining blueberries. Bake until toothpick inserted in center comes out clean, about 20 minutes. Cool muffins on wire rack 10 minutes.

4 Meanwhile, mix confectioners' sugar, lemon zest, and enough milk in small bowl to make a pourable glaze. Drizzle glaze over muffins after they have cooled.

(Some More Ideas)

* Make these muffins with raspberries or blackberries.

* Change the vanilla extract to almond or orange.

Health Points

* Blueberries are one of the best fruit sources of anti-oxidants. In fact, the very pigments that help give berries their color (called anthocyanins) sweep free radicals out of your bloodstream and may even help stave off memory loss.

Each serving provides

Key Nutrients 210 Calories, 50 Calories from Fat, 5g Fat, 2g Saturated Fat, 1g Trans Fat, 4g Protein, 37g Carb, 1g Fiber, 270mg Sodium
Blood Pressure Nutrients 3mg Vitamin C, 3mg Magnesium, 63mg Potassium, 105mg Calcium

Blueberry Muffins
with Lemon Glaze *p30*

Pop-Up Scallion Popovers *p29*

Cherry-Oatmeal Muffins *p32*

Peaches and Cream Quick Bread *p34*

Cherry-Oatmeal Muffins

Most modern-day muffins should be ashamed—they're oversized, lacking in fiber, loaded with fat, and dripping with sugar. These tender golden muffins are bundles of whole grains that will please your heart and your palate.

Preparation time **15 minutes**   Cooking time **40 minutes**   *Serves 12*

1 cup old-fashioned rolled oats
3/4 cup all-purpose flour
3/4 cup whole-wheat flour
1/3 cup toasted wheat germ
1/3 cup plus 1 tablespoon sugar
1 teaspoon baking powder
1/2 teaspoon baking soda
Salt to taste
1 1/3 cups buttermilk
3 tablespoons olive oil
1 large egg
1 tablespoon grated orange zest
3/4 cup dried cherries, cranberries, or raisins

1 Preheat oven to 375°F. Line twelve 2 1/2-inch muffin cups with paper liners. Toast oats in a jelly-roll pan until golden brown and crisp, stirring occasionally, about 10 minutes. Transfer to large bowl and let cool to room temperature.

2 Add all-purpose flour, whole-wheat flour, wheat germ, 1/3 cup of sugar, baking powder, baking soda, and salt to oats, stirring to combine. Whisk together buttermilk, oil, egg, and orange zest in small bowl until blended.

3 Make well in center of dry ingredients and pour in buttermilk mixture. Stir just until dry ingredients are moistened. Fold in cherries, using a wooden spoon.

4 Spoon batter into muffin cups. Sprinkle top of each muffin with 1/4 teaspoon sugar. Bake until golden brown and a toothpick inserted in center of a muffin comes out clean, about 30 minutes. Remove muffins from pan to wire rack to cool.

(Some More Ideas)

• Make these muffins with a lemon flavor. Substitute grated lemon zest for the orange zest.

• Add chopped dates or dried apples to the batter.

Health Points

• At 3 grams of fiber per serving, this muffin is a good source of fiber, making it a worthy part of the morning meal.

• Using olive oil in the batter increases the amount of monounsaturated versus saturated fat. Most commercially prepared muffins have far too much saturated fat.

photo, page 31

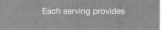
Each serving provides

Key Nutrients 200 Calories, 45 Calories from Fat, 5g Fat, 1g Saturated Fat, 0g Trans Fat, 6g Protein, 34g Carb, 3g Fiber, 90mg Sodium
Blood Pressure Nutrients 1mg Vitamin C, 23mg Magnesium, 147mg Potassium, 59mg Calcium

Dutch Apple Muffins

We bet the Muffin Man never offered such healthful fare! Applesauce replaces some of the fat, and fresh apples and oatmeal add nutritious fiber. But they're still as delicious as any homemade muffin you can remember.

Preparation time **10 minutes**   Cooking time **20 minutes**   *Serves 12*

1 2/3 cups all-purpose flour
3/4 cup firmly packed brown sugar
2 packages (about 1 1/2 ounces each) apple-cinnamon instant oatmeal
2 tablespoons margarine
1 teaspoon baking soda
1/2 teaspoon apple pie spice
Salt to taste
1 1/4 cups unsweetened applesauce
1/4 cup vegetable oil
1/2 cup fat-free egg substitute
1 large apple, chopped

1 Preheat oven to 375°F. Line 12-cup muffin pan with paper liners. Combine 1/3 cup flour, 1/4 cup brown sugar, 1 package oatmeal, and margarine in small bowl. Stir together with fingertips until margarine is incorporated into dry ingredients (mixture will be crumbly). Set aside.

2 Mix remaining flour, remaining oatmeal, baking soda, apple pie spice, and salt in medium bowl and make well in center of mixture.

3 Stir together applesauce, oil, remaining brown sugar, and egg substitute in another medium bowl until brown sugar dissolves. Pour all at once into well. Stir just until combined (do not overmix; batter should be lumpy). Stir in apple.

4 Spoon batter into muffin cups. Sprinkle with reserved crumb topping. Bake until toothpick inserted in center comes out clean, about 20 minutes.

(Some More Ideas)

• Add a pear instead of the apple in Step 3. Add 1/2 cup dried raisins to the batter.

• For a denser muffin with even more fiber, substitute whole-wheat flour for the all-purpose flour.

Health Points

• Oats are a nutritional winner. They are high in soluble fiber, B vitamins, and vitamin E, as well as heart-healthy minerals. Oats may help to reduce blood cholesterol.

photo, page 37

Each serving provides

Key Nutrients 220 Calories, 70 Calories from Fat, 7g Fat, 1g Saturated Fat, 0g Trans Fat, 3g Protein, 35g Carb, 2g Fiber, 150mg Sodium
Blood Pressure Nutrients 1mg Vitamin C, 16mg Magnesium, 159mg Potassium, 43mg Calcium

Peaches and Cream Quick Bread

Fresh peaches and lush (but fat-free) sour cream combine in a delicious tea bread. This bread is at its very best when you can get freshly picked, tree-ripened local fruit.

Preparation time **15 minutes**   Cooking time **1 hour plus cooling**   *Serves 16*

2 medium peaches
1 1/2 cups all-purpose flour
3/4 cup whole-wheat flour
1/4 cup toasted wheat germ
3/4 cup sugar
1 teaspoon baking soda
Salt to taste
1/2 cup fat-free sour cream
1 large egg plus 2 large egg whites
2 tablespoons extra-light olive oil
1 teaspoon almond extract

1 Preheat oven to 350°F. Lightly spray 9 x 5-inch loaf pan with nonstick cooking spray.

2 Blanch peaches in medium saucepan of boiling water for 20 seconds. Peel, pit, and finely chop peaches (you should have about 1 cup).

3 Combine all-purpose flour, whole-wheat flour, wheat germ, sugar, baking soda, and salt in large bowl.

4 Combine sour cream, whole egg, egg whites, oil, and almond extract in small bowl. Make well in dry ingredients, pour in sour-cream mixture, and stir just until combined. Fold in peaches.

5 Spoon batter into pan, smoothing top. Bake until cake tester inserted in center comes out clean, about 1 hour. Cool in pan on rack for 10 minutes, then turn out onto rack to cool completely before slicing.

(Some More Ideas)

• Try using plums or nectarines in place of peaches. Blanch them the same way you would do the peaches.

• If fresh peaches are unavailable, canned peaches are fine.

Health Points

• Peaches are an excellent source of vitamins A and C. Clinical studies suggest that vitamin C may have a benefit by widening blood vessels and promoting excretion of environmental toxins, such as lead, which can contribute to high blood pressure.

photo, page 31

Each serving provides

Key Nutrients 140 Calories, 20 Calories from Fat, 3g Fat, 0g Saturated Fat, 0g Trans Fat, 4g Protein, 25g Carb, 1g Fiber, 100mg Sodium
Blood Pressure Nutrients 1mg Vitamin C, 18mg Magnesium, 86mg Potassium, 17mg Calcium

Maple and Toasted-Walnut Quick Bread

This healthy quick bread has it all: just the right amount of sweetness, a delicious moist crumb, and the toothsome crunch of nuts throughout. The only thing it doesn't have is lots of fat and cholesterol.

Preparation time 15 minutes   Cooking time **50 minutes plus cooling**   *Serves 16*

2 3/4 cups self-rising flour
1/3 cup margarine
1 cup maple syrup
1 egg, lightly beaten
2/3 cup evaporated fat-free milk
1 teaspoon vanilla
1/2 cup walnuts, toasted and chopped

1 Preheat oven to 350°F. Lightly coat 9 x 5-inch loaf pan with nonstick cooking spray. Put flour into large bowl and make a well in center.

2 Beat margarine in medium bowl with wooden spoon until creamy; blend in syrup. Beat in egg, and then milk and vanilla. Pour mixture into well of flour and stir just until flour disappears. (Do not overbeat; a few lumps are okay.) Stir in walnuts.

3 Scrape batter into loaf pan. Bake until golden brown and a toothpick inserted in center comes out with moist crumbs, about 50 minutes. If bread browns too fast, loosely cover with foil (shiny-side up) during last 15 minutes of baking.

4 Cool in pan on wire rack 10 minutes. Turn bread onto rack to cool.

(Some More Ideas)

• For a different nutty flavor, use toasted pecans or toasted slivered almonds in place of the walnuts.

• This bread is equally delicious with almond extract instead of vanilla.

Health Points

• There is some evidence to suggest that eating unsalted nuts may help relieve high blood pressure. Nuts are a good source of mono-unsaturated fat and are high in fiber. Walnuts, in particular, are heart-healthy: They contain alpha-linolenic acid, an omega-3 fat that may lower risk for heart attack, and ellagic acid, an antioxidant compound. Store nuts in a cool, dry place or in the refrigerator for longer-lasting freshness.

photo, page 37

photo, page 37

Each serving provides

Key Nutrients 200 Calories, 60 Calories from Fat, 7g Fat, 1g Saturated Fat, 1g Trans Fat, 4g Protein, 31g Carb, 1g Fiber, 280mg Sodium
Blood Pressure Nutrients 0mg Vitamin C, 15mg Magnesium, 130mg Potassium, 117mg Calcium

Herb and Cheddar Drop Biscuits

Revive the tradition of homemade bread in your house with these fast and easy fresh-baked biscuits. There's no rolling or cutting required, so they go from flour bin to oven in just 15 minutes.

Preparation time **15 minutes**   Cooking time **12 minutes**   *Serves 18*

1 3/4 cups self-rising flour

1 tablespoon snipped fresh chives

1 teaspoon chopped fresh thyme

1/4 teaspoon baking soda

3 tablespoons margarine, cut into pieces

1/2 cup shredded reduced-fat cheddar cheese

3/4 cup low-fat buttermilk

1 egg white, lightly beaten

1 Preheat oven to 450°F. Line baking sheet with parchment paper or coat with nonstick cooking spray. Mix flour, chives, thyme, and baking soda in large bowl.

2 Cut in margarine with pastry blender or two knives until mixture resembles coarse crumbs. Stir in 1/4 cup cheddar. Make a well in center and pour in buttermilk. Mix with fork until a soft, sticky dough forms.

3 Drop heaping tablespoons of dough onto baking sheet, making 18 biscuits. Brush biscuits with egg white and sprinkle with remaining cheddar. Bake until puffy and golden, about 12 minutes.

(Some More Ideas)

• Use other herbs instead of chives and thyme. Snipped basil and sage are good choices.

• Try low-fat mozzarella or Jack cheese as a change from cheddar.

Health Points

• Despite its name, buttermilk is a low-fat beverage as well as an excellent liquid for baking. It will make these biscuits extra light in flavor. If you don't have buttermilk on hand, just stir 1 tablespoon of either vinegar or lemon juice into 1 cup fat-free milk and let it stand until the milk curdles.

Each serving provides

Key Nutrients 70 Calories, 20 Calories from Fat, 3g Fat, 1g Saturated Fat, 0g Trans Fat, 2g Protein, 10g Carb, 0g Fiber, 22mg Sodium
Blood Pressure Nutrients 0mg Vitamin C, 3mg Magnesium, 21mg Potassium, 58mg Calcium

Home-Style Corn Bread *p38*

Dutch Apple Muffins *p33*

Maple and Toasted-Walnut
Quick Bread *p35*

Herb and Cheddar Drop Biscuits *p36*

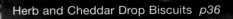

Home-Style Corn Bread

Warm-from-the-oven corn bread is always a treat, and somehow the pleasure's doubled when you've made it yourself. This traditional recipe complements any style meal—from Tex-Mex to soul food.

Preparation time **10 minutes**   Cooking time **20 minutes**   *Serves 16*

1 ear corn or 2/3 cup frozen corn, thawed
1 cup all-purpose flour
3/4 cup cornmeal
1 tablespoon baking powder
Salt to taste
2/3 cup low-fat (1%) milk
1/4 cup olive oil
1 egg
1 tablespoon honey

1 Preheat oven to 425°F. Lightly grease 8 x 8 x 2-inch baking pan with vegetable oil spray. Using sharp knife, remove corn kernels. Set aside.

2 In medium bowl, thoroughly mix all-purpose flour, corn-meal, baking powder, and salt. In small bowl, combine corn, milk, oil, egg, and honey, and beat well to mix.

3 Pour egg mixture into bowl with flour and cornmeal. Quickly and thoroughly mix together. Pour batter into baking pan, scraping any batter off sides of bowl into pan. Spread batter evenly with spatula.

4 Bake until lightly browned and knife inserted in the center comes out clean, about 20–25 minutes. Cut into 3/4-inch squares and serve at once.

(Some More Ideas)

• Add 1 cup frozen, thawed corn to the batter.

• Like your corn bread spicy? Using spices instead of salt will add flavor and no unwanted sodium. Add 1/2 teaspoon chili powder and 1/4 teaspoon ground cumin to the flour mixture and skip the salt.

Health Points

• Store-bought and restaurant-made corn breads have lots of fat and sodium in them. So always opt for homemade.

• Corn has a surprisingly large mix of important nutrients. It is particularly rich in folate, which helps reduce the risk of heart disease. It also contains lutein, which is healthy for your eyes. Plus, corn is rich with protease inhibitors, chemical compounds that may help to prevent cancerous tumors from developing.

photo, page 37

Each serving provides

Key Nutrients 100 Calories, 35 Calories from Fat, 4g Fat, 1g Saturated Fat, 0g Trans Fat, 2g Protein, 13g Carb, 1g Fiber, 15mg Sodium
Blood Pressure Nutrients 0mg Vitamin C, 11mg Magnesium, 140mg Potassium, 56mg Calcium

appetizers

Double-Cheese Pizza Bites

What a delicious way to welcome your guests! These personal-sized pizzas are loaded with fresh tomato slices and jazzed up with two kinds of cheese, black olives, and fresh herbs.

Preparation time **30 minutes plus rising**   Cooking time **10 minutes**   *Serves 24*

2 3/4–3 cups all-purpose flour
1 teaspoon sugar
1 packet rapid-rise yeast
1 cup very warm water (120°F–130°F)
1 tablespoon extra-virgin olive oil
Salt to taste
1 pint cherry tomatoes
4 ounces fontina cheese, shredded (1 cup)
3 tablespoons freshly grated Parmesan cheese
12 kalamata olives, pitted and cut into slivers
Fresh oregano leaves

1 Mix 1 cup flour, sugar, and yeast in bowl. Stir in the water and oil until blended. Pulse 1 3/4 cups flour and salt in food processor to mix. Add yeast mixture and pulse until blended. With motor running, add remaining flour, 1 tablespoon at a time, until soft dough forms (you will need to process about 2 minutes).

2 Dust work surface lightly with flour. Turn out dough and knead until smooth, 1–2 minutes. Shape into ball. Cover with clean kitchen towel; let rest 10 minutes.

3 Preheat oven to 450°F. Line two baking sheets with parchment paper. Divide dough into 4 pieces. Wrap 3 in plastic; refrigerate. Cut remaining dough into 12 equal pieces; shape each into 1 1/2-inch ball. Arrange on baking sheets; flatten into 3-inch rounds. Lightly coat with nonstick cooking spray.

4 Thinly slice tomatoes; fan out slices. Top each pizza with 2 or 3 slices. Sprinkle with 1 teaspoon fontina, a little Parmesan, plus a few olive slivers and oregano leaves. Bake until bubbly and crust is golden, about 10 minutes. Repeat with remaining dough.

(Some More Ideas)

• Use mozzarella or cheddar cheese instead of fontina cheese.

• Try green olives as a twist instead of the black.

Health Points

• This recipe is a good example of how to use higher-fat, higher-sodium foods in small quantities. The olives provide such a flavor boost, but admittedly they do have fat and salt. By using just a few, you get the taste you need with fewer of the things you don't.

Each serving (2 pizza bites) provides

Key Nutrients 90 Calories, 25 Calories from Fat, 3g Fat, 1g Saturated Fat, 0g Trans Fat, 3g Protein, 12g Carb, 1g Fiber, 75mg Sodium
Blood Pressure Nutrients 2mg Vitamin C, 6mg Magnesium, 53mg Potassium, 34mg Calcium

Double-Cheese Pizza Bites *p40*

Roasted-Pepper Pinwheels *p42*

Beef Satay with Asian
Dipping Sauce *p43*

Portobello Pizzas *p46*

Roasted-Pepper Pinwheels

Wraps are a quick way to roll tasty fillings into a fun-to-eat package. Take a wrap and cut it crosswise and you get a different spin—bite-size spiraled pinwheel sandwiches equally at home in a lunchbox or on a holiday buffet.

Preparation time **15 minutes**   Cooking time **10 minutes plus chilling**   *Serves 24*

3 red bell peppers, cut length-wise into flat panels

1 1/2 cups canned chickpeas, rinsed and drained

3 tablespoons plain fat-free yogurt

1 teaspoon dark sesame oil

1 teaspoon grated lemon zest

2 tablespoons fresh lemon juice

2 tablespoons water

Salt to taste

3 spinach- or basil-flavored flour tortillas (8 inches)

4 cups mixed salad greens

1 Preheat broiler. Broil pepper pieces, skin-side up, 4 inches from heat, until charred, about 10 minutes. Transfer to a plate. When cool enough to handle, peel and cut into 1/2-inch-wide strips.

2 Combine chickpeas, yogurt, sesame oil, lemon zest, lemon juice, water, and salt in food processor and puree until smooth.

3 Spread mixture evenly over one side of each tortilla, leaving 1/2-inch border all around. Top with salad greens and roasted peppers. Roll up jelly-roll fashion.

4 Wrap tightly in foil or plastic wrap and refrigerate for at least 1 hour or up to 4 hours. (The rolls will get softer and easier to slice if they sit in the refrigerator for a while before serving.) Unwrap and slice each roll crosswise into 8 pieces (1 inch wide) to serve.

(Some More Ideas)

• Use roasted yellow or orange peppers, or combine several colors of peppers for a particularly attractive pinwheel.

• Use white kidney beans or small navy beans in place of the chickpeas.

Health Points

• Bell peppers are among the best natural sources of vitamin C. One cup of fresh bell peppers has 1 1/2 times as much vitamin C as a cup of fresh orange juice. And colored peppers have even more vitamin C than a green pepper! Vitamin C is particularly good for fighting high blood pressure, so always keep peppers in the vegetable bin.

photo, page 41

Each serving (1 pinwheel) provides

Key Nutrients 45 Calories, 10 Calories from Fat, 1g Fat, 0g Saturated Fat, 0g Trans Fat, 2g Protein, 8g Carb, 1g Fiber, 80mg Sodium
Blood Pressure Nutrients 31mg Vitamin C, 10mg Magnesium, 90mg Potassium, 22mg Calcium

Beef Satay with Asian Dipping Sauce

Tempting Asian-style steak bites, all dressed up for a party! Let these snacks-on-a-skewer kick off your next gathering. Prepare them ahead, so they're ready for grilling in an instant. They're lean enough to be heart-healthy!

Preparation time **25 minutes**   Cooking time **15 minutes**   *Serves 12*

Satay

1 boneless beef sirloin steak (1 inch thick, 12 ounces), trimmed

3 large yellow or red bell peppers, cut into 8 triangles each

4 scallions, sliced into 3-inch pieces

Salt to taste

Dipping Sauce

1/2 cup rice vinegar

1/2 cup finely chopped red bell pepper

2 tablespoons sugar

1 tablespoon finely chopped shallot

1 1/2 teaspoons grated peeled fresh ginger

1–1 1/2 teaspoons chile garlic sauce

1/2 teaspoon grated lemon zest

1 Soak twenty-four 6-inch wooden or bamboo skewers in water 30 minutes. Freeze steak 20 minutes.

2 To make dipping sauce, combine vinegar, red pepper, sugar, shallot, ginger, chile garlic sauce, and lemon zest in small serving bowl.

3 Blanch yellow peppers in boiling water 1 minute. Drain, rinse with cold water, and pat dry with paper towels. Toss in medium bowl with 2 tablespoons dipping sauce.

4 Preheat broiler. Slice steak into 24 very thin strips and sprinkle with salt. Thread 1 beef strip, 1 yellow pepper triangle, and 1 scallion piece onto each skewer, twisting meat as you go. Broil until cooked through, 3–5 minutes on each side.

(Some More Ideas)

• Satay is versatile! Make these with chicken, pork, and even turkey.

• You can also vary the vegetables to be grilled. Anything goes: mushrooms, zucchini, Chinese pea pods—whatever you enjoy!

• Lower the spice in this dish by omitting the chile garlic sauce.

Health Points

• Lean meat can still be part of a healthy food program as long as you consume it in healthy portion sizes and lay off the salt. Lean beef is an important source of B vitamins and iron, and provides outstanding protein that your body needs. Make sure, though, that your meals contain far more vegetables and whole grains than beef.

photo, page 41

Each serving (2 skewers) provides

Key Nutrients 70 Calories, 15 Calories from Fat, 2g Fat, 1g Saturated Fat, 0g Trans Fat, 7g Protein, 7g Carb, 1g Fiber, 25mg Sodium
Blood Pressure Nutrients 91mg Vitamin C, 12mg Magnesium, 201mg Potassium, 10mg Calcium

Little Chicken Salad Rolls

There's absolutely no added fat in this Asian-inspired appetizer. Chicken is poached in ginger-flavored broth, shredded and tossed with a soy-vinegar dressing and vegetables, then rolled in lettuce leaves for a scrumptious snack or appetizer.

Preparation time **40 minutes**   Cooking time **15 minutes**   *Serves 16*

Rolls

1 cup reduced-sodium chicken broth

2 slices (1/4 inch thick) fresh ginger

1 pound skinless, boneless chicken thighs or breasts

3 tablespoons rice vinegar

1 tablespoon reduced-sodium soy sauce

1 carrot, shredded

1 red bell pepper, slivered

16 Boston lettuce leaves

16 fresh mint leaves

3 tablespoons finely chopped dry-roasted peanuts

Dipping Sauce

3 tablespoons reduced-sodium soy sauce

1 tablespoon rice vinegar

1 teaspoon sugar

1 To make dipping sauce, combine soy sauce, vinegar, and sugar in small saucepan. Stir over low heat until sugar has dissolved. Set aside to cool.

2 Bring broth and ginger to a boil in large skillet over medium heat. Add chicken, reduce to simmer, cover, and cook until chicken is opaque, turning chicken over midway through cooking, about 12 minutes. Remove chicken from skillet, discarding broth. When cool enough to handle, shred chicken.

3 Stir together vinegar and soy sauce in medium bowl. Add shredded chicken, carrot, and bell pepper. Toss to combine.

4 Place lettuce leaves, hollow-side up, on work surface. Place a mint leaf in each. Dividing evenly, spoon chicken mixture into lettuce leaves and sprinkle peanuts on top. Roll leaves up and serve with dipping sauce.

(Some More Ideas)

• Make this recipe with tofu. Sauté 1/2 pound tofu, cut into cubes, in a little sesame oil. Combine the tofu with the vegetables.

• Use lean turkey instead of chicken.

Health Points

• When you're thinking health, think color. The more colors you have in a meal, the more likely there will be a wider variety of vitamins and minerals. This dish is particularly colorful with leafy greens, red peppers, and carrots. It's perfect for great eating—and lowering blood pressure.

Each serving (1 salad roll) provides

Key Nutrients 50 Calories, 10 Calories from Fat, 2g Fat, 0g Saturated Fat, 0g Trans Fat, 8g Protein, 3g Carb, 1g Fiber, 160mg Sodium
Blood Pressure Nutrients 16mg Vitamin C, 15mg Magnesium, 139mg Potassium, 10mg Calcium

Portobello Pizzas

Portobello mushrooms have a wide, flat cap that makes an innovative base for mini-pizzas. For a fabulous first course, top the "crust" with a bean puree flavored with fresh basil and Parmesan, then layer on shredded mozzarella and tomatoes.

Preparation time **10 minutes**   Cooking time **15 minutes**   *Serves 8*

8 large portobello mushrooms
(2 ounces each), stems
removed

1 can (19 ounces) pinto beans,
rinsed and drained

1/2 cup water

1/2 cup chopped fresh basil

3 tablespoons grated
Parmesan

1/2 teaspoon pepper

Salt to taste

3/4 cup shredded fat-free
mozzarella (3 ounces)

3 large plum tomatoes, halved,
seeded, and diced or slivered

1 Preheat oven to 400°F. With spoon, scrape out and discard the black gills from mushrooms. Spray jelly-roll pan with nonstick cooking spray. Place mushrooms stemmed-side down in pan. Cover pan with foil and bake until mushrooms are tender, about 5 minutes. Remove mushrooms from pan and drain stemmed-side down on paper towels. Leave oven on.

2 Meanwhile, combine beans, water, basil, Parmesan, pepper, and salt in medium bowl and mash until smooth with a potato masher or large fork.

3 Return mushrooms, stemmed-side up, to jelly-roll pan. Spoon bean mixture into mushroom hollow and bake 5 minutes.

4 Top with mozzarella and tomatoes and bake until cheese has melted and bean mixture is hot, about 5 minutes.

(Some More Ideas)

• Use the filling to stuff a pound of small cremini mushrooms instead of the portobello.

• Use any other cheese you desire; try reduced-fat cheddar or Swiss.

• Kidney beans are also good in place of the pinto beans.

Health Points

• Beans are one of the highest-fiber foods you can consume. Try to purchase beans packed without sodium.

• Fresh or dried basil is teeming with powerful antioxidants. In addition, flavonoid and terpene phytochemicals in basil are under review for their potential benefit in reducing cholesterol.

photo, page 41

Each serving (1 pizza) provides

Key Nutrients 110 Calories, 10 Calories from Fat, 2g Fat, 1g Saturated Fat, 0g Trans Fat, 9g Protein, 14g Carb, 4g Fiber, 280mg Sodium
Blood Pressure Nutrients 4mg Vitamin C, 22mg Magnesium, 400mg Potassium, 139mg Calcium

Heavenly Deviled Eggs

A low-cholesterol deviled egg? Yes, indeed! Filled with a delicious blend of egg yolks, vegetables, and spices, these are lighter and creamier than traditional deviled eggs, yet have a richer flavor.

Preparation time **15 minutes**   Cooking time **25 minutes**   *Serves 10*

12 large eggs
3/4 cup nonfat sour cream
2 scallions, finely chopped
1/3 cup finely chopped green bell pepper
1/3 cup finely chopped red bell pepper
2 teaspoons Dijon mustard
Salt to taste
3 tablespoons finely chopped parsley
Paprika, for dusting

1 Bring eggs and cold water to a full boil in large saucepan. Remove from heat, cover, and let stand 15 minutes. Drain eggs and rinse under cold water to cool them. Peel eggs, then cut lengthwise in half, and remove yolks. Discard 8 yolks.

2 Arrange 20 egg white halves on platter. Chop remaining 4 egg white halves very finely. Mash 4 yolks with fork. Transfer whites and yolks to medium bowl. Stir in sour cream, scallions, green and red peppers, mustard, and salt.

3 Pipe or spoon egg mixture into egg white halves. Sprinkle with parsley and dust with paprika.

(Some More Ideas)

• Make these eggs spicy! Add 1/2 teaspoon chili powder or 1/4 teaspoon cayenne to the egg mixture. Or substitute a very finely minced jalapeño pepper into the egg mixture.

Health Points

• Eggs are not a "no-no" food. Their low saturated-fat content, high protein levels, low price, and versatility make them a useful part of your food plan. And they have less cholesterol than formerly believed.

photo, page 49

Each serving (2 eggs) provides

Key Nutrients 110 Calories, 60 Calories from Fat, 6g Fat, 2g Saturated Fat, 0g Trans Fat, 8g Protein, 5g Carb, 0g Fiber, 125mg Sodium
Blood Pressure Nutrients 16mg Vitamin C, 8mg Magnesium, 108mg Potassium, 60mg Calcium

Sausage-Stuffed Cremini Mushrooms

For a delicious meal starter, stuff fresh mushrooms with savory chicken sausage, veggies, a sprinkling of cheese, and a dash of spice. They're surprisingly low in fat and calories and equally high in taste.

Preparation time 20 minutes   **Cooking time 22 minutes**   *Serves 6*

12 large cremini mushrooms

3/4 cup plain dry bread crumbs

2 tablespoons grated Parmesan cheese

2 ounces chicken sausage links, casings removed

1 large onion, finely chopped

1 small red bell pepper, finely chopped

1/4 teaspoon black pepper

1 Preheat oven to 400°F. Remove stems from mushrooms and finely chop stems. Mix 2 tablespoons bread crumbs and Parmesan in small bowl.

2 Lightly coat large nonstick skillet with nonstick cooking spray and set over medium heat. Cook sausages until they begin to brown, breaking up with side of spoon, about 5 minutes. Stir in onion, red pepper, and mushroom stems, and then cook until vegetables are soft, about 5 minutes. Stir in remaining bread crumbs and black pepper. Remove from heat.

3 Mound stuffing in mushrooms and arrange, stuffing-side up, in 13 x 9-inch baking dish. Sprinkle with Parmesan mixture. Bake until heated through, about 9 minutes.

(Some More Ideas)

• Use the stuffing to fill 2 large portobello mushrooms with the gills removed.

• Try using a low-fat spicy chicken or turkey sausage.

• For a softer filling, make your own bread crumbs. Purchase whole-wheat bread, and crumble it in a food processor or blender.

Health Points

• Mushrooms may not be particularly dense with many vitamins and minerals, but researchers are discovering that they are rich in healing phytochemicals. While the cremini or portobello mushrooms suggested above are healthy, among the healthiest mushrooms are shiitakes. If you can afford them, consider using them more in your cooking.

Each serving (2 mushrooms) provides

Key Nutrients 90 Calories, 20 Calories from Fat, 2g Fat, 1g Saturated Fat, 0g Trans Fat, 5g Protein, 14g Carb, 1g Fiber, 140mg Sodium
Blood Pressure Nutrients 25mg Vitamin C, 15mg Magnesium, 239mg Potassium, 53mg Calcium

Sausage-Stuffed Cremini Mushrooms *p48*

Heavenly Deviled Eggs *p47*

Chicken Dumplings with Sesame Dipping Sauce *p50*

Parmesan Breadsticks *p51*

Chicken Dumplings with Sesame Dipping Sauce

Water chestnuts and chopped cilantro combine with chicken, scallions, ginger, and pepper to create a Far East-style treat to tempt every palate. These tasty packets are boiled, not fried, to keep them low-fat and low-calorie.

Preparation time **30 minutes**   Cooking time **15 minutes**   *Serves 12*

Dumplings

1/2 pound ground chicken

1/4 cup thinly sliced scallions

1/4 cup minced canned water chestnuts

1/4 cup chopped cilantro

4 teaspoons reduced-sodium soy sauce

1/2 teaspoon ground ginger

1/4 teaspoon freshly ground black pepper

24 wonton wrappers (3-inch square)

Dipping Sauce

1/4 cup lower-sodium soy sauce

1 tablespoon sesame oil

2 teaspoons rice vinegar

1/2 teaspoon sugar

1/4 cup thinly sliced scallions

1 In medium bowl, combine chicken, scallions, water chestnuts, cilantro, soy sauce, ginger, and pepper. Mix well.

2 Working with several wonton wrappers at a time and keeping remainder loosely covered with dampened cloth, start filling wontons: Place generous teaspoonful of filling on bottom half of wrapper. With wet finger or pastry brush, moisten two sides of wonton. Fold two moistened sides over filling and press to seal and form triangle. Repeat with remaining wonton wrappers and filling.

3 In small bowl, make the dipping sauce: Whisk together soy sauce, sesame oil, vinegar, sugar, and scallions.

4 Bring large pot of water to boil. Add dumplings and cook until they float to surface and chicken is cooked through (filling will be firm to the touch), about 4 minutes. Drain. Serve with dipping sauce.

(Some More Ideas)

Vegetarian dumplings: Mix together shredded carrots, finely diced red peppers, and 1 cup sautéed spinach leaves. Mix with the scallions, water chestnuts, cilantro, soy sauce, ginger, and black pepper.

Health Points

• These dumplings are so low in fat because they are boiled, not fried. The added texture of the water chestnuts satisfies the desire for crunchy foods.

• Soy sauce is particularly heavy with sodium, so should be used sparingly and always in a low-sodium version. By keeping most of the soy sauce to the dipping sauce, you can regulate your intake more carefully.

photo, page 49

Each serving (2 dumplings) provides

Key Nutrients 90 Calories, 30 Calories from Fat, 4g Fat, 0g Saturated Fat, 0g Trans Fat, 6g Protein, 10g Carb, 0g Fiber, 220mg Sodium
Blood Pressure Nutrients 2mg Vitamin C, 6mg Magnesium, 36mg Potassium, 14mg Calcium

Parmesan Breadsticks

Freshly grated Parmesan, a bite of black pepper, and just a hint of fresh rosemary—baked into crispy golden twists. Great to eat now, perfect to give away as gifts, or to offer for a celebratory feast!

Preparation time **25 minutes plus standing**   Cooking time **36 minutes**   *Makes 40*

3 1/4 cups all-purpose flour

1 cup Parmesan cheese

2 teaspoons chopped fresh rosemary or 1/2 teaspoon dried

Salt to taste

1 teaspoon pepper

1 teaspoon rapid-rise dry yeast

1 1/4 cups very warm water (120°F–130°F)

1/4 cup semolina flour or cornmeal

1 teaspoon olive oil

1 Mix 1 1/2 cups flour, Parmesan, rosemary, salt, pepper, and yeast in large bowl. Blend in water. Add 1 1/2 cups more flour to form soft dough. Dust work surface with remaining flour. Turn dough onto floured surface and knead until smooth and elastic, about 10 minutes, working in remaining flour to keep dough from sticking. Divide dough into two equal pieces. Cover with damp kitchen towel and let rest 10 minutes.

2 Sprinkle two 16 x 12-inch sheets of wax paper with 1 tablespoon semolina each and pat dough pieces into 10 x 6-inch rectangles. Brush with oil and cover with kitchen towel. Let rise in warm place until doubled, about 30 minutes. Refrigerate 1 piece of dough.

3 Preheat oven to 400°F. Line two baking sheets with parchment paper and sprinkle with half of remaining semolina. Cut unrefrigerated dough crosswise into 20 equal strips, each about 8 inches long. Hold dough strips by the ends, twisting and stretching until about 12 inches long. Place twists 1 inch apart on baking sheets. Let rise, uncovered, 10 minutes.

4 Lightly coat breadsticks with nonstick cooking spray. Bake 10 minutes. Remove breadsticks from oven and lightly coat again with cooking spray. Bake until golden and crisp, about 8 minutes longer. Transfer to a wire rack and cool completely. Repeat with remaining dough.

(Some More Ideas)

• Add very finely chopped walnuts to the batter for added crunch and flavor.

• Combine Parmesan and another stronger grated cheese such as pecorino Romano for a more robust cheese flavor.

Health Points

• Rosemary is believed to offer relief to ailments of the nervous system, and is rich in such anticancer compounds as carnosol, rosmanol, and a variety of flavonoids. Additional anticancer substances in rosemary—cineole, geraniole, and pinene—show promise blocking tumor growth. Rosemary is highly aromatic, so be careful not to overuse it.

photo, page 49

Each serving (2 breadsticks) provides

Key Nutrients 90 Calories, 10 Calories from Fat, 2g Fat, 0g Saturated Fat, 0g Trans Fat, 4g Protein, 16g Carb, 0g Fiber, 40mg Sodium
Blood Pressure Nutrients 0mg Vitamin C, 6mg Magnesium, 36mg Potassium, 28mg Calcium

Guacamole with a Kick

Chunks of onion, tomato, and jalapeño peppers add so much zing to this zesty dip, your mouth will sing! Low-fat yogurt and nonfat sour cream lighten the mix and stretch two avocados to feed a horde of hungry dunkers.

Preparation time **20 minutes plus standing**   *Serves 16*

1/2 cup low-fat plain yogurt
2 small jalapeño peppers
2 plum tomatoes, finely chopped
1 small white onion, finely chopped
2 tablespoons minced cilantro
1/2 teaspoon salt
1/2 cup nonfat sour cream
2 large avocados
2 tablespoons fresh lime juice
3 ounces baked tortilla chips

1 Line the bottom of a strainer with cheesecloth, a coffee filter, or paper towels and set over a medium bowl (strainer should not touch bottom of bowl). Spoon in yogurt, cover, and refrigerate 8 hours or overnight, until yogurt cheese is thick and creamy.

2 Remove seeds and ribs from jalapeños with melon baller (wear gloves when handling, as the peppers can burn); mince. Mix jalapeños, tomatoes, onion, cilantro, and salt in large bowl. Fold in yogurt cheese and sour cream.

3 Halve, pit, and peel avocados. Mash with potato masher; sprinkle with lime juice. Quickly fold into tomato mixture. Makes 3 cups guacamole. Serve with tortilla chips.

(Some More Ideas)

• For an even greater kick, add 1 small diced serrano pepper instead of the jalapeño.

• Add a peeled, diced mango to crown the top of the guacamole for a festive look.

• To keep a lid on the fat, serve baked, not fried, tortilla chips with the guacamole.

Health Points

• Avocados are amazingly rich in vitamins, minerals, and phytochemicals—so much so that the U.S. government has revised its nutrition guidelines to urge Americans to eat more of them. True, they are dense with calories, but in healthy portions they are excellent sources of magnesium, fiber, and other nutrients essential to battle high blood pressure.

Each serving provides

Key Nutrients 90 Calories, 50 Calories from Fat, 6g Fat, 1g Saturated Fat, 0g Trans Fat, 2g Protein, 8g Carb, 2g Fiber, 80mg Sodium
Blood Pressure Nutrients 6mg Vitamin C, 13mg Magnesium, 201mg Potassium, 34mg Calcium

Gulf Coast Hot Crab Dip

All along the Gulf Coast, there's a lot of crabbing going on—followed by large beach parties called crab boils. Skip the melted butter and enjoy this favorite seafood in a hot and creamy dip with chunks of crab in every bite.

Preparation time **10 minutes**   Cooking time **20 minutes**   *Serves 24*

12 ounces fresh lump crabmeat or 2 cans (6 ounces each) crabmeat, drained

8 ounces fat-free cream cheese, softened

1 cup nonfat sour cream

1 small onion, finely chopped

1 tablespoon prepared horseradish

2 teaspoons Worcestershire sauce

1/4 teaspoon hot red pepper sauce

3 tablespoons plain dry bread crumbs

1/2 teaspoon paprika

1 Preheat oven to 350°F. Coat gratin dish or deep-dish pie plate with nonstick cooking spray. Pick through crabmeat; discard any shells and cartilage. Rinse crabmeat and drain.

2 Stir cream cheese in medium bowl until smooth. Blend in sour cream, onion, horseradish, Worcestershire, and hot pepper sauce. Gently fold in crabmeat. Spoon into baking dish; smooth out top.

3 Combine bread crumbs and paprika and sprinkle evenly over crabmeat mixture. Bake until bubbly, about 20 minutes. Serve piping hot with crackers.

(Some More Ideas)

• Make this dip with canned tuna or salmon.

• Add 2 tablespoons grated Parmesan to the dip for extra flavor.

Health Points

• Low in saturated fat, seafood is more desirable than beef as a protein source. Shellfish have one of the lowest saturated-fat contents of foods in the seafood world. And their omega-3 fatty acids may help blood to circulate more freely, lowering blood pressure.

Each serving (3 crackers) provides

Key Nutrients 50 Calories, 10 Calories from Fat, 2g Fat, 0g Saturated Fat, 0g Trans Fat, 3g Protein, 7g Carb, 0g Fiber, 105mg Sodium
Blood Pressure Nutrients 1mg Vitamin C, 7mg Magnesium, 48mg Potassium, 39mg Calcium

Crudités with Three Dips

Few foods can be healthier than raw vegetable sticks, so make the most of them by serving them with tempting low-fat dips for a snack or instead of a formal first course. Or, for a light lunch, these quantities will serve 4.

Preparation time **25 minutes, plus 30 minutes soaking**   *Serves 8*

Pesto-Yogurt Dip

1 cup fresh basil leaves
1 garlic clove, crushed
1 tablespoon pine nuts
1 cup plain low-fat yogurt

Fresh Herb Dip

3/4 cup low-fat sour cream
1 scallion, finely chopped
2 tablespoons finely chopped parsley
1 tablespoon finely snipped fresh chives
1 teaspoon tarragon vinegar

Italian-Style Tomato Dip

1/2 cup sun-dried tomatoes (dry-packed)
1/2 cup low-fat cottage cheese
1/4 cup plain low-fat yogurt
1/4 cup fresh basil leaves
Salt and pepper to taste

To Serve

1 pound vegetable crudités, such as baby carrots, zucchini sticks, green beans (blanched for 1 minute), pepper strips, and broccoli florets

1 For the pesto-yogurt dip, use a pestle and mortar to crush the basil, garlic, and pine nuts to a paste. Work in the yogurt a spoonful at a time, until thoroughly combined. Add seasoning to taste. Alternatively, puree all the ingredients together in a food processor or blender. Transfer to a bowl, cover, and chill.

2 For the fresh herb dip, stir all the ingredients together in a bowl until well blended. Cover tightly and chill until required.

3 For the Italian-style tomato dip, place the sun-dried tomatoes in a heatproof bowl and pour over boiling water to cover them. Leave to soak until the tomatoes are plump and tender, about 30 minutes. Drain the tomatoes well, then pat them dry and finely chop them.

4 Puree the cottage cheese with the yogurt in a food processor or blender. Alternatively, press the cheese through a sieve and stir in the yogurt. Transfer to a bowl and stir in the tomatoes. Cover and chill until required.

5 Just before serving the Italian-style tomato dip, finely shred the basil and stir in with seasoning to taste.

6 Serve the bowls of dips on a large platter with the crudités arranged around them.

(Some More Ideas)

• There is a wide choice of vegetables for making crunchy, delicious crudités. For example, try celery or cucumber sticks, whole radishes, baby plum tomatoes halved lengthwise, small cauliflower florets (raw or briefly cooked), and baby new potatoes cooked until tender.

• You could also offer a selection of fruit and warm pita bread for dipping, as well as vegetables.

Health Points

• Broccoli is one of the most studied vegetables, and for good reason: It has an extra-ordinary number of nutrients. In fact, broccoli may be as close to a blood-pressure superfood as there is, with its rich stores of calcium, potassium, anti-oxidants, and other heart-friendly phyto-chemicals.

• Pine nuts are rich in a variety of minerals: magnesium, potassium, iron, zinc, and copper.

Each serving (equal amounts of each dip) provides

Key Nutrients 80 Calories, 40 Calories from Fat, 4g Fat, 2g Saturated Fat, 0g Trans Fat, 6g Protein, 7g Carb, 0g Fiber, 110mg Sodium
Blood Pressure Nutrients 5mg Vitamin C, 25mg Magnesium, 297mg Potassium, 119mg Calcium

Spiced Root-Vegetable Wedges with Creamy Mustard Dip *p56*

Crudités with Three Dips *p54*

Spiced Fruits, Nuts, and Seeds *p58*

Pita Crisps with Hummus *p57*

Spiced Root-Vegetable Wedges with Creamy Mustard Dip

Lightly crushed coriander seeds and a hint of cinnamon accentuate the flavors of sweet potatoes, parsnips, and carrots, baked in wedges to make dippers for a tangy mustard and yogurt dip.

Preparation and cooking time **about 1 1/4 hours**   *Serves 4*

Wedges

2 large carrots

2 parsnips

Juice of 1 lime

2 tablespoons canola oil

2 tablespoons lightly crushed coriander seeds

1/2 teaspoon ground cinnamon

1 1/2 pounds sweet potatoes, peeled

Salt and pepper

Dip

2 teaspoons Dijon mustard

1 teaspoon sugar

Grated zest of 1 lime

7 ounces plain low-fat yogurt

3 tablespoons chopped fresh dill, plus extra to garnish

1 Preheat the oven to 425°F. Cut the carrots across in half. Cut the narrow halves in half lengthwise and each of the larger halves into quarters lengthwise. Cut up the parsnips in the same way. Place the prepared vegetables in a saucepan and pour in just enough water to cover them. Bring to the boil, then reduce the heat slightly and part cover the pan. Leave the vegetables to cook for 2 minutes.

2 Meanwhile, mix together the lime juice, oil, coriander, cinnamon, and salt and pepper to taste in a large roasting pan. Cut the sweet potatoes across in half, then into thick wedges, about the same size as the pieces of carrot and parsnip. Add the sweet potato wedges to the pan and turn them in the spice mixture until they are well coated, then push them to one side of the pan.

3 Drain the carrots and parsnips and add them to the roasting pan. Use a spoon and fork to turn the hot vegetables and coat them with the spice mixture. Place the roasting pan in the oven and bake, stirring and turning the vegetables twice, until they are well browned in places and just tender, about 40 minutes.

4 While the vegetables are baking, make the dip. Mix together the mustard, sugar, and lime zest, then stir in the yogurt and dill. Transfer the dip to a serving bowl, cover, and set aside until the vegetables are ready.

5 Remove the vegetable wedges from the oven and leave them to cool slightly. Garnish the mustard dip with a little extra dill, and serve with the vegetables.

(Some More Ideas)

Chile and herb dip: Mix plain low-fat yogurt with 1 tablespoon chopped fresh mint, 2 tablespoons chopped fresh cilantro, 1 small fresh green chile, seeded and finely chopped, and grated zest of 1 lemon. Use juice from lemon in spice mixture for coating vegetables instead of lime juice.

• Coat vegetables with a spice mixture made from lemon juice instead of lime juice, 1 tablespoon caraway seeds instead of coriander seeds, and ground mace instead of cinnamon. Use lemon zest instead of lime zest.

Health Points

• Parsnips were eaten by both the Greeks and the Romans, but the variety common today was not developed until the Middle Ages. Parsnips were an important staple food before the introduction of the potato.

photo, page 55

Each serving provides

Key Nutrients 380 Calories, 80 Calories from Fat, 9g Fat, 1g Saturated Fat, 0g Trans Fat, 8g Protein, 69g Carb, 11g Fiber, 150mg Sodium
Blood Pressure Nutrients 57mg Vitamin C, 47mg Magnesium, 776mg Potassium, 196mg Calcium

Pita Crisps with Hummus

This simple, easy-to-prepare snack is surprisingly rich in heart-healthy nutrients. Soft pita breads are transformed into crisp fingers by grilling. They pair perfectly with the creamy hummus dip.

Preparation and cooking time **about 15 minutes, plus cooling**   *Serves 4*

Hummus

1 can (15 ounces) chickpeas, drained and rinsed

1/2 teaspoon ground cumin

2 garlic cloves, crushed

2 tablespoons lemon juice

2 teaspoons olive oil

5 1/2 ounces low-fat sour cream

Salt and pepper to taste

Paprika and ground cumin to garnish *(optional)*

Lemon wedges to serve

Pita Crisps

6 small pita breads

1 1/2 tablespoons olive oil

1 1/4 ounces sesame seeds

1 Put the chickpeas, cumin, garlic, lemon juice, olive oil and sour cream in a food processor. Blend until very smooth, stopping and scraping down the sides of the container once or twice, 1–2 minutes.

2 Alternatively, place the ingredients in a bowl, preferably with a flat bottom, and puree with a handheld blender. For a slightly chunkier result, mash the chickpeas with a potato masher or fork until quite smooth, then stir in the other ingredients.

3 Season the hummus with salt and pepper to taste, then spoon into a bowl. Cover and keep in the fridge until ready to serve.

4 To prepare the pita crisps, preheat the grill to high. Spread out the pita breads on a baking tray and lightly brush the top side with half of the olive oil. Sprinkle with half of the sesame seeds. Grill until both the bread and seeds are golden brown, about 1 minute.

5 Turn the pitas over, brush with the remaining olive oil, and sprinkle with the remaining sesame seeds. Return to the hot grill and toast until the bread and seeds are golden brown, about 1 minute. Using scissors, quickly cut the warm pitas across into 3/4-inch fingers. Leave to cool and become crisp.

6 Sprinkle the hummus with a pinch each of paprika and cumin, if desired, then serve with the pita crisps and lemon wedges. (The pita crisps can be kept in an airtight container for 1–2 days.)

(Some More Ideas)

Eggplant dip: Grill 2 medium eggplants, turning frequently, until soft and charred. Put in a plastic bag and leave until cool enough to handle. Cut into quarters and peel. Leave the flesh to drain in a colander for 15 minutes, then gently squeeze out remaining liquid. Puree eggplant flesh in food processor with 1 crushed garlic clove, 1 teaspoon ground cumin, juice of 1 lemon, 4 tablespoons tahini paste, 1 tablespoon olive oil, 2 tablespoons chopped fresh mint, and salt and pepper. Garnish with cayenne pepper and small fresh mint leaves.

Lebanese flat bread: Split pita breads through middle and open them. Put 2 tablespoons toasted sesame seeds, 2 tablespoons poppy seeds, and 2 tablespoons chopped fresh thyme in a mortar. Crush lightly with a pestle. Stir in 3 tablespoons olive oil. Spread over inner sides of halves. Grill until golden brown. Leave to cool. Break into dipping-size pieces.

photo, page 55

Each serving provides

Key Nutrients 420 Calories, 170 Calories from Fat, 19g Fat, 4g Saturated Fat, 0g Trans Fat, 13g Protein, 51g Carb, 9g Fiber, 580mg Sodium
Blood Pressure Nutrients 8mg Vitamin C, 65mg Magnesium, 320mg Potassium, 118mg Calcium

Spiced Fruits, Nuts, and Seeds

This mildly spiced mix of crunchy nuts, pumpkin and sunflower seeds, tangy dried cranberries, and sweet raisins is great for nibbling as a healthy snack or with drinks. Children love it too!

Preparation and cooking time **about 1 1/4 hours**   *Serves 16 (makes 2 pounds)*

1 teaspoon cardamom pods
1 (1 inch) piece cinnamon stick
2 whole cloves
1 teaspoon black peppercorns
1 teaspoon cumin seeds
1 teaspoon coriander seeds
2 teaspoons finely chopped fresh root ginger
1 large egg white
1/4 cup fine or medium oatmeal
1/2 cup blanched almonds
1/2 cup pecan nut halves
1/2 cup Brazil nuts
1/4 cup pumpkin seeds
1/4 cup sunflower seeds
1/2 cup raisins
1/2 cup dried cranberries

1 Preheat the oven to 250°F. Lightly crush the cardamom pods with a pestle and mortar, or the side of a large knife, and discard the husks. Place the tiny seeds in a spice mill or a pestle and mortar, together with the cinnamon stick, cloves, peppercorns, and cumin and coriander seeds, and grind to a fairly fine powder.

2 Mix the ground spices with the ginger, egg white, and oatmeal in a large bowl. Add the almonds, pecan halves, Brazil nuts, pumpkin seeds, and sunflower seeds, and toss well to coat them all evenly with the spice mixture.

3 Spread the nuts and seeds onto a large baking sheet and spread out evenly in a single layer. Bake, stirring occasionally, until lightly browned and crisp, for about 1 hour. Remove from the oven and leave to cool on the baking sheet.

4 Put the nuts and seeds in a bowl. Add the raisins and cranberries, mixing well. The mixture is ready to serve, or it can be stored in an airtight container for up to 2 weeks.

(Some More Ideas)

• If you don't have a spice mill, you can use 1 tablespoon ready-made curry powder instead of the whole spices.

Hot-spiced nuts and seeds: add 1/2 teaspoon crushed dried chiles and 1–2 cloves crushed garlic to spice mixture. Use nuts and seeds only, omitting raisins and cranberries.

Sweet-spiced fruits, nuts, and seeds: Replace all spices used in main recipe with 1 teaspoon ground cinnamon, 1/2 teaspoon ground ginger, and 1/2 teaspoon freshly grated nutmeg. Stir these into the egg white and oatmeal, and use to coat nuts and seeds. Bake and cool. Mix with 1/2 cup each chopped dried mango, dried cherries, and chopped dried apple.

Health Points

• Almonds are a good source of unsaturated fat. They are also rich in vitamin E and provide protein, fiber, and zinc.

photo, page 55

Each serving provides

Key Nutrients 150 Calories, 110 Calories from Fat, 12g Fat, 2g Saturated Fat, 0g Trans Fat, 4g Protein, 9g Carb, 2g Fiber, 5mg Sodium
Blood Pressure Nutrients 1mg Vitamin C, 58mg Magnesium, 177mg Potassium, 39mg Calcium

meat

Sizzling Beef Fajitas

This Mexican fiesta-on-a-plate consists of strips of marinated steak, bell peppers, and onions presented smoking-hot from the broiler. It's a treat for the family, but also ideal party fare, so double or triple the recipe if you're entertaining a crowd.

Preparation time **10 minutes**   Cooking time **20 minutes**   *Serves 4*

1/4 cup fresh lime juice
1 teaspoon chili powder
3/4 teaspoon oregano
3/4 teaspoon ground coriander
1/4 teaspoon black pepper
12 ounces well-trimmed beef sirloin
2 large onions, thickly sliced
2 large red bell peppers, cut lengthwise into flat panels
1/4 cup minced cilantro
4 (7 inch) flour tortillas
4 cups shredded romaine lettuce
1/4 cup fat-free sour cream

1 Combine lime juice, chili powder, oregano, coriander, and black pepper in medium bowl.

2 Place beef in a shallow bowl and spoon 2 tablespoons of lime mixture on top; turn to coat both sides. Let stand while you broil the vegetables.

3 Preheat broiler. Spray broiler pan with nonstick cooking spray. Place onions and pepper pieces, skin-side up, on broiler pan. Broil 4 inches from heat until peppers are charred and onions are golden brown, about 10 minutes. Remove, and when cool enough to handle, peel peppers and thickly slice. Add peppers and onions to lime juice mixture in bowl. Add cilantro and toss.

4 Broil beef until done to medium, about 8 minutes, turning it over midway. Let stand 5 minutes before thinly slicing. Broil tortillas until lightly browned, about 15 seconds per side.

5 Place beef, peppers, onions, lettuce, sour cream, and flour tortillas in serving containers. Let each person fill his or her own tortilla.

(Some More Ideas)

• Use two (5 ounce) skinless, boneless chicken breasts in place of the steak. Slice the chicken into 1/2-inch strips and sauté in 2 teaspoons olive oil until cooked through, about 5 minutes. Add chicken in place of the steak in Step 5.

• Use orange or yellow peppers in place of the red ones.

• For a twist, place the meat mixture into large lettuce leaves instead of tortillas.

Health Points

• The vegetable mixture for these fajitas provides more than twice your daily requirement for vitamin C. This important vitamin works as an antioxidant to fight off a wide range of diseases.

• Olive oil is rich in unique disease-fighting phytochemicals, vitamin E, and monounsaturated fat, which all help to clear cholesterol from arteries. Research also suggests that olive oil may manage diabetes, rheumatoid arthritis, stroke, and various cancers.

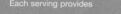Each serving provides

Key Nutrients 370 Calories, 90 Calories from Fat, 10g Fat, 3g Saturated Fat, 0g Trans Fat, 36g Protein, 34g Carb, 6g Fiber, 135mg Sodium
Blood Pressure Nutrients 184mg Vitamin C, 52mg Magnesium, 935mg Potassium, 88mg Calcium

Sizzling Beef Fajitas *p60*

Heartland Meat Loaf *p62*

Seared Sirloin with Garden Vegetables *p66*

Roast-Beef Hash *p63*

Heartland Meat Loaf

Meat loaf is often made only with beef. But with a few smart substitutions and techniques, you can keep all the flavor and texture of this old-fashioned favorite but get rid of excess fat, while adding many more nutrients.

Preparation time **30 minutes**   Cooking time **1 hour 20 minutes**   *Serves 8*

2 large onions, chopped

2 large celery ribs, chopped

1 large green bell pepper, chopped

3 garlic cloves, minced

2 pounds lean (95%) ground beef

1 cup fresh bread crumbs (about 2 slices)

1 egg white

1 teaspoon salt

1/2 teaspoon freshly ground black pepper

2 cups chopped canned tomatoes in puree

1/4 cup no-salt-added ketchup

1 Preheat oven to 350°F. Lightly coat 13 x 9-inch baking dish and large nonstick skillet with nonstick cooking spray. Set skillet over medium-high heat. Sauté onions, celery, green pepper, and garlic until soft, about 5 minutes. Transfer vegetables to large bowl.

2 Add beef, bread crumbs, egg white, salt, and pepper to vegetables in bowl and mix with your hands. Combine tomatoes and ketchup in small bowl, add half to meat-loaf mixture, and mix again.

3 Transfer meat-loaf mixture to baking dish and shape into 10 x 7-inch loaf, mounding slightly in center. Make length-wise groove down center with the side of your hand. Pour remaining tomato mixture into groove. Bake meat loaf until instant-read thermometer inserted in center reaches 165°F, about 1 hour 15 minutes. Let stand 10 minutes before slicing.

(Some More Ideas)

• If you're pressed for time, make mini meat loaves in a regular-sized muffin pan. Bake loaves at 350°F for about 25 minutes (this can cut total cooking time by 50 minutes!). Freeze any leftovers in ziplock plastic bags up to 1 month. To serve, cover with foil and reheat in a 350°F oven until hot, about 15 minutes.

• For added flavor and fiber, decrease the bread crumbs to 3/4 cup. Add 1/4 cup toasted wheat germ.

• Add one chopped or shredded carrot to the loaf.

Health Points

• Garlic is close to being a superfood when it comes to heart and arterial health. A phytochemical called ajoene apparently gives garlic its anti-clotting properties. Allicin, the chemical responsible for garlic's pungent smell, has antibacterial qualities. Sulfur compounds in garlic help prevent tumors and battle against free radicals in the bloodstream.

photo, page 61

Each serving provides

Key Nutrients 360 Calories, 130 Calories from Fat, 14g Fat, 6g Saturated Fat, 1g Trans Fat, 34g Protein, 23g Carb, 3g Fiber, 470mg Sodium
Blood Pressure Nutrients 29mg Vitamin C, 56mg Magnesium, 846mg Potassium, 74mg Calcium

Roast-Beef Hash

The question of what to do with leftover roast beef has never been answered more deliciously or healthfully: Pan-fry chunks of last night's roast with golden corn kernels and nuggets of potato and carrot for a filling, family-pleasing supper.

Preparation time **10 minutes**   Cooking time **30 minutes**   *Serves 4*

1 pound small red-skinned potatoes, cut into 1/4-inch dice

2 carrots, quartered lengthwise and thinly sliced

1 tablespoon, plus 2 teaspoons olive oil

1 medium onion, finely chopped

2 cloves garlic, minced

1 1/4 cups frozen corn

3/4 teaspoon salt

1/4 teaspoon pepper

6 ounces cooked roast beef, cut into 1/3-inch dice

1 Cook potatoes in medium saucepan of boiling water until almost tender, about 6 minutes. Add carrots and cook 2 minutes longer. Drain.

2 Spray a large nonstick skillet with nonstick cooking spray. Add 1 tablespoon oil and heat over medium-low heat. Add onion and garlic to skillet and cook, stirring frequently, until onion is golden brown, about 7 minutes.

3 Increase heat to medium-high. Add remaining 2 teaspoons oil. Add potatoes and carrots, corn, salt, and pepper, and cook, stirring occasionally, until mixture starts to form a crust, about 10 minutes.

4 Stir in beef and press down on mixture to help form a crust. Cook until crusty on the bottom, about 5 minutes.

(Some More Ideas)

• Cut sweet potatoes into 1/4-inch dice in place of the red-skinned potatoes.

• Use 6 ounces cooked chicken breast, diced, in place of the roast beef.

• Serve the hash with a salad of mixed greens and slivered red onions.

Health Points

• Though corned-beef hash may be more traditional, it is a far fattier dish than roast-beef hash, because corned beef is made from brisket, one of the fattiest cuts of beef. And because it is brined, corned beef is also very high in sodium.

• Eating potatoes with their skin on is good for your heart. The skins supply notable heart-healthy nutrients, including potassium, B vitamins, and plenty of cholesterol-lowering fiber.

photo, page 61

Each serving provides

Key Nutrients 250 Calories, 60 Calories from Fat, 7g Fat, 1g Saturated Fat, 0g Trans Fat, 13g Protein, 35g Carb, 4g Fiber, 560mg Sodium
Blood Pressure Nutrients 9mg Vitamin C, 8mg Magnesium, 149mg Potassium, 62mg Calcium

Stir-Fried Beef Salad with Mango

This colorful Thai-style dish is bursting with fresh flavors and deliciously contrasting textures. The dressing is completely oil-free, so despite the beef and nuts, this dish is light in calories.

Preparation time **30 minutes**　　Cooking time **about 10 minutes**　　*Serves 4*

Stir-Fry

1 pound lean steak, such as sirloin

3 garlic cloves, finely chopped

1 teaspoon sugar

2 teaspoons low-sodium soy sauce

1 1/2 tablespoons canola oil

Dressing

2 teaspoons paprika

2 teaspoons mild chili powder

1 1/2 tablespoons honey

1-inch piece fresh ginger, grated

1 cup water

4 tablespoons vinegar

Juice of 1 lime or lemon

Salad

1 mango, peeled and cut into strips

2 plums, sliced

1/4 medium red cabbage

2 cups watercress leaves

1/2 cucumber

1/2 red pepper

3–4 scallions, cut into diagonal pieces

1/4 cup mixed fresh mint and cilantro

2 tablespoons chopped roasted unsalted peanuts

1 To make the dressing, put the paprika, chili powder, honey, ginger, and rice or cider vinegar in a saucepan and slowly add one cup water, stirring. Bring to boil, then reduce the heat and simmer for 5 minutes. Remove from the heat and stir in the lime or lemon juice. Set aside.

2 Shred the cabbage, cut the cucumber into matchsticks, and cut the pepper into thin strips. Combine all the salad ingredients, except the peanuts, in a large shallow serving dish and toss gently together until evenly mixed. Set aside.

3 Cut the steak into thin strips for stir-frying. Put the steak in a bowl with the garlic, sugar, and soy sauce and mix together so the strips of steak are seasoned. Heat a wok or nonstick pan on a high heat, then add the oil. Add the beef and stir-fry until the strips are evenly browned and cooked to taste.

4 Spoon the stir-fried beef over the salad. Drizzle the dressing over the top and sprinkle with the peanuts. Serve immediately.

(Some More Ideas)

• Add cubes of fresh or canned pineapple (canned in juice rather than syrup) or kiwifruit to the salad, to increase the fruit content.

• Spice up the salad with very thin strips of fresh red chile pepper—particularly if you have a cold, as scientists have suggested that eating chiles can help to alleviate nasal congestion.

• Replace the mango with 2 nectarines, unpeeled and sliced.

• For a vegetarian version, omit the stir-fried beef and increase the quantity of peanuts to 5 1/2 ounces. Peanuts are an excellent source of protein and contain much less saturated fat than meat.

Health Points

• Apart from adding its delicious spiciness to the dressing, ginger also aids digestion.

Each serving provides

Key Nutrients 470 Calories, 170 Calories from Fat, 19g Fat, 5g Saturated Fat, 0g Trans Fat, 42g Protein, 33g Carb, 5g Fiber, 200mg Sodium
Blood Pressure Nutrients 90mg Vitamin C, 77mg Magnesium, 1036mg Potassium, 75mg Calcium

Seared Sirloin with Garden Vegetables

Looking for a healthful steak? Here it is: a scrumptious sirloin, flash-cooked to seal in all its fabulous flavors and surrounded by plenty of fresh veggies. Sirloin is among the leanest cuts of steak, yet is full of flavor.

Preparation time **20 minutes**   Cooking time **35 minutes**   *Serves 8*

2 garlic cloves, minced

1 teaspoon salt

1/2 teaspoon pepper

1 bone-in beef sirloin steak (1 1/4 inches thick, about 2 1/4 pounds)

1 pound medium red potatoes, quartered

1 pound green beans

1 large red onion, very thinly sliced

2 tablespoons white wine vinegar

2 teaspoons extra-virgin olive oil

1/4 teaspoon sugar

1 Preheat oven to 375°F. Mash garlic, 1/2 teaspoon salt, and 1/4 teaspoon pepper with side of chef's knife to form chunky paste. Rub on both sides of steak. Set aside.

2 Bring potatoes and enough water to cover to a boil in saucepan. Reduce heat and simmer 5 minutes. Add beans and cook until potatoes are tender and beans are crisp-tender, 3–4 minutes. Drain, rinse with cool water, and transfer to large bowl.

3 Put onion in colander and rinse with hot tap water. Mix vinegar, oil, 1/4 teaspoon salt, remaining pepper, and sugar in small bowl. Set vinaigrette aside.

4 Heat large heavy ovenproof skillet over medium-high heat until very hot but not smoking. Sprinkle skillet with remaining salt. Add steak and sear until browned, about 3 minutes on each side. Transfer to oven. For medium-rare (135°F–140°F), cook 15–18 minutes; medium (140°F–145°F), 20–23 minutes. Let stand 5 minutes. Trim any remaining fat and thinly slice steak. Arrange potatoes, beans, and onions around steak and drizzle with vinaigrette before serving.

(Some More Ideas)

• For a tasty change, roast the potatoes instead of boiling them. (This variation is featured on our cover.)

• Use 1 pound cubed sweet potatoes in place of the red potatoes.

• Use snow or sugar snap peas in place of the green beans.

• For an extra zesty flavor, toss the red onion in balsamic vinegar instead of white wine vinegar.

Health Points

• A 4 1/2-ounce serving of beef (which is what you get in this recipe) provides a whopping supply of vitamin B12. It is also an excellent source of iron and zinc.

• The red onion in this dish is particularly healthy for your cardiovascular system. In addition to being high in fiber, it offers large amounts of antioxidants, particularly quercetin, a potent flavonoid linked to a reduced risk of cancer, cardiovascular disease, and cataracts.

photo, page 61

Each serving provides

Key Nutrients 410 Calories, 160 Calories from Fat, 18g Fat, 5g Saturated Fat, 1g Trans Fat, 45g Protein, 15g Carb, 3g Fiber, 470mg Sodium
Blood Pressure Nutrients 16mg Vitamin C, 58mg Magnesium, 925mg Potassium, 47mg Calcium

Fusilli and Meatballs

Hearty, healthy, and everyone's favorite Italian dish—don't you want pasta and meatballs for dinner tonight? Unlike traditional recipes, these meatballs are low in fat, yet they're full of the terrific taste you crave.

Preparation time **30 minutes**   Cooking time **1 hour 20 minutes**   *Serves 6*

1 large onion, chopped
2 garlic cloves, minced
1 can (28 ounces) no-salt-added Italian tomatoes
1 can (28 ounces) no-salt-added whole tomatoes in puree
1/4 cup chopped fresh basil
1 tablespoon fresh oregano or 1 teaspoon dried
2 slices firm-textured, dry white bread
1 pound lean (93%) ground beef
1 large egg
2 tablespoons reduced-fat (2%) milk
1/2 teaspoon salt
1/2 teaspoon pepper
12 ounces long fusilli

1 Coat large saucepan with nonstick cooking spray and set over medium-high heat. Sauté onion and garlic until soft, about 5 minutes. Transfer 2 tablespoons onion mixture to large bowl.

2 Process Italian and whole tomatoes in food processor until fairly smooth. Add to saucepan. Bring to a boil over medium-high heat. Reduce heat to medium-low. Cover and simmer, stirring often, 30 minutes. Add basil and oregano during the last 15 minutes.

3 Process bread until crumbs form. Add crumbs, beef, egg, milk, salt, and pepper to onion mixture and mix just until blended. Shape into twenty 1-inch meatballs. Coat medium skillet with nonstick cooking spray and set over medium-high heat. Cook meatballs in batches until browned on all sides, about 8 minutes. Drain on paper towels. Add meatballs to sauce. Cover and cook, stirring occasionally, 20 minutes.

4 Meanwhile, cook pasta according to package directions. Drain and toss with 1 1/2 cups sauce in large heated serving bowl. Spoon 1 cup sauce over pasta. Serve meatballs and remaining sauce alongside.

(Some More Ideas)

• Make turkey or chicken meatballs in place of ground beef. Use 1 pound lean ground white-meat turkey or chicken breasts.

• Make spicy meatballs: Add 1/2 teaspoon or more of crushed red pepper flakes to the meat mixture.

• Try any shaped pasta for the fusilli. For added fiber, substitute whole-wheat noodles for the white-flour ones.

• Serve with a vegetable course for a more well-rounded meal. A fast sauté of zucchini, peppers, green beans, or asparagus in a teaspoon of olive oil, plus garlic and black pepper, is fast and delicious.

Health Points

• Pasta and meatballs is a healthy dish, especially when you include cooked tomatoes. Studies have shown that lycopene, a phytochemical in tomatoes, is best absorbed by the body if the tomatoes are cooked.

photo, page 69

Each serving provides

Key Nutrients 470 Calories, 60 Calories from Fat, 6g Fat, 2g Saturated Fat, 0g Trans Fat, 31g Protein, 77g Carb, 8g Fiber, 340mg Sodium
Blood Pressure Nutrients 30mg Vitamin C, 126mg Magnesium, 1549mg Potassium, 119mg Calcium

Pesto-Coated Pork Chops

Pork chops on a menu for lower blood pressure? You bet! Pork is about 50% leaner than just a few years ago, which means it's lower in saturated fat as well. To keep these chops succulent, top them with a homemade pesto.

Preparation time **15 minutes**   Cooking time **8 minutes**   *Serves 4*

6 ounces eggless noodles

2 cups fresh basil leaves

3 garlic cloves, peeled

Salt to taste

1/2 teaspoon freshly ground black pepper

2 tablespoons plain dry bread crumbs

2 tablespoons olive oil

4 center-cut pork loin chops (1/2 inch thick, about 4 ounces each)

1 Prepare noodles according to package directions. Drain and keep hot. Meanwhile, preheat broiler.

2 Put basil, garlic, and a pinch each of salt and pepper in food processor. Pulse until roughly chopped. Add bread crumbs and process until incorporated, about 30 seconds. With motor running, slowly add oil through feed tube until pureed. Set aside.

3 Coat large heavy ovenproof skillet and broiler rack with nonstick cooking spray. Set skillet over high heat until very hot but not smoking. Sprinkle both sides of chops with remaining salt and pepper. Sauté chops until browned, about 1 minute on each side. Remove from heat. Spread chops on both sides with pesto and transfer to broiler pan.

4 Broil chops until pesto is slightly darker and juices run clear, about 2 minutes on each side. Divide noodles evenly among 4 plates and top with a pork chop.

(Some More Ideas)

• Use skinless, boneless chicken breasts or thighs in place of the pork. Sauté the chicken on both sides for about 5–6 minutes per side.

Health Points

• Pork is a good source of zinc and it provides useful amounts of iron, as well as vitamins from the B group, particularly B1, B6, B12, and niacin.

• Garlic truly is a superfood when it comes to treating high blood pressure. A review of eight independent studies shows that people who took a daily preparation of garlic powder saw a nearly 8 point decline in their systolic blood-pressure measure when compared with those on a placebo. The diastolic measure also fell, by an average of 5 points.

Each serving provides

Key Nutrients 480 Calories, 170 Calories from Fat, 19g Fat, 5g Saturated Fat, 0g Trans Fat, 39g Protein, 36g Carb, 2g Fiber, 100mg Sodium
Blood Pressure Nutrients 5mg Vitamin C, 72mg Magnesium, 669mg Potassium, 74mg Calcium

Pesto-Coated Pork Chops *p68*

Fusilli and Meatballs *p67*

Cidered Pork with Red Cabbage *p70*

Lamb Curry *p71*

Cidered Pork with Red Cabbage

Slow cooking makes this hearty stew perfect for cool autumn days. Experiment with different types of apples— Granny Smith are tart and tangy; Golden Delicious are juicy and mild.

Preparation time **20 minutes**   Cooking time **2 1/4–2 1/2 hours**   *Serves 6*

1 tablespoon canola oil

1 pound lean boneless pork shoulder, cut into bite-size chunks

2 onions, chopped

2 baking apples, peeled, cored, and diced

1 carrot, diced

2 tablespoons raisins

2 cups apple cider

1 cup reduced-sodium chicken broth

2 bay leaves

1/4 teaspoon fresh thyme leaves, or to taste

Pinch ground cinnamon

Pinch ground allspice

12 pitted prunes

1/2 red cabbage, cut into bite-size pieces

1 tablespoon tomato puree

1 pound pasta in small sizes, such as shells (conchiglie) or ears (orecchiette)

2 tablespoons chopped fresh parsley

Salt and pepper to taste

1 Heat the oil in a heavy-based saucepan or flameproof casserole, add the chunks of pork, and cook until they are starting to brown. Add the onions and continue to cook until the pork and onions are both lightly browned, stirring occasionally.

2 Stir in the apples, carrot, raisins, cider, broth, bay leaves, thyme, cinnamon, and allspice. Bring to the boil, then reduce the heat and cover the pan. Cook over a very low heat for about 1 hour.

3 Mix in the prunes and red cabbage and cover the pan again. Continue to cook gently until the meat is very tender, about 1 hour.

4 Stir in the tomato puree. Leave to cook gently, covered, while you cook the pasta.

5 Cook the pasta in boiling water according to the package instructions, until al dente, 10–12 minutes.

6 Drain the pasta, then divide among 6 bowls. Ladle the cidered pork over. Sprinkle with parsley and serve.

(Some More Ideas)

Chunky borscht: Increase the broth to 3 cups. Add 3–4 grated cooked beets, 1 tablespoon sugar, and the juice of 1 lemon with the cabbage. Taste for sweet-sour balance, adding a little extra lemon juice or sugar, and ladle the borscht over pasta shells in deep bowls. Serve with a dollop of plain low-fat yogurt on each portion, and a sprinkling of dill.

Health Points

• Over the last 20 years, farmers have been breeding leaner pigs, and pork now contains considerably less fat than it did in the past. It also contains higher levels of the "good" polyunsaturated fats. The average fat content of lean pork is just 3.5%, much the same as skinless chicken breast.

• Prunes provide useful amounts of potassium, iron, and vitamin B6. They are also a good source of dietary fiber.

photo, page 69

Each serving provides

Key Nutrients 460 Calories, 100 Calories from Fat, 11g Fat, 3g Saturated Fat, 0g Trans Fat, 29g Protein, 65g Carb, 7g Fiber, 85mg Sodium
Blood Pressure Nutrients 50mg Vitamin C, 62mg Magnesium, 792mg Potassium, 87mg Calcium

Lamb Curry

This scrumptious curried lamb dish is prepared with everyday ingredients—most you probably have on hand right now—yet you'll be wowed by its authentic flavor. For your blood pressure's sake, we've used the leanest cut of lamb.

Preparation time **25 minutes**   Cooking time **55 minutes**   *Serves 4*

1 teaspoon olive oil

12 ounces well-trimmed boneless lamb loin, cut into 3/4-inch chunks

1 medium onion, finely chopped

4 cloves garlic, minced

1 tablespoon grated fresh ginger

1 tablespoon curry powder

4 cups cauliflower florets

1 cup no-salt-added canned crushed tomatoes

Salt to taste

1/2 cup water

1 1/2 cups frozen peas

1/3 cup chopped cilantro

1/2 cup plain fat-free yogurt

2 tablespoons flour

1 Heat oil in nonstick Dutch oven over medium heat. Add lamb and cook until browned, about 5 minutes. With slotted spoon, transfer lamb to bowl or plate.

2 Add onion, garlic, and ginger to pan and cook, stirring frequently, until onion is tender, about 5 minutes. Add curry powder and cauliflower, stirring to coat.

3 Add tomatoes, salt, and water to pan and bring to a boil. Return lamb to pan and reduce to a simmer. Cover and cook until lamb and cauliflower are tender, about 40 minutes.

4 Add peas and cilantro, and cook until peas are heated through, about 3 minutes. Stir yogurt and flour together in small bowl. Stir yogurt mixture into pan and cook over low heat, stirring, until slightly thickened, about 2 minutes.

(Some More Ideas)

• Use 12 ounces well-trimmed beef roast, cut into 3/4-inch chunks, in place of the lamb.

Shrimp curry: Omit cooking the lamb in Step 1 and substitute 1 pound peeled and deveined large shrimp. Cook the shrimp for 3 minutes and remove to a bowl. In Step 3 omit the lamb and cook only the cauliflower for 20 minutes. Add the shrimp back to the dish after adding the yogurt mixture to the pan in Step 4.

Health Points

• Turmeric, a principal component of curry powder, may help lower LDL ("bad") cholesterol and prevent blood clots.

• The combination of onion, garlic, and ginger that is so common in Asian cooking is an extraordinary one-two-three punch of nutrition. All are rich in antioxidants and phytochemicals that fight cancer, heart disease, hypertension, and other chronic illnesses.

photo, page 69

Each serving provides

Key Nutrients 280 Calories, 60 Calories from Fat, 7g Fat, 2g Saturated Fat, 0g Trans Fat, 27g Protein, 30g Carb, 8g Fiber, 190mg Sodium
Blood Pressure Nutrients 92mg Vitamin C, 79mg Magnesium, 953mg Potassium, 125mg Calcium

MEAT

Fragrant Lamb with Spinach

This enticing curry is warmly spiced rather than fiery hot with chiles. Serve it with basmati rice, chapatis, and a fresh tomato and cucumber chutney for a healthy Indian-style meal.

Preparation time **20–25 minutes**   Cooking time **1 hour 20 minutes**   *Serves 4*

2 tablespoons canola oil

2 onions, finely chopped

4 garlic cloves, crushed

2-inch piece fresh ginger, peeled and chopped

1 red chile pepper, seeded and sliced

2 teaspoons paprika

2 teaspoons ground cumin

2 teaspoons ground coriander

1 teaspoon ground white pepper

1/2 teaspoon ground cinnamon

Seeds from 8 green cardamom pods, crushed

2 bay leaves

Salt to taste

1 cup plain nonfat yogurt

2/3 cup water

1 pound lean boneless lamb, cubed

2 large tomatoes, chopped

8 ounces fresh baby spinach

4 tablespoons chopped fresh cilantro

Sprigs of fresh cilantro *(garnish)*

1 Heat the oil in a large saucepan or flameproof casserole. Add the onions, garlic, and ginger, and sauté, stirring frequently, until the onions are golden, about 15 minutes.

2 Stir in the chile, paprika, cumin, coriander, white pepper, cinnamon, crushed cardamom seeds, bay leaves, and salt. Stir briefly over a moderate heat, then stir in the yogurt and water. Add the lamb, mix well, and cover the pan. Simmer gently until the lamb is tender, about 1 1/4 hours.

3 Add the tomatoes, spinach, and chopped cilantro. Cook, stirring, until the tomatoes have softened slightly and the spinach has wilted, 2–3 minutes. Taste for seasoning and remove the bay leaf. Serve garnished with fresh cilantro.

(Some More Ideas)

• The basic curry sauce in this recipe can be used to cook other meats or vegetables. Cubes of skinless, boneless chicken or turkey breast (fillet) are delicious, as are lean boneless pork chops. All of these need only 40 minutes simmering in the sauce. A mixture of vegetables—halved new potatoes, cauliflower florets, sliced carrots, and chunks of parsnip—is good too. Use 1 1/2 pounds total weight and cook for 30 minutes.

Tomato Chutney: Serve this with the curry. Finely chop and mix together 4 plum tomatoes, 1/2 cucumber, 1 small onion, 1 seeded fresh green chile pepper, and 4 tablespoons chopped fresh cilantro.

Health Points

• Cardamom is believed to help relieve digestive problems such as indigestion, flatulence, and stomach cramps, and it can help prevent acid regurgitation and belching.

Each serving provides

Key Nutrients 320 Calories, 130 Calories from Fat, 14g Fat, 3g Saturated Fat, 0g Trans Fat, 30g Protein, 21g Carb, 5g Fiber, 170mg Sodium
Blood Pressure Nutrients 81mg Vitamin C, 100mg Magnesium, 1035mg Potassium, 195mg Calcium

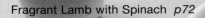

Fragrant Lamb with Spinach *p72*

Veal Marsala *p75*

Veal Cutlets with Lemon-Garlic Sauce *p76*

Leg of Lamb with Double-Mint Sauce *p74*

Leg of Lamb with Double-Mint Sauce

Whether it's spring or not, treat yourself to lamb! A small leg serves 6 and is surprisingly low in fat. The crowning jewel of a fresh mint sauce simmers up in seconds, yet tastes as if it took much more time.

Preparation time **20 minutes**   Cooking time **55 minutes plus standing**   *Serves 6*

Sauce

2/3 cup mint jelly
2 tablespoons fresh lemon juice
1/4 cup chopped fresh mint

Lamb

1 boneless leg of lamb, well trimmed (about 2 1/4 pounds)
2 garlic cloves, chopped
1 tablespoon chopped fresh rosemary
Salt to taste
1/2 teaspoon pepper
1 large lemon, halved
2/3 cup dry white wine or reduced-sodium chicken broth

1 Preheat oven to 400°F. Lightly coat roasting pan with non-stick cooking spray. Combine mint jelly, lemon juice, and fresh mint in small saucepan. Stir constantly over medium heat until jelly melts, about 5 minutes. Remove from heat and set aside.

2 Meanwhile, cut lamb horizontally three-quarters through with sharp knife. Open and spread flat like a book. Put meat between two pieces of plastic wrap and pound with meat mallet or rolling pin to about 1 inch thick.

3 Brush about 2 tablespoons sauce on lamb, and then sprinkle with garlic, rosemary, salt, and pepper. Squeeze juice from one lemon half over lamb. Roll up lamb from one wide side. Tie with kitchen string, in both directions. Transfer to pan, seam-side down. Squeeze remaining lemon half over lamb and pour on wine.

4 Roast until done to taste or an instant-read thermometer inserted in center reaches 140°F (medium), about 50 minutes. Let stand 10 minutes before slicing. Reheat remaining sauce. Remove strings from lamb and cut lamb into 1/2-inch slices. Serve with mint sauce.

(Some More Ideas)

• Although lamb and mint sauce is a traditional pairing, you could substitute a 2 1/4-pound beef or pork loin roast for the lamb.

• Pair this meal with steamed asparagus and roasted new potatoes.

Health Points

• Lamb is a rich-tasting meat, but over the years, it has grown leaner thanks to marketplace demand for less fatty meats. While still not as lean as pork or poultry, lamb meat is extremely flavorful, and can often be served in smaller portions as part of a well-rounded meal.

photo, page 73

Each serving provides

Key Nutrients 310 Calories, 70 Calories from Fat, 7g Fat, 3g Saturated Fat, 0g Trans Fat, 36g Protein, 26g Carb, 1g Fiber, 115mg Sodium
Blood Pressure Nutrients 17mg Vitamin C, 50mg Magnesium, 540mg Potassium, 30mg Calcium

Veal Marsala

Elegant enough for company, easy enough for every day! Lean veal cutlets cook in a jiffy, and the Marsala sauce with mushrooms adds plenty of class.

Preparation time **15 minutes**   Cooking time **12 minutes**   *Serves 4*

12 large white mushrooms
(about 10 ounces)

1 pound veal cutlets

1/2 teaspoon pepper

Salt to taste

1/4 cup all-purpose flour

2 tablespoons margarine,
cut into 4 pieces

3/4 cup dry Marsala wine

3 tablespoons chopped
flat-leaf parsley

1 Preheat oven to 250°F. Place baking sheet on middle rack of oven. Trim ends of mushrooms. Thinly slice mushrooms. Set aside.

2 Place veal cutlets between pieces of wax paper and pound with meat mallet, from center out, to 1/8-inch thickness. Sprinkle with pepper and salt. Place flour in ziplock plastic bag. Add veal, a few slices at a time, and shake to coat.

3 Coat large nonstick skillet with nonstick cooking spray and set over high heat. Melt 1 piece margarine in skillet, tilting to coat. Sauté a few pieces of veal at a time until browned, about 1 minute on each side, turning only once (do not crowd skillet!). Transfer cutlets to baking sheet in oven. Repeat with remaining veal, adding margarine as needed.

4 Sauté mushrooms in skillet until golden, about 3 minutes. Pour in Marsala, scraping up browned bits left in the skillet. Cook until pan juices are reduced to 1/2 cup, about 2 minutes. Return veal to skillet, stacking if necessary. Turn to coat with hot pan juices. Sprinkle with parsley.

(Some More Ideas)

• For a lower grocery bill, substitute equal amounts of skinless, boneless chicken or turkey breasts for the pricier veal.

• Substitute two large, fresh portobello mushrooms—they provide a rich, meaty taste and texture that elevate the delicate flavor of the veal from sublime to divine! Or consider using shiitake mushrooms, which also have an earthy, full flavor and feature heart-healthy phytochemicals not found in other mushrooms.

Health Points

• Compared with many beef and lamb cuts, veal is lower in both fat and saturated fat. It's also a good source of the B vitamins niacin and riboflavin, which aid in metabolizing fat.

• Mushrooms are a good source of copper, a mineral that is important for healthy bones. Copper also helps the body to absorb iron from food.

photo, page 73

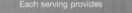
Each serving provides

Key Nutrients 290 Calories, 80 Calories from Fat, 9g Fat, 2g Saturated Fat, 1g Trans Fat, 26g Protein, 14g Carb, 1g Fiber, 180mg Sodium
Blood Pressure Nutrients 5mg Vitamin C, 43mg Magnesium, 329mg Potassium, 32mg Calcium

Veal Cutlets with Lemon-Garlic Sauce

There's a whole head of garlic in this recipe, but after slow roasting, it comes out of the oven tasting mild and sweet. The mashed roast garlic adds a sublime but subtle perfume to the sauce.

Preparation time **5 minutes**   Cooking time **50 minutes**   *Serves 4*

Sauce

1 head garlic
2/3 cup reduced-sodium chicken broth
1/4 cup fresh lemon juice
2 teaspoons cornstarch
1/4 teaspoon salt

Veal

4 veal cutlets (4 ounces each)
1/4 teaspoon salt
1 tablespoon Dijon mustard
1 lemon, very thinly sliced

1 Preheat oven to 375°F. Wrap garlic in foil and bake until tender (package will feel soft when pressed), about 45 minutes. When cool enough to handle, cut off top of bulb, squeeze out garlic pulp into small bowl, and mash until smooth.

2 Preheat broiler. Sprinkle cutlets with 1/4 teaspoon salt and brush with mustard. Top each cutlet with 3 lemon slices. Broil cutlets 4 inches from heat until cooked through, about 2 minutes. Transfer cutlets to platter and cover loosely with foil to keep warm.

3 In small saucepan, whisk broth and lemon juice into cornstarch. Whisk in 1/4 teaspoon salt and roasted garlic. Bring to a boil over medium heat and boil until sauce is lightly thickened, about 1 minute. Spoon sauce over veal on platter.

(Some More Ideas)

Garlic Bread: Use roasted garlic as it is prepared in Step 1 to spread over slices of whole-grain bread instead of butter.

• You can substitute chicken or pork cutlets for the veal.

Health Points

• The sulfur compounds in garlic may protect blood vessels against the accumulation of fatty plaque that can lead to heart disease and stroke.

photo, page 73

Each serving provides

Key Nutrients 160 Calories, 35 Calories from Fat, 4g Fat, 1g Saturated Fat, 0g Trans Fat, 24g Protein, 8g Carb, 2g Fiber, 450mg Sodium
Blood Pressure Nutrients 30mg Vitamin C, 34mg Magnesium, 461mg Potassium, 53mg Calcium

poultry

Citrus-Grilled California Chicken with Melon Salsa

Capture the spirit of the Golden State and set it on your dinner table! This sunny mix of melon, salad greens, chicken, and citrus, spiked with jalapeños, is healthful, carefree eating at its best.

Preparation time **20 minutes**   Cooking time **10 minutes**   *Serves 4*

Chicken

4 skinless, boneless chicken breast halves (about 4 ounces each)

Salt to taste

1/2 teaspoon black pepper

1 jalapeño pepper

6 tablespoons fresh lime juice, divided

1 garlic clove, minced

2 teaspoons light soy sauce

Salsa

1 large cucumber

1 small cantaloupe, cut into 1-inch cubes

1/2 pint cherry tomatoes, halved

2 tablespoons very thinly sliced fresh basil

To Serve

6 cups mesclun (about 3 ounces)

1 Preheat grill to medium or preheat broiler. Sprinkle chicken on both sides with salt and black pepper. Devein and seed jalapeño pepper with melon baller (wear gloves when handling, as it can burn); mince. Stir 2 tablespoons lime juice, garlic, soy sauce, and 1 teaspoon jalapeño in pie plate. Add chicken and turn to coat. Marinate at room temperature, turning once, while preparing Melon Salsa.

2 Halve cucumber lengthwise. Remove seeds by dragging tip of spoon down center. Place cucumber cut-side down on board, and slice 1/8 inch thick. Toss cucumber, cantaloupe, tomatoes, basil, and remaining jalapeño and lime juice in medium bowl. Set aside.

3 Discard marinade. Lightly coat both sides of chicken with nonstick cooking spray (preferably olive oil flavored). Grill or broil chicken until juices run clear, about 5 minutes on each side, turning only once.

4 Transfer chicken to cutting board and cut diagonally into strips, about 1/2 inch wide. Toss with cucumber mixture. Divide mesclun among 4 plates and spoon one-fourth melon mixture on top of each.

(Some More Ideas)

• This recipe can use any kind of lean meat instead of chicken. Use turkey, pork, or lean beef for variety.

• For a dish with less heat, omit the jalapeño and substitute 1 teaspoon mild chili powder. Use half in the marinade for the chicken and half in the salsa.

• Add 1 cup pineapple chunks (fresh or canned in its own juice) to the salsa.

• Serve over torn romaine lettuce leaves instead of mesclun.

Health Points

• Cantaloupe is an excellent source of beta-carotene, a powerful antioxidant with anti-carcinogenic properties.

• Hot peppers such as jalapeño have ample amounts of vitamin C; more than bell peppers do. And capsaicin, the chemical that causes the heat, is also very healthy.

Each serving provides

Key Nutrients 180 Calories, 15 Calories from Fat, 2g Fat, 0g Saturated Fat, 0g Trans Fat, 28g Protein, 14g Carb, 2g Fiber, 210mg Sodium
Blood Pressure Nutrients 66mg Vitamin C, 56mg Magnesium, 814mg Potassium, 47mg Calcium

Chicken with Apples *p80*

Citrus-Grilled California Chicken with Melon Salsa *p78*

Chicken and Cashew Pancakes *p86*

Greek Chicken Pitas *p83*

Chicken with Apples

Looking for a meal that can be on the table in 30 minutes yet is elegant enough for a dinner party? This dish looks and tastes like it comes from a fine French bistro, but with far healthier ingredients.

Preparation time **10 minutes**   Cooking time **20 minutes**   *Serves 4*

Apples

2 medium shallots, finely chopped

2 tart apples, peeled and cut into 1/4-inch slices

1 cup apple juice

3/4 cup reduced-sodium chicken broth

1 tablespoon Calvados, applejack, or apple juice

Chicken

1/4 cup all-purpose flour

Salt to taste

1/2 teaspoon freshly ground black pepper

4 skinless, boneless chicken breast halves (5 ounces each)

2 tablespoons heavy cream

1 Lightly coat large heavy nonstick skillet with nonstick cooking spray and set over medium-high heat. Sauté shallots until soft, about 2 minutes. Add apples and sauté until lightly browned, about 3 minutes. Add apple juice, broth, and Calvados. Cook, stirring, until apples are tender, about 5 minutes. Transfer to medium bowl. Wipe skillet clean.

2 Meanwhile, combine flour, salt, and pepper on sheet of wax paper. Coat chicken breasts with seasoned flour, pressing with your hands so flour adheres and chicken is flattened evenly.

3 Lightly coat skillet again with cooking spray and set over medium-high heat. Cook chicken until browned and almost cooked through, about 3 minutes on each side. Return apple mixture and any juices to skillet and bring to a boil. Reduce heat and simmer 2 minutes. Stir in cream and remove from heat.

(Some More Ideas)

• Serve this dish with wild rice, sautéed green beans, and diced mango for dessert.

• Substitute turkey cutlets for chicken breasts.

• Stirring in a smidgen of heavy cream at the end gives the sauce a lush satiny smoothness. A small amount adds a satisfying richness to sauces without ruining your healthy eating goals.

Health Points

• Apples contain ellagic acid, an antioxidant substance that protects against heart disease and cancer. They also contain rutin, a chemical that teams up with vitamin C to maintain blood-vessel health.

photo, page 79

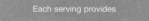
Each serving provides

Key Nutrients 320 Calories, 50 Calories from Fat, 5g Fat, 3g Saturated Fat, 0g Trans Fat, 35g Protein, 33g Carb, 3g Fiber, 120mg Sodium
Blood Pressure Nutrients 10mg Vitamin C, 53mg Magnesium, 626mg Potassium, 43mg Calcium

Basmati Chicken Pilaf

This colorful one-pot dish is very simple to make and ideal for a tasty and nutritious midweek meal. Coconut milk, gentle spices, and fresh cilantro add an exotically fragrant note. Serve with a mixed green salad for a well-rounded dinner.

Preparation time **10 minutes**   Cooking time **20–25 minutes**   *Serves 4*

2 tablespoons olive oil

1 onion, chopped

1 garlic clove, crushed

1 red bell pepper, seeded and diced

1 pound skinless, boneless chicken breasts, cut into thin strips

6 ounces button mushrooms, halved

2 small zucchini, sliced

1 cup basmati rice, rinsed

1 teaspoon ground coriander

1 teaspoon ground cumin

1 teaspoon ground cinnamon

1/2 cup light coconut milk

1 1/2 cups hot reduced-sodium chicken broth

2 tablespoons chopped fresh cilantro

Salt and pepper to taste

Sprigs of fresh cilantro *(garnish)*

1 Heat the oil in a saucepan and add the onion, garlic, red pepper, and chicken. Cook, stirring, over a fairly high heat until the chicken has lost its pinkness, 4–5 minutes.

2 Add the mushrooms, zucchini, rice, ground coriander, cumin, and cinnamon. Cook, stirring, for 1 minute.

3 Pour in the coconut milk and hot broth, and season with salt and pepper to taste. Bring to the boil, then cover, reduce the heat, and simmer until the rice is tender and has absorbed the liquid, 10–15 minutes.

4 Remove from the heat. Stir in the chopped cilantro, then cover again and leave to stand for 5 minutes. Serve hot, garnished with cilantro sprigs.

(Some More Ideas)

Ginger-turkey pilaf: Sauté a turkey breast steak in the oil with 2 sliced leeks, 1 crushed garlic clove, a 1-inch piece of fresh ginger, finely chopped, and 1 seeded and finely chopped fresh red chile pepper. Add the basmati rice with 1 cup sliced baby corn and 1 cup frozen peas. In Step 3, replace the coconut milk with dry white wine or additional broth, then cook as in the main recipe. In Step 4, stir in chopped fresh flat-leaf parsley instead of cilantro, and leave to stand for 5 minutes before serving.

• Use shiitake, cremini, or portobello mushrooms instead of button mushrooms.

Health Points

• By using a light coconut milk, you'll save 2–3 grams of fat for this recipe. Coconut milk can provide a rich, creamy taste to foods, and with only 5 grams of fat per cup for the light, it can be a boon to many Asian-inspired dishes.

Each serving provides

Key Nutrients 480 Calories, 160 Calories from Fat, 18g Fat, 8g Saturated Fat, 0g Trans Fat, 34g Protein, 47g Carb, 5g Fiber, 125mg Sodium
Blood Pressure Nutrients 70mg Vitamin C, 67mg Magnesium, 784mg Potassium, 81mg Calcium

Poached Chicken Breasts in Vegetable-Herb Sauce

A tender chicken breast absorbs the essence of a seasoned poaching liquid, which keeps the meat moist and flavorful. Here the chicken picks up the gentle onion flavor of leeks and the fresh taste of tarragon.

Preparation time **15 minutes**   Cooking time **36 minutes**   *Serves 4*

2 cups dry white wine or 1 cup each apple juice and water

3 medium stalks celery, chopped

1 large leek, thoroughly washed and chopped

1 medium carrot, chopped

1 cup reduced-sodium chicken broth

1 tablespoon chopped parsley

1 tablespoon chopped fresh tarragon

4 skinless, boneless chicken breast halves

1 tablespoon all-purpose flour

1 tablespoon butter

Salt to taste

1/4 teaspoon black pepper

1 In large skillet over moderately high heat, bring wine, celery, leek, carrot, broth, parsley, and tarragon to a boil. Add chicken, reduce heat to low, and simmer, covered, for 25 minutes. Remove chicken from skillet, cover with foil, and keep warm.

2 Increase heat under skillet to moderate and boil skillet mixture, uncovered, for 5 minutes.

3 Remove 1/4 cup skillet mixture to small bowl. Add flour and whisk until smooth. Stir back into skillet and cook, stirring, until sauce boils and thickens slightly, about 3 minutes.

4 Remove from heat and swirl in butter. Add salt and pepper. Transfer chicken to warmed serving plates and top with sauce.

(Some More Ideas)

Poached fish in vegetable-herb sauce: Substitute 1 pound sole or flounder fillets for the chicken. Add to the poaching liquid in Step 1. Simmer covered, for about 5–6 minutes and remove from the skillet. Proceed with the recipe, pouring the sauce over the fish when completed.

• Change the herbs in the recipe. Substitute chopped basil or thyme for the tarragon.

• Use skinless, boneless turkey fillets for the chicken.

Health Points

• While celery is relatively high in sodium for a vegetable (35mg per stalk), it also contains unique compounds called phthalides that are believed to lower blood pressure. How phthalides work is under review—preliminary studies indicate the compounds may reduce the level of some hormones that constrict blood vessels.

Each serving provides

Key Nutrients 280 Calories, 45 Calories from Fat, 5g Fat, 3g Saturated Fat, 0g Trans Fat, 29g Protein, 9g Carb, 2g Fiber, 150mg Sodium
Blood Pressure Nutrients 9mg Vitamin C, 59mg Magnesium, 588mg Potassium, 63mg Calcium

Greek Chicken Pitas

These chicken pitas are packed with tasty salad leaves and a sauce made from cucumbers and yogurt. They are incredibly easy to prepare, so when you are short of time, skip the fast food and try these instead.

Preparation time **15 minutes**   Cooking time **about 8 minutes**   *Serves 4*

Pitas

1 1/2 pounds skinless, boneless chicken breasts

4 tablespoons instant polenta

1/2 teaspoon onion powder

1 teaspoon paprika

1 teaspoon cumin seeds

1 teaspoon coarsely ground black pepper

Salt to taste

2 tablespoons olive oil, divided

4 pita breads, whole-wheat or white

4 ounces mixed herb salad leaves

Sauce

3-inch piece cucumber, grated

1 cup plain low-fat yogurt

1 large garlic clove, crushed

1 teaspoon mint jelly

1 tablespoon chopped fresh mint

1. Cut the chicken breasts into thin strips. Mix together the polenta, onion powder, paprika, cumin seeds, pepper, and salt in a plastic bag. Add the chicken strips, a few at a time, and toss well to coat all over. Remove, shaking off the excess, and set aside on a plate while making the sauce.

2. Prepare sauce: Squeeze the grated cucumber, in handfuls, to remove excess moisture, then put into a bowl. Add the remaining ingredients and stir to mix. Set aside.

3. Heat a grill pan or heavy skillet and add half the oil, swirling it around the pan until lightly coated. Add half the chicken strips and cook over a high heat until golden brown all over and cooked through, turning once, 2–3 minutes. Keep hot while cooking the remaining chicken strips, using the rest of the oil.

4. Meanwhile, warm the pita breads under the grill for 1 minute on each side. Split down the side of each pita to make a pocket.

5. Fill the pita pockets with the salad leaves. Pile in the chicken strips, spoon over the sauce and serve.

(Some More Ideas)

Middle Eastern chicken sandwich: Put 4 whole chicken breasts between sheets of plastic wrap and bat out with a rolling pin to a thickness of about 1/2 inch all over. Lightly beat 1 egg and pour onto a plate. Put 1/2 cup fine fresh white bread crumbs on another plate. Season each chicken fillet with salt and pepper, then dip into the egg and coat both sides in bread crumbs, patting them on lightly. Heat half the oil in a grill pan or skillet and add 2 of the chicken breasts. Cook for 6 minutes, turning once, until golden. Keep hot while cooking the other 2 chicken breasts. Meanwhile, finely shred half of one small head each of white and red cabbage, and thinly slice 1 sweet white onion such as Vidalia. Toss with 2 tablespoons chopped parsley and 2 tablespoons lemon juice. Spoon 1 tablespoon hummus into each warmed pita pocket, add some cabbage salad, and fill with the hot chicken fillets.

photo, page 79

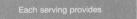
Each serving provides

Key Nutrients 430 Calories, 90 Calories from Fat, 11g Fat, 2g Saturated Fat, 0g Trans Fat, 41g Protein, 43g Carb, 5g Fiber, 380mg Sodium
Blood Pressure Nutrients 10mg Vitamin C, 77mg Magnesium, 570mg Potassium, 146mg Calcium

Sautéed Chicken with Caramelized Onions

Savory sautéed chicken breasts are piled high with sweet mounds of cooked onions for a dinner that will have your family clucking with pleasure! Double the recipe to feed a larger flock.

Preparation time **7 minutes**   Cooking time **22 minutes**   *Serves 4*

1 1/2 pounds medium onions

4 skinless, boneless chicken breast halves (4 ounces each)

Salt to taste

1/2 teaspoon pepper

4 teaspoons margarine

2 tablespoons superfine sugar

1/3 cup reduced-sodium chicken broth

1 teaspoon chopped fresh rosemary

1 teaspoon chopped fresh thyme

1 tablespoon red wine vinegar

1. Cut onions into 6 wedges each. Sprinkle chicken with 1/4 teaspoon salt and 1/4 teaspoon pepper.

2. Coat a large nonstick skillet with nonstick cooking spray. Add 2 teaspoons margarine and melt over medium-high heat. Sauté chicken until browned, about 3 minutes on each side; transfer to plate.

3. Reduce heat to medium and melt remaining margarine in skillet. Sauté onions, 1 tablespoon sugar, and remaining salt and pepper until onions turn golden brown and caramelize, about 8 minutes. Stir frequently, breaking onions apart as they cook. Add broth and boil until it evaporates, about 2 minutes.

4. Stir in rosemary, thyme, and remaining sugar. Return chicken to skillet and sprinkle with vinegar. Cook, uncovered, until juices of chicken run clear, about 4 minutes.

(Some More Ideas)

• Use caramelized onions to top any kind of homemade pizza, or stuff into pita bread along with fresh vegetables for a vegetarian sandwich. Or just serve as a side vegetable.

• Use this recipe with boneless pork loin chops or turkey fillets instead of chicken.

• Does chopping onions make you cry? It's the sulfuric compounds in the vegetable. Remedies: Leave the root end intact; it's where the compounds are concentrated. Or freeze the onion for 20 minutes before cutting to inhibit the chemical release. One trick we use at home: Light a candle near your chopping board as you cut the onions.

Health Points

• Caramelizing the onions enhances the rich flavor, making them much more palatable. The same cooking process can bring out the best flavor in other vegetables as well, including peppers and carrots.

Each serving provides

Key Nutrients 240 Calories, 50 Calories from Fat, 6g Fat, 1g Saturated Fat, 1g Trans Fat, 29g Protein, 19g Carb, 3g Fiber, 140mg Sodium
Blood Pressure Nutrients 13mg Vitamin C, 50mg Magnesium, 565mg Potassium, 55mg Calcium

Chicken and Cashew Pancakes

Chicken stir-fried with carrots, celery, and cabbage, then lightly flavored with orange and sesame, makes a delicious filling for pancakes. This dish is sure to meet with your family's approval.

Preparation time **15–20 minutes**   Cooking time **about 30 minutes**   *Serves 4*

Pancakes

1/2 cup all-purpose flour
1 egg, beaten
1 1/4 cups fat-free milk
1 teaspoon canola oil
Salt and pepper to taste

Filling

2 ounces unsalted cashews
1 tablespoon canola oil
1/2 pound skinless, boneless chicken breasts, cut into strips
1 garlic clove, crushed
1 teaspoon finely chopped fresh ginger
1 fresh red chile pepper, seeded and finely chopped (optional)
2 carrots, cut into matchstick strips
2 celery stalks, cut into matchstick strips
Grated zest of 1/2 orange
1/2 cup shredded Savoy cabbage
1 tablespoon reduced-sodium soy sauce
1 tablespoon toasted sesame oil

1 To make the pancakes, sift the flour into a bowl and add a little salt and pepper to taste. Make a well in the center. Mix the egg with the milk, then pour into the well. Gradually whisk the flour into the egg and milk to form a smooth batter.

2 Use a little of the oil to lightly grease a griddle or large skillet and place it on a medium heat. Pour in a little of the batter and swirl it evenly across the surface, then cook for 2 minutes to form a pancake. Toss the pancake or flip it over with a spatula and cook on the other side for about 30 seconds. Slide out onto a warm heatproof plate and cover with a sheet of wax paper.

3 Cook the remaining batter in the same way, making 8 pancakes in all and stacking them up, interleaved with wax paper. Add a little more oil to the pan between pancakes as necessary. When all the pancakes have been made, cover the pancake stack with foil, sealing it well. Set aside and keep warm.

4 Heat a wok or large skillet. Add the cashews and stir-fry them over a medium heat for a few minutes or until golden. Remove to a plate and set aside.

5 Add the oil to the pan, then add the chicken, garlic, ginger, and chile, if using. Stir-fry for 3 minutes. Add the carrots and celery and stir-fry for a further 2 minutes. Add the orange zest and cabbage, and stir-fry for 1 minute. Sprinkle over the soy sauce and sesame oil, and stir-fry for another minute. Return the cashews to the pan and toss to mix with the other ingredients.

6 Divide the stir-fry filling among the warm pancakes and fold them over or roll up. Serve immediately, with a little extra soy sauce to sprinkle.

(Some More Ideas)

Sesame duck pancakes: Stir-fry 1 pound skinless, boneless, sliced duck breast with 1 crushed garlic clove and 2 teaspoons finely chopped fresh ginger in 1 tablespoon canola oil for 3–4 minutes. Add 1 tablespoon dry sherry, 1 tablespoon reduced-sodium soy sauce, and 1 teaspoon honey and stir, then add 1/2 cup bean sprouts and toss to mix. While the duck is cooking, boil 3 ounces fine Chinese egg noodles in boiling water for 2–3 minutes; drain and add to the stir-fry with 1 teaspoon toasted sesame oil and 6 chopped scallions. Toss together until hot, then divide the stir-fry among the pancakes and roll up or fold over.

Health Points

• Cashews are a rich source of protein, fiber, and minerals such as iron, magnesium, and selenium. Though cashews are high in fat, the majority of it is the "healthy" monounsaturated type.

photo, page 79

Each serving provides

Key Nutrients 320 Calories, 130 Calories from Fat, 15g Fat, 3g Saturated Fat, 0g Trans Fat, 22g Protein, 26g Carb, 3g Fiber, 260mg Sodium
Blood Pressure Nutrients 10mg Vitamin C, 77mg Magnesium, 578mg Potassium, 138mg Calcium

Baked Chicken Bundles with Carrots and Zucchini

This colorful dish shows how easy it can be to make a healthful chicken entrée without sacrificing flavor—or slaving over a hot stove.

Preparation time **15 minutes**   Cooking time **30 minutes**   *Serves 4*

4 skinless, boneless chicken breast halves (1 1/2 pounds)

4 ounces mushrooms, sliced

2 carrots, cut into 1 1/2-inch matchsticks

2 zucchini, cut into 1 1/2-inch matchsticks

2 tablespoons olive oil

1 tablespoon chopped basil

2 tablespoons lemon juice

Salt to taste

1/8 teaspoon pepper

1 Preheat oven to 375°F. Cut 4 sheets of aluminum foil, about 12 inches square. Place 1 chicken breast on each; arrange a quarter of vegetables on top.

2 Prepare seasoning mixture: In small bowl, whisk together oil, chopped basil, lemon juice, salt, and pepper until combined. Spoon a quarter of seasoning mixture evenly over each chicken and vegetable mound.

3 With the mound in center of foil, fold 2 sides over, and then fold the other sides over and tuck the ends under.

4 Bake bundles in baking dish for about 30 minutes. Unwrap each bundle and transfer chicken and vegetables to serving platter with juices or to individual plates.

(Some More Ideas)

• Substitute skinless, boneless turkey breasts for the chicken.

• Cut matchstick pieces of fennel and use in place of either the carrots or zucchini.

• Substitute yellow summer squash cut into matchstick strips for the zucchini.

Health Points

• The vegetables add heart-healthy beta-carotene and vitamins A and C; the mushrooms have a high content of glutamic acid, which is believed to boost the immune system.

• When you bake poultry, herbs, and vegetables in a sealed aluminum packet, the foods will cook in their own juices, creating exquisite flavor with little fat or sodium.

Each serving provides

Key Nutrients 270 Calories, 80 Calories from Fat, 9g Fat, 2g Saturated Fat, 0g Trans Fat, 41g Protein, 5g Carb, 1g Fiber, 125mg Sodium
Blood Pressure Nutrients 12mg Vitamin C, 59mg Magnesium, 687mg Potassium, 32mg Calcium

Country Captain Chicken

In the nineteenth century, when no place seemed more exotic to Americans than India, this "foreign" chicken dish offered a welcome change from plain old chicken stew.

Preparation time **10 minutes**   Cooking time **35 minutes**   *Serves 4*

2 teaspoons olive oil

4 skinless, boneless chicken breast halves (5 ounces each)

1 small onion, thinly sliced

3 cloves garlic, minced

1 tablespoon curry powder

1 1/3 cups no-salt-added canned crushed tomatoes

1/4 cup dried apricots, thinly sliced

Salt to taste

1/2 teaspoon dried thyme

1/4 teaspoon pepper

1/4 cup sliced almonds

1 Heat oil in large nonstick Dutch oven over medium heat. Add chicken and sauté until golden brown, about 3 minutes per side. With tongs or slotted spoon, transfer chicken to plate.

2 Add onion and garlic to pan and cook until onion is tender, about 5 minutes.

3 Stir in curry powder and cook for 1 minute. Add tomatoes, apricots, salt, thyme, and pepper, and bring to a boil.

4 Return chicken (and any accumulated juices) to Dutch oven. Reduce to a simmer, cover, and cook until chicken is cooked through, about 20 minutes. (Recipe can be made ahead to this point and refrigerated. Reheat in 325°F oven.) Serve sprinkled with almonds.

(Some More Ideas)

• Substitute boneless turkey fillets for the chicken breasts.

• Add 1/2 cup dark raisins to the sauce.

• When in peak season, use fresh tomatoes instead of canned ones. Coarsely chop 3 peeled, cored, and seeded medium tomatoes.

Health Points

• Tomatoes are an excellent source of the phytochemical lycopene, which may help fight heart disease. Lycopene is most available when the tomatoes are cooked with a little fat, as they are in this recipe.

• Dried apricots are a good source of vitamin A and fiber. They are portable, making them an equally good snack.

• Orange and red fruits and vegetables, such as mangoes, red cabbage, and red peppers, are excellent sources of beta-carotene and vitamin C—both antioxidants that help to protect against heart disease and cancer. The vitamin C aids the absorption of valuable iron from the steak.

Each serving provides

Key Nutrients 290 Calories, 70 Calories from Fat, 7g Fat, 1g Saturated Fat, 0g Trans Fat, 36g Protein, 19g Carb, 4g Fiber, 125mg Sodium
Blood Pressure Nutrients 14mg Vitamin C, 82mg Magnesium, 952mg Potassium, 65mg Calcium

Moroccan Chicken with Couscous

Aromatic cumin, coriander, and cinnamon give these chicken breasts a Mediterranean flavor, and serving them with chickpeas further enhances the ethnic theme. Zucchini and sugar snap peas add color, flavor, and all the benefits of fresh vegetables.

Preparation and cooking time **30 minutes**   *Serves 4*

Chicken

1 pound skinless, boneless chicken breasts
1 tablespoon olive oil
1 large onion, finely chopped
2 garlic cloves, finely chopped
1 teaspoon ground cumin
1 teaspoon ground coriander
1 cinnamon stick
2 large zucchini, halved lengthwise and sliced
1 can (14 ounces) diced tomatoes
1 cup reduced-sodium vegetable broth
1/2 pound sugar snap peas
1 can (15 ounces) chickpeas, drained and rinsed

Couscous

1 cup couscous
1 tablespoon olive oil
1 1/2 cups boiling water
2 teaspoons butter
Salt and pepper to taste
Chopped fresh cilantro *(garnish)*

1 Cut the chicken on the diagonal into strips about 1/2 inch thick. Heat 1 tablespoon oil in a wok or heavy skillet. Add the chicken, onion, and garlic, and cook over a medium-high heat, stirring constantly, until the chicken turns white with golden brown flecks, about 2 minutes.

2 Reduce the heat to low and add the cumin, coriander, and cinnamon stick. Cook, stirring constantly, for 1 minute. Add the zucchini and stir well, then add the tomatoes with their juice and the broth. Cook for 5 minutes, stirring occasionally.

3 Meanwhile, put the couscous in a saucepan and pour over the boiling water. Add 1 tablespoon oil. Stir well, cover, and leave to soak, off the heat, for 5 minutes.

4 Add the sugar snap peas and chickpeas to the chicken mixture. Cook for a further 5 minutes, stirring frequently.

5 Stir the butter into the couscous and cook over a moderate heat for 3 minutes, fluffing up with a fork to separate the grains. Pile the couscous onto a serving platter. Spoon the chicken on top and garnish with chopped cilantro. Serve hot.

(Some More Ideas)

Shrimp and bean couscous: Replace the chicken with 1 pound cooked peeled and deveined shrimp (thawed if frozen), and replace the chickpeas with canned black-eyed peas. In Step 1, cook the onion and garlic in the oil for 2 minutes. In Step 2, omit the zucchini. In Step 4, add the shrimp and black-eyed peas, and instead of sugar snap peas, add 1/2 pound frozen peas, thawed.

Health Points

• Believing chickpeas to be powerful aphrodisiacs, the Romans fed them to their stallions to improve their performance. Although this reputation seems to be long forgotten, chickpeas do contribute good amounts of soluble fiber and useful amounts of iron, folate, vitamin E, and manganese to the diet.

Each serving provides

Key Nutrients 600 Calories, 110 Calories from Fat, 12g Fat, 3g Saturated Fat, 0g Trans Fat, 43g Protein, 80g Carb, 14g Fiber, 650mg Sodium
Blood Pressure Nutrients 36mg Vitamin C, 141mg Magnesium, 1300mg Potassium, 181mg Calcium

Skillet Chicken with
Rosemary-Orange Sauce *p92*

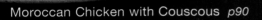

Moroccan Chicken with Couscous *p90*

Chicken Jamboree *p94*

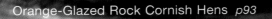

Orange-Glazed Rock Cornish Hens *p93*

Skillet Chicken with Rosemary-Orange Sauce

There's no denying that skinless chicken breast is the most versatile and healthful of meats. Try this herb-citrus skillet sauce for a chicken dish with minimal fat and maximum flavor.

Preparation time **10 minutes**   Cooking time **15 minutes**   *Serves 4*

Chicken

2 teaspoons olive oil

4 skinless, boneless chicken breast halves (5 ounces each)

1/4 teaspoon salt

Sauce

2 shallots, finely chopped

1/4 teaspoon salt

1 1/2 teaspoons grated orange zest

1/2 teaspoon rosemary, minced

1/4 teaspoon pepper

2/3 cup orange juice

1 tablespoon orange marmalade

1 tablespoon fresh lemon juice

1 teaspoon cornstarch blended with 1 tablespoon water

1 Heat oil in large nonstick skillet over medium heat. Sprinkle chicken with 1/4 teaspoon salt and cook until golden brown on one side, about 5 minutes. Turn chicken and cook until golden brown on second side and cooked through, about 5 minutes. Transfer chicken to plate and cover loosely with foil to keep warm.

2 Add shallots to pan and cook, stirring, until light golden, about 3 minutes. Stir in 1/4 teaspoon salt, orange zest, rosemary, pepper, orange juice, and marmalade and bring to a boil. Stir in lemon juice.

3 Stir in cornstarch mixture and cook, stirring, until sauce is slightly thickened, about 1 minute. Slice chicken and serve with sauce spooned on top.

(Some More Ideas)

• Use skinless, boneless turkey fillets or boneless pork chops instead of chicken.

• Substitute apricot preserves for the orange marmalade.

• Serve this meal with steamed brown rice and grilled vegetables.

Health Points

• The potassium in the orange juice will lower your risk of stroke, and the pectin found in the marmalade is a cholesterol-lowering type of soluble fiber.

• Shallots, whose taste falls somewhere between onion and garlic, are a good source of vitamin B6, which helps manufacture amino acids in the body.

photo, page 91

Each serving provides

Key Nutrients 220 Calories, 35 Calories from Fat, 4g Fat, 1g Saturated Fat, 0g Trans Fat, 33g Protein, 11g Carb, 0g Fiber, 330mg Sodium
Blood Pressure Nutrients 6mg Vitamin C, 43mg Magnesium, 405mg Potassium, 23mg Calcium

Orange-Glazed Rock Cornish Hens

Rock Cornish hens are a cross between two different breeds of chicken, and typically weigh just over a pound. With this recipe, the hens are glazed as they roast with a delicious orange-tea marmalade.

Preparation time **20 minutes**   Cooking time **1 minutes plus standing**   *Serves 4*

1 tea bag, such as Earl Grey

2 medium oranges

1/2 cup no-sugar-added orange marmalade

4 Rock Cornish hens (1 pound each), thawed if frozen

1/2 teaspoon pepper

Salt to taste

2 medium onions, sliced

8 sprigs fresh rosemary

8 sprigs fresh thyme

1 Preheat oven to 375°F. Fit a roasting pan with rack. Steep tea bag in 1/4 cup boiling water 5 minutes in small saucepan. Discard tea bag. Squeeze juice from 1 orange into tea, and then stir in marmalade until melted. Keep warm. Cut remaining orange into quarters (do not peel).

2 Remove and discard giblets from hens. Wash hens and dry thoroughly, and then sprinkle cavities with pepper and salt. Loosen breast skin slightly. Stuff large cavity of each hen with 1 orange quarter, one-fourth of the onion slices, 1 rosemary sprig, and 1 thyme sprig. Tie legs together with kitchen string. Place hens, breast-side up, on rack in roasting pan. Brush hens over and under skin with about one-fourth of glaze. Pour enough water into pan to cover bottom (water should not reach rack).

3 Roast hens on middle oven rack, basting over and under skin every 20 minutes with remaining glaze, until browned and juices run clear, about 1 hour. Let hens stand 10 minutes. Discard rosemary, thyme, onions, and orange from cavities of hens. Garnish with remaining rosemary and thyme sprigs. Discard skin before eating.

(Some More Ideas)

Orange-roasted chicken: Substitute a whole roasting chicken for the Rock Cornish hens. Prepare the chicken as in the recipe for the Rock Cornish hens. Roast a 2-pound chicken at 400°F until the juices run clear, about 1–1 1/2 hours.

• Try using no-sugar apricot preserves instead of the orange marmalade.

Health Points

• Rock Cornish hens with skins removed are relatively low in fat, especially saturated fat, while providing a rich, gamy flavor.

• You don't often think of onions as a useful vegetable, but they provide allium, a phytochemical believed to alleviate high blood pressure and possibly help to reduce cholesterol.

photo, page 91

Each serving provides

Key Nutrients 1040 Calories, 570 Calories from Fat, 64g Fat, 18g Saturated Fat, 0g Trans Fat, 79g Protein, 33g Carb, 3g Fiber, 280mg Sodium
Blood Pressure Nutrients 41mg Vitamin C, 95mg Magnesium, 1281mg Potassium, 90mg Calcium

Chicken Jamboree

This healthy chicken and vegetable casserole makes an easy midweek meal. To make it even quicker, you could use supermarket washed-and-cut carrots and broccoli, ready to go from package to pan.

Preparation time **10 minutes**   Cooking time **about 20 minutes**   *Serves 4*

2 tablespoons canola oil

1 pound skinless, boneless chicken breasts, cut into small cubes

1 small onion, chopped

1/2 pound button mushrooms

1 bay leaf

2 large sprigs fresh thyme or 1/2 teaspoon dried thyme

3 large sprigs fresh tarragon or 1/2 teaspoon dried tarragon *(optional)*

Grated zest of 1 small lemon or 1/2 large lemon

1/2 cup dry sherry

1 1/4 cups boiling water

1/2 pound baby carrots

1/2 pound broccoli florets

1 tablespoon flour

2 tablespoons cold water

3 tablespoons chopped parsley

Salt and pepper to taste

1 Heat the oil in a large sauté pan with a lid. Add the chicken and brown the pieces over a high heat for 3 minutes, stirring constantly. Reduce the heat to medium. Stir in the onion, mushrooms, bay leaf, thyme, tarragon, if used, and lemon zest. Cook until the onion and mushrooms are beginning to soften, about 4 minutes.

2 Pour in the sherry and water. Add the carrots and seasoning to taste, and stir to mix all the ingredients. Bring to the boil, then reduce the heat and cover the pan. Simmer for 5 minutes.

3 Stir in the broccoli florets. Increase the heat to bring the liquid back to a steady simmer. Cover the pan and cook until the pieces of chicken are tender and the vegetables are just cooked, about 5 minutes. Remove and discard the bay leaf, and the sprigs of thyme and tarragon, if used.

4 Blend the flour to a smooth paste with the cold water. Stir the flour paste into the casserole and simmer, stirring constantly, until thickened and smooth, about 2 minutes. Check the seasoning, then stir in the parsley and serve.

(Some More Ideas)

Creamy chicken and mushroom casserole: Increase the quantity of button mushrooms to 1 pound and omit the broccoli. Simmer for 5 minutes longer in Step 2. Stir in 4 tablespoons half-and-half after thickening the casserole with the flour, then heat for a few more seconds.

• Small pattypan squash are good in this casserole. Trim off and discard the stalk ends from 1/2 pound squash and slice them horizontally in half. Add them to the pan with the broccoli. When cooked, the pattypan should be tender but still slightly crunchy.

• Mixed wild and long-grain rice goes well with the casserole.

Health Points

• This recipe uses vegetables to extend a modest amount of chicken. Served with whole grains such as brown rice, it makes a well-balanced meal, especially if followed by fresh fruit for a vitamin boost.

photo, page 91

Each serving provides

Key Nutrients 270 Calories, 80 Calories from Fat, 9g Fat, 1g Saturated Fat, 0g Trans Fat, 31g Protein, 14g Carb, 4g Fiber, 115mg Sodium
Blood Pressure Nutrients 66mg Vitamin C, 65mg Magnesium, 915mg Potassium, 67mg Calcium

Chicken-Apricot Casserole

Chicken thighs are excellent in a casserole, being very tender and full of flavor. Fresh apricots and a bulb of fennel make good partners, especially when spiced up with cumin.

Preparation time **15 minutes**   Cooking time **50 minutes**   *Serves 4*

2 tablespoons canola oil

8 chicken thighs, about 1 pound

1 onion, sliced

2 garlic cloves, chopped

2 teaspoons ground cumin

2 teaspoons ground coriander

1 1/4 cups reduced-sodium chicken broth

3 carrots, halved crosswise, then each half cut into 6–8 thick fingers

1 bulb of fennel, halved lengthwise, then cut crosswise into slices

5 apricots, pitted and quartered

Salt and pepper to taste

Chopped fennel leaves from the bulb *(garnish)*

1 Heat the oil in a large skillet and sauté the chicken thighs, turning occasionally, until golden brown all over, 5–10 minutes. Remove from the pan. Add the onion and garlic to the pan and sauté until soft and golden, about 5 minutes.

2 Stir in all the spices and fry for 1 minute, then add the broth. Return the chicken to the pan together with the carrots and fennel. Bring to the boil. Stir well, then cover and simmer gently until the chicken is tender, about 30 minutes. Remove the lid. If there is too much liquid, boil to reduce it slightly.

3 Add the apricots to the casserole and stir gently to mix. Simmer over a low heat for a further 5 minutes.

4 Season to taste with salt and pepper. Sprinkle with the fennel leaves and serve.

(Some More Ideas)

• Replace the apricots with 1 fresh mango, cut into slices or chunks. Sprinkle with fresh cilantro instead of fennel leaves.

• Use 1 can (15 ounces) apricot halves in natural juice, drained and cut in half, instead of fresh apricots.

• Plain boiled rice, or saffron rice, is a good accompaniment to this dish, as are boiled new potatoes or baked potatoes.

Health Points

• Both apricots and carrots provide some vitamin A in the form of beta-carotene, which gives them their distinctive color, but carrots are by far the better source, providing about 20 times more of this nutrient per 3 1/2 ounces than apricots. Vitamin A is essential for proper vision and increasingly valued for its role as an antioxidant, helping to prevent cancer and coronary heart disease.

Each serving provides

Key Nutrients 280 Calories, 110 Calories from Fat, 13g Fat, 2g Saturated Fat, 0g Trans Fat, 26g Protein, 18g Carb, 6g Fiber, 180mg Sodium
Blood Pressure Nutrients 21mg Vitamin C, 51mg Magnesium, 831mg Potassium, 87mg Calcium

Turkey Piccata

Company coming on a weeknight? Versatile turkey breast to the rescue! In this case, the turkey is cooked like veal cutlets, in a classic garlic-lemon sauce with capers. You'll have dinner ready in the time it takes to set a pretty table.

Preparation time **10 minutes**   Cooking time **10 minutes**   *Serves 4*

Turkey

1 tablespoon olive oil
4 turkey cutlets (4 ounces each)
2 tablespoons flour

Sauce

2 cloves garlic, minced
1 teaspoon grated lemon zest
1/4 cup lemon juice
1 cup reduced-sodium chicken broth
1 teaspoon cornstarch blended with 1 tablespoon water
2 teaspoons capers, rinsed and drained
2 tablespoons chopped parsley

1 Heat oil in large nonstick skillet over medium heat. Dredge turkey in flour, shaking off excess. Sauté turkey until golden brown and cooked through, about 2 minutes per side. With tongs or slotted spoon, transfer turkey to plate; cover loosely with foil to keep warm.

2 Add garlic to pan and cook, stirring, until tender, about 1 minute. Add lemon zest, lemon juice, and chicken broth to pan and bring to a boil. Boil 1 minute.

3 Stir in cornstarch mixture and capers, and cook until slightly thickened, about 1 minute. Stir in parsley. Serve turkey with sauce spooned on top.

(Some More Ideas)

• One way to increase the flavor of lean meat is to coat it with flour before sautéing. A dusting of flour helps lock in the juices so the turkey cooks up tender and juicy, with a tempting golden crust.

• Chicken and veal cutlets are also delicious prepared piccata style.

• Serve this dish with brown rice with slivered almonds, and steamed broccoli. Poached plums would be perfect for dessert.

Health Points

• Not only does lemon zest enhance flavor, but its high vitamin C content is a potent antioxidant.

Each serving provides

Key Nutrients 210 Calories, 40 Calories from Fat, 5g Fat, 1g Saturated Fat, 0g Trans Fat, 36g Protein, 6g Carb, 0g Fiber, 130mg Sodium
Blood Pressure Nutrients 11mg Vitamin C, 37mg Magnesium, 372mg Potassium, 26mg Calcium

Turkey Cutlets with Pineapple-Cranberry Sauce *p98*

Turkey Piccata *p96*

Turkey Stroganoff *p99*

Spicy Turkey Chili with Spaghetti *p100*

Turkey Cutlets with Pineapple-Cranberry Sauce

Summer berries have to compete with one another for attention, but come fall, the cranberry stands alone. Its jewel-like color makes it not just an attractive addition to any dish but a healthful one as well.

Preparation time **10 minutes**   Cooking time **15 minutes**   *Serves 4*

Cutlets

1 tablespoon olive oil

4 turkey cutlets (4 ounces each), halved crosswise

1 tablespoon cornstarch

1/2 cup reduced-sodium chicken broth

Salt to taste

Sauce

1 cup fresh or frozen cranberries

1/4 cup frozen pineapple juice concentrate, thawed

2 teaspoons dark brown sugar

2 teaspoons grated lime zest

1/4 teaspoon crushed red pepper flakes

3/4 cup canned pineapple chunks

1 Combine cranberries, pineapple juice concentrate, brown sugar, lime zest, and red pepper flakes in small saucepan. Bring to a boil over medium heat and cook, stirring occasionally, until cranberries have popped and are glossy, about 10 minutes. Stir in pineapple. (Cranberry mixture can be made up to 3 days ahead and refrigerated. Return to room temperature before proceeding.)

2 Heat oil in large nonstick skillet over medium heat. Dust turkey with cornstarch and cook until golden brown and cooked through, about 1 minute per side. Transfer turkey to platter and cover loosely with foil to keep warm.

3 Stir broth and salt into skillet and bring to a boil. Remove from heat, stir in cranberry mixture, and spoon over turkey.

(Some More Ideas)

• Use pork or chicken cutlets in place of turkey.

• For an orange flavor, substitute orange juice concentrate for the pineapple juice concentrate. Substitute orange zest for the lime zest.

Health Points

• Adding fruit to main meals helps you to reach your 5-a-day goal, while adding personality and sweetness to otherwise routine flavors.

• Cranberries, while not often thought of as a fruit you eat often, are brimming with vitamin C and antioxidant properties, as well as heart-healthy fiber.

photo, page 97

Each serving provides

Key Nutrients 240 Calories, 40 Calories from Fat, 5g Fat, 1g Saturated Fat, 0g Trans Fat, 29g Protein, 20g Carb, 2g Fiber, 70mg Sodium
Blood Pressure Nutrients 16mg Vitamin C, 49mg Magnesium, 510mg Potassium, 33mg Calcium

Turkey Stroganoff

Here's a creamy dish of comfort you can gobble up without guilt! Substitute turkey for the customary beef and boost the flavor with portobello mushrooms. It's just as tasty as the original but so much better for your blood pressure.

Preparation time **10 minutes**   Cooking time **18 minutes**   *Serves 4*

8 ounces eggless noodles

2 teaspoons poppy seeds

12 ounces fresh-roasted turkey breast, cut into 2 x 1/2-inch strips

Salt to taste

1/2 teaspoon freshly ground black pepper

2 portobello mushrooms (4 ounces each)

1 small red onion, thinly sliced

1 tablespoon margarine

1 1/2 tablespoons all-purpose flour

1 1/2 cups reduced-sodium beef broth

1/2 cup reduced-fat sour cream

1 1/2 teaspoons Dijon mustard

1 Cook noodles according to package directions; toss with poppy seeds, and return to empty cooking pot to keep warm. Sprinkle turkey strips with salt and pepper; toss to coat. Remove and discard stems from mushrooms. Cut mushroom caps into quarters and thinly slice.

2 Meanwhile, lightly coat large nonstick skillet with nonstick cooking spray and set over medium-high heat. Sauté onion 2 minutes. Add mushrooms and sauté until mushrooms are tender, 5–6 minutes. Transfer to large bowl.

3 Melt margarine in skillet over medium heat. Add flour and cook, stirring, 1 minute. Gradually whisk in broth. Cook, stirring with wooden spoon, until sauce thickens and boils, about 4 minutes.

4 Reduce heat to low. Blend in sour cream and mustard. Return turkey and reserved vegetables with accumulated juices to skillet. Cook until heated through (do not boil). Divide noodles among 4 plates and spoon stroganoff on top.

(Some More Ideas)

• Prepare this recipe with fresh roasted chicken breast instead of turkey.

• Use shiitake, cremini, or white button mushrooms in place of portobellos.

Health Points

• The leanest of poultry is skinless turkey breast—3 ounces of cooked meat has only about 1 gram of fat.

• The reduced-fat sour cream makes this dish creamy with half the fat of the original recipe. Avoid curdled sauces when cooking with reduced-fat sour cream by cooking over low heat and never letting the sauce boil.

• Onions contain a type of dietary fiber called fructooligosaccharides (FOS), which is also found in chicory, leeks, garlic, Jerusalem artichokes, asparagus, barley, and bananas. It is believed to stimulate the growth of friendly bacteria in the gut while inhibiting bad bacteria.

photo, page 97

Each serving provides

Key Nutrients 450 Calories, 80 Calories from Fat, 9g Fat, 4g Saturated Fat, 0g Trans Fat, 36g Protein, 52g Carb, 3g Fiber, 160mg Sodium
Blood Pressure Nutrients 2mg Vitamin C, 60mg Magnesium, 821mg Potassium, 101mg Calcium

Spicy Turkey Chili with Spaghetti

Sweet peppers and warm spices flavor this family-style chili, made with minced turkey rather than the traditional beef for a lower fat content, and served on spaghetti to boost the carbohydrate value.

Preparation time **10 minutes**   Cooking time **about 25 minutes**   *Serves 4*

Chili

1 tablespoon canola oil
1 large garlic clove, crushed
1 onion, finely chopped
2 red or green peppers, seeded and finely chopped
1 1/2 teaspoons cayenne pepper, or to taste
2 teaspoons ground cumin
1 teaspoon dried oregano
1 pound ground white-meat turkey
2 cans (14 ounces each) no-salt-added diced tomatoes
1 can (15 ounces) red kidney beans, drained and rinsed
Salt and pepper to taste
1 pound spaghetti

Topping

1/2 cup plain low-fat yogurt
1 scallion, finely chopped
4 tablespoons finely chopped mixed fresh herbs, such as parsley, cilantro, and chives

1 First make the topping. Mix the yogurt with the scallion and herbs. Cover and chill until needed.

2 Heat the oil in a large skillet, Add the garlic and sauté for 30 seconds. Add the onion and red or green peppers, and sauté, stirring occasionally, until softened, about 5 minutes.

3 Stir in the cayenne pepper, ground cumin, and oregano, and continue to cook, stirring occasionally, for about 2 minutes. Add the turkey and cook, stirring occasionally, until it is browned and crumbly.

4 Stir in the tomatoes and kidney beans, and add seasoning to taste. Bring to the boil, then reduce the heat and simmer for 15 minutes.

5 Meanwhile, cook the spaghetti in boiling water 10–12 minutes, according to the package instructions, until al dente. Drain well.

6 Divide the spaghetti among 4 plates and spoon an equal amount of turkey chili over each serving. Top with the herb-flavored yogurt and serve.

(Some More Ideas)

• Use black or pinto beans instead of kidney beans.

• Omit the turkey entirely and just have a bean chili. To do so, increase the beans to two cans.

• To increase the fiber content of this dish, use whole-wheat spaghetti or noodles.

Health Points

• Turkey is a good source of zinc and many B vitamins, particularly B1, B12, and niacin. It also provides iron.

• Red kidney beans are low in fat. They provide good amounts of vitamins B1, niacin, and B6, and useful amounts of iron. They are also a good source of soluble fiber, which can help to reduce high cholesterol levels in the blood.

photo, page 97

Each serving provides

Key Nutrients 790 Calories, 150 Calories from Fat, 16g Fat, 4g Saturated Fat, 0g Trans Fat, 44g Protein, 116g Carb, 13g Fiber, 510mg Sodium
Blood Pressure Nutrients 142mg Vitamin C, 134mg Magnesium, 1209mg Potassium, 158mg Calcium

seafood

Poached Salmon with Cucumber-Dill Sauce

You've hooked a prizewinning catch with this one! Supper for four in just 20 minutes—fresh salmon fillets topped with creamy cucumber-dill sauce. And it's oh-so-good for you.

Preparation time **10 minutes**   Cooking time **10 minutes**   *Serves 4*

Salmon

1 cup dry white wine or reduced-sodium chicken broth

2 scallions, sliced

8 black peppercorns

4 salmon fillets (4 ounces each)

Sauce

3/4 cup nonfat sour cream

1/3 cup diced peeled cucumber

2 tablespoons snipped fresh dill

1 tablespoon fresh lemon juice

Salt to taste

1/8 teaspoon freshly ground black pepper

Fresh dill sprigs *(garnish)*

1 Pour 1 1/2 cups water into large nonstick skillet; stir in wine, scallions, and peppercorns. Put salmon in skillet in single layer; bring just to a boil over high heat.

2 Reduce heat to medium-low, cover, and simmer until fish flakes when tested with a fork, about 6 minutes.

3 Meanwhile, stir sour cream, cucumber, dill, lemon juice, salt, and pepper in medium bowl to make sauce. Refrigerate if not serving immediately.

4 Carefully transfer fillets with a slotted spatula to large platter. Garnish with fresh dill sprigs. Serve hot or chilled with sauce.

(Some More Ideas)

• Do you like your salmon hot or cold? This recipe works either way. To serve cold, squeeze lemon juice over the poached fillets, cover with plastic, and refrigerate until well chilled, at least 2 hours or overnight. Mix the dill sauce right before it's time to serve.

• Serve the salmon hot with steamed jasmine rice tossed with toasted almonds or cold on a bed of mixed greens. Accompany with French or green beans topped with vinaigrette and slices of cantaloupe.

Health Points

• Although the fat in salmon is of the heart-friendly type, it is still high in calories. By poaching the salmon instead of pan sautéing it, you bypass the fat calories from the oil and also rid the salmon of some of its fat.

• Nonfat sour cream tastes rich enough when enhanced with crispy cucumbers and fresh snipped dill that it will taste creamy and rich, despite its lightness.

Each serving provides

Key Nutrients 300 Calories, 110 Calories from Fat, 12g Fat, 3g Saturated Fat, 0g Trans Fat, 24g Protein, 10g Carb, 0g Fiber, 130mg Sodium

Blood Pressure Nutrients 9mg Vitamin C, 43mg Magnesium, 522mg Potassium, 89mg Calcium

Lemon-Glazed Flounder Fillets

Floundering over what to make for supper? Here's a smart solution—grill fish fillets on top of fresh lemon slices. Top them with a light citrus sauce. It's all ready in less than 25 minutes.

Preparation time **15 minutes**   Cooking time **8 minutes**   *Serves 4*

Fillets

5 large lemons
6 large fresh basil leaves
1 tablespoon olive oil
1 garlic clove, minced
4 flounder fillets (4 ounces each)
1/2 teaspoon salt
1/4 teaspoon pepper

Sauce

1/2 cup reduced-sodium chicken broth
1 1/2 teaspoons cornstarch
2 teaspoons sugar

1 Roll 1 lemon on surface to get juices flowing; grate zest from this lemon and squeeze juice. Cut 3 lemons into twelve 1/4-inch slices. Slice remaining lemon into 8 wedges. Make basil chiffonade: Stack basil leaves and roll up tightly (to resemble a long cigar). Slice across the roll, making cuts about 1/16 inch apart. Set aside for garnish. Heat oil in small saucepan over medium heat. Add garlic and cook until golden, about 2 minutes. Whisk in lemon juice, and then remove from heat.

2 Coat grill rack or broiler pan rack with nonstick cooking spray. Preheat grill to medium or preheat broiler. Lightly brush both sides of fish with garlic mixture and sprinkle with salt and pepper. Place 3 lemon slices on grill or broiler rack and put 1 flounder fillet on top. Repeat with remaining lemon slices and fish. Grill or broil fish, without turning, until just opaque throughout, about 6 minutes. Cook lemon wedges alongside until browned, about 2 minutes on each side.

3 Meanwhile, blend broth and cornstarch in cup until smooth. Whisk cornstarch mixture, sugar, and 1/4 teaspoon lemon zest into remaining garlic mixture. Bring to a boil over medium-high heat and cook until sauce thickens, about 1 minute.

4 Transfer fish to plates, lemon slices down. Spoon sauce over fish and sprinkle with basil chiffonade and remaining lemon zest. Garnish with grilled lemon wedges.

(Some More Ideas)

• If flounder is not available, substitute fillets of any other white flatfish in this recipe. Halibut, sole, and turbot are good choices.

Health Points

• Lemon and other citrus fruits are particularly good for hypertension. They are rich with vitamin C, potassium, pectin, and phytochemicals that may benefit numerous other conditions as well, including allergies, asthma, cancer, cataracts, heart disease, stroke, and even the common cold.

• Most nutrition experts recommend eating at least 6 ounces of fish per week. Fish has more protein, fewer calories, and less fat than most meats.

photo, page 105

Each serving provides

Key Nutrients 180 Calories, 50 Calories from Fat, 5g Fat, 1g Saturated Fat, 0g Trans Fat, 23g Protein, 18g Carb, 6g Fiber, 340mg Sodium
Blood Pressure Nutrients 106mg Vitamin C, 52mg Magnesium, 613mg Potassium, 107mg Calcium

Sole en Papillote

A packet, a pocket, a papillote—an elegant envelope with supper inside! If you've never cooked fish this way, give it a try. Cooking en papillote seals in the food's natural flavor and juices, and the presentation is bound to impress!

Preparation time **15 minutes**   Cooking time **15 minutes**   *Serves 4*

5 ounces fresh spinach, washed and trimmed

1 medium onion, chopped

4 sole fillets (4–6 ounces each)

Salt to taste

1/2 teaspoon pepper

2 medium tomatoes, chopped

4 medium carrots, cut into matchstick strips

4 scallions, sliced

1/2 cup dry white wine or chicken broth

2 teaspoons olive oil

8 thin lemon slices

4 sprigs fresh thyme

1 Preheat oven to 400°F. Cut four 15-inch squares of parchment paper and fold in half diagonally, forming triangles. Open and coat with nonstick cooking spray.

2 Divide spinach and onion among parchment pieces. Cut sole fillets in half crosswise and top each portion of vegetables with 2 fillet halves, overlapping them slightly. Sprinkle each with 1/4 teaspoon salt and 1/8 teaspoon pepper. Top evenly with tomatoes, carrots, and scallions. Drizzle each with 2 tablespoons wine and 1/2 teaspoon oil. Top each with 2 lemon slices and 1 thyme sprig.

3 Fold parchment over filling. Fold two open sides of triangle over to seal. Fold over points at ends of creased side, making a five-sided packet. Lightly coat packets with nonstick cooking spray and set on jelly-roll pan.

4 Bake until packets puff, about 15 minutes. Transfer to plates and cut open tops of packets (be careful of steam). Serve immediately.

(Some More Ideas)

• Cooking in a packet is so versatile. Use any other kind of fish in place of sole, although lean fishes, such as flounder, are better for this method, as they cook up moist even though they have little fat. But fatty fishes such as salmon are also delicious prepared in a packet.

• Skip the fish entirely and just prepare vegetables en papillote. The vegetables will cook up moist and flavorful.

Health Points

• By cooking fish in a confined space, such as parchment paper, more of the natural juices are left intact. When you cook small pieces of lean fish in an oven, the dry heat pulls out the moisture, causing your fish to become tasteless.

• Spinach has a tremendous wealth of disease-fighting carotenoids and phytochemicals that team up with vitamins to help protect against cancer, high cholesterol, and vision problems.

Each serving provides

Key Nutrients 260 Calories, 45 Calories from Fat, 5g Fat, 1g Saturated Fat, 0g Trans Fat, 35g Protein, 14g Carb, 5g Fiber, 200mg Sodium
Blood Pressure Nutrients 37mg Vitamin C, 104mg Magnesium, 1210mg Potassium, 108mg Calcium

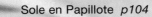
Sole en Papillote *p104*

Lemon-Glazed Flounder Fillets *p103*

Scallop and Cherry Tomato Sauté *p106*

Crispy Tuna Steaks in Citrus Sauce *p107*

Scallop and Cherry Tomato Sauté

Scallops are infinitely adaptable, pairing well with many vegetables and herbs, spices, and sauces. Here these succulent shellfish are sautéed with cherry tomatoes, seasoned with garlic and basil, and enlivened with a vermouth-based sauce.

Preparation time **5 minutes**   Cooking time **10 minutes**   *Serves 4*

1 pound sea scallops

4 teaspoons cornstarch

2 teaspoons olive oil

3 cloves garlic, minced

1 pint cherry tomatoes

2/3 cup dry vermouth, white wine, or chicken broth

Salt to taste

1/3 cup chopped fresh basil

1 tablespoon cold water

1 Dredge scallops in 3 teaspoons cornstarch, shaking off excess. Heat oil in large nonstick skillet over medium heat. Add scallops and sauté until golden brown and cooked through, about 3 minutes. With slotted spoon, transfer scallops to bowl.

2 Add garlic to pan and cook 1 minute. Add tomatoes and cook until they begin to collapse, about 4 minutes. Add vermouth, salt, and basil to pan. Bring to a boil and cook for 1 minute.

3 Meanwhile, stir together remaining 1 teaspoon cornstarch and cold water in small bowl. Add cornstarch mixture to pan and cook, stirring, until sauce is slightly thickened, about 1 minute.

4 Return scallops to pan, reduce to a simmer, and cook just until heated through, about 1 minute.

(Some More Ideas)

Shrimp and cherry tomato sauté: Substitute 1 pound large peeled and deveined shrimp for the scallops and cook as in Step 1. Then return to the pan as in Step 4.

• Delete the scallops entirely and just prepare the tomato and basil mixture as a side vegetable dish. Prepare the recipe beginning with Step 2, but add the olive oil to sauté the garlic. Omit Step 4.

Health Points

• When a dish is very low in calories (like this one), the percentage of calories from fat can seem high, even though there is just a small amount of fat in the recipe. The fat that is used here is heart-friendly olive oil, which is a healthy monounsaturated fat. Moreover, the mineral-rich scallops are naturally low in both saturated and total fat.

photo, page 105

Each serving provides

Key Nutrients 180 Calories, 30 Calories from Fat, 4g Fat, 0g Saturated Fat, 0g Trans Fat, 20g Protein, 10g Carb, 1g Fiber, 190mg Sodium
Blood Pressure Nutrients 21mg Vitamin C, 88mg Magnesium, 637mg Potassium, 60mg Calcium

Crispy Tuna Steaks in Citrus Sauce

Their beefy texture makes tuna steaks a favorite with confirmed meat eaters. In this tangy recipe, the seasoned cornmeal seals in the tuna's juicy flavor. Who could resist?

Preparation time **15 minutes**   Cooking time **9 minutes**   *Serves 4*

Sauce

2 large oranges

1 1/2 cups orange juice

2 tablespoons dry white wine
(optional)

2 tablespoons cornstarch

Tuna Steaks

2 tablespoons chopped fresh
cilantro

2 tablespoons cornmeal

Salt to taste

1/4 teaspoon pepper

4 tuna steaks (1/2 inch thick,
6 ounces each)

4 teaspoons olive oil

1 Peel and section oranges. Whisk orange juice, wine (if using), and cornstarch in small saucepan until smooth. Bring to a boil over medium-high heat and cook, stirring, until sauce boils and thickens, about 2 minutes. Remove from heat and stir in orange sections. Keep warm.

2 Mix cilantro, cornmeal, salt, and pepper in pie plate. Coat both sides of tuna steaks with cornmeal mixture, pressing firmly so mixture adheres.

3 Heat 2 teaspoons oil in large cast-iron skillet over medium-high heat until hot but not smoking. Sear tuna until done to taste, 2–3 minutes on each side for medium-rare. Add remaining oil just before turning fish. Serve with the sauce.

(Some More Ideas)

• Of the many varieties of tuna, the most common kind sold fresh is yellowfin. It's a good choice for this recipe because it holds its shape and is flavorful enough to stand up to the seasonings in the crust and sauce. For variety, try this recipe with salmon, swordfish, or mahi-mahi.

Health Points

• Tuna is a member of the mackerel family. It is high in omega-3 fatty acids. Like most fish, tuna is especially rich in B vitamins, including niacin, thiamine, and vitamin B6.

photo, page 105

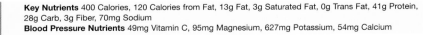

Each serving provides

Key Nutrients 400 Calories, 120 Calories from Fat, 13g Fat, 3g Saturated Fat, 0g Trans Fat, 41g Protein, 28g Carb, 3g Fiber, 70mg Sodium
Blood Pressure Nutrients 49mg Vitamin C, 95mg Magnesium, 627mg Potassium, 54mg Calcium

Spaghettini with Seafood

Cooked in a delicious wine-enriched tomato sauce, a nutritious mix of seafood makes an elegant partner for the long, thin pasta called spaghettini. Prepare a leafy mixed side salad to go with this dinner party main course.

Preparation time **25 minutes**   Cooking time **about 45 minutes**   *Serves 4*

2 tablespoons olive oil

1 onion, chopped

2–3 garlic cloves, chopped

2 tablespoons chopped fresh parsley

1 cup dry white wine

1 can (15 ounces) chopped tomatoes

Pinch crushed dried chiles

1/4 teaspoon sugar

Pinch saffron threads

8–12 mussels, scrubbed and beards removed

2 squid, cleaned, then tentacles cut into bite-size pieces and bodies cut into rings

1 pound large shrimp, peeled and deveined

1 pound spaghettini

Salt and pepper to taste

Sprigs of fresh oregano or marjoram *(garnish)*

1 Heat the oil in a large saucepan, add the onion, and sauté until softened but not browned, 5–7 minutes. Add the garlic and parsley and cook for 1 minute.

2 Pour in the wine and bring to the boil. Regulate the heat so that the wine boils steadily, and cook until the wine has almost all evaporated, about 15 minutes.

3 Stir in the tomatoes with their juice, the crushed chiles, sugar, and saffron. Reduce the heat and cook gently for 15 minutes. Season to taste.

4 Add the mussels. Cover and cook over a medium heat until the mussels start to open, about 5 minutes. Add the squid and shrimp, and cook until the shrimp turn from blue-gray to pink, another 3–4 minutes. Remove from the heat. Discard any mussels that have not opened, then cover the pan to retain the heat.

5 Meanwhile, cook the spaghettini in boiling water for 10 minutes, or according to the package instructions, until al dente. Drain and return to the empty pan. Add some of the tomato sauce and toss the pasta until coated.

6 Serve the pasta with the remaining tomato sauce and seafood piled on top, garnished with small sprigs of fresh oregano or marjoram.

(Some More Ideas)

• When tomatoes are in season, use 2 1/4 pounds ripe plum tomatoes, peeled and diced, instead of canned. The cooking time for the sauce will be about 5 minutes longer. (You may need a little more sugar to balance the tangy flavor of fresh tomatoes.)

• Omit the squid and replace it with 1 cup cooked or canned, drained cannellini beans.

Health Points

• Shellfish contain useful amounts of B vitamins, particularly B12, and they are a good source of the antioxidant selenium.

• Wine and tomatoes make a sauce that is far lower in fat than the usual cream-based dressings.

• Onions and garlic contain allicin, which has antifungal and antibiotic properties.

Each serving provides

Key Nutrients 750 Calories, 110 Calories from Fat, 12g Fat, 2g Saturated Fat, 0g Trans Fat, 52g Protein, 97g Carb, 5g Fiber, 390mg Sodium
Blood Pressure Nutrients 33mg Vitamin C, 145mg Magnesium, 990mg Potassium, 115mg Calcium

Classic Grilled Dover Sole *p110*

Spaghettini with Seafood *p108*

Grilled Salmon with
Pepper-Corn Relish *p114*

Steamed Fish with Ginger and Sesame *p111*

Classic Grilled Dover Sole

The superb taste of Dover sole is brought to full realization when gently grilled, as in this recipe. New potatoes with fresh mint and baby leaf spinach complement this most elegant of fish dishes.

Preparation and cooking time **30 minutes**   *Serves 4*

4 small Dover sole (1/2 pound each), cleaned and skinned

2 pounds baby new potatoes, scrubbed

1 large sprig fresh mint

1 tablespoon unsalted butter

Finely grated zest and juice of 1 large lemon

1 pound baby leaf spinach

Freshly grated nutmeg *(optional)*

Salt and pepper to taste

Sprigs of fresh mint *(garnish)*

Lemon wedges *(garnish)*

1 Preheat the oven broiler to high. Cut a piece of foil to fit the grill pan and lay the fish on top.

2 Put the potatoes in a saucepan, cover with boiling water and add the sprig of mint. Cook until the potatoes are just tender, about 15 minutes.

3 Meanwhile, melt the butter in a small saucepan and mix in the lemon zest and juice. Season with salt and pepper. Brush the lemon butter over the fish and broil until the flesh close to the bone flakes easily when pierced with a knife, 5–6 minutes. Carefully turn the fish over, brush again with the lemon butter and broil for 5–6 minutes.

4 While the fish is cooking, steam the spinach until just wilted, 2–3 minutes. Season with salt, pepper and nutmeg to taste.

5 Drain the potatoes and put into a warmed serving dish. Add plenty of black pepper, toss gently, and garnish with mint sprigs. Transfer the sole to warmed dinner plates and spoon over any cooking juices from the grill pan. Add lemon wedges and serve, with the potatoes and spinach.

(Some More Ideas)

• Other, less expensive flatfish such as halibut or lemon sole are also delicious when grilled with lemon butter. Allow 4–5 minutes cooking each side. Instead of spinach, serve with broccoli florets steamed until barely tender, 2–3 minutes.

• Smooth, creamy mashed potatoes flavored with herbs are another good accompaniment for grilled sole. Peel and cut up 2 pounds potatoes and cook in boiling water until tender, 15–20 minutes. Drain thoroughly, then mash until smooth. Beat in 1/2 cup 1% milk and 2 teaspoons butter. Season to taste, then mix in 3 tablespoons chopped fresh herbs; a combination of parsley and chives is particularly good.

Health Points

• Sole is a useful source of vitamin B12, which plays a critical role in the production of DNA and RNA, the genetic material in cells.

photo, page 109

Each serving provides

Key Nutrients 470 Calories, 60 Calories from Fat, 6g Fat, 3g Saturated Fat, 0g Trans Fat, 51g Protein, 55g Carb, 7g Fiber, 290mg Sodium
Blood Pressure Nutrients 77mg Vitamin C, 218mg Magnesium, 2369mg Potassium, 169mg Calcium

Steamed Fish with Ginger and Sesame

Steaming is unbeatable when it comes to heart-healthy cooking. Since no fat is used in the cooking, these ginger-and-cilantro-scented fillets have the luxury of a dash of aromatic sesame oil added at the end.

Preparation time **10 minutes**   Cooking time **10 minutes**   *Serves 4*

Fish

2 tablespoons grated fresh ginger

3 cloves garlic, minced

1/2 teaspoon grated lime zest

1/4 cup chopped cilantro

4 cod or tilapia fillets (5 ounces each)

Salt to taste

2 1/2 teaspoons dark sesame oil

Sauce

2 tablespoons fresh lime juice

1/2 cup water

1 teaspoon cornstarch blended with 1 tablespoon water

1/4 cup cilantro

1 Combine ginger, garlic, lime zest, and 1/4 cup cilantro in small bowl. Lay fillets skinned-side up on work surface and sprinkle with salt and cilantro mixture. Fold fillets in half. Drizzle sesame oil over folded fish and place fish on heatproof plate.

2 Place a cake rack in a skillet large enough to hold plate of fish and add water to just fall short of cake rack. Cover and bring to a simmer.

3 Carefully place plate of fish on rack over simmering water. Cover and steam until cooked through, about 5 minutes. With slotted spatula, transfer fish to platter and cover loosely to keep warm.

4 To make the sauce: Pour cooking liquids on plate used for steaming into small saucepan. Add lime juice and water and bring to a boil. Stir in cornstarch mixture and cook, stirring, until sauce is lightly thickened, about 1 minute. Stir in 1/4 cup cilantro. Pass sauce at the table in small serving bowl.

(Some More Ideas)

• Fillets of sole or flounder work equally well in place of tilapia.

Steamed fish, Italian style: In place of the ginger, garlic, lime zest, and cilantro, make a mixture of chopped garlic, finely diced onion, chopped basil, and diced seeded tomato. Fill the tilapia with this mixture. For the sauce in Step 4, add lemon juice instead of lime to the cooking liquids and replace the cilantro with chopped thyme, oregano, or basil.

Health Points

• A single 4-ounce serving of tilapia has 20 grams of protein and less than 1 gram of fat, all of it heart-healthy omega-3 oil. Tilapia is becoming increasingly popular, not only due to its mild taste and sumptuous texture, but also thanks to improved aquafarming techniques.

• The more flavorful you can prepare fish, the greater the chances you'll meet the recommendation of eating seafood twice a week.

photo, page 109

Each serving provides

Key Nutrients 170 Calories, 40 Calories from Fat, 5g Fat, 1g Saturated Fat, 0g Trans Fat, 27g Protein, 3g Carb, 0g Fiber, 120mg Sodium
Blood Pressure Nutrients 16mg Vitamin C, 50mg Magnesium, 584mg Potassium, 42mg Calcium

Shrimp Scampi

Ever wonder how some people can give great dinner parties on short notice? They have a secret: fast, "fancy" dishes they've long since mastered. And adding show-stopping side dishes like asparagus never hurts the presentation.

Preparation time **20 minutes**   Cooking time **10 minutes**   *Serves 6*

1 1/2 pounds large shrimp

2 teaspoons olive oil

3 cloves garlic, minced

2/3 cup bottled clam juice or reduced-sodium, low-fat chicken broth

3 tablespoons fresh lemon juice

Salt to taste

1/8 teaspoon crushed red pepper flakes

1 teaspoon cornstarch blended with 1 tablespoon water

1/4 cup chopped parsley

1 Shell the shrimp. If you wish to devein, make a shallow cut along the back of each shrimp and remove the black vein.

2 Spray large nonstick skillet with nonstick cooking spray. Add oil and heat over medium heat. Add garlic and cook until tender, about 2 minutes.

3 Add shrimp and cook, stirring frequently, until almost cooked through, about 3 minutes. Add clam juice, lemon juice, salt, and red pepper flakes and bring to a boil. Cook until shrimp are opaque throughout, about 1 minute.

4 With slotted spoon, transfer shrimp to serving plates. Bring liquid in skillet to a boil, stir in cornstarch mixture, and cook, stirring, until sauce is lightly thickened, about 1 minute. Stir in parsley and spoon sauce over shrimp.

(Some More Ideas)

Scallop scampi: In place of the shrimp, use large sea scallops and add them as in Step 3. Cook the scallops for only 1 minute before adding the clam and lemon juices. Cook one more minute.

• Add more garlic if you are a true garlic lover!

• Serve with rice and steamed asparagus, with fresh pineapple for dessert.

Health Points

• Despite a reputation for being high in cholesterol, shrimp are actually good for your heart. They are rich in omega-3 fatty acids, selenium, zinc, and vitamin B12, and their cholesterol levels, ounce for ounce, are not much different from that in lean beef or poultry.

• Asparagus contains asparagine, a phytochemical that acts as a diuretic. The vegetable also contains rutin, a flavonoid that helps to maintain blood-vessel health, and saponins, compounds that prevent absorption of cholesterol.

Each serving provides

Key Nutrients 210 Calories, 35 Calories from Fat, 4g Fat, 1g Saturated Fat, 0g Trans Fat, 40g Protein, 2g Carb, 0g Fiber, 480mg Sodium
Blood Pressure Nutrients 12mg Vitamin C, 70mg Magnesium, 425mg Potassium, 85mg Calcium

Grilled Salmon with Pepper-Corn Relish

The rich flavor of salmon is a clue to its bountiful supply of heart-healthy omega-3 fatty acids—and just about everybody loves the taste. Here the spice-rubbed fish is served with a colorful confetti of diced vegetables.

Preparation time **10 minutes**   Cooking time **10 minutes**   *Serves 4*

1/4 teaspoon plus
2 tablespoons sugar

1 teaspoon ground coriander

Salt to taste

1/2 teaspoon cinnamon

1/4 teaspoon cardamom

1/4 teaspoon black pepper

4 salmon steaks
(6 ounces each)

1/2 teaspoon yellow
mustard seeds

1/3 cup distilled white vinegar

1 zucchini, cut into
1/4-inch dice

1 orange or red bell pepper,
cut into 1/4-inch dice

1 cup corn kernels, fresh or
thawed frozen

1 Spray grill rack with nonstick cooking spray. Preheat grill to medium. Combine 1/4 teaspoon sugar, coriander, salt, cinnamon, cardamom, and black pepper in small saucepan. Measure out 1 1/4 teaspoons of spice mixture and rub into one side of each salmon steak.

2 For relish, add remaining 2 tablespoons sugar, mustard seeds, and vinegar to spice mixture in saucepan, and bring to a boil over medium heat. Add zucchini, bell pepper, and corn, and cook until bell pepper is crisp-tender, about 4 minutes.

3 Place salmon, spice-side down, on grill and cook, without turning, until just done, about 5 minutes. Serve salmon topped with relish.

(Some More Ideas)

• Use swordfish or tuna steaks in place of the salmon.

• Serve the pepper-corn relish as a side dish to grilled beef, chicken, or pork.

• Serve this dish with grilled new potatoes and arugula salad, with fresh blueberries for dessert.

Health Points

• Whether you use fresh or frozen corn, you will still get the same nutrients: fiber, folate, potassium, and vitamin C. Yellow corn also provides the added nutritional benefit of carotenoids, which are important disease-fighting phytochemicals.

• Salmon is a rich source of omega-3 fatty acids, a type of polyunsaturated fat thought to help protect against coronary heart disease and strokes by making blood less "sticky" and therefore less likely to clot. A diet rich in omega-3 fatty acids may also be helpful in preventing and treating arthritis.

photo, page 109

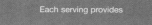
Each serving provides

Key Nutrients 300 Calories, 120 Calories from Fat, 13g Fat, 3g Saturated Fat, 0g Trans Fat, 25g Protein, 18g Carb, 2g Fiber, 70mg Sodium
Blood Pressure Nutrients 86mg Vitamin C, 39mg Magnesium, 509mg Potassium, 29mg Calcium

Fish Baked on a Bed of Broccoli, Corn, and Red Pepper

Baking fish fillets on top of cut fresh vegetables creates an easy and nutritious meal. You can change the vegetables depending on what is in season at the market or to suit your personal tastes.

Preparation time **15 minutes**   Cooking time **50 minutes**   *Serves 4*

4 sole or any firm white fillets (4–6 ounces each), fresh or frozen and thawed

2 tablespoons reduced-sodium, fat-free Italian dressing

1 tablespoon fine dry unseasoned bread crumbs

1 tablespoon grated Parmesan cheese

1/4 teaspoon paprika

1 tablespoon olive oil

2 cups broccoli florets

1 cup fresh or frozen corn kernels, thawed

1 red bell pepper, cut into thin strips

1 small red onion, thinly sliced

2 tablespoons chopped parsley

1 tablespoon chopped fresh basil

Salt to taste

1/8 teaspoon pepper

1 Place fish in shallow baking dish and brush lightly with Italian dressing. Cover and refrigerate. In small bowl, combine bread crumbs with Parmesan cheese and paprika until blended.

2 Preheat oven to 425°F. Brush 4 individual ovenproof dishes (or one 13 x 9 x 2-inch dish) with oil. In large bowl, combine broccoli, corn, red pepper, onion, parsley, basil, salt, and pepper.

3 Divide vegetable mixture evenly among cooking dishes. Cover with aluminum foil and bake until vegetables are just tender, about 35–40 minutes.

4 Uncover dishes and top vegetables with fish fillets. Cover again and bake until fish is barely cooked and still moist in thickest part, about 8–10 minutes. Uncover dishes, sprinkle with bread crumb mixture, and continue to bake, uncovered, until topping is golden, about 2–3 minutes.

(Some More Ideas)

• Use the crumb mixture to top any cooked vegetable.

• Substitute 1 pound peeled and deveined shrimp for the fish fillets. Bake the shrimp as in Step 4 for only 4 minutes. Uncover the dishes, sprinkle with the crumb mixture, and continue to bake 1–2 minutes.

Health Points

• This recipe is a good example of how to plan for portion sizes. When it is served in individual dishes, just the right amount of protein and vegetables is supplied.

• Broccoli is one of the most important, nutrient-rich vegetables. It is a member of the cruciferous family and contains ample amounts of fiber, vitamin C, and phyto-chemicals for all kinds of disease prevention.

Each serving provides

Key Nutrients 200 Calories, 50 Calories from Fat, 6g Fat, 1g Saturated Fat, 0g Trans Fat, 24g Protein, 14g Carb, 3g Fiber, 240mg Sodium
Blood Pressure Nutrients 96mg Vitamin C, 51mg Magnesium, 637mg Potassium, 63mg Calcium

Summer Salmon and Asparagus

Fresh young vegetables and succulent salmon make this an excellent speedy casserole to prepare for special occasions.
The leek, tender asparagus, and sugar snap peas all cook quickly and look superb.

Preparation time **10 minutes**   Cooking time **about 20 minutes**   *Serves 4*

4 (5 ounce) salmon fillets

1 leek, bottom half only, washed and sliced

1/2 pound tender asparagus spears

1/4 pound sugar snap peas

4 tablespoons dry white wine

1 cup reduced-sodium vegetable broth

1 tablespoon unsalted butter, cut into small pieces

Salt and pepper to taste

1 tablespoon snipped fresh chives *(garnish)*

1 Run your fingertips over each salmon fillet to check for any stray bones, pulling out any that remain between the flakes of fish. Arrange the leek slices in a single layer in the bottom of a large, shallow flameproof casserole. Lay the pieces of salmon on top. Surround the fish with the asparagus and sugar snap peas. Pour in the wine and stock, and dot the butter over the fish. Season with salt and pepper.

2 Bring to a boil, then cover the casserole with a tight-fitting lid and reduce the heat so the liquid simmers gently. Cook the fish and vegetables until the salmon is pale pink all the way through and the vegetables are tender, 12–14 minutes. Sprinkle the chives over the salmon and serve.

(Some More Ideas)

Mackerel and carrots: Season mackerel fillets and fold them loosely in half, with the skin outside. Use baby carrots, or large carrots cut into short, thick sticks, instead of the asparagus, and medium-dry cider instead of the wine. Add 2 sprigs fresh rosemary to the vegetables before arranging the mackerel on top and pouring in the cider and broth.

Asian-style fish casserole: Use cod or halibut fillet instead of salmon, 4 scallions instead of the leek, and 1/2 pound whole button mushrooms instead of the asparagus. Arrange the vegetables and fish as in the main recipe, adding 4 tablespoons Chinese rice wine or dry sherry with the broth instead of the white wine. Omit the butter and sprinkle 1 tablespoon low-sodium soy sauce, 1 tablespoon grated fresh ginger, and 1 tablespoon toasted sesame oil over the fish. Garnish with chopped fresh cilantro instead of chives and serve with plain boiled rice.

Each serving provides

Key Nutrients 340 Calories, 170 Calories from Fat, 18g Fat, 5g Saturated Fat, 0g Trans Fat, 31g Protein, 9g Carb, 3g Fiber, 870mg Sodium
Blood Pressure Nutrients 18mg Vitamin C, 59mg Magnesium, 734mg Potassium, 68mg Calcium

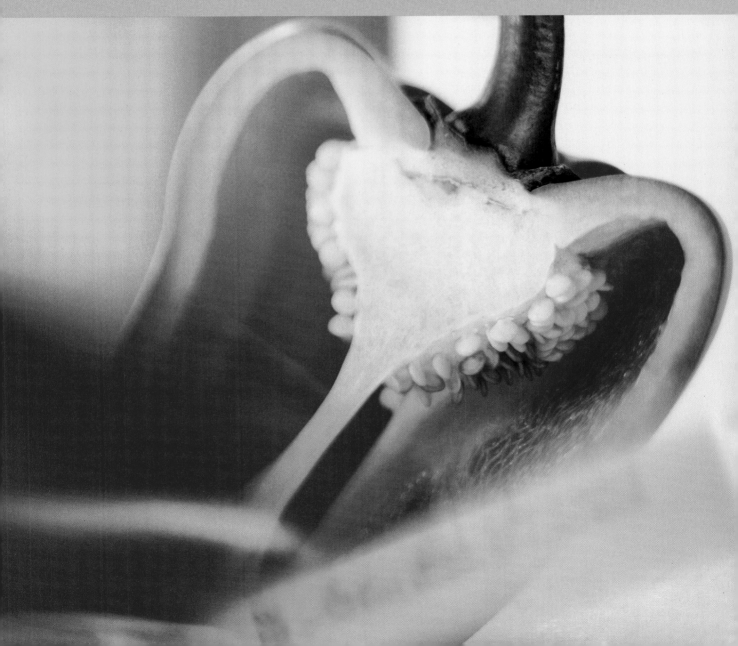

vegetarian

Baked Rice with Wild Mushrooms and Cheese

Brown rice, with its toasty taste, takes well to robust mix-ins like wild mushrooms and sun-dried tomatoes. Add in some snappy cheese, and a little goes a long way.

Preparation time **20 minutes**   Cooking time **50 minutes**   *Serves 6*

1/3 cup dried porcini mushrooms

2 1/2 cups hot water

1/3 cup sun-dried tomatoes (not oil-packed)

1 teaspoon olive oil

1 large onion, finely chopped

3 cloves garlic, minced

1 cup brown rice

Salt to taste

1/2 teaspoon rubbed sage

1/2 teaspoon pepper

1/2 cup shredded reduced-fat sharp cheddar cheese

2 tablespoons grated Parmesan cheese

1 Place porcini in small bowl and pour 1 1/2 cups hot water over them. Place sun-dried tomatoes in a separate small bowl and pour remaining 1 cup hot water over them. Let both stand until softened, about 20 minutes.

2 Scoop mushrooms out of soaking liquid. Finely chop mushrooms. Strain soaking liquid through fine-meshed sieve into a bowl. Strain sun-dried tomato soaking liquid into same bowl and set aside. Coarsely chop tomatoes.

3 Preheat oven to 350°F. Heat olive oil and 3 tablespoons of mushroom-tomato soaking liquid in medium saucepan over medium heat. Add onion and garlic to pan and cook until onion is golden, about 7 minutes.

4 Add rice, stirring to coat. Add mushrooms, tomatoes, remaining soaking liquid, salt, sage, and pepper to pan and bring to a boil. Transfer rice mixture to 8-inch square glass baking dish. Cover with foil, transfer to oven, and bake until rice is tender and liquid has been absorbed, about 40 minutes. Sprinkle hot rice with cheddar and Parmesan cheeses.

(Some More Ideas)

• If you cannot locate porcini mushrooms, try dried shiitake mushrooms, also known as Chinese black mushrooms. Or use fresh sliced mushrooms and replace the mushrooms soaking water with about 1 cup water in Step 4.

• To vary the flavor, try other reduced-fat cheeses such as Swiss or provolone.

Health Points

• The concentrated flavor of dried porcinis and dried tomatoes doubles the flavor without adding any more fat, sugar, or sodium. These wonderful enhancers can also stay on your pantry shelf for a long time.

• Brown rice is a particularly good grain for blood pressure. It is rich in magnesium, folate, and other nutrients, as well as insoluble fiber. Many of these nutrients get stripped out in the milling process that is used to make white rice.

photo, page 123

Each serving provides

Key Nutrients 190 Calories, 25 Calories from Fat, 3g Fat, 1g Saturated Fat, 0g Trans Fat, 8g Protein, 32g Carb, 3g Fiber, 140mg Sodium
Blood Pressure Nutrients 3mg Vitamin C, 55mg Magnesium, 228mg Potassium, 71mg Calcium

Spanish Rice

Traditional versions of this red-rice dish begin with fatty sausage. This version focuses on vegetables— toss with shrimp, chicken, or chicken sausage to turn it into a meat eater's main attraction.

Preparation time **20 minutes**   Cooking time **33 minutes**   *Serves 6*

1 medium onion, finely chopped

1 large green bell pepper, finely chopped

1 celery stalk, finely chopped

2 garlic cloves, minced

4 ounces white mushrooms, sliced

1 cup long-grain white rice

1 1/2 cups no-salt-added tomato juice

1 cup reduced-sodium chicken or vegetable broth

Salt to taste

1/4 teaspoon black pepper

1 bay leaf

6 plum tomatoes, halved, seeded, and diced

1 Lightly coat deep nonstick skillet with nonstick cooking spray. Sauté onion, green pepper, celery, and garlic until onion is almost soft, about 3 minutes. Stir in mushrooms and rice and sauté until rice turns golden, about 2 minutes.

2 Stir in tomato juice, broth, salt, black pepper, and bay leaf. Bring to a boil over medium-high heat. Cover, reduce heat, and simmer, stirring occasionally, 15 minutes. Stir in tomatoes.

3 Cover and cook until the rice is tender and liquid is absorbed, about 10 minutes longer. Fluff with fork to test for doneness and to keep rice from sticking together. Remove from heat and discard bay leaf.

(Some More Ideas)

Shrimp paella: Add 1 1/2 pounds shelled, deveined, large shrimp and 2 cups peas in Step 3 during the last 8 minutes of cooking.

• Although not traditional, you could make Spanish rice with brown rice instead of the white, and greatly boost both the toothiness of the dish, as well as its healthiness. In Step 3, cover and cook brown rice until tender, 40–50 minutes.

Health Points

• Tomato juice is an excellent liquid to cook with. It adds flavor and color to your dishes, and also helps minimize fattier add-ins like butter or oil. Best of all, it is rich in nutrients great for blood pressure and the heart, such as beta-carotene, lycopene, and vitamin C.

Each serving provides

Key Nutrients 80 Calories, 5 Calories from Fat, 1g Fat, 0g Saturated Fat, 0g Trans Fat, 3g Protein, 18g Carb, 2g Fiber, 40mg Sodium
Blood Pressure Nutrients 50mg Vitamin C, 24mg Magnesium, 452mg Potassium, 26mg Calcium

Rice Pilaf with Dried Fruits and Almonds

Pilaf always begins with a grain—often rice. But the ingredients can vary: One day add dried fruits and sweet spice; another, vegetables and herbs. This version overflows with flavor.

Preparation time **15 minutes**   Cooking time **40 minutes, plus standing**   *Serves 6*

12 dried apricot halves
1 tablespoon margarine
1 medium onion, chopped
1 cup jasmine or white rice
1/4 teaspoon ground cardamom
Salt to taste
1/4 teaspoon pepper
2 1/2 cups reduced-sodium chicken or vegetable broth
1/2 cup golden raisins
1/3 cup slivered almonds, toasted
Fresh rosemary sprigs *(garnish)*

1 Snip apricots with kitchen shears into small slivers (you need about 1/3 cup).

2 Melt margarine in large nonstick saucepan over medium heat. Sauté onion, rice, cardamom, salt, and pepper until rice is toasted, about 8 minutes.

3 Stir in broth, raisins, almonds, and apricots and bring to a boil. Reduce heat to medium-low. Cover and simmer until broth is absorbed, about 25 minutes. Remove from heat and let stand 5 minutes. Fluff with fork. Garnish with rosemary sprigs.

(Some More Ideas)

Savory rice pilaf: Use 1 cup brown rice instead of jasmine rice. Sauté 1 chopped green bell pepper along with the rice and onion and use 2 teaspoons fresh thyme and 1 teaspoon fresh rosemary instead of the cardamom. Use 1/3 cup toasted chopped pecans in place of the raisins, almonds, and apricots.

Health Points

• Dried apricots are fat-free and full of nutrients good both for blood pressure and cholesterol, such as potassium, lycopene, beta-carotene, and pectin. Plus, apricots are a particularly rich source of iron. While the drying process hurts apricots' store of vitamin C, many other nutrients get enhanced.

Each serving provides

Key Nutrients 250 Calories, 50 Calories from Fat, 6g Fat, 1g Saturated Fat, 0g Trans Fat, 5g Protein, 44g Carb, 3g Fiber, 75mg Sodium
Blood Pressure Nutrients 1mg Vitamin C, 21mg Magnesium, 260mg Potassium, 37mg Calcium

VEGETARIAN

Bulgur with Spring Vegetables

The sparkling taste of lemon juice plus the refreshing fragrance of mint make this a dish that will brighten any meal. Bulgur is a form of cracked wheat that cooks fast and easily.

Preparation time **45 minutes**   Cooking time **10 minutes**   *Serves 6*

1 1/4 cups bulgur
3 1/2 cups boiling water
2 tablespoons olive oil
3 tablespoons fresh lemon juice
Salt to taste
1/2 teaspoon pepper
2 leeks, halved lengthwise, cut crosswise into 1-inch pieces, and well washed
2 cloves garlic, minced
12 asparagus spears, cut into 2-inch lengths
1 cup frozen peas
1/4 cup chopped fresh mint

1 Combine bulgur and boiling water in large heatproof bowl. Let stand until bulgur is tender, about 30 minutes; stir after 15 minutes. Drain bulgur in large fine-meshed sieve to get rid of any remaining liquid.

2 Whisk together 1 tablespoon of oil, the lemon juice, salt, and pepper in large bowl. Add drained bulgur and fluff with a fork to separate the grains and combine them with the lemon mixture.

3 Heat remaining 1 tablespoon oil in medium skillet over low heat. Add leeks and garlic to skillet and cook until leeks are tender, about 5 minutes. Transfer to bowl with bulgur.

4 In steamer set over a pan of boiling water, steam asparagus until tender, about 4 minutes. Add peas during final 30 seconds of steaming. Add vegetables to bowl of bulgur along with mint and toss to combine. Serve at room temperature or chilled.

(Some More Ideas)

• Use couscous instead of bulgur wheat using the same proportions, but couscous only needs 5 minutes to absorb.

• Serve this hearty dish with lean sliced beef and roasted red peppers. Offer fresh figs for dessert.

• Add cubes of cooked chicken breast, turkey, or roast beef.

Health Points

• Bulgur wheat provides a number of nutrients: protein, niacin, insoluble fiber, phyto-estrogens, and vitamin E, all of which work to keep your heart healthy. Plus, it is a great source of potassium and magnesium, two minerals important to blood pressure.

• Bulgur wheat is a good, low-fat complex carbohydrate. It contains useful amounts of some of the B vitamins, particularly B1, as well as copper and iron.

Each serving provides

Key Nutrients 190 Calories, 50 Calories from Fat, 5g Fat, 1g Saturated Fat, 0g Trans Fat, 6g Protein, 32g Carb, 8g Fiber, 140mg Sodium
Blood Pressure Nutrients 19mg Vitamin C, 68mg Magnesium, 292mg Potassium, 44mg Calcium

Baked Rice with Wild Mushrooms and Cheese *p118*

Bulgur with Spring Vegetables *p122*

Quinoa Pilaf with Cherries and Walnuts *p126*

Barley Pilaf with Herbs *p125*

Sunny Risotto with Carrots

The moment you take a bite of this rich-tasting, aromatic risotto you'll forget how healthy it is. The secret to its incredibly appealing texture is the liquid-absorbing rice starch.

Preparation time **15 minutes**   Cooking time **35 minutes**   *Serves 4*

2 teaspoons olive oil
1 small onion, finely chopped
2 large carrots, cut into 1/4-inch dice
1 cup arborio rice
1/2 cup dry white wine
1 can (14 1/2 ounces) reduced-sodium chicken or vegetable broth
1 cup carrot juice
Salt to taste
1/4 cup grated Parmesan cheese
1/4 teaspoon pepper

1 In medium nonstick saucepan, heat oil over moderate heat. Add onion and sauté until tender, about 5 minutes. Add carrots and sauté until crisp-tender, about 4 minutes. Add rice, stirring to coat.

2 Add wine and cook, stirring occasionally, until evaporated by half, about 2 minutes.

3 In medium bowl, combine broth, carrot juice, 1/2 cup water, and salt. Add broth mixture, 1/2 cup at a time, to rice and cook, stirring, until absorbed, before adding the next 1/2 cup. (Total time will be about 20 minutes.) Remove from heat. Stir in Parmesan cheese and pepper.

(Some More Ideas)

• For a deeper color and a more Spanish flavor, add a pinch of saffron threads to the broth mixture in Step 3.

• To cut calories even more without sacrifice, substitute two tablespoons of a stronger cheese such as Romano for the Parmesan.

• This is a good dish to make when you have friends or family in the kitchen with you. Have one of them do the stirring!

Health Points

• The beta-carotene in carrots that is so good for vision is equally important for healthy skin and hair. One cup of cooked carrots provides three times the recommended intake of beta-carotene.

• Carrots were known to the Greeks and Romans, although they were not widely used in Europe until the Middle Ages. Early varieties were red, purple, or black; the familiar orange variety was developed in Holland in the 17th century.

Each serving provides

Key Nutrients 320 Calories, 45 Calories from Fat, 5g Fat, 2g Saturated Fat, 0g Trans Fat, 9g Protein, 65g Carb, 3g Fiber, 135mg Sodium
Blood Pressure Nutrients 10mg Vitamin C, 19mg Magnesium, 403mg Potassium, 73mg Calcium

Barley Pilaf with Herbs

Like rice, barley can be cooked as fluffy, separate kernels, or made risotto-style, as in this delicious dish—gently, steadily stirred with liquid to make a smooth, creamy texture.

Preparation time **10 minutes**   Cooking time **55 minutes**   *Serves 6*

2 teaspoons olive oil
1 medium onion, finely chopped
3 cloves garlic, minced
2 carrots, thinly sliced
3/4 cup pearl barley
Salt to taste
3/4 teaspoon rubbed sage
3/4 teaspoon thyme
3 1/4 cups water
1 teaspoon slivered lemon zest
3/4 teaspoon pepper
1/4 cup grated Parmesan cheese

1 Heat oil in medium saucepan over medium heat. Add onion and garlic to pan and cook until onion is tender and golden brown, about 5 minutes.

2 Add carrots to pan and cook until tender, about 5 minutes. Add barley, stirring to combine.

3 Add salt, sage, thyme, and water to pan and bring to a boil. Reduce to a simmer and cook, stirring frequently, until barley is tender, about 45 minutes.

4 Stir in lemon zest, pepper, and Parmesan until evenly combined.

(Some More Ideas)

• This recipe is great with brown rice too. Add the rice instead of barley in Step 2 and follow the same directions.

• Other herbs such as basil or oregano are equally good. Substitute 3/4 teaspoon each for the sage and the thyme

Health Points

• Barley is abundant with lignans, which are phyto-chemicals that help lower cholesterol. The plant sterols found in barley may also assist in reducing total and LDL cholesterol. Barley is also rich in selenium and vitamin E.

photo, page 123

Each serving provides

Key Nutrients 130 Calories, 20 Calories from Fat, 3g Fat, 1g Saturated Fat, 0g Trans Fat, 4g Protein, 24g Carb, 5g Fiber, 46mg Sodium
Blood Pressure Nutrients 4mg Vitamin C, 27mg Magnesium, 176mg Potassium, 44mg Calcium

Quinoa Pilaf with Cherries and Walnuts

Grainlike quinoa (pronounced KEEN-wah) is not a grain at all, but the seed of a plant related to Swiss chard. Here it is made with a creative mix of tastes: thyme, cherries, and walnuts.

Preparation time **10 minutes**   Cooking time **30 minutes**   *Serves 12*

2 teaspoons olive oil
1 large onion, finely chopped
2 cups quinoa
2 cups boiling water
Salt to taste
1 teaspoon pepper
1/2 teaspoon thyme
1 cup dried cherries
1/2 cup walnuts, toasted and coarsely chopped

1 Heat oil in nonstick Dutch oven over medium heat. Add onion and cook, stirring frequently, until golden brown, about 7 minutes.

2 Meanwhile, place quinoa in large ungreased skillet over medium heat and cook, stirring often, until lightly toasted, about 5 minutes.

3 Add quinoa to onion in Dutch oven. Stir in boiling water, salt, pepper, and thyme. Return to a boil, cover, and gently boil 10 minutes. Uncover and cook, stirring occasionally, until liquid has been absorbed and quinoa is tender, 10–12 minutes.

4 Remove from heat and stir in cherries and walnuts. Serve hot, at room temperature, or chilled.

(Some More Ideas)

• To turn this dish into a meaty meal, add some leftover cooked chicken breast, strips of roast pork tenderloin, or cubes of cooked lean beef.

• Make this pilaf with brown rice. Use 1 cup rice and 2 cups boiling water. Follow the directions for Steps 2 and 3 cooking the brown rice for 40–50 minutes.

Health Points

• Quinoa is suddenly popular, but it is an ancient grain, dating back about 4,000 years and consumed by the Aztecs. It is particularly high in lysine, an amino acid necessary for the synthesis of protein, making it one of the best sources of plant protein. Plus, it provides lots of magnesium, potassium, zinc, vitamin E, iron, and fiber.

• Walnuts provide useful amounts of vitamin E, many of the B vitamins, and potassium.

photo, page 123

Each serving provides

Key Nutrients 190 Calories, 50 Calories from Fat, 5g Fat, 0g Saturated Fat, 0g Trans Fat, 6g Protein, 30g Carb, 3g Fiber, 10mg Sodium
Blood Pressure Nutrients 1mg Vitamin C, 72mg Magnesium, 259mg Potassium, 31mg Calcium

Millet with Spinach and Pine Nuts

Bright green spinach and golden apricots add rich color and flavor to this easy grain-and-vegetable dish. Serve it with stews and casseroles that have plenty of sauce.

Preparation time **10 minutes**   Cooking time **20–25 minutes**   *Serves 4*

1 cup millet

2 ounces dried apricots, roughly chopped

3 cups reduced-sodium vegetable broth

1/4 cup pine nuts

1/2 pound baby spinach leaves

Juice of 1/2 lemon

Salt and pepper

1 Put the millet and dried apricots into a large saucepan and stir in the broth. Bring to a boil, then lower the heat. Simmer until all the broth has been absorbed and the millet is tender, 15–20 minutes.

2 Meanwhile, toast the pine nuts in a small skillet until they are golden brown and fragrant. Set aside.

3 Add the spinach and lemon juice to the millet, with salt and pepper to taste. Cover the pan and leave over a very low heat for 4–5 minutes to wilt the spinach.

4 Stir the millet and spinach mixture gently, then spoon into a serving bowl. Scatter the toasted pine nuts on top and serve immediately.

(Some More Ideas)

Eggplant with millet and sesame seeds: Cut 2 medium eggplants into dice. Heat 2 tablespoons olive oil in large frying pan, add the eggplant, and brown over a high heat, stirring constantly. Remove from the heat and stir in 1 cup millet and 3 cups vegetable broth. Return to the heat and bring to the boil. Stir, then reduce the heat and simmer until the broth has been absorbed and the millet is tender, 15– 20 minutes. Season with salt and pepper to taste. Transfer to a serving bowl and scatter over 2 tablespoons chopped fresh cilantro, 1 tablespoon thinly sliced scallions, and 2 tablespoons toasted sesame seeds.

Health Points

• Millet provides useful amounts of iron and B vitamins, and as it is not highly milled, it retains all its nutritional value.

• Pine nuts are a good source of vitamin E and potassium. They also contribute useful amounts of magnesium, zinc, and iron.

Each serving provides

Key Nutrients 310 Calories, 60 Calories from Fat, 7g Fat, 1g Saturated Fat, 0g Trans Fat, 10g Protein, 53g Carb, 8g Fiber, 390mg Sodium
Blood Pressure Nutrients 21mg Vitamin C, 122mg Magnesium, 656mg Potassium, 85mg Calcium

Kasha with Onions and Mushrooms

Imagine a meal you'd relish in the depth of a Russian winter and you'll understand the warming, sustaining qualities of kasha, which in America means roasted buckwheat.

Preparation time **10 minutes**   Cooking time **35 minutes**   *Serves 4*

1 tablespoon olive oil

2 large onions, halved and thinly sliced

2 teaspoons sugar

12 ounces shiitake mushrooms, stems discarded and caps thickly sliced

1/2 teaspoon rubbed sage

1/2 teaspoon pepper

1 cup whole-grain kasha

1 cup water

3/4 cup carrot juice

Salt to taste

1 Heat oil in large skillet over medium-high heat. Add onions, sprinkle with sugar, and cook, stirring frequently, until onions are golden brown and tender, about 15 minutes.

2 Add mushrooms, sage, and pepper and cook, stirring frequently until mushrooms are tender, about 5 minutes.

3 Meanwhile, place kasha in medium skillet over medium heat and cook, stirring frequently, until lightly toasted, about 5 minutes.

4 Combine water, carrot juice, and salt in medium saucepan over medium heat and bring to boil. Add kasha, cover, and cook until tender, about 10 minutes. Fluff with a fork, then transfer to pan with onion mixture and toss together to combine.

(Some More Ideas)

• This recipe works well for other grains as well. For example, choose 1 cup couscous and cook for 5 minutes in Step 4. Or choose brown rice and cook for 40 minutes in Step 2.

• Serve the kasha with roast salmon and sugar snap peas, with lemon sorbet for dessert.

Health Points

• Although buckwheat has the word "wheat" in its name, it is not wheat at all, but the grain-like fruit of a leafy plant related to rhubarb. Robust in flavor and texture, buckwheat cooks up like a wheat grain. And it contains plenty of cholesterol-lowering soluble fiber, along with protein, magnesium, and B vitamins.

• The addition of carrot juice and shiitake mushrooms, both antioxidant powerhouses, makes this a particularly healthy dish for blood pressure and the heart.

Each serving provides

Key Nutrients 260 Calories, 40 Calories from Fat, 5g Fat, 1g Saturated Fat, 0g Trans Fat, 8g Protein, 48g Carb, 7g Fiber, 40mg Sodium
Blood Pressure Nutrients 11mg Vitamin C, 105mg Magnesium, 382mg Potassium, 35mg Calcium

Kasha with Onions and Mushrooms *p128*

Lentil Risotto *p130*

Wild Rice with Walnuts *p131*

Nutted Lemon Barley *p132*

Lentil Risotto

Lentils add extra flavor and texture to this Italian-style mushroom risotto. Serve with roasted or grilled vegetables, such as peppers and zucchini, or a mixed salad, for a satisfying lunch.

Preparation time **30 minutes**   Cooking time **45 minutes**   *Serves 4*

1 cup green lentils
2 cups water
4 cups reduced-sodium vegetable broth
1 tablespoon olive oil
1 onion, finely chopped
1 garlic clove, crushed
3 celery stalks, chopped
1 red bell pepper, seeded and diced
1 teaspoon ground coriander
1 teaspoon ground cumin
1/2 pound sliced mushrooms
1 cup arborio rice
1 cup dry white wine
3 tablespoons coarsely chopped fresh cilantro, plus extra to garnish
1/4 cup grated Parmesan cheese
Salt and pepper to taste

1 Place the lentils and the water in a saucepan and bring to a boil. Lower the heat and simmer, covered, for about 20–30 minutes. Drain and set aside. Place the broth in the saucepan and bring to simmering point over a medium heat. Lower the heat so the broth is simmering gently.

2 Heat the oil in another large saucepan, add the onion, garlic and celery, and cook until softened, stirring occasionally, about 5 minutes. Add the red pepper and the ground coriander and cumin, and cook for 1 minute, stirring.

3 Add the mushrooms, rice, and cooked lentils and stir to mix. Pour in the wine and add a ladleful of the hot broth. Bring to a gentle boil and bubble until most of the liquid has been absorbed, stirring frequently.

4 Add another ladleful of broth and cook until it is absorbed, stirring frequently. Repeat this gradual addition of the hot broth until it has all been added. The rice should be creamy and tender but still with some bite, and the lentils cooked.

5 Stir in the chopped cilantro and season with salt and pepper to taste. Serve hot, sprinkled with the Parmesan shavings and extra chopped cilantro.

(Some More Ideas)

• Instead of regular-sized lentils, try the tiny Puy lentils.

Pearl barley risotto: Soften 2 sliced leeks and 1 crushed garlic clove in 1 tablespoon olive oil. Add 1 seeded and diced red or yellow bell pepper, 1 cup pearl barley, 2 teaspoons dried herbes de Provence, 1 cup dry white wine, and 1/2 cup hot vegetable broth. Simmer for 45 minutes, gradually adding a further 3 cups hot broth and stirring frequently, until the pearl barley is cooked and tender. Meanwhile, steam 1/2 pound broccoli florets and 6 ounces frozen peas. Stir these into the barley risotto and heat gently until hot. Season with salt and pepper to taste and serve, topped with the Parmesan.

Health Points

• Lentils are the small seeds of a variety of leguminous plants. They are a good source of protein, complex carbohydrate, dietary fiber, and B vitamins.

photo, page 129

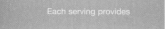
Each serving provides

Key Nutrients 510 Calories, 60 Calories from Fat, 6g Fat, 2g Saturated Fat, 0g Trans Fat, 21g Protein, 84g Carb, 12g Fiber, 560mg Sodium
Blood Pressure Nutrients 66mg Vitamin C, 22mg Magnesium, 879mg Potassium, 135mg Calcium

Wild Rice with Walnuts

Usher in autumn with this wholesome blend of wild rice, nuts, and dried fruit. Wild rice is often said to have a nutlike flavor, so teaming it with toasty walnuts makes perfect sense.

Preparation time **15 minutes**   Cooking time **1 hour 20 minutes**   *Serves 4*

2 teaspoons olive oil
1 small onion, finely chopped
2 cloves garlic, minced
2 celery stalks, cut into 1/2-inch dice
1 carrot, quartered lengthwise and thinly sliced crosswise
1 cup wild rice
1 1/2 cups carrot juice
1 1/2 cups water
Salt to taste
1/2 teaspoon pepper
1/4 teaspoon thyme
1/4 cup coarsely chopped walnuts
1/4 cup dried cranberries or raisins

1 Heat oil in medium nonstick saucepan over low heat. Add onion and garlic to pan and cook, stirring frequently, until onion is tender, about 7 minutes.

2 Add celery and carrot to pan and cook, stirring frequently, until carrot is tender, about 5 minutes.

3 Stir in wild rice. Add carrot juice, water, salt, pepper, and thyme to pan and bring to a boil. Reduce to a simmer, cover, and cook until wild rice is tender, about 1 hour (check after 45 minutes).

4 Meanwhile, toast walnuts in small skillet over low heat, stirring frequently, until walnuts are crisp and fragrant, about 5 minutes. Stir walnuts and cranberries into wild rice just before serving.

(Some More Ideas)

• Wild rice is expensive, especially if you buy the kind that's harvested by hand from the northern Great Lakes region. To stretch your supply, use half brown rice and half wild; they take the same amount of time to cook and their flavors and textures are complementary.

• Use raisins and almonds in place of the cranberries and walnuts.

Health Points

• Cooking the rice in carrot juice rather than broth or water adds a touch of sweetness and color to the dish and boosts its beta-carotene content.

• Wild rice isn't a true rice, but the seed of an aquatic grass from a different botanical family. It has more protein than other rices, and is a good source of potassium, zinc, and B vitamins.

photo, page 129

Each serving provides

Key Nutrients 300 Calories, 70 Calories from Fat, 8g Fat, 1g Saturated Fat, 0g Trans Fat, 10g Protein, 52g Carb, 6g Fiber, 55mg Sodium
Blood Pressure Nutrients 13mg Vitamin C, 111mg Magnesium, 707mg Potassium, 63mg Calcium

Nutted Lemon Barley

Barley is a slightly chewy grain with a sweet flavor that is too often consigned to just soup. Cooked in a spicy broth, barley makes a welcome change from potatoes or rice.

Preparation time **10 minutes**   Cooking time **55–60 minutes**   *Serves 8*

2 tablespoons olive oil
2 onions, finely chopped
3 stalks celery, finely chopped
1 cup pearl barley, rinsed
2 1/2 cups low-sodium canned chicken or vegetable broth
1 teaspoon finely grated lemon zest
1/2 teaspoon dried oregano
Salt to taste
1/8 teaspoon pepper
2 tablespoons sunflower seeds
1 tablespoon fresh lemon juice
1/4 cup golden raisins
2 tablespoons chopped parsley

1 In wide heavy saucepan, heat oil over moderate heat. Add onions and celery and sauté, stirring, until softened and lightly browned, about 7 minutes. Stir in barley until coated with oil. Pour in broth and add lemon zest, oregano, salt, and pepper.

2 Bring broth to boil, then reduce heat; cover pan and simmer, stirring occasionally, until barley is nearly cooked through and almost all liquid is absorbed, about 40 minutes.

3 Meanwhile, toast sunflower seeds in dry nonstick skillet over moderate heat, stirring frequently or shaking pan until golden brown. Remove from heat and transfer to plate.

4 Stir lemon juice and raisins into barley mixture and cover saucepan. Remove saucepan from heat and allow mixture to stand about 5 minutes, then gently stir toasted sunflower seeds and chopped parsley into barley until just mixed.

(Some More Ideas)

• Substitute orange zest and orange juice for the lemon zest and juice.

• Add the same amount of pumpkin seeds to the pilaf in place of the sunflower seeds.

• Use snipped dried apricots or dates in place of the golden raisins.

Health Points

• Barley is one of the first crops cultivated by man and has been a staple of healthy diets since biblical times. Barley has 6 grams of fiber per cup, making it one of the more fiber-rich grains available. It is also a great source of potassium, B vitamins, and iron.

• Toasted sunflower seeds contain a wide variety of useful minerals, including phosphorous, magnesium, and copper as well as fiber and protein.

photo, page 129

Each serving provides

Key Nutrients 170 Calories, 50 Calories from Fat, 5g Fat, 1g Saturated Fat, 0g Trans Fat, 5g Protein, 28g Carb, 5g Fiber, 50mg Sodium
Blood Pressure Nutrients 5mg Vitamin C, 35mg Magnesium, 220mg Potassium, 32mg Calcium

Cracked-Wheat Pilaf with Tomato and Onions

Next time you're looking for a simple, healthy dish to serve, try this nutty-tasting grain as a delicious switch from rice.

Preparation time **15 minutes**   Cooking time **45 minutes**   *Serves 8*

1 cup cracked wheat

2 tablespoons olive or canola oil

3 onions, thinly sliced

1 clove garlic, finely chopped

1 1/2 cups vegetable broth

1 1/2 cups reduced-sodium tomato juice

1 tomato, coarsely chopped

2 tablespoons chopped fresh basil or 1 tablespoon dried

Salt to taste

1/8 teaspoon pepper

1 Place cracked wheat in fine sieve and rinse under cold running water. Stir so that all the grains are well rinsed, then drain.

2 Heat oil in a large nonstick skillet. Add onions and garlic and sauté, stirring often, until softened and dark golden brown. Stir in broth and tomato juice. Bring to a boil; add drained wheat.

3 Cover and simmer 15 minutes, stirring occasionally. Stir in tomato, basil, salt, and pepper. Simmer a few minutes longer, until liquid is absorbed. Serve warm.

(Some More Ideas)

• Add leftover cooked poultry to this pilaf for a one-pot supper.

• Or serve it as the main event for lunch, with a mixed green salad and crusty roll on the side.

• Make this dish spicy! Use reduced-sodium spicy tomato juice and add 1 jalapeño pepper, minced, to the onions and garlic in Step 2.

Health Points

• Cracked wheat is made from whole-wheat berries, so it's high in fiber and B vitamins.

• The combination of olive oil, garlic, basil, and tomatoes is not only a classical Mediterranean flavor, but is a one-two-three punch against bad health. Each ingredient contains unique nutrients that help the heart and fight disease.

Each serving provides

Key Nutrients 150 Calories, 35 Calories from Fat, 4g Fat, 1g Saturated Fat, 0g Trans Fat, 4g Protein, 26g Carb, 5g Fiber, 95mg Sodium
Blood Pressure Nutrients 15mg Vitamin C, 34mg Magnesium, 311mg Potassium, 27mg Calcium

Refried Bean Burritos

The creamy texture of pinto beans makes them the perfect partner for strong flavors and spices. The beans aren't actually refried, but are simmered first, then cooked gently in a little oil.

Preparation and cooking time **1 3/4 hours, plus 8 hours soaking**   *Serves 6*

Beans

1 cup dried pinto beans, soaked for at least 8 hours

2 onions, 1 quartered and 1 finely chopped

3 garlic cloves, 2 whole and 1 finely chopped

2 bay leaves

1 1/2 tablespoons canola oil

Salt and pepper to taste

Salsa

1 pound firm, ripe tomatoes, diced

1 fresh green chile, seeded and finely chopped

Finely grated zest and juice of 1 lime

Pinch of sugar

3 tablespoons chopped fresh cilantro

To Serve

8 large flour tortillas

1/2 cup reduced-fat cheddar or Monterey Jack cheese

1 head romaine lettuce, shredded

1/2 cup plain nonfat yogurt

1 Drain the soaked beans and rinse under cold running water. Put them in a large pan, cover with plenty of fresh water, and add the quartered onion, 2 peeled garlic cloves, and the bay leaves. Bring to a boil and boil rapidly for 10 minutes, then reduce the heat, partly cover, and simmer gently until tender, 45– 60 minutes.

2 Meanwhile, make the salsa by mixing together the tomatoes, chile, lime zest and juice, sugar, and cilantro in a bowl. Cover and leave at room temperature until ready to serve.

3 When the beans have finished cooking, spoon out 3/4 cup of the cooking liquid and reserve. Drain the beans, discarding the onion and bay leaves but reserving the garlic.

4 Heat the oil in a large skillet, add the finely chopped onion and garlic, and cook gently until soft, about 10 minutes. Add the reserved whole garlic cloves, a ladleful of the beans, and a few spoonfuls of the reserved cooking liquid. Mash with a fork to break up the beans and garlic cloves.

5 Continue adding the beans, a ladleful at a time, with a little of the liquid, cooking over a low heat and mashing, to make a dryish, slightly textured puree. Season with salt and pepper to taste.

6 Meanwhile, heat the tortillas in the oven or in a microwave according to the package instructions.

7 Spoon the refried beans into the middle of the tortillas. Sprinkle with the cheese followed by the shredded lettuce, then add the yogurt. Roll up the tortillas to enclose the filling and serve immediately with the tomato and chile salsa.

(Some More Ideas)

Refried bean quesadillas: Use 1/2 cup shredded reduced-fat cheddar or Monterey Jack cheese. Heat a large skillet over a medium-low heat. Take one of 8 large flour tortillas, place it in the pan, and spoon 2–3 tablespoons of the refried beans in the middle. Sprinkle one-eighth of the cheese over the bean puree and around the edge of the tortilla. Fold the tortilla over the filling to make a half-moon shape and press the edges together gently, so that the melting cheese seals them. Cook for 1 minute, then turn over and cook the other side for 1 minute. You can also fill and fold the tortillas ahead of time, then cook them to order. Serve with a mango salsa made by mixing 1 finely chopped ripe mango with 2 seeded and sliced fresh chiles (1 green and 1 red) and the juice of 1/2 lime.

Health Points

• Tortillas provide complex carbohydrate, and make a great alternative to bread.

Each serving provides

Key Nutrients 520 Calories, 110 Calories from Fat, 12g Fat, 3g Saturated Fat, 1g Trans Fat, 20g Protein, 85g Carb, 13g Fiber, 540mg Sodium
Blood Pressure Nutrients 49mg Vitamin C, 94mg Magnesium, 889mg Potassium, 167mg Calcium

Tuscan-Style Baked Polenta *p136*

Refried Bean Burritos *p134*

Three Beans and Rice *p138*

Chickpea and Vegetable Omelet *p137*

Tuscan-Style Baked Polenta

Polenta is the much loved "mashed potatoes" of northern Italy. In this recipe, Parmesan-flavored "soft" polenta provides the topping for beans and a creamy mushroom sauce.

Preparation time **45 minutes**   Cooking time **20 minutes**   *Serves 4*

1 ounce dried porcini mushrooms

2 cups fat-free milk

1 1/2 tablespoons olive oil

1 tablespoon butter

2 celery stalks, thinly sliced

1/2 pound cremini mushrooms, sliced

3 tablespoons flour

2 teaspoons lemon juice

1 can (15 ounces) pinto beans, drained and rinsed

1 cup instant polenta

2 eggs, lightly beaten

1/4 cup freshly grated Parmesan cheese

Salt and pepper to taste

1 Place the dried mushrooms and 1 cup of the milk in a small saucepan. Bring just to a boil, then remove from the heat and set aside to soak.

2 Heat the oil and butter in a wide saucepan over a moderate heat. Add the celery and cook gently, stirring occasionally, until softened, 3–4 minutes. Raise the heat, add the cremini mushrooms, and cook, stirring, until softened, about 3 minutes.

3 Add the flour and cook, stirring, for 2 minutes. Gradually mix in the remaining milk and cook, stirring well, until the mixture just comes to a boil and thickens.

4 Strain the milk from the porcini mushrooms and add it to the mushroom and celery sauce. Bring back to the boil, stirring. Coarsely chop the porcini and add to the pan. Simmer for 2 minutes, then add the lemon juice and season with salt and pepper to taste.

5 Pour the mushroom sauce into a shallow ovenproof dish and spread out in an even layer. Scatter the beans on top. Set aside.

6 Preheat the oven to 400°F. In a heavy saucepan, cook the polenta in 2 1/2 cups boiling water, or according to the package instructions, until it is thick. Remove from the heat and briskly stir in the eggs and about half of the grated Parmesan. Season with salt and pepper to taste.

7 Pour the polenta mixture over the mushrooms and beans. Sprinkle the remaining Parmesan cheese over the top. Bake for about 20 minutes or until the filling is bubbling and the top is lightly browned. Serve hot.

(Some More Ideas)

• Replace the pinto beans with cannellini beans.

• Spread 1 pound spinach, steamed, well drained, and coarsely chopped, over the mushroom sauce before adding the beans.

Health Points

• Polenta is very versatile: It can be served soft with fish, meat, and vegetable dishes as an alternative to pasta or rice, or it can be left to set, then cut up and grilled or sautéed. It is a refreshing change from wheat products.

photo, page 135

Each serving provides

Key Nutrients 480 Calories, 140 Calories from Fat, 15g Fat, 5g Saturated Fat, 0g Trans Fat, 23g Protein, 63g Carb, 10g Fiber, 540mg Sodium
Blood Pressure Nutrients 16mg Vitamin C, 58mg Magnesium, 847mg Potassium, 331mg Calcium

Chickpea and Vegetable Omelet

This thick and chunky Arab omelet is served flat, not rolled or folded, and is more like a cake. It is packed with vegetables and chickpeas, and is equally delicious hot or cold.

Preparation and cooking time **30 minutes**   *Serves 4*

2 tablespoons olive oil, divided
1 small onion, chopped
1 garlic clove, crushed
1 teaspoon ground cumin
1 teaspoon ground coriander
Pinch cayenne pepper
1/2 pound new potatoes, scrubbed and cut into 1/2-inch dice
1 small red bell pepper, seeded and diced
1 small eggplant, cut into 1/2-inch dice
1 can (15 ounces) chickpeas, drained and rinsed
6 eggs
2 tablespoons chopped fresh cilantro
Salt and pepper to taste

1 Heat 1 tablespoon of the oil in a 10-inch nonstick skillet pan with a flameproof handle. Add the onion and cook until starting to soften, 2–3 minutes. Stir in the garlic, cumin, ground coriander, and cayenne pepper, and continue cooking for 1 minute, stirring constantly.

2 Add the additional 1 tablespoon of oil to the pan, then add the potatoes, red pepper, and eggplant. Continue sautéing for 5 minutes, stirring frequently, until the vegetables are lightly browned.

3 Add 5 tablespoons water, cover, and steam for 5 minutes. Then remove the lid and continue cooking until all excess liquid has evaporated. Stir in the chickpeas.

4 Lightly beat the eggs in a large mixing bowl. Add the chopped cilantro and season with salt and pepper to taste. Add in the vegetable and chickpea mixture from the pan and stir to mix.

5 Preheat the grill to high. Spray the skillet with cooking spray over a medium heat. Pour in the egg mixture, spreading the vegetables out evenly. Cook the omelet, shaking the pan from time to time, until almost set, 3–4 minutes; there will still be some uncooked egg mixture on the top.

6 Place the pan under the grill and cook the omelet until the top looks set, about 2 minutes. Remove from the heat and allow the omelet to rest in the pan for 2 minutes, then slide it onto a serving plate or board. Serve hot, cut into wedges.

(Some More Ideas)

Salmon omelet: Omit the cumin, coriander, and eggplant, and add 2 diced zucchini with the water in Step 3. In Step 4, add 1 can (7 ounces) salmon, drained and flaked, 2 tablespoons chopped fresh dill, 1 tablespoon snipped fresh chives, and the finely grated zest of 1 lemon to the beaten eggs with the vegetables and chickpeas.

Health Points

• New potatoes cooked in their skins have a higher fiber content than peeled potatoes. The nutrients just under the skin are also preserved when potatoes are only scrubbed and not peeled.

• Eggs are still an inexpensive source of protein. A whole egg only has a total of 5 grams of fat, making it part of a healthful food plan.

photo, page 135

Each serving provides

Key Nutrients 360 Calories, 140 Calories from Fat, 16g Fat, 4g Saturated Fat, 0g Trans Fat, 18g Protein, 37g Carb, 10g Fiber, 105mg Sodium
Blood Pressure Nutrients 53mg Vitamin C, 92mg Magnesium, 897mg Potassium, 117mg Calcium

VEGETARIAN

Three Beans and Rice

Three-bean salad is an American classic that is as easy to make as it is nutritious. When you add rice and more vegetables, it becomes a substantial main dish.

Preparation time **about 50 minutes**   *Serves 4*

1 cup long-grain rice
2 cups water
2 carrots, thinly sliced
1/4 pound green beans, cut into 1-inch lengths
1 can (15 ounces) red kidney beans, drained and rinsed
1 can (15 ounces) black-eyed peas, drained and rinsed
1 can (15 ounces) chickpeas, drained and rinsed
1 large ripe tomato, coarsely chopped
1 small red bell pepper, seeded and chopped
1 small red onion, chopped
1 tablespoon canola oil
1 tablespoon coarse mustard
2 teaspoons sugar
3 tablespoons red wine vinegar, or to taste
1 tablespoon chopped fresh thyme
1 garlic clove, chopped
Salt and pepper to taste

1 Put the rice in a saucepan, cover with water, and bring to a boil. Reduce the heat and simmer according to the package instructions, until tender about 15 minutes. Drain and leave to cool.

2 Meanwhile, drop the carrots into another pan of boiling water and cook for 3 minutes. Add the green beans and cook until the vegetables are tender, another 4 minutes. Drain and refresh under cold running water.

3 Place the carrots and green beans in a mixing bowl and add the kidney beans, black-eyed peas, chickpeas, tomato, red pepper, and red onion.

4 Whisk together the oil, mustard, sugar, vinegar, thyme, garlic, and salt and pepper to taste in a small bowl. Drizzle this dressing over the bean salad and toss well to combine everything. Serve the bean salad over the rice, or gently fold the rice into the bean salad.

(Some More Ideas)

• Replace the green beans with 1/2 pound broccoli, broken into small florets.

Mexican-style bean and corn salad: Combine 1 package (10 ounces) cooked frozen corn kernels, drained, with 1 can (15 ounces) pinto beans, drained and rinsed. Add 1 small red and 1 small green bell pepper, seeded and chopped; 1 chopped large ripe tomato; 3 scallions, sliced; and 3 tablespoons chopped fresh cilantro. Make the dressing with 2 tablespoons olive oil, the juice of 1 large lime, 2 chopped garlic cloves, 1/2 teaspoon mild chili powder, 1/2 teaspoon ground cumin, and seasoning to taste. Add to the salad and toss well. Toast 3 corn tortillas under a hot grill for 1 minute or until crisp, then crumble them over the salad.

Health Points

• This salad provides excellent amounts of fiber, both the soluble and insoluble types.

photo, page 135

Each serving provides

Key Nutrients 530 Calories, 70 Calories from Fat, 8g Fat, 1g Saturated Fat, 0g Trans Fat, 23g Protein, 94g Carb, 21g Fiber, 350mg Sodium
Blood Pressure Nutrients 57mg Vitamin C, 199mg Magnesium, 1176mg Potassium, 166mg Calcium

Spicy Lentils with Potatoes and Cauliflower

This is an Indian-style curry dish called a dal, made even more interesting with vegetables and chutney. Don't let the ingredient list deter you: The mildly spicy sauce is delicious.

Preparation time **25 minutes**　　Cooking time **about 55 minutes**　　*Serves 4*

Dal

2 tablespoons canola oil

1 large onion, chopped

1– 2 garlic cloves, crushed

2 tablespoons finely chopped fresh ginger

2 tablespoons mild curry paste

1 cup red lentils

1 teaspoon ground cumin

1 teaspoon turmeric

1 pound small new potatoes

1 small cauliflower, broken into florets

1 red bell pepper, seeded and coarsely chopped

4 tomatoes, skinned and quartered

2 cups baby spinach leaves

Handful fresh cilantro leaves, chopped

Chutney

3 carrots, coarsely grated

1 green chile, seeded and finely chopped

Juice of 1 lime

2 tablespoons chopped fresh cilantro

Raita

2 firm bananas

1 cup plain low-fat yogurt

1/4 cup sliced almonds

Each serving provides

1　Heat the oil in a large saucepan over medium-low heat. Add the onion, garlic, and ginger, and cook for 5 minutes. Stir in the curry paste and stir for a further 2 minutes.

2　Stir in the lentils, cumin, turmeric, and 3 cups water. Bring to a boil, then cover the pan and simmer gently for 10 minutes. Stir in halved potatoes and cook for 10 minutes, then add the cauliflower and cook for another 10 minutes. Add the pepper and tomatoes, and simmer for 5 minutes.

3　Meanwhile, prepare the side dishes. Mix together the carrots, chile, lime juice, and cilantro for the chutney. Transfer to a serving dish. Now make the raita: Toast the almonds. Slice the bananas into a serving bowl. Stir in the yogurt and sprinkle with the almonds.

4　Stir the spinach into the curry and cook until just wilted, about 2 minutes. Stir in the cilantro and serve with the chutney and raita.

(Some More Ideas)

• The vegetables can be varied according to whatever is available. Try chunks of zucchini and eggplant with, or instead of, the cauliflower, or small whole okra or cut green beans with the tomatoes.

• Additional beans can be added. Black-eyed peas and chickpeas are particularly good. If using dried beans, soak them overnight, then drain and cook them in boiling water until almost tender, 45–60 minutes, before adding them to the curry. Canned beans, well drained, should be added toward the end of the cooking time.

Health Points

• This curry is full of vegetables. Together with the lentils, they provide valuable dietary fiber, vitamins, and minerals.

• Uncooked accompaniments like the chutney and raita boost the vitamin content of a meal as well as providing a variety of complementary textures and flavors.

Key Nutrients 530 Calories, 110 Calories from Fat, 13g Fat, 2g Saturated Fat, 0g Trans Fat, 23g Protein, 90g Carb, 19g Fiber, 130mg Sodium
Blood Pressure Nutrients 188mg Vitamin C, 130mg Magnesium, 2193mg Potassium, 266mg Calcium

Falafel Pitas

Falafel, the traditional Middle Eastern bean patties, are usually deep-fried. This version, delicately spiced and crunchy with grated carrot, is baked for a lower-fat result, but is just as delicious.

Preparation time **15 minutes**   Cooking time **15–20 minutes**   *Serves 4*

1 can (15 ounces) chickpeas, drained and rinsed
1 teaspoon olive oil
1/2 teaspoon ground cumin
Good pinch of cayenne pepper
Good pinch of turmeric
1 garlic clove, crushed
1 tablespoon lemon juice
1 medium carrot, finely grated
1 tablespoon chopped fresh cilantro
4 large pita breads
1 heart of romaine lettuce, shredded
2 plum tomatoes, thinly sliced
8 tablespoons plain low-fat yogurt
2 tablespoons chopped fresh mint
Salt and pepper to taste

1 Preheat the oven to 400°F. Line a baking sheet with baking parchment. Put the chickpeas in a bowl with the oil and use a potato masher to mash them until smooth. Mix in the cumin, cayenne pepper, turmeric, garlic, lemon juice, carrot, cilantro, and salt and pepper to taste. Alternatively, mix all the ingredients, except the carrot and coriander, in a food processor. Transfer the mixture to a bowl and stir in the carrot and cilantro.

2 Shape the mixture into 16 flat, round patties, each about 1 1/4 inches across, and place them on the parchment-lined baking sheet. Bake until crisp and lightly browned, 15–20 minutes, turning them over halfway through the cooking time.

3 About 3 minutes before the falafel have finished cooking, put the pita breads in the oven to warm. Then split the breads in half widthwise and gently open out each half to make a pocket.

4 Half-fill the pita bread pockets with the shredded lettuce and sliced tomatoes, then divide the falafel among them. Mix together the yogurt and mint, season with salt and pepper to taste, and drizzle over the falafel. Serve hot.

(Some More Ideas)

• The falafel are also delicious cold, with the minted yogurt, salad, and warm pita bread.

• Choose whole-wheat pita breads for more fiber.

• Serve the falafel as a party appetizer without the bread. Spear each patty with a frill pick and serve the yogurt mint sauce as a dipping sauce.

Health Points

• Chickpeas, also known as garbanzos, are used throughout the world, although they are best known for their use in Middle Eastern and Indian dishes. They are close to being a perfect food—high in protein, complex carbohydrates, and fiber; low in fat, cholesterol, and salt; and loaded with important nutrients, including potassium, folate, and iron.

photo, page 143

Each serving provides

Key Nutrients 310 Calories, 40 Calories from Fat, 4g Fat, 0g Saturated Fat, 0g Trans Fat, 14g Protein, 57g Carb, 10g Fiber, 370mg Sodium
Blood Pressure Nutrients 13mg Vitamin C, 101mg Magnesium, 456mg Potassium, 110mg Calcium

Lentils with Macaroni

This highly spiced dish from Egypt is perfect for both vegetarians and meat lovers because it is so rich with protein. You'll love the interesting texture and mix of flavors.

Preparation time **10–15 minutes**   Cooking time **about 1 hour**   *Serves 4*

Lentils

1 1/4 cup lentils, rinsed
2 teaspoons ground cumin
2 teaspoons ground coriander
1/4 teaspoon cayenne pepper

Onions

1/2 tablespoon canola oil
1 large onion, very thinly sliced
1 teaspoon sugar

Tomato Sauce

1 tablespoon canola oil
1 large garlic clove, crushed
1/2 teaspoon turmeric
2 cans (14 ounces each) no-salt-added chopped tomatoes
Pinch sugar

To serve

8 ounces macaroni
2 tablespoons finely chopped fresh cilantro or parsley
Salt and pepper to taste

1 Put the lentils in a heavy saucepan and pour in enough water to cover them by 3 inches. Bring to a boil and boil vigorously for about 10 minutes, skimming the surface as necessary. Reduce the heat and simmer until tender, 30–40 minutes. Drain well and keep warm.

2 Meanwhile, heat 1/2 tablespoon canola oil in a large non-stick skillet over a high heat. Add the onion and stir to coat with the oil, then reduce the heat and cook, stirring frequently, until soft, about 20 minutes. Stir in the sugar, raise the heat, and continue cooking, stirring, until the onion becomes dark brown and crisp. Immediately pour onto paper toweling to drain, and set aside.

3 To make tomato sauce, heat 1 tablespoon oil in the skillet. Add the garlic and sauté for 30 seconds, stirring. Stir in the turmeric and continue sautéing for a further 30 seconds. Pour in the tomatoes with their juice and add a pinch of sugar. Bring to a boil, stirring. Reduce the heat and simmer, stirring occasionally, until the sauce thickens a little, 10–15 minutes. Season to taste.

4 Heat the cumin, coriander, and cayenne pepper in a sauce-pot and cook for 30 seconds. Add the lentils and stir in seasoning to taste. Keep warm over a very low heat.

5 Cook the macaroni in boiling water according to the package instructions, until al dente, 10–12 minutes. Drain well.

6 Spoon the macaroni onto a serving platter, and top with the spiced lentils and the tomato sauce. Sprinkle with the chopped cilantro and top with the crisp onions. Serve at once.

(Some More Ideas)

• Add 1 seeded and thinly sliced red bell pepper to the lentil mixture, cooking it in the oil until slightly softened before adding the spices and cooked lentils.

Health Points

• Lentils are an excellent source of iron and of dietary fiber, particularly the soluble type. They also provide useful amounts of many B vitamins.

• The onion topping is traditionally deep fried, but here it is cooked in a small amount of vegetable oil in a nonstick pan to reduce the fat content.

photo, page 143

Each serving provides

Key Nutrients 530 Calories, 70 Calories from Fat, 7g Fat, 1g Saturated Fat, 0g Trans Fat, 27g Protein, 92g Carb, 24g Fiber, 95mg Sodium
Blood Pressure Nutrients 23mg Vitamin C, 96mg Magnesium, 709mg Potassium, 100mg Calcium

Saffron Couscous with Peppers

Serve this salad warm or cool as a main dish for four, or as a main course accompaniment for six. Either way, it is a flavorsome vegetarian dish that has real meal appeal.

Preparation time **about 1 hour, plus optional cooling**   *Serves 4*

Dressing

1 large garlic clove, crushed

3 tablespoons olive oil

4 1/2 teaspoons lemon juice

Harissa or other chile sauce, to taste

Vegetables

1 large yellow bell pepper, seeded and cut into wide strips

1 large red bell pepper, seeded and cut into wide strips

2 zucchini, halved lengthwise, then cut into 1-inch chunks

4 large sprigs fresh rosemary

2 tomatoes, skinned, seeded and diced

Salt and pepper to taste

Couscous

2 1/2 cups reduced-sodium vegetable broth

10–12 saffron threads

1 1/2 cups couscous

1 bay leaf, torn in half

1/2 cup raisins

2 teaspoons butter

2 scallions, trimmed and finely chopped

Large handful fresh cilantro, mint, parsley, or a combination of these, coarsely chopped

1 Preheat the oven to 400°F. Place the garlic and oil in a small bowl and set aside to infuse while the oven heats. Lay the rosemary sprigs in a roasting pan.

2 Meanwhile, for the couscous, put the broth and saffron in a saucepan. Bring to a boil, then cover, remove from the heat, and leave to infuse.

3 Using your hands, rub the pepper and zucchini pieces with a little of the garlic-flavored oil so they are well coated. Place the peppers in the roasting pan on top of the rosemary and roast for 10 minutes. Then add the zucchini and continue roasting, turning the vegetables over once or twice, until they are just tender and slightly charred, 20– 25 minutes.

4 Pour the remaining garlic-infused oil into a large bowl. Whisk in the lemon juice, and harissa and seasoning to taste, to make the dressing.

5 As soon as the vegetables are cooked, transfer them to the bowl containing the dressing and add the tomatoes. Stir to coat with the dressing, then set aside to cool.

6 Bring the saffron-infused broth to the boil. Add the couscous, bay leaf, and raisins. Stir well, then cover and remove from the heat. Leave to stand for 5 minutes.

7 Add the butter to the couscous and place over a medium heat. Cook for 1–2 minutes, fluffing with a fork to separate the grains. Remove the bay leaf. Stir in the scallions and season to taste. Leave the couscous to cool until just warm or allow it to cool completely, as preferred.

8 Place the couscous on a serving platter. Top with the vegetables and any dressing remaining in the bowl, scatter the chopped herbs over, and serve. Lightly grilled pita bread, cut into strips, is the ideal accompaniment.

(Some More Ideas)

• For a heartier dish, add 1 can (15 ounces) chickpeas, drained and rinsed, to the hot vegetables.

• For a meat-based main course, add spicy roasted pork. Combine 2 teaspoons olive oil with 1 teaspoon each ground coriander and cumin and a pinch of cayenne pepper. Rub this mixture over 1 pound boneless pork loin chops and marinate for 30 minutes. When the vegetables are cooked, place the pork on a broiler pan and broil for 3–4 minutes per side. Remove from the oven and leave to rest for 5 minutes, then slice thinly.

Health Points

• Couscous is low in fat and a good source of fiber, particularly if you purchase whole-wheat couscous. Mixing couscous with delicious roasted vegetables makes a main dish that can be a lower-fat alternative to a high-fat stew.

Each serving provides

Key Nutrients 490 Calories, 120 Calories from Fat, 13g Fat, 3g Saturated Fat, 0g Trans Fat, 12g Protein, 83g Carb, 8g Fiber, 310mg Sodium
Blood Pressure Nutrients 194mg Vitamin C, 78mg Magnesium, 871mg Potassium, 75mg Calcium

Saffron Couscous with Peppers *p142*

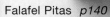

Falafel Pitas *p140*

Braised Vegetables with Falafel and Yogurt Sauce *p144*

Lentils with Macaroni *p141*

Braised Vegetables with Falafel and Yogurt Sauce

Try these bite-size falafel with a simple vegetable casserole. Made with canned chickpeas and then baked, these falafel are quick and easy to prepare. They're good cold as well as hot.

Preparation time **30 minutes**   Cooking time **about 1 hour**   *Serves 4*

Falafel

2 cans (15 ounces each) chickpeas, drained and rinsed
8 scallions, chopped
6 tablespoons chopped parsley
2 tablespoons chopped fresh cilantro
2 tablespoons ground coriander

Vegetables

2 tablespoons olive oil
1 garlic clove, crushed
2 large onions, sliced
2 large yellow or red bell peppers, seeded and sliced
2 medium zucchini
1 1/4 cups reduced-sodium vegetable broth
1 pint cherry tomatoes, halved
Salt and pepper to taste
Fresh mint sprigs (garnish)

Sauce

1/2 cucumber, grated
3 ounces watercress leaves, finely shredded
3 ounces arugula, finely shredded
3 tablespoons chopped fresh mint
Grated zest of 1 lime
1 cup plain low-fat yogurt

1 Brush a shallow baking dish with a little oil. Put the chickpeas in a bowl and use a potato masher to mash them, then mix in the scallions, parsley, fresh cilantro, and ground coriander, and seasoning to taste. Alternatively, mix the ingredients in a food processor. With your hands, shape the mixture into 24 balls slightly larger than walnuts, placing them in the prepared dish. Set aside.

2 Preheat the oven to 400°F. Heat the oil in a flameproof casserole. Add the garlic, onions, and peppers. Stir well, then cover and cook gently, stirring frequently, until the vegetables are soft but not browned, about 15 minutes.

3 Stir in the zucchini and broth. Bring to a boil, then cover the casserole and transfer it to the oven. Place the falafel in the oven at the same time. Cook for 20 minutes.

4 Add the tomatoes to the casserole and stir. Cover and return it to the oven. Use a spoon and fork to turn the falafel, taking care not to break them. Cook the casserole and falafel until the vegetables are tender and the falafel are crisp and lightly browned, about 20 minutes.

5 Meanwhile, to make the yogurt sauce, squeeze the cucumber in handfuls to remove excess moisture. Put it into a bowl. Stir in the watercress, arugula, mint, lime zest, and yogurt. Add seasoning to taste and transfer to a serving dish. Cover and chill until ready to serve.

6 Transfer the falafel to a serving dish. Taste the casserole for seasoning, garnish with mint sprigs, and serve with the falafel and yogurt sauce.

(Some More Ideas)

Ratatouille: Use 1 large onion, and add 1 diced eggplant with the zucchini. Replace cherry tomatoes with 1 pound skinned and quartered plum tomatoes.

• Garlic lovers will enjoy additional garlic in the falafel; add 2 crushed garlic cloves and the grated zest of 1 lemon for a punchy flavor.

• Basil is splendid in the yogurt sauce; shred a handful of fresh leaves and add them with or instead of the arugula.

Health Points

• Watercress has been considered something of a superfood for many centuries. Hippocrates wrote about its medicinal values in 460 BC and built the world's first hospital next to a stream so he could grow fresh watercress. Watercress provides vitamins C and E, and carotenoid compounds. It also contributes substantial amounts of folate, niacin, and vitamin B6.

photo, page 143

Each serving provides

Key Nutrients 420 Calories, 110 Calories from Fat, 12g Fat, 2g Saturated Fat, 0g Trans Fat, 21g Protein, 62g Carb, 17g Fiber, 230mg Sodium
Blood Pressure Nutrients 216mg Vitamin C, 183mg Magnesium, 1562mg Potassium, 382mg Calcium

Green Pasta with White Beans

Here's proof that pasta sauce doesn't need meat to be hearty. Rosemary and garlic-flavored tomato juice thickened with mashed beans makes a light sauce that nicely coats this elegant but easy spinach penne.

Preparation time **10 minutes**   Cooking time **15 minutes**   *Serves 4*

1 tablespoon olive oil

1 carrot, thinly sliced on the diagonal

5 cloves garlic, minced

1/2 teaspoon dried rosemary, minced

1 cup low-sodium tomato juice

1/2 teaspoon salt

1 can (19 ounces) white beans, rinsed and drained

12 ounces spinach penne

1/2 teaspoon cracked black pepper

1 Heat oil in large skillet over low heat. Add carrot, garlic, and rosemary. Cook, stirring occasionally, until carrot is tender, about 5 minutes.

2 Stir in tomato juice and salt, and bring to a boil. Add white beans and, with a potato masher, mash about one-fourth of beans.

3 Meanwhile, cook pasta in large pot of boiling water according to package directions. Drain, reserving 1/2 cup pasta cooking liquid.

4 Transfer hot pasta to large bowl. Add reserved pasta cooking liquid, bean mixture, and pepper, and toss to combine.

(Some More Ideas)

• Serve this dish with roasted red peppers as an antipasto with whole-grain bread. Offer fresh fruit salad for dessert.

• Use red kidney beans in place of white beans.

Health Points

• This recipe contains a lot of garlic! Evidence suggests that the potent phytochemicals in garlic may lower blood pressure. For best benefit, always eat fresh garlic, not garlic powder or garlic salt. Garlic in capsule form does not give you the same effect as the fresh.

• One cup of cooked beans provides nearly 8 grams of fiber, making beans one of the best food sources of heart-healthy fiber.

photo, page 147

Each serving provides

Key Nutrients 500 Calories, 50 Calories from Fat, 6g Fat, 1g Saturated Fat, 0g Trans Fat, 22g Protein, 94g Carb 11g Fiber, 280mg Sodium
Blood Pressure Nutrients 14mg Vitamin C, 141mg Magnesium, 1133mg Potassium, 165mg Calcium

Pepper-Squash Couscous

Wonderfully exotic and colorful, this vegetarian salad captures the flavors of ancient Persian cooking. Dates, raisins, squash, peppers, and orange combine in a uniquely great flavor.

Preparation time **about 1 hour**   *Serves 4*

Vegetables

1 large butternut squash
1 red bell pepper, halved and seeded
1 yellow bell pepper, halved and seeded
1/2 pound baby pattypan squashes, halved if large
1 orange, unpeeled, cut into large chunks
4 bay leaves
1 cinnamon stick, halved
2 garlic cloves, chopped
1 tablespoon olive oil

Couscous

1 tablespoon olive oil
1 onion, finely chopped
2 garlic cloves, chopped
10 pitted dates, chopped
1/2 cup raisins
1 cinnamon stick
3/4-inch piece fresh ginger
1/2 cup dry white wine
1 cup couscous
1 can (15 ounces) chickpeas, drained and rinsed
1 1/2 cups boiling water
2 tablespoons chopped parsley
2 tablespoons chopped fresh mint
Juice of 1 orange

1 Preheat the oven to 400°F. Peel and cut the butternut squash in half lengthwise, remove the seeds, and cut across into thick slices. Cut each pepper half into 12 pieces. Put the squash and peppers in a roasting pan with the pattypans, orange, bay leaves, cinnamon stick, and garlic. Drizzle over the olive oil and sprinkle with 1/2 teaspoon crushed dried chiles, if desired. Roast, turning once, until the vegetables are browned and tender, about 25 minutes.

2 Meanwhile, prepare the couscous. Heat the oil in a saucepan, add the onion and garlic, and sauté for 5 minutes. Add the dates, raisins, cinnamon, finely chopped ginger, and wine. Cover and cook gently for 5 minutes. Remove from the heat. Stir in the couscous and chickpeas, then add the boiling water. Cover and leave for 5 minutes.

3 Add the parsley, mint, and orange juice to the couscous, and season with salt and pepper to taste. Mix and fluff up with a fork. Spoon onto 4 plates and top with the roasted vegetables. Add salt and pepper to taste. Serve warm or at room temperature.

(Some More Ideas)

Eggplant and pearl barley salad: Use 2 eggplants instead of the butternut squash, and roast with the peppers as in the main recipe. Instead of the date and raisin couscous, put 1 cup pearl barley in a saucepan with 1 chopped onion, 1 halved cinnamon stick, and 3 cups vegetable or chicken broth. Bring to a boil, then cover and simmer until the barley is just tender, about 1 hour. Drain if necessary and cool, then toss with 1/4 cup toasted walnut pieces, 1 tablespoon chopped fresh mint, 1 tablespoon chopped parsley, the grated zest and juice of 1 lemon, and 1 tablespoon olive oil. Serve topped with the vegetables.

Health Points

• Dried dates are rich in potassium, niacin, copper, iron, and magnesium. Both dried dates and raisins are a valuable source of soluble fiber.

Each serving provides

Key Nutrients 590 Calories, 80 Calories from Fat, 9g Fat, 1g Saturated Fat, 0g Trans Fat, 16g Protein, 113g Carb, 16g Fiber, 20mg Sodium
Blood Pressure Nutrients 205mg Vitamin C, 152mg Magnesium, 1484mg Potassium, 186mg Calcium

Green Pasta with White Beans *p145*

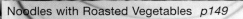

Pepper-Squash Couscous *p146*

Noodles with Roasted Vegetables *p149*

Penne Primavera *p148*

Penne Primavera

This classic Italian pasta dish once used young spring vegetables from the garden.
Today vegetables are available year-round, so this dish can be made anytime.

Preparation time **15 minutes**   Cooking time **15 minutes**   *Serves 4*

12 ounces penne or other pasta shapes

1/2 pound asparagus

1/2 pound green beans, trimmed and cut into 1/4-inch lengths

1/2 pound shelled fresh peas

1 tablespoon olive oil

1 onion, chopped

1 garlic clove, chopped

1 can (15 ounces) chickpeas, drained

1/4 pound button mushrooms, chopped

1 tablespoon flour

1 cup dry white wine

2 tablespoons half-and-half

2 tablespoons chopped mixed fresh parsley and thyme

4 shredded fresh sage leaves or tarragon

Salt and pepper to taste

1 Cook the pasta in boiling water, according to the package instructions, until al dente, 10–12 minutes. Drain well.

2 While the pasta is cooking, cut the asparagus into 1 1/2-inch lengths, keeping the tips separate. Drop the pieces of asparagus stalk, the green beans and peas into a saucepan of boiling water. Bring back to a boil and cook for 5 minutes. Add the asparagus tips and cook for 2 minutes. Drain thoroughly.

3 Heat the oil in a saucepan. Add the onion and cook until softened, 3–4 minutes. Add the garlic, chickpeas, and mushrooms, and continue to cook, stirring occasionally, for 2 minutes.

4 Stir in the flour, then gradually pour in the wine and bring to the boil, stirring. Simmer until the sauce is thickened. Stir in the half-and-half and herbs with seasoning to taste. Add the vegetables to the sauce and heat gently for 1–2 minutes, without boiling.

5 Divide the pasta among 4 serving bowls and spoon the sauce over the top. Serve immediately.

(Some More Ideas)

• For a meaty version, substitute 3 ounces lean chopped pancetta or Canadian bacon, chickpeas, and omit the sage leaves and tarragon.

• Use frozen peas instead of fresh, adding them with the asparagus tips.

Health Points

• Peas provide good amounts of the B vitamins B1, niacin, and B6. They also provide dietary fiber, particularly the soluble variety, some folate,

photo, page 147

Each serving provides

Key Nutrients 510 Calories, 70 Calories from Fat, 7g Fat, 2g Saturated Fat, 0g Trans Fat, 22g Protein, 81g Carb, 8g Fiber, 320mg Sodium
Blood Pressure Nutrients 36mg Vitamin C, 92mg Magnesium, 709mg Potassium, 71mg Calcium

Noodles with Roasted Vegetables

Oven-roasted vegetables, tender and scented with garlic, make a chunky dressing that is great with wide noodles. A sprinkling of crunchy sunflower seeds adds texture.

Preparation time about **20 minutes**   Cooking time **about 45 minutes**   *Serves 4*

Vegetables

1 eggplant, cut into large chunks

2 zucchini, cut into large chunks

2 red bell peppers, quartered and seeded

1 green bell pepper, quartered and seeded

4 ripe tomatoes, halved

2 red onions, quartered

1 head garlic, cloves separated but unpeeled, plus 2 garlic cloves, chopped

3 tablespoons olive oil

Cayenne pepper

Pasta

1/4 cup unsalted sunflower seeds

Light soy sauce to taste

12 ounces wide pasta noodles, such as reginette, lasagnette, or pappardelle

3 tablespoons no-salt-added tomato puree, or to taste

Handful of fresh basil leaves or parsley, coarsely chopped

Salt and pepper to taste

1 Preheat the oven to 375°F. Arrange the eggplant, zucchini, red and green peppers, tomatoes, red onions, and whole garlic cloves in a single layer in a large ovenproof dish or roasting pan. Sprinkle with about 2 tablespoons of the olive oil, a little cayenne pepper, half the chopped garlic, and salt and pepper.

2 Roast until the vegetables are tender but not soft and mushy, and are charred in places, about 45 minutes. Turn the vegetables once or twice during cooking, and increase the heat slightly if they are not cooking quickly enough.

3 Lightly brush a skillet with just a few drops of olive oil, then heat the pan. Add the sunflower seeds and toss and turn them for a few moments until they begin to toast. Shake in a few drops of soy sauce and turn the seeds quickly, letting the soy sauce evaporate as the seeds toast and brown lightly. This should take about 4–5 minutes in total. Remove from the heat just before the seeds are crisp and leave them to cool in the pan. They will crisp up as they cool.

4 Cook the pasta in boiling water according to the package instructions, until al dente, 10–12 minutes. Drain well and keep hot.

5 Using a knife and fork, cut the roasted vegetables into bite-size chunks. Toss the vegetables and garlic with the remaining raw chopped garlic, the tomato puree, and basil or parsley. Taste for seasoning.

6 Toss the pasta with the vegetables and serve immediately, sprinkled with the toasted sunflower seeds.

(Some More Ideas)

• Crush a few saffron threads in a mortar using a pestle and add them to the roasted vegetables along with the tomato puree.

• Serve each portion of roasted vegetable pasta topped with sesame seeds instead of toasted sunflower seeds.

• Pumpkin seeds can also be used instead of sunflower seeds.

Health Points

• As well as all the benefits from the excellent mixture of vegetables in this dish, the sunflower seeds provide a useful source of iron, vitamin B1, and phosphorus.

photo, page 147

Each serving provides

Key Nutrients 580 Calories, 150 Calories from Fat, 17g Fat, 3g Saturated Fat, 0g Trans Fat, 19g Protein, 95g Carb, 13g Fiber, 30mg Sodium
Blood Pressure Nutrients 193mg Vitamin C, 150mg Magnesium, 1287mg Potassium, 91mg Calcium

Pasta with Mushroom Medley

Choose a variety of exotic and wild mushrooms for this feast of fungi. Their flavors are complemented by red wine in a dish that will fit perfectly into a well-balanced diet.

Preparation time **15 minutes, plus 15 minutes soaking**   Cooking time **30 minutes**   *Serves 4*

Sauce

1/4 ounce dried porcini mushrooms

1/2 cup boiling water

1 tablespoon olive oil, divided

3 shallots, chopped

1/2 pound button mushrooms, sliced

1/2 cup Marsala wine

1 garlic clove, finely chopped (optional)

1 pound mixed mushrooms, such as shiitake, oyster, cremini, chanterelle or other wild mushrooms, sliced or halved

2 large tomatoes, skinned, seeded, and sliced

2 teaspoons fresh thyme leaves or 1 teaspoon dried thyme

2 tablespoons chopped fresh parsley

Salt and pepper to taste

To Serve

1 pound tagliatelle or other pasta

1 Put the dried porcini mushrooms in a bowl and cover with the boiling water. Set aside to soak for 15 minutes, then drain, reserving the soaking liquid. Slice the rehydrated mushrooms, discarding any tough stalks.

2 Heat half the olive oil in a saucepan and sauté the shallots until they are tender and golden, about 3 minutes. Add the button mushrooms and cook until all the juice from the mushrooms has evaporated, 8–10 minutes.

3 Add the Marsala and the soaking liquid from the dried mushrooms. Simmer until the sauce has reduced by half, about 10 minutes.

4 Meanwhile, cook the tagliatelle in boiling water for 10–12 minutes, or according to the package instructions, until al dente.

5 About 5 minutes before the pasta is done, heat the remaining oil in a large skillet. Add the garlic, if using, and the mixed mushrooms. Cook over a moderate heat, shaking the pan often, until the mushrooms are lightly cooked, 3–5 minutes.

6 Stir the tomatoes, thyme, and parsley into the mushroom sauce and heat through for 1–2 minutes. Add the mixed mushrooms, season to taste, and remove from the heat.

7 Drain the tagliatelle and divide it among 4 serving dishes. Spoon the mushroom sauce on top and serve immediately.

(Some More Ideas)

• For a creamy sauce, stir in 4 tablespoons low-fat sour cream or plain nonfat yogurt.

• White or red wine can be used in place of the Marsala.

Health Points

• Mushrooms are a useful source of the B vitamins niacin, B6, and folate, and they provide a good source of copper, one of the all-important minerals that form part of a healthy diet.

• Most recipes use mushrooms in small quantities, so that the nutritional contribution they make to the diet is limited. However, this dish contains a substantial amount of fresh mushrooms, plus dried ones for additional flavor.

Each serving provides

Key Nutrients 580 Calories, 50 Calories from Fat, 6g Fat, 1g Saturated Fat, 0g Trans Fat, 21g Protein, 104g Carb, 5g Fiber, 30mg Sodium
Blood Pressure Nutrients 30mg Vitamin C, 85mg Magnesium, 1143mg Potassium, 55mg Calcium

Pasta with Mushroom Medley *p150*

Cold Sesame Noodles and Vegetables *p152*

Spaghetti with Chickpeas, and
Spicy Tomato Sauce *p153*

Linguine with No-Cook Sauce *p154*

Cold Sesame Noodles and Vegetables

A longtime favorite at Chinese restaurants, cold sesame noodles make a great main or side dish. We've replaced hard-to-find sesame paste with peanut butter and sesame oil.

Preparation time **15 minutes**   Cooking time **1 hour 20 minutes**   *Serves 4*

Noodles

8 ounces whole-wheat linguine

Sauce

1/3 cup cilantro leaves

2 tablespoons low-sodium peanut butter

2 tablespoons reduced-sodium soy sauce

2 1/2 teaspoons honey

1 tablespoon rice vinegar or cider vinegar

1 tablespoon dark sesame oil

2 cloves garlic, peeled

Salt to taste

1/4 teaspoon cayenne

1/2 carrots, slivered

1 red bell pepper, slivered

1 large stalk celery, slivered

2 scallions, slivered

1 Cook linguine in large pot of boiling water according to package directions. Drain, reserving 1/2 cup cooking water.

2 Meanwhile, combine cilantro, peanut butter, soy sauce, honey, vinegar, sesame oil, garlic, salt, and cayenne in food processor. Puree. Transfer to large bowl.

3 Whisk in reserved pasta cooking water. Add linguine, carrots, bell pepper, celery, and scallions. Toss. Chill at least 1 hour before serving.

(Some More Ideas)

· Add blanched cauliflower or broccoli florets to the vegetable mixture.

· Serve this dish warm by heating the sauce and adding cubes of cooked tofu.

Health Points

· The pasta cooking water, which carries some of the pasta's starch, is used here to stretch the sauce. It's a traditional Italian technique for thinning or smoothing a sauce so that it coats the noodles better. And the water replaces what might otherwise be a lot more fat.

photo, page 151

Each serving provides

Key Nutrients 320 Calories, 80 Calories from Fat, 9g Fat, 2g Saturated Fat, 0g Trans Fat, 11g Protein, 52g Carb, 4g Fiber, 290mg Sodium
Blood Pressure Nutrients 67mg Vitamin C, 53mg Magnesium, 356mg Potassium, 43mg Calcium

Spaghetti with Chickpeas and Spicy Tomato Sauce

Here's a colorful and easy pasta and bean dish that makes a satisfying main course all on its own. Garlic, olive oil, onion, Tabasco, and grating cheese add up to tons of sunny flavor.

Preparation and cooking time **20–25 minutes** *Serves 4*

Sauce

2 tablespoons olive oil

1 onion, chopped

1 garlic clove, crushed

1 celery stalk, finely chopped

1 can (14 ounces) no-salt-added chopped tomatoes

Pasta

12 ounces spaghetti

2 cans (15 ounces each) chickpeas, drained and rinsed

1/2 teaspoon Tabasco sauce, or to taste

2 cups baby spinach leaves

Salt and pepper to taste

1/4 cup pecorino Romano cheese

Fresh parsley leaves *(garnish)*

1 Heat the olive oil in a heavy saucepan, add the onion and garlic, and cook over a moderate heat, stirring occasionally, until softened, 3– 4 minutes.

2 Add the celery and sauté, stirring, for 1– 2 minutes, then stir in the chopped tomatoes with their juice and bring to a boil. Reduce the heat and simmer gently, stirring occasionally, until thick, about 15 minutes.

3 Meanwhile, cook the spaghetti in a large pan of boiling water, according to the package instructions, until al dente, 10–12 minutes.

4 When the sauce is cooked, stir in the chickpeas and Tabasco sauce. Add the spinach leaves and simmer, stirring, until the spinach wilts, 1–2 minutes. Season with salt and pepper to taste.

5 Drain the spaghetti and toss with the chickpeas and tomato sauce. Scatter over the parsley leaves, and serve immediately, sprinkled with the pecorino cheese.

(Some More Ideas)

Tagliatelle with cannellini beans: Use tagliatelle or fettuccine instead of spaghetti, and replace the chickpeas with canned cannellini. Instead of spinach, add 1/2 pound cooked asparagus spears, cut into 1-inch lengths, to the sauce.

Health Points

• Despite its name, the chickpea is not really a pea but a bean. Chickpeas contain good amounts of iron, manganese, and folate, and are richer in vitamin E than most other beans.

• Cooking the spinach leaves in the sauce very briefly, just to wilt them, retains all their juices and the maximum nutrients.

photo, page 151

Each serving provides

Key Nutrients 630 Calories, 110 Calories from Fat, 12g Fat, 3g Saturated Fat, 0g Trans Fat, 26g Protein, 103g Carb, 13g Fiber, 180mg Sodium
Blood Pressure Nutrients 14mg Vitamin C, 155mg Magnesium, 705mg Potassium, 242mg Calcium

Linguine with No-Cook Sauce

Of the hundreds of ways to dress linguine, this quick and easy sauce is bound to become the most requested pasta topper in your house. It bursts with fresh-from-the-garden flavor.

Preparation time **20 minutes, plus standing**   Cooking time **12 minutes**   *Serves 4*

Sauce

3 pounds plum tomatoes, seeded and chopped

2/3 cup chopped fresh basil

1/4 cup olive oil

1/4 cup chopped flat-leaf parsley

2 tablespoons chopped fresh mint

2 teaspoons grated orange zest

3 garlic cloves, minced

Salt to taste

1/2 teaspoon pepper

To Serve

12 ounces linguine

1/4 cup Parmesan cheese *(garnish)*

1 Mix tomatoes, basil, oil, parsley, mint, orange zest, garlic, salt, and pepper in bowl. Let stand at least 30 minutes or up to 2 hours at room temperature.

2 Cook pasta according to package directions. Drain well and put into a large pasta bowl. Top with sauce and sprinkle with Parmesan.

(Some More Ideas)

• Place the tomato topping on toasted rounds of Italian bread and serve as an appetizer.

• Spoon the tomato topping over any green salad.

• Use the tomato mixture as a filling for baked potatoes.

Health Points

• One serving of the fresh tomatoes in this dish supplies more than a full day's requirement of vitamin C.

• Prolonged heating of foods can cause them to lose some of their nutrients. Only in rare cases does cooking enhance nutrition. In general, try to shorten your cooking times whenever possible. This recipe is a good example of how to preserve all the nutrients of fresh produce with no cooking.

photo, page 151

Each serving provides

Key Nutrients 520 Calories, 150 Calories from Fat, 17g Fat, 3g Saturated Fat, 0g Trans Fat, 16g Protein, 81g Carb, 7g Fiber, 80mg Sodium
Blood Pressure Nutrients 74mg Vitamin C, 93mg Magnesium, 955mg Potassium, 87mg Calcium

main dish salads

Asian Chicken Salad

That old-fashioned chicken salad has adopted a new-fashioned Asian accent. Grilled chicken is tossed with a healthy mix of oranges, scallions, snow peas, and lychees and is then crowned with a drizzle of creamy peanut dressing.

Preparation time **20 minutes**   Cooking time **10 minutes**   *Serves 4*

Salad

1 pound romaine lettuce

4 ounces snow peas

1 can (20 ounces) lychees, drained and cut in half

1 large navel orange, peeled and cut into sections

1 red plum, pitted and sliced

4 scallions, thinly sliced

12 ounces skinless, boneless chicken breast halves

Dressing

1/3 cup nonfat mayonnaise

3 tablespoons creamy reduced-sodium peanut butter

1 garlic clove, minced

1 Finely shred romaine and put into large salad bowl. Trim snow peas and remove strings with fingers. Cut peas in half on the diagonal and add to salad bowl. Add lychees, orange, plum, and scallions; toss to mix.

2 Coat nonstick ridged grill pan with nonstick cooking spray and set over medium-high heat until hot, about 2 minutes. Grill chicken breasts until cooked through, about 4 minutes on each side.

3 Meanwhile, whisk mayonnaise, peanut butter, and garlic in a small measuring cup until dressing is blended. Diagonally cut chicken into thin slices and add to salad bowl. Right before serving, drizzle the salad with dressing and toss to coat.

(Some More Ideas)

• This salad works with many types of cooked lean meat and seafood. In place of the chicken, grill the same amount of boneless lamb, turkey breast, pork tenderloin, or beef, or large peeled shrimp.

• Use spinach leaves in place of the romaine.

Health Points

• Lychees are a tropical fruit that originated in southern China but have since gone international. A lychee is about 1–1 1/2 inches in size, with a bumpy red skin and an oval shape. Peel the skin and you discover a juicy, translucent flesh not unlike a grape, but sweeter. Lychees have a relatively short growing season, so you'll only find them fresh in stores around springtime, sold in large clusters. Canned versions are available year-round. Lychees are high in vitamin C and potassium.

Each serving provides

Key Nutrients 330 Calories, 80 Calories from Fat, 9g Fat, 2g Saturated Fat, 0g Trans Fat, 27g Protein, 41g Carb, 7g Fiber, 230mg Sodium
Blood Pressure Nutrients 171mg Vitamin C, 79mg Magnesium, 1071mg Potassium, 102mg Calcium

Barley, Black Bean, and Avocado Salad

We think of barley as a soup ingredient, but it's also a delicious "dinner grain," served hot or cold. When combined with black beans, tomato, and avocado, it adds up to a salad that could hardly be more healthful or delicious.

Preparation time **10 minutes**   Cooking time **20 minutes**   *Serves 4*

1 cup carrot juice
1/2 teaspoon thyme
Salt to taste
1/8 teaspoon cayenne
1/2 cup quick-cooking barley
3 tablespoons fresh lemon juice
1 tablespoon olive oil
1 can (19 ounces) black beans, rinsed and drained
1 cup fresh diced tomatoes
1/2 cup diced avocado

1 Combine carrot juice, thyme, salt, and cayenne in medium saucepan. Bring to a boil over medium heat, add barley, and reduce to a simmer. Cover and cook until barley is tender, about 15 minutes.

2 Meanwhile, whisk together lemon juice and oil in large bowl. Transfer barley and any liquid remaining in pan to bowl with lemon juice mixture; toss to coat.

3 Add beans and tomatoes and toss to combine. Add avocado and gently toss. Serve at room temperature or chilled. For best flavor, remove from the refrigerator 20 minutes before serving.

(Some More Ideas)

• Make this salad with brown rice in place of barley. Add 1/2 cup reduced-sodium chicken broth to the carrot juice mixture. Add 1/2 cup rinsed brown rice, cover, and cook until the rice is tender, about 40–50 minutes.

• Use red kidney or pinto beans instead of black beans.

Health Points

• This salad is a powerful combination of healthy foods. An exceptional amount of fiber comes from the barley and the beans. The avocado supplies vitamins A and E, and the beans and avocado are rich in the B vitamin folate.

photo, page 161

Each serving provides

Key Nutrients 250 Calories, 60 Calories from Fat, 7g Fat, 1g Saturated Fat, 0g Trans Fat, 10g Protein, 46g Carb, 13g Fiber, 320mg Sodium
Blood Pressure Nutrients 19mg Vitamin C, 47mg Magnesium, 784mg Potassium, 80mg Calcium

Warm Sesame-Chicken Salad

Strips of chicken in a crisp coating of sesame seeds, bread crumbs, and cornflakes are served atop a crunchy vegetable salad dressed with a fresh herb vinaigrette. A little chili powder in the coating gives a bit of a kick.

Preparation time **15 minutes**   Cooking time **15–20 minutes**   *Serves 4*

Chicken

1 pound skinless, boneless chicken breasts

1/2 cup fresh white bread crumbs

1 cup low-sodium cornflakes, lightly crushed

4 teaspoons sesame seeds, plus extra to garnish

1 teaspoon hot chili powder, or to taste

2 eggs

Salt and pepper to taste

Salad

1/4 white cabbage

1/2 frisée (curly endive)

2 heads chicory

Dressing

1 teaspoon chopped parsley

1 teaspoon chopped fresh oregano

1 tablespoon chopped fresh tarragon

1 tablespoon white wine vinegar

4 tablespoons olive oil

1 teaspoon honey

1 Preheat the oven to 400°F. Slice each chicken breast in half horizontally, then cut lengthwise into strips.

2 Put the bread crumbs, cornflakes, sesame seeds, and chili powder in a plastic bag and shake to mix well. Break the eggs into a shallow dish and beat together lightly.

3 Dip the chicken strips, one at a time, in the egg, then drop into the plastic bag. When a few pieces of chicken are in the bag, shake to coat evenly with the sesame seed mixture. As the chicken strips are coated, transfer to 2 nonstick baking trays, spreading out the pieces.

4 Bake the chicken strips for 15–20 minutes, turning the pieces over halfway through the baking time.

5 Meanwhile, make the salad. Finely shred the cabbage and place in a large mixing bowl. Pull the frisée and chicory leaves apart and tear any large ones into smaller pieces. Add to the mixing bowl.

6 In a small screw-top jar, shake together the dressing ingredients. Season to taste. Pour the dressing over the salad and toss well.

7 Divide the salad among 4 plates and pile the cooked chicken pieces on top. Garnish with a few more sesame seeds, then serve.

(Some More Ideas)

Chinese-style chicken salad: Beat 1 egg with 2 teaspoons five-spice powder, 1 tablespoon poppy seeds, 2 tablespoons no-salt-added tomato puree, 2 tablespoons sherry, and 2 tablespoons reduced-sodium soy sauce in a bowl. Stir in the chicken strips. Lift them out and coat with the bread-crumb mixture (omit the sesame seeds and chili powder). Bake as in main recipe. Meanwhile, finely shred 1 head Chinese leaves, discarding some of the core. Place in a bowl; add 4 ounces bean sprouts and 1 bunch scallions, thinly sliced into rings. Toss with the dressing made with 1 1/2 tablespoons each parsley and fresh cilantro. Serve the hot chicken strips on top of the salad.

Health Points

• Cabbage belongs to a family of vegetables that contain phytochemicals that help protect against some cancers. Cabbage is also a source of folate.

photo, page 161

Each serving provides

Key Nutrients 410 Calories, 180 Calories from Fat, 20g Fat, 3g Saturated Fat, 0g Trans Fat, 34g Protein, 25g Carb, 5g Fiber, 300mg Sodium
Blood Pressure Nutrients 38mg Vitamin C, 63mg Magnesium, 763mg Potassium, 139mg Calcium

Curry Chicken and Rice Salad

This curry-flavored salad with a fruity rice pilaf can become a traditional summer dish. Instead of using a cream and mayonnaise sauce, this version lightens up by reducing the mayo and adding yogurt.

Preparation time **about 1 1/2 hours, plus cooling** *Serves 6*

Salad

1 pound skinless, boneless chicken breasts

1 onion, sliced

1 large carrot, coarsely chopped

1 celery stalk, chopped

6 black peppercorns

1 bay leaf

1 large banana

2 zucchini, cut into thin ribbons with a vegetable peeler

Sprigs of fresh mint *(garnish)*

Dressing

1 cup plain low-fat yogurt

4 tablespoons reduced-fat mayonnaise

2 tablespoons curry paste

Grated zest of 1 large lemon

1 tablespoon lemon juice

2 tablespoons snipped fresh chives

2 tablespoons chopped fresh mint

2 tablespoons chopped parsley

Salt and pepper to taste

Pilaf

1 cup basmati rice, rinsed

1/2 cup raisins

1/2 cup chopped dried mango

1/4 cup pecans

1 Place the chicken breasts in a large saucepan and cover with water. Add the onion, carrot, and celery, and bring almost to boiling point, skimming the surface as necessary. When bubbles begin to break through the surface, reduce the heat so the water is just simmering. Add the peppercorns, lightly crushed, and bay leaf, and simmer until the juices run clear from the chicken, about 15 minutes.

2 Remove the chicken from the liquid and set aside to cool. Pour the cooking liquid through a fine sieve into a measuring jug. Discard the vegetables.

3 To make the pilaf, put the rice in a saucepan and add 2 cups of the strained cooking liquid. Stir in the raisins and mango. Bring to the boil, then reduce the heat, cover, and simmer, according to the package instructions, until all the liquid has been absorbed and the rice is tender, about 20 minutes.

4 Remove the rice from the heat and set aside, covered, for 5 minutes. Then transfer the rice to a bowl and leave to cool completely.

5 Meanwhile, make the dressing. Put the yogurt, mayonnaise, curry paste, and lemon zest and juice in a large mixing bowl and mix until well blended. Stir in the chives, mint, and parsley and seasoning to taste.

6 When the chicken is completely cool, cut the meat into bite-size pieces. Fold them into the curry dressing. (If you like, cover the chicken and chill; remove from the refrigerator 15 minutes before serving.) Slice the banana and gently stir it into the chicken mixture.

7 Stir the pecans into the rice pilaf and spoon onto 6 plates. Arrange the zucchini ribbons on the pilaf and top with the chicken mixture. Garnish with fresh mint sprigs and serve.

(Some More Ideas)

• Use halved seedless green grapes instead of sliced banana.

• Use skinless, boneless turkey in place of the chicken.

Health Points

• Using the chicken stock to cook the rice ensures that you retain the water-soluble vitamins that seeped into the water while the chicken was being poached.

Each serving provides

Key Nutrients 450 Calories, 80 Calories from Fat, 9g Fat, 2g Saturated Fat, 0g Trans Fat, 24g Protein, 72g Carb, 5g Fiber, 190mg Sodium
Blood Pressure Nutrients 16mg Vitamin C, 68mg Magnesium, 783mg Potassium, 127mg Calcium

Curry Chicken and Rice Salad *p160*

Barley, Black Bean, and Avocado Salad *p158*

Warm Sesame-Chicken Salad *p159*

Marinated Duck and Kasha Salad *p162*

Marinated Duck and Kasha Salad

Kasha, or buckwheat grain, is available either plain or roasted. When plain kasha is toasted and then simmered in stock, it develops a rich, nutty flavor. It works perfectly with duck in this hearty main-dish salad.

Preparation and cooking time **50 minutes**   *Serves 4*

1 pound skinless, boneless duck breasts

2 garlic cloves, chopped

Juice of 1 lemon

12 sprigs fresh thyme

1 teaspoon chopped fresh rosemary

2 tablespoons olive oil

1 cup kasha (buckwheat grain)

2 1/4 cups reduced-fat chicken broth

4 1/2 ounces green beans

4 cups mixed salad greens

5 sprigs fresh basil, finely shredded

1/2 red onion, thinly sliced

4 green olives, pitted *(optional)*

4 black olives, pitted *(optional)*

2 medium zucchini, thinly sliced lengthwise

12 small scallions

12 small tomatoes

1 1/2 tablespoons red wine vinegar, or a combination of sherry and balsamic vinegars

Salt and pepper to taste

1 Remove all the fat and skin from the duck breasts. With a sharp knife, score the flesh on both sides in a criss-cross pattern. Put the breasts in a bowl and add about two-thirds of the garlic, the lemon juice, half of the thyme sprigs, the rosemary, and 1 tablespoon of the oil. Turn to coat the breasts with the flavorings, then marinate while you prepare the rest of the ingredients.

2 Put the kasha in a heavy skillet and toast over medium heat, stirring and tossing, until it has become slightly darker in color, 4–5 minutes. Remove from the heat.

3 Bring the broth to the boil in a saucepan, then stir in the toasted kasha. Bring back to the boil. Reduce the heat, cover, and cook over a low heat until the broth has been absorbed and the kasha is tender, 10–15 minutes. Remove from the heat and set aside, still covered, until ready to use.

4 Heat a grill pan for 5 minutes. Meanwhile, drop the green beans into a saucepan of boiling water and blanch for 1–2 minutes. Drain and refresh under cold running water. Cut the beans in half and put into a salad bowl. Add the salad leaves, basil, red onion, and olives, and toss to mix.

5 Remove the duck breasts from the marinade and place on the hot grill pan. Cook for 3 minutes, then turn the breasts over and cook for another 3 minutes (the meat will be rare, so cook longer if you prefer it well done). Remove the duck to a board. Place the zucchini, whole scallions, and whole tomatoes on the grill pan and cook until lightly charred all over, 1–2 minutes.

6 Combine the remaining garlic and 2 tablespoons oil with the vinegar in a small bowl, and add the leaves from the remaining thyme sprigs. Whisk together, then drizzle over the salad. Spoon on the kasha, and arrange the hot grilled zucchini, scallions, and tomatoes on top. Slice the duck breasts, place over the vegetables, and serve.

(Some More Ideas)

Duck and pumpkin salad: Rub the duck breasts with a mixture of 2 chopped garlic cloves, 1/2 teaspoon ground cumin, 1/4 teaspoon ground cinnamon, and 1/2 teaspoon cocoa powder, and put in a mixing bowl. Add 1 cup peeled and seeded pumpkin or butternut squash, thinly sliced, and sprinkle over the juice of 1 lemon, the juice of 1 orange, and 1 tablespoon extra-virgin olive oil. Turn the ingredients to mix them, then leave to marinate for at least 30 minutes. Make the green bean and leaf salad and sprinkle with 1/2 cup dried cherries and 1 orange, peeled and segmented. For the dressing, whisk the juice of 1 orange with 2 tablespoons olive oil, 2 teaspoons sugar, and 1/4 teaspoon paprika. Grill the duck breasts as in the main recipe, then slice. Grill the pumpkin for 4–5 minutes. Pour the dressing over the salad, add the kasha, and arrange the duck and pumpkin slices on top.

photo, page 161

Each serving provides

Key Nutrients 530 Calories, 150 Calories from Fat, 16g Fat, 4g Saturated Fat, 0g Trans Fat, 47g Protein, 55g Carb, 12g Fiber, 240mg Sodium
Blood Pressure Nutrients 98mg Vitamin C, 208mg Magnesium, 1853mg Potassium, 117mg Calcium

Crab and Grapefruit Salad

Here's the surprise of the season: Crab and grapefruit are the perfect partners for a quick, no-cook salad. The sweetness of the crabmeat and dressing contrast with the tartness of the grapefruit and the slight bitterness of the greens.

Preparation time **25 minutes**   *Serves 4*

4 grapefruits

2 tablespoons light mayonnaise

1 tablespoon finely chopped mango chutney

2 teaspoons Dijon mustard

1 teaspoon sesame oil

Salt to taste

1/4 teaspoon pepper

3/4 pound lump crabmeat, picked over to remove any cartilage

2 cups watercress, tough stems trimmed

1 Belgian endive, cut crosswise into 1/2-inch-wide strips

1 head Bibb lettuce, separated into leaves

1 With small paring knife, peel grapefruits. Working over a large bowl to catch juice, separate grapefruit sections from membranes; reserve any juice that collects in bowl.

2 In medium bowl, whisk together mayonnaise, chutney, mustard, sesame oil, salt, pepper, and 3 tablespoons reserved grapefruit juice.

3 Add crabmeat, tossing to combine. Add watercress, endive, and grapefruit sections, and toss. Serve salad on a bed of Bibb lettuce.

(Some More Ideas)

• Crabmeat is a classic choice for this refreshing salad, but you could opt for shrimp, lobster, scallops, or good-sized cubes of poached chicken breasts.

• Substitute oranges for the grapefruits.

Health Points

• By using pink or red grapefruits, not only do you add high amounts of vitamin C to the recipe, but the colored grapefruits are packed with beta-carotene as well. All grapefruit is high in fiber and low in calories.

Each serving provides

Key Nutrients 250 Calories, 50 Calories from Fat, 5g Fat, 1g Saturated Fat, 0g Trans Fat, 20g Protein, 35g Carb, 8g Fiber, 410mg Sodium
Blood Pressure Nutrients 137mg Vitamin C, 85mg Magnesium, 1332mg Potassium, 222mg Calcium

Mango Chicken Salad

Here is a very special salad: new potatoes, slices of tender grilled chicken, and asparagus tossed in a mellow fresh orange dressing and then mixed with juicy mango slices and baby salad leaves. It makes a well-balanced meal all on its own.

Preparation and cooking time **50 minutes, plus 15 minutes marinating**   *Serves 4*

Salad

1 garlic clove, crushed

1 teaspoon grated fresh ginger

1 tablespoon light soy sauce

2 teaspoons canola oil

2 skinless, boneless
chicken breasts

1 3/4 pounds new potatoes,
scrubbed

2 large sprigs fresh mint

4 1/2 ounces asparagus spears

1 mango, peeled and sliced

4 cups mixed baby
salad leaves

Dressing

1/2 teaspoon finely grated
orange zest

1 tablespoon orange juice

1 teaspoon Dijon mustard

1 tablespoon canola oil

1 tablespoon walnut oil

Salt and pepper to taste

1 Put the garlic, ginger, soy sauce, and sunflower oil in a bowl and whisk together. Add the chicken breasts and turn to coat both sides, then leave to marinate for 15 minutes.

2 Put the potatoes in a saucepan, pour over boiling water to cover, and add the mint sprigs. Cook until tender, 15–20 minutes. At the same time, put the asparagus in a steamer basket or metal colander, cover, and set over the pan of potatoes to steam. Cook thin spears for 4–5 minutes, thick spears 8–10 minutes, or until just tender. Drain the potatoes (discard the mint) and leave until cool enough to handle, then cut into thick slices. Cut the asparagus diagonally into 2 1/2-inch lengths.

3 Preheat the grill to moderate. Remove the chicken from the marinade and place it on the grill rack. Grill, brushing frequently with the marinade and turning once, until cooked through and the juices run clear when the chicken is pierced with the tip of a knife, about 15 minutes. Leave to rest for 3–4 minutes, then slice.

4 To make the dressing, put the orange zest and juice, mustard, and canola and walnut oils in a large serving bowl, and whisk together until slightly thickened. Season with salt and pepper to taste.

5 Transfer the warm sliced chicken, potatoes, and asparagus to the serving bowl and gently toss together to coat with the dressing. Add the mango and salad leaves and toss gently again. Serve immediately while still warm.

(Some More Ideas)

• For a sharper citrus dressing, use lime zest and juice instead of orange.

Turkey salad with fresh blueberries: Use turkey breast fillets, and marinate and grill as for the chicken in the main recipe. Cut 2 pounds new potatoes into 3/4-inch dice and cook in boiling salted water until just tender, about 10 minutes. Drain well and toss with the warm turkey slices in the fresh orange dressing. Put 1 cup blueberries in a small pan with 1 tablespoon balsamic vinegar and 2 teaspoons honey. Gently bubble until the blueberries are tender, 3–4 minutes. Add salad leaves to the turkey and potato mixture and toss together, then drizzle over blueberries.

Health Points

• Mango is an excellent source of antioxidants that help to protect against damage by free radicals. Mango is also a good source of vitamin A.

Each serving provides

Key Nutrients 390 Calories, 100 Calories from Fat, 11g Fat, 1g Saturated Fat, 0g Trans Fat, 19g Protein, 56g Carb, 6g Fiber, 230mg Sodium
Blood Pressure Nutrients 54mg Vitamin C, 91mg Magnesium, 1278mg Potassium, 63mg Calcium

Mango Chicken Salad *p164*

Indian-Style Rice with Turkey *p166*

Marinated Duck Salad with Bulgur *p167*

Pork and Pear Salad with Pecans *p168*

Indian-Style Rice with Turkey

The spicy aromas of this satisfying salad make it tempting fare at any time of year. The rice, with its slightly chewy texture and Indian spicing, provides the perfect backdrop for the turkey, vegetables, grapes, and nuts.

Preparation time **50 minutes, plus cooling**   *Serves 6*

Salad

1 tablespoon canola oil

2 cups brown basmati rice, well rinsed

1 onion, finely chopped

1 teaspoon grated fresh ginger

1/4 teaspoon garam masala

1/4 teaspoon ground coriander

1/2 teaspoon curry powder

4 1/2 cups hot reduced-fat chicken broth

1 bay leaf

3 large celery stalks, chopped

4 scallions, chopped

1 large carrot, grated

1 cup seedless red grapes, halved

1 pound skinless cooked turkey or chicken meat, cubed

3 tablespoons chopped parsley

Soft lettuce leaves

1/2 cup toasted pecans, coarsely chopped

Vinaigrette

4 tablespoons orange juice

2 teaspoons lime juice

4 teaspoons canola oil

1 tablespoon snipped fresh chives

Salt and pepper to taste

1 Heat the oil in a large saucepan over a moderate heat. Add the rice and stir to coat thoroughly, then cook, stirring frequently, for 1 minute. Add the onion, ginger, garam masala, coriander, and curry powder, and continue cooking, stirring, until the onion starts to soften, 3–4 minutes.

2 Add the broth and bay leaf, and bring to the boil. Reduce the heat, cover, and simmer until the rice is tender, about 25 minutes. Discard the bay leaf and transfer the rice to a large bowl to cool.

3 Meanwhile, to make the dressing, whisk together the orange and lime juices, oil, and chives. Season with salt and pepper to taste.

4 Add the celery, scallions, and carrot to the cooled rice. Reserve half the grapes and add the remainder to the rice together with the chicken or turkey and the parsley. Drizzle over the dressing and turn the salad gently to combine everything.

5 Arrange a bed of lettuce leaves on each of 4 plates and pile the rice salad on top. Scatter the remaining grapes and the pecans over the salad and serve.

(Some More Ideas)

Herbed brown rice salad with salmon: Cook the rice with the onion as in the main recipe, but omit spices and ginger. Leave to cool, then stir in mixed fresh herbs,1 tablespoon chopped fresh tarragon or dill, 2 tablespoons snipped fresh chives, and 4 tablespoons chopped parsley plus half a peeled cucumber, quartered lengthwise and sliced; 1 large grated carrot; 3 sliced celery stalks; and 5 radicchio leaves, torn into thin ribbons. Dress with the citrus vinaigrette and toss gently. Heat 1 teaspoon olive oil in a small skillet and sauté 1 pound skinless salmon fillet for 3 minutes on each side or until just cooked through. Break into large flakes and fold into the rice salad, taking care not to break up the fish too much. Garnish with halved cherry tomatoes.

• Peel 3 oranges and divide into segments, working over a bowl to catch the juice. Use the juice in the dressing and garnish the salads with the orange segments.

photo, page 165

Each serving provides

Key Nutrients 500 Calories, 150 Calories from Fat, 17g Fat, 2g Saturated Fat, 0g Trans Fat, 26g Protein, 62g Carb, 4g Fiber, 170mg Sodium
Blood Pressure Nutrients 14mg Vitamin C, 46mg Magnesium, 487mg Potassium, 88mg Calcium

Marinated Duck Salad with Bulgur

The contrast of sweet citrus, spicy chile, earthy grains, tangy basil, and tender duck is marvelous. This seems like an ambitious, unusual dish, but if you buy the ingredients in advance, it comes together quickly. It's worth the effort!

Preparation time **45 minutes**   Cooking time **10 minutes**   *Serves 4*

3/4 cup bulgur wheat

4 small boneless duck breasts (about 1 1/2 pounds)

3 garlic cloves, chopped

1 1/2 tablespoons mild chili powder

1 1/2 teaspoons ground cumin

4 tablespoons finely shredded fresh basil

Grated zest and juice of 1 orange, plus juice of 2 more oranges

Juice of 1 1/2 lemons

2 tablespoons olive oil

16 kumquats

1 1/2 tablespoons sugar

1 cup water

3 scallions, thinly sliced

3 tablespoons chopped fresh cilantro

1/2 pound mixed salad greens

2 teaspoons balsamic vinegar, or to taste

1/4 cucumber, finely diced

1/2 large tomato, finely diced

Salt and pepper to taste

1 Place the bulgur wheat in a bowl and cover with boiling water. Leave to soak for about 30 minutes.

2 Meanwhile, remove skin and fat from breasts. Put the breasts in a dish and add half of garlic, chili powder, cumin, and basil, all zest and juice of 1 orange, juice of 1/2 lemon, and 1/2 tablespoon olive oil. Mix well, turn breasts, then set aside to marinate.

3 To prepare the kumquats, cut a small slit in each one (do not cut all the way through). Place the kumquats in a saucepan with the juice of 1 orange, the sugar, and 1 cup of water. Bring to the boil and simmer over a moderate heat, turning the kumquats so that they cook evenly, until they are just tender and the liquid has reduced by about half, 15–20 minutes. Remove from the heat and leave to cool in the liquid.

4 Drain the soaked bulgur wheat and return it to the bowl. Add the scallions, the remaining garlic, chili powder, cumin, lemon juice and orange juice, 1 tablespoon of the remaining olive oil, and the cilantro. Season to taste.

5 Heat a large nonstick skillet. Remove the duck from its marinade and brown on both sides over a high heat. Cook for a further 4–5 minutes, turning the breasts frequently so that they don't stick. The meat will be rosy in color in the center (cook a little longer if you prefer it well done). Remove the breasts to a carving board and slice very thinly against the grain.

6 Arrange the salad leaves and remaining basil on 4 plates and place 4 kumquats on each bed of leaves. Drizzle with the remaining 1/2 tablespoon olive oil, the balsamic vinegar, and a little of the kumquat cooking liquid. Place a portion of the bulgur wheat salad in the center of each plate, and arrange the duck slices around it. Scatter on the diced cucumber and tomato, and serve immediately.

(Some More Ideas)

• Instead of bulgur wheat, use quinoa, a nutty little grain that comes from Peru. Rinse 1 cup quinoa grains well (they are coated with a sticky substance), then place in a saucepan and add 2 cups boiling water. Bring to the boil, then cover and simmer until the grains are just tender and have absorbed the liquid, about 10 minutes. Fluff up with a fork and then dress as for the bulgur wheat.

• Add a North African flavor to the marinade for the duck breasts. In addition to the spices above, add 1/4 teaspoon each of ground ginger, cinnamon, and coriander and 1/4 teaspoon mild or medium curry powder. Double the amount of lemon juice.

Health Points

• Oranges and kumquats are both an excellent source of vitamin C. They also contain compounds called coumarins, which are believed to help thin the blood, thus helping to prevent stroke and heart attacks.

photo, page 165

Each serving provides

Key Nutrients 430 Calories, 120 Calories from Fat, 13g Fat, 3g Saturated Fat, 0g Trans Fat, 30g Protein, 52g Carb, 13g Fiber, 240mg Sodium
Blood Pressure Nutrients 96mg Vitamin C, 103mg Magnesium, 922mg Potassium, 139mg Calcium

Pork and Pear Salad with Pecans

This is a simple yet substantial salad with lots of interesting ingredients that you wouldn't ordinarily think of combining. The dressing is delicately flavored with ginger juice, squeezed from fresh ginger.

Preparation time **35 minutes**   *Serves 4*

Salad

2 ounces pecans

2 pounds new potatoes, scrubbed

4 ounces red radishes, cut into quarters

2 pears

1 head red leaf lettuce, separated into leaves

2 cups watercress, tough stalks discarded

12 ounces cooked roast pork loin, fat removed and thinly sliced

Dressing

1 (1-inch) piece peeled ginger

2 teaspoons coarse mustard

2 teaspoons white wine vinegar

2 tablespoons olive oil

2 teaspoons hazelnut oil

Salt and pepper to taste

1 Heat a skillet and toast the pecans over a moderate heat for 6–7 minutes. Cool, then chop roughly. Set aside.

2 Cook the potatoes in a saucepan of boiling water until tender, about 15 minutes. Drain. When cool enough to handle, cut into quarters and place in a mixing bowl.

3 To make the dressing, first put the ginger in a garlic crusher and press to squeeze out the juice (this will have to be done in 3 or 4 batches). You need 2 teaspoons of this ginger juice. Put the ginger juice, mustard, vinegar, olive and hazelnut oils, and salt and pepper to taste, in a screw-top jar. Shake well to mix. Pour about one-third of the dressing over the warm potatoes and toss gently to coat. Leave to cool.

4 Meanwhile, in another bowl, toss the red radishes with half of the remaining dressing, to prevent them from browning. Halve the pears lengthwise and scoop out the cores, then cut into long wedges. Toss with the radishes.

5 Arrange the lettuce leaves and watercress in a shallow salad bowl. Add the radish mixture to the potatoes and gently mix together. Pile onto the middle of the salad leaves, and arrange the pork slices on top.

6 Stir the toasted pecans into the remaining dressing and drizzle over the top of the salad. Serve immediately.

(Some More Ideas)

• Instead of pears, use other fresh fruit, such as 2 peaches or 4 apricots.

Pork and apple salad with hazelnuts: Replace the pears with red-skinned apples. Add 2 carrots, cut into matchstick strips. Finish with toasted hazelnuts instead of pecans.

Health Points

• Radishes offer useful amounts of fiber and vitamin C and, in common with other members of the cruciferous family, they contain phytochemicals that may help to protect against cancer. Most of the enzymes responsible for the hot taste are found in the skin. If you find the taste overpowering, peeling will help to reduce the heat.

photo, page 165

Each serving provides

Key Nutrients 590 Calories, 260 Calories from Fat, 29g Fat, 5g Saturated Fat, 0g Trans Fat, 31g Protein, 54g Carb, 11g Fiber, 80mg Sodium
Blood Pressure Nutrients 73mg Vitamin C, 106mg Magnesium, 1721mg Potassium, 125mg Calcium

Garden Pasta Salad

This Italian salad (known in its homeland as insalata alla giardiniera) uses the freshest picks from the vegetable patch to provide it with a wonderful mix of colors, flavors, and nutrients. It stores well and is even better the next day.

Preparation time **30 minutes, plus marinating**   Cooking time **25 minutes**   *Serves 6*

Salad

Salt to taste

1/2 teaspoon pepper

3 cups broccoli florets

1 large red bell pepper, cut into thin strips

1 medium yellow squash, thinly sliced

1 small red onion, chopped

10 ounces radiatore pasta (about 3 cups)

1/2 pint yellow or red pear tomatoes, halved

Dressing

2/3 cup cider vinegar

1/4 cup extra-virgin olive oil

1/3 cup finely chopped parsley

2 tablespoons finely chopped fresh dill

1 Set out large bowl of ice water. Fill pasta pot or large saucepan with water, add salt to taste and 1/4 teaspoon pepper, and bring to a boil over high heat. Put broccoli, red pepper, squash, and onion in perforated liner or large strainer. Blanch just until colors brighten, about 2 minutes. Quickly transfer to colander; plunge into ice water.

2 Cook pasta in boiling water according to package directions. Rinse with cold water and drain; put in large pasta bowl. Drain vegetables and add to pasta; add tomatoes and toss.

3 Put vinegar, oil, parsley, and dill in jar with tight-fitting lid and shake until combined. Pour over salad and toss to coat. Cover and refrigerate at least 8 hours, or overnight. Toss again before serving.

(Some More Ideas)

• In place of cider vinegar, white wine or tarragon vinegar may be used. But avoid white distilled vinegar, as it overpowers this salad.

• Replace the broccoli with an equal amount of fresh asparagus tips.

• For more fiber, substitute whole-wheat pasta for the radiatore.

Health Points

• This salad gives you four 1/2-cup servings of vegetables, getting you most of the way toward the daily goal of at least five servings of produce. Add in a few pieces of fruit as snacks and a cooked vegetable at either lunch or dinner, and you will have had a truly healthy day of eating.

Each serving provides

Key Nutrients 320 Calories, 90 Calories from Fat, 10g Fat, 2g Saturated Fat, 0g Trans Fat, 11g Protein, 49g Carb, 6g Fiber, 100mg Sodium
Blood Pressure Nutrients 143mg Vitamin C, 62mg Magnesium, 512mg Potassium, 109mg Calcium

Roast Beef and Rice Salad

This family-style salad is packed with vitamins, minerals, and fiber. It is an excellent way of using up leftover roast beef, and the vegetables can be varied to suit all tastes. It makes a hearty meal in itself.

Preparation time **about 1 hour**   *Serves 4*

Salad

1 pound cooked roast beef, cubed into 1/2-inch pieces

1/2 cup rehydrated sun-dried tomatoes

4 scallions, thinly sliced

2 tablespoons snipped fresh chives

1 cup basmati rice, rinsed

1 celery stalk, thinly sliced

1 carrot, coarsely grated

1 zucchini, coarsely grated

3 ounces button mushrooms, thinly sliced

4 tablespoons chopped parsley

Radicchio or other salad leaves *(optional)*

Dressing

1 1/2 teaspoons dry mustard

1/2 teaspoon sugar

2 tablespoons cider vinegar

3 tablespoons olive oil

Salt and pepper to taste

1 First make the dressing. Put the dry mustard and sugar in a large mixing bowl and stir in the vinegar until smooth. Whisk in the oil until thoroughly blended. Season with salt and pepper to taste.

2 Add the beef, sun-dried tomatoes, scallions, and chives to the bowl and stir to coat all the ingredients with the dressing. Cover and refrigerate for at least 30 minutes (or up to 8 hours).

3 Meanwhile, cook the rice in a saucepan of boiling water until just tender, 8–10 minutes. Drain well and spread out on a tray to cool completely.

4 When the rice is cool, transfer it to a bowl and stir in the celery, carrot, zucchini, mushrooms, and parsley. Cover and chill until needed.

5 About 10 minutes before serving, remove the marinated beef and the rice salad from the refrigerator. If you like, line 4 plates with radicchio or other salad leaves. Add the marinated beef mixture to the rice salad and gently stir together until well mixed. Spoon onto the bed of leaves and serve.

(Some More Ideas)

Chicken, peach, and rice salad: Use cubes of cooked chicken instead of beef, and replace the sun-dried tomatoes and onions with 2 sliced peaches and the chives with chopped parsley. In the rice salad, instead of the celery, carrot, zucchini, and mushrooms, use 1 cup corn kernels, 2 thinly sliced leeks, and 1 cup chopped fennel.

• For extra texture and healthiness, add alfalfa sprouts.

Health Points

• Beef is now much leaner than it used to be. Cuts of beef, such as top round, can contain less than 3% fat.

• Vinegar has been used for healing, preserving, cleaning, and cooking for more than 10,000 years. Almost anything that contains sugar can be made into vinegar. First, yeast converts the sugar in the liquid to alcohol; then bacteria convert the alcohol to acid. White vinegar is made from grain alcohol; fruit vinegars have a much milder, more pleasant taste and are best for cooking.

Each serving provides

Key Nutrients 500 Calories, 160 Calories from Fat, 18g Fat, 4g Saturated Fat, 0g Trans Fat, 31g Protein, 57g Carb, 4g Fiber, 95mg Sodium

Blood Pressure Nutrients 17mg Vitamin C, 52mg Magnesium, 773mg Potassium, 61mg Calcium

Roast Beef and Rice Salad *p170*

Tabbouleh with Goat Cheese *p172*

Tropical Beef and Rice Salad *p173*

Lemony Lentil and Vegetable Salad *p174*

Tabbouleh with Goat Cheese

Tabbouleh is a classic Middle Eastern salad made with bulgur wheat. While the wheat is soaking, you have just enough time to chop the vegetables and herbs, and make the dressing. Serve with pita bread.

Preparation time **about 30 minutes**   *Serves 4*

Tabbouleh

1 1/4 cups bulgur wheat

1 yellow bell pepper, seeded and chopped

20 cherry tomatoes, quartered

1 small red onion, finely chopped

1 small cucumber, seeded and chopped

1 large carrot, grated

5 tablespoons chopped parsley

2 tablespoons chopped fresh cilantro

2 tablespoons chopped fresh mint

1 small fresh red chile, seeded and finely chopped *(optional)*

2/3 cup reduced-fat soft goat cheese, crumbled

Salt and pepper to taste

Dressing

1/4 teaspoon ground cumin

1 small garlic clove, very finely chopped

1 tablespoon lemon juice

3 tablespoons olive oil

To Serve

Lettuce leaves

12 radishes, sliced

1 Put the bulgur wheat in a mixing bowl, pour over enough boiling water to cover, and stir well. Leave to soak for 15–20 minutes.

2 Meanwhile, make the dressing. Whisk together the cumin, garlic, and lemon juice in a small bowl, then whisk in the olive oil.

3 Drain the bulgur wheat in a sieve, pressing out excess water, then return it to the bowl. Add the pepper, tomatoes, onion, cucumber, carrot, parsley, cilantro, and mint, plus the chile, if using. Pour the dressing over the top and season with salt and pepper to taste. Fold gently to mix well.

4 Arrange the lettuce leaves on 4 plates or a serving platter. Pile the bulgur salad on the leaves and sprinkle the goat cheese over the top. Garnish with the radishes and serve.

(Some More Ideas)

Spicy tabbouleh with chicken: Replace the goat cheese with 2 cooked skinless, boneless chicken breasts, about 10 ounces in total, cut into cubes. Mix the soaked bulgur wheat with the chicken, pepper, onion, carrot, and parsley (omit the other vegetables and herbs). For the dressing, gently warm 3 tablespoons olive oil in a small skillet with 1 finely chopped garlic clove. Add 1/2–1 teaspoon each of ground cumin, ground coriander, dry mustard, and curry powder, and continue cooking for 1 minute. Stir in 2 tablespoons lemon juice and seasoning to taste. Pour the dressing over the salad and stir gently to combine. Garnish with sliced cucumber rounds. Serves 6.

Health Points

• Goat cheese is a tasty source of protein and calcium and lower in fat than cheeses such as cheddar and Parmesan.

photo, page 171

Each serving provides

Key Nutrients 300 Calories, 110 Calories from Fat, 12g Fat, 2g Saturated Fat, 0g Trans Fat, 8g Protein, 46g Carb, 11g Fiber, 50mg Sodium
Blood Pressure Nutrients 122mg Vitamin C, 100mg Magnesium, 659mg Potassium, 52mg Calcium

Tropical Beef and Rice Salad

Ginger, honey, orange, and chile add exciting flavors to this colorful salad. It is perfect for a relaxed lunch, as it can be mostly prepared ahead. To finish, add the papaya and salad leaves and sprinkle with toasted sesame seeds.

Preparation and cooking time **about 45 minutes**   *Serves 4*

Salad

12 ounces fillet steak, trimmed of all fat, cut into 3/4-inch slices

1 cup mixed basmati and wild rice

1 papaya, peeled, seeded, and sliced

6 scallions, sliced diagonally

4 cups mixed baby salad leaves

1 tablespoon sesame seeds, toasted

Salt and pepper to taste

Marinade

3 tablespoons sherry vinegar

1 large garlic clove, crushed

2 teaspoons canola oil

1 teaspoon finely chopped fresh ginger

Grated zest of 1 orange

1 teaspoon light brown sugar

Dressing

2 tablespoons canola oil

2 tablespoons orange juice

2 teaspoons red wine vinegar

1 teaspoon honey

1 teaspoon finely chopped fresh ginger

1 large fresh red chile, seeded and finely chopped

1 Put all the ingredients for the marinade in a large shallow dish. Add salt and pepper to taste and mix well. Place the steak in the marinade, then cover and chill for 30 minutes, turning the slices over after 15 minutes so that both sides absorb the flavors.

2 Meanwhile, put the rice in a pan, add 2 cups water, and bring to a boil. Cover and simmer very gently until the rice is tender and has absorbed all the water, about 20 minutes. Remove from the heat.

3 While the rice is cooking, put all the ingredients for the dressing in a large salad bowl and whisk to combine. Season to taste. When the rice is cooked, add it to the bowl and stir gently to mix with the dressing.

4 Preheat the grill to medium. Remove the steak slices from the marinade and place on the rack of the grill pan. Grill until cooked to your taste, 5–6 minutes, turning over halfway through cooking and brushing with any remaining marinade. Transfer the steak to a board and cut the slices across the grain into narrow strips. Add to the rice. (Cool and chill, if desired.)

5 Just before serving, add the papaya, scallions, and salad leaves, and toss gently together. Sprinkle with the sesame seeds and serve.

(Some More Ideas)

• Substitute skinless, boneless chicken breasts for steak. Marinate and grill the chicken for 5–6 minutes per side.

Health Points

• Not long ago, tropical fruits like papaya were considered exotic and strange. But with widespread distribution, people are discovering how delicious and versatile they are. Papaya is extremely healthy, too, with lots of nutrients good for blood pressure, such as vitamin C, potassium, fiber, folate, and carotenoids.

• Sesame seeds can provide useful amounts of calcium.

photo, page 171

Each serving provides

Key Nutrients 410 Calories, 120 Calories from Fat, 13g Fat, 2g Saturated Fat, 0g Trans Fat, 23g Protein, 55g Carb, 6g Fiber, 65mg Sodium
Blood Pressure Nutrients 79mg Vitamin C, 65mg Magnesium, 599mg Potassium, 79mg Calcium

Lemony Lentil and Vegetable Salad

This is a deliciously healthy and filling Middle Eastern salad. The lentils are cooked with lemon and spices, then dressed while warm. Vegetables add color, and dried apricots, goat cheese, and sunflower seeds finish off the feast.

Preparation and cooking time **about 50 minutes**   *Serves 4*

Salad

1 cup lentils, rinsed

1 garlic clove

Good pinch of ground cumin

1 slice lemon

1 small red onion, finely chopped

1/2 cup roughly chopped dried apricots

3 small bell peppers (1 red, 1 yellow, and 1 green), seeded and cut into 3/4-inch squares

1/4 pound broccoli, broken into small florets

1 ounce reduced-fat goat cheese

2 tablespoons toasted sunflower seeds

Dressing

Juice of 1 lemon

3 tablespoons olive oil

2 tablespoons finely chopped fresh cilantro

Salt and pepper to taste

1 Put the lentils in a large saucepan, cover with water, and bring to the boil, skimming off any scum. Add the peeled garlic, cumin, and lemon slice, then reduce the heat and simmer until the lentils are tender, about 30 minutes.

2 Meanwhile, to make the dressing, put the lemon juice, oil, cilantro, and salt and pepper to taste into a large salad bowl, and whisk together.

3 Drain the lentils, discarding the lemon and garlic, and add them to the salad bowl. Toss gently to mix with the dressing.

4 Add the onion, apricots, peppers, and broccoli florets, and mix gently. Crumble the cheese over the top, scatter over the sunflower seeds, and serve immediately.

(Some More Ideas)

• Instead of goat cheese, top the salad with slices of hard-boiled eggs.

Health Points

• Lentils are a good source of soluble fiber, which can help to reduce high blood cholesterol levels. Lentils also offer protein and B vitamins.

• The sunflower was first brought to Europe around 1510 as a decorative plant, but it wasn't until the 18th century that sunflowers began to be grown as a crop for the production of sunflower oil. Sunflower seeds are rich in healthy polyunsaturated fats and they are a good source of the antioxidant vitamin E, which helps to protect cell membranes from damage by free radicals and vitamin B1. They also provide useful amounts of the minerals zinc, iron, copper, phosphorus, selenium, and magnesium.

photo, page 171

Each serving provides

Key Nutrients 370 Calories, 130 Calories from Fat, 14g Fat, 2g Saturated Fat, 0g Trans Fat, 18g Protein, 49g Carb, 19g Fiber, 50mg Sodium
Blood Pressure Nutrients 177mg Vitamin C, 93mg Magnesium, 968mg Potassium, 69mg Calcium

Turkey Salad with Red Cabbage

This is a lovely, crunchy salad for winter, full of contrasting tastes and tossed with an unusual dressing made from cranberry sauce and walnut oil. Red cabbage tends to stain the other ingredients, so serve the salad as soon as it's made.

Preparation time **about 20 minutes**   *Serves 4*

Salad

2 ounces pecans, coarsely chopped

1/2 teaspoon caraway seeds

12 ounces cold roast turkey meat, without skin, diced

1 cup finely shredded red cabbage

3 celery stalks, sliced

2 carrots, grated

1/4 cup dark raisins

Dressing

2 tablespoons cranberry sauce

1 tablespoon olive oil

1 tablespoon walnut oil

2 tablespoons red wine vinegar

Salt and pepper to taste

1 Put all the ingredients for the dressing into a salad bowl and whisk together until well blended and starting to emulsify.

2 Place the pecans and caraway seeds in a small, dry skillet and toast over a low heat, stirring occasionally, until the pecans are golden and you can smell the nutty fragrance, 3–5 minutes. Add to a bowl and leave to cool slightly.

3 Put the turkey, red cabbage, celery, and carrots into the bowl with the dressing. Add the toasted pecans and caraway seeds and the raisins, and mix until all the ingredients are well coated with the dressing. Serve immediately.

(Some More Ideas)

Summer turkey salad: Make the dressing with 3 tablespoons olive oil, 2 teaspoons Dijon mustard, 1 tablespoon honey, 2 tablespoons lemon juice, 2 teaspoons finely grated fresh ginger, and seasoning to taste. Stir the diced turkey into the dressing. Steam 1/2 pound fresh asparagus, cut into bite-size pieces, 1/2 pound small sugar snap peas, and 1/2 pound sliced new potatoes. Toss the vegetables with the turkey and dressing while still hot. Fold in 2 tablespoons snipped fresh chives. Serve warm or at room temperature.

• Use white cabbage instead of red, and substitute apples for the carrots and raisins.

Health Points

• Cranberries contain a compound that helps to prevent *E. coli* bacteria from causing urinary tract infections.

• Red cabbage provides the B vitamin folate, vitamin C, and potassium, making it a potent food for healthier blood pressure.

Each serving provides

Key Nutrients 360 Calories, 180 Calories from Fat, 20g Fat, 3g Saturated Fat, 0g Trans Fat, 28g Protein, 19g Carb, 4g Fiber, 95mg Sodium
Blood Pressure Nutrients 18mg Vitamin C, 56mg Magnesium, 629mg Potassium, 65mg Calcium

Fresh Artichoke and Crab Salad

This salad is a real treat when globe artichokes are in season. The large outer leaves are removed and the succulent, meaty bottom part, or heart, is cooked, then served with fresh crabmeat in a lemony dressing.

Preparation time **1 1/2 hours, plus cooling**   *Serves 4*

Artichokes

4 large globe artichokes

2 lemons, halved

Vinaigrette

1 tablespoon lemon juice

3 tablespoons olive oil

1 tablespoon finely chopped fresh chervil or parsley

1 tablespoon finely chopped fresh chives

Salt and pepper to taste

Salad

2 tablespoons plain low-fat yogurt

2 tablespoons reduced-fat mayonnaise

1/2 teaspoon grated lemon zest

1 teaspoon lemon juice

1 1/2 tablespoons chopped fresh chives

1 pound fresh crabmeat, preferably lump

Soft lettuce leaves

1 To prepare each artichoke, cut off the top two-thirds and trim the stalk level with the base. Rub the cut surfaces with lemon juice as you work. Pull off the large outer leaves, starting from the bottom, to expose the soft, pale inner leaves. Holding the artichoke in one hand, trim the top edge to form a rounded shape, and trim around the sides and base to remove all the green parts and expose the pale yellow flesh. Drop the artichoke into a bowl of water with the juice of half a lemon added to it. Prepare the remaining artichokes in the same way.

2 Put the artichokes in a saucepan large enough to hold them in a single layer, cover with boiling water, and add the juice of half a lemon. Cover the pan and simmer until a leaf can be pulled away easily and the hearts are tender, about 40 minutes. Remove from the pan and leave to drain upside down until cool.

3 To make the herb vinaigrette, put the lemon juice in a bowl, whisk in the olive oil, and season with salt and pepper to taste. Stir in the chervil or parsley and chives.

4 Quarter the artichokes and use a teaspoon to scoop out the fuzzy choke just underneath the center leaves. Add the artichoke pieces to the herb vinaigrette and turn to coat.

5 For the crab salad, put the yogurt, mayonnaise, lemon zest and juice, and chives in a mixing bowl and stir to combine. Add the crab and mix in gently. Taste and add more lemon juice if you wish.

6 Arrange 2–3 lettuce leaves on each of 4 plates to form a small bed or cup and spoon on the crab salad. Add the artichoke quarters with their dressing, and serve at once.

(Some More Ideas)

Artichoke, mushroom, and chicken salad: Replace the crabmeat with 1/2 pound button mushrooms and 10 ounces cooked chicken breast, cut into thin slivers. Use 1 teaspoon grated lemon zest and 2 teaspoons Dijon mustard in the dressing. Cut the artichokes into eighths, and instead of tossing them in the herb vinaigrette, fold them into the mushroom and chicken salad. Pile onto lettuce leaves, and garnish with a good sprinkling of chopped fresh chives and chervil or parsley.

Health Points

• Crab, like other shellfish, is a good source of low-fat protein. It also provides useful amounts of vitamin B2, potassium, and zinc.

• Chives are a member of the same family as onions and garlic and share the same antibiotic healing powers.

• Globe artichokes are rich in cynarin, a phytochemical that is believed to help reduce high blood cholesterol levels.

Each serving provides

Key Nutrients 310 Calories, 130 Calories from Fat, 14g Fat, 2g Saturated Fat, 0g Trans Fat, 27g Protein, 25g Carb, 11g Fiber, 550mg Sodium
Blood Pressure Nutrients 69mg Vitamin C, 145mg Magnesium, 1090mg Potassium, 223mg Calcium

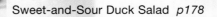

Sweet-and-Sour Duck Salad *p178*

Fresh Artichoke and Crab Salad *p176*

Shrimp with Dill Dressing *p181*

Steakhouse Salad *p179*

Sweet-and-Sour Duck Salad

With ripe nectarines, red grapes, peppery lettuces, and slices of tender grilled duck, this is a particularly pretty salad. The unusual dressing complements and brings together all the ingredients.

Preparation time **about 1 hour, plus cooling**   *Serves 4*

Salad

1 cup mixed basmati and wild rice

1 pound skinless, boneless duck breasts

2 teaspoons olive oil

2 cups watercress, tough stalks discarded

1 cup seedless green grapes, halved

4 scallions, thinly sliced

3 celery stalks, thinly sliced

4 nectarines

8 radicchio leaves or other red salad leaves

3 tablespoons toasted pumpkin seeds

Salt and pepper to taste

Dressing

1 teaspoon grated fresh ginger

1 small garlic clove, very finely chopped

1 tablespoon apricot jam

2 teaspoons raspberry vinegar or white wine vinegar

2 tablespoons hazelnut oil

1 Cook the rice in a saucepan of boiling water, according to the package instructions, until tender, about 20 minutes. Drain, then transfer to a bowl and allow to cool.

2 Heat a ridged grill pan. Meanwhile, remove all excess fat from the duck breasts, and brush them on both sides with the olive oil. Place on the grill pan and cook over a moderately high heat for 3 minutes on each side (the meat will be rare, so cook longer if you prefer it well done). Allow the duck breasts to cool.

3 To make the dressing, put the ginger, garlic, apricot jam, vinegar, and hazelnut oil in a small bowl and stir to combine. Season with salt to taste.

4 Chop half the watercress and add to the rice together with the grapes, scallions, and celery. Drizzle over half the dressing and mix gently.

5 Cut the duck breasts into thin slices. Thinly slice the nectarines. Arrange the radicchio and reserved watercress leaves on 4 plates and divide the rice salad among them. Arrange the duck and nectarine slices on top, drizzle over the remaining dressing, and sprinkle with the pumpkin seeds.

(Some More Ideas)

Grilled duck, sweet potato, and apple salad: Cook 1 1/2 pounds peeled and cubed sweet potatoes in enough boiling water to cover, until tender, 6–8 minutes. Drain well and cool slightly. For the dressing, stir 2 1/2 tablespoons each reduced-fat mayonnaise and plain low-fat yogurt with 1 tablespoon Dijon mustard in a small bowl. Core and chop 1 large apple and toss with 2 tablespoons lemon juice in a large mixing bowl. Add 3 celery stalks and 4 scallions, all thinly sliced, and stir in the dressing. Fold in the sweet potatoes and the hot sliced duck. Serve warm on a bed of mixed salad leaves.

• Use 4 peaches instead of the nectarines.

Health Points

• Nectarines are high in vitamin C, fiber, and beta-carotene (the darker the color of the flesh, the higher the carotenoid content). They also offer B-complex vitamins.

photo, page 177

Each serving provides

Key Nutrients 600 Calories, 180 Calories from Fat, 20g Fat, 4g Saturated Fat, 0g Trans Fat, 41g Protein, 68g Carb, 6g Fiber, 135mg Sodium
Blood Pressure Nutrients 35mg Vitamin C, 130mg Magnesium, 1141mg Potassium, 69mg Calcium

Steakhouse Salad

How can steak be part of a smart diet? Very easily! Grill the finest of steaks, filet mignon, and arrange it atop fresh greens and plenty of vegetables to make a delicious "composed" salad.

Preparation time **20 minutes**   Cooking time **16 minutes**   *Serves 4*

Steak

4 medium red bell peppers
10 ounces trimmed filet mignon
1/2 teaspoon salt
1/2 teaspoon pepper
1 garlic clove
1 pound green beans, trimmed

Dressing

3 tablespoons balsamic vinegar
2 teaspoons extra-virgin olive oil
1 garlic clove
2 tablespoons minced shallot

To Serve

8 cups mesclun (about 4 ounces)
6 medium tomatoes, cut into 1/4-inch wedges

1 Preheat grill or broiler. Put red peppers on grill rack or broiler pan. Cook until skins are blistered and blackened, about 10 minutes, turning frequently. Put in paper bag, seal tightly, and let steam 10 minutes. Peel away blackened skins from peppers, seed, and cut into chunks.

2 Meanwhile, lay filet flat on cutting board and slit lengthwise three-fourths of the way through. Open like a book and press flat. Sprinkle with 1/4 teaspoon salt and 1/4 teaspoon pepper. Cut 1 garlic clove in half and rub cut sides all over beef. Grill or broil beef until done to taste, about 3 minutes on each side for medium. Thinly slice beef.

3 Cook beans in boiling water until crisp-tender, about 5 minutes. Drain and rinse immediately with cold water.

4 Mince remaining garlic clove. Whisk vinegar, oil, garlic, shallot, and remaining salt and pepper in small bowl. Divide mesclun among plates and arrange steak, red peppers, beans, and tomatoes on top. Drizzle with dressing.

(Some More Ideas)

• Use other lean cuts of meat such as sirloin or top round in place of filet mignon.

• Use roasted yellow or orange bell peppers instead of red ones.

• Make an herb dressing. To the vinegar and oil mixture, add 2 teaspoons finely chopped thyme and basil.

Health Points

• Choosing the right cuts and controlling your portion sizes are the secret to making beef a part of a healthy, lean diet. Beef can range widely in its healthiness—3 ounces of cooked rib roast, for example, has 24 grams of fat, while the same amount of top round has 5.4 grams of fat. Filet mignon, which is used in this recipe, falls in the middle. Beef is rich with potassium, zinc, and vitamin B12, as well as protein.

photo, page 177

Each serving provides

Key Nutrients 360 Calories, 150 Calories from Fat, 17g Fat, 6g Saturated Fat, 0g Trans Fat, 25g Protein, 31g Carb, 11g Fiber, 100mg Sodium
Blood Pressure Nutrients 311mg Vitamin C, 107mg Magnesium, 1056mg Potassium, 137mg Calcium

Peachy Cottage Cheese Salad

This fresh-tasting salad combines luscious, sweet peaches and crisp green vegetables with a generous portion of creamy cottage cheese. It is quick and easy to put together, taking only a little longer to make than a sandwich.

Preparation time **about 30 minutes**   *Serves 4*

Salad

1/2 pound sugar snap peas

1/4 pound arugula, washed, dried, and torn

1/4 pound butter lettuce, washed, dried, and torn

4 ripe peaches, pitted and thinly sliced

1 pound low-sodium, low-fat (1%) cottage cheese

4 tablespoons toasted sliced almonds

Cayenne pepper

Sprigs of fresh dill *(garnish)*

Dressing

2 tablespoons olive oil

Grated zest and juice of 1 lemon

1 teaspoon Dijon mustard

2 teaspoons honey

2 tablespoons chopped fresh dill

Salt and pepper to taste

1 Add the sugar snap peas to a pot of boiling water. Cook for 2–3 minutes and drain.

2 To make the dressing, put the oil, lemon zest and juice, mustard, honey, chopped dill, and salt and pepper to taste in a mixing bowl. Whisk well.

3 Add the sugar snap peas, arugula, and butter lettuce to the dressing and toss to coat well with the dressing.

4 Divide the dressed vegetables among 4 serving plates. Scatter over the peach slices and top with the cottage cheese. Sprinkle with the sliced almonds and a little cayenne pepper. Garnish with dill sprigs and serve.

(Some More Ideas)

• Top this salad with nectarines or fresh apricots.

• Mix in 1/2 cup low-fat plain yogurt to make the cottage cheese taste creamier.

• Serve with warmed sunflower seed, walnut, or pumpkin bread for a well-balanced lunch.

Health Points

• A half-cup of 1% cottage cheese has only 82 calories, compared to 144 calories for the same amount of part-skim mozzarella, or 170 calories for part-skim ricotta. Moreover, the cottage cheese has only 1.2 grams of fat, compared with 9 and 9.8 grams for mozzarella and ricotta. Cottage cheese is a great source of B vitamins as well.

• Fresh peaches are a good source of vitamin C and provide some beta-carotene.

Each serving provides

Key Nutrients 280 Calories, 100 Calories from Fat, 11g Fat, 2g Saturated Fat, 0g Trans Fat, 19g Protein, 25 Carb, 5g Fiber, 510mg Sodium
Blood Pressure Nutrients 24mg Vitamin C, 47mg Magnesium, 534mg Potassium, 175mg Calcium

Shrimp with Dill Dressing

In this good-looking salad, shrimp are served piled on a mixture of aromatic basmati and wild rice, crunchy broccoli florets, snow peas, and yellow bell pepper tossed in a fresh dill and lime juice dressing.

Preparation time **40 minutes, plus cooling**   *Serves 4*

1 cup mixed basmati and wild rice, rinsed

Thinly pared zest and juice of 1 lime

2 tablespoons canola oil, divided

2 teaspoons toasted sesame oil

1 tablespoon light soy sauce

1/2 pound broccoli, broken into small florets

1/2 pound snow peas, halved lengthwise

1 pound large, peeled, and deveined shrimp, tails left on

1 small yellow bell pepper, seeded and thinly sliced

3 scallions, sliced

4 tablespoons coarsely chopped fresh dill

Salt and pepper to taste

1 Cook the rice with the lime zest in a saucepan of boiling water, according to the package instructions, until tender, about 20 minutes. Drain the rice and add it to a wide salad bowl. Discard the lime zest.

2 Whisk together 1 tablespoon of the lime juice, 1 tablespoon of the canola oil, the sesame oil, soy sauce, and salt and pepper to taste in a small bowl. Drizzle this dressing over the rice and stir to mix. Spread out the rice in the bowl and leave to cool.

3 Meanwhile, put the broccoli in a steamer basket set over a pan of boiling water and steam for 4 minutes. Add the snow peas and steam until the vegetables are tender but still crisp, another 2 minutes. Drain the vegetables into a colander and refresh under cold running water.

4 Heat the remaining 1 tablespoon of canola oil in a large skillet. Add the shrimp and cook over a high heat until pink and cooked through, 1–2 minutes on each side. Remove from the heat and sprinkle with the remaining lime juice.

5 Add the bell pepper and scallions and 3 tablespoons of the dill to the rice and stir gently to mix. Pile the shrimp on top and scatter the remaining 1 tablespoon of dill for garnish.

(Some More Ideas)

• The salad can be made in advance and refrigerated until needed. Let it stand at room temperature for 30 minutes before serving.

• For a high-fiber salad, use brown long-grain rice instead of basmati and wild rice.

• Instead of broccoli and snow peas, use asparagus tips and sliced small zucchini.

• To save time, cooked peeled shrimp and simply toss them in the lime juice.

• Instead of shrimp, use 16 scallops, searing them in the hot oil for about 1 minute on each side or until golden brown.

Health Points

• Shrimp are low in fat and calories. They contain a useful amount of vitamin B12, which is essential for the formation of red blood cells and maintaining a healthy nervous system. They also provide good amounts of copper, phosphorus, iodine, and the antioxidant selenium.

photo, page 177

Each serving provides

Key Nutrients 420 Calories, 100 Calories from Fat, 11g Fat, 2g Saturated Fat, 0g Trans Fat, 32g Protein, 50g Carb, 6g Fiber, 410mg Sodium
Blood Pressure Nutrients 182mg Vitamin C, 112mg Magnesium, 743mg Potassium, 118mg Calcium

Corn and Whole-Grain Salad

Grains of whole wheat have a distinctive sweet, nutty flavor and slightly chewy texture. Here they are mixed with grilled fresh corn, toasted walnuts, and crisp vegetables in a fragrant orange dressing to make a nutritious salad.

Preparation and cooking time **35 minutes, plus cooling**   *Serves 4*

Salad

1 cup wheat berries

3 cups water

1 bay leaf

2 corn on the cob, peeled and silks removed

1/2 tablespoon canola oil

1/2 cup coarsely chopped walnuts

1 red bell pepper, seeded and diced

1/4 pound button mushrooms, sliced

1/2 cucumber, cut into small chunks

1 tablespoon chopped fresh mint

1 egg, hard-boiled and sliced

Salt and pepper to taste

Sprigs of fresh mint *(garnish)*

Dressing

1 teaspoon Dijon mustard

1/2 teaspoon finely grated orange zest

1 tablespoon orange juice

1 tablespoon canola oil

1 tablespoon walnut oil

1 Bring the wheat berries and water to a boil in a medium saucepan. Add the bay leaf. Simmer until the grain is tender and all the liquid has been absorbed, 15–20 minutes. Discard the bay leaf and add the grains into a mixing bowl.

2 Preheat the grill to medium-high. Brush the corn cobs all over with the canola oil, then put them on the rack of the grill pan. Grill, turning frequently, until tender and lightly charred in places, about 10 minutes. Set aside to cool slightly.

3 Meanwhile, spread out the walnuts in a baking sheet. Put them under the grill and cook until lightly toasted, 2–3 minutes, turning them frequently and watching them all the time, as they burn easily. Set aside.

4 When the corn is cool enough to handle, cut the kernels off the cobs with a sharp knife. Add them to the grains.

5 To make the dressing, whisk together the mustard, orange zest and juice, canola oil, and walnut oil. Season with salt and pepper to taste. Drizzle the dressing over the warm grains and corn, and toss well to mix. Leave to cool completely.

6 Add the red pepper, mushrooms, cucumber, mint, and toasted walnuts to the grain mixture and toss gently together. Taste and add more seasoning, if needed. Serve at room temperature, garnished with slices of hard-boiled egg and sprigs of mint.

(Some More Ideas)

Barley and egg salad: Heat 2 teaspoons canola oil in a large saucepan, add 1 1/2 cups pearl barley and 1 crushed garlic clove, and cook gently for about 1 minute. Add a bay leaf and pour in 4 cups boiling reduced-sodium vegetable broth. Bring to the boil, then reduce the heat and simmer until the barley is tender, 35–40 minutes. Drain off any excess stock, then add the barley into a bowl and leave to cool. Mix in 1 cup broccoli florets, 1/2 cup cauliflower florets, 1 seeded and sliced yellow bell pepper, and a bunch of sliced scallions. For the dressing, whisk together 2 tablespoons canola oil, 1 teaspoon toasted sesame oil, 2 teaspoons sherry vinegar, 2 teaspoons light soy sauce, and pepper to taste. Drizzle over the salad. Add 2 table-spoons toasted sunflower seeds and 1 tablespoon toasted sesame seeds and toss together. Gently mix in 4 hard-boiled eggs, cut into wedges, just before serving at room temperature.

Each serving provides

Key Nutrients 430 Calories, 190 Calories from Fat, 21g Fat, 2g Saturated Fat, 0g Trans Fat, 15g Protein, 55g Carb, 10g Fiber, 55mg Sodium
Blood Pressure Nutrients 63mg Vitamin C, 122mg Magnesium, 655mg Potassium, 43mg Calcium

Corn and Whole-Grain Salad *p182*

Avocado and Shrimp Cups *p184*

Pasta Salad with Cucumber Salsa *p187*

Warm Kasha and Seafood Salad *p188*

Avocado and Shrimp Cups

Here lettuce-lined salad bowls are filled with a fun mix of ingredients, then topped with a creamy yogurt for a real hot and cold taste explosion. Serve for lunch with whole-wheat bread.

Preparation time **25 minutes, plus cooling**   *Serves 4*

1 pound new potatoes, scrubbed and diced

2 tablespoons canola oil

1 small red onion, thinly sliced

1 garlic clove, crushed

1 fresh mild red chile, seeded and finely chopped

1 teaspoon coriander seeds, roughly crushed

1 teaspoon cumin seeds, roughly crushed

1 large avocado

1 pound peeled and deveined cooked large shrimp, thawed if frozen

Juice of 2 limes

6 tablespoons plain low-fat yogurt

3 tablespoons chopped fresh cilantro

Soft lettuce leaves

Salt and pepper to taste

1 Cook the potatoes in a saucepan of boiling water until just tender, about 8 minutes. Drain and refresh under cold running water. Dry in a clean towel.

2 Heat the oil in a large skillet, add the onion, and fry until softened and lightly browned, about 5 minutes. Add the garlic, chile, and crushed coriander and cumin seeds, and cook for 1 more minute, stirring. Stir in the potatoes and cook over a high heat for 3 minutes. Remove from the heat and leave to cool.

3 Peel the avocado, remove the pit, and cut the flesh into cubes. Add to the potatoes together with the shrimp and lime juice. Season with salt and pepper to taste, and toss gently.

4 Mix together the yogurt, chopped cilantro, and seasoning to taste. Arrange 2 lettuce leaves in each of 4 bowls. Spoon the salad into them and top with the cilantro yogurt.

(Some More Ideas)

Avocado, potato, and tofu salad: Replace the shrimp with 8 ounces plain tofu, drained and cubed. Add the tofu in Step 2 with the garlic and spices.

• Use just 10 ounces potatoes, and spoon the salad into 4 warmed round whole-wheat pita breads. Top each with shredded lettuce and a spoonful of the yogurt and chopped cilantro mixture.

Health Points

• Substances in avocados stimulate the production of collagen, which is why they have a reputation for being good for the skin.

• Coriander and cumin seeds are particularly healthy spices. Both appear to have antibacterial properties. Coriander also contains limonene, a flavonoid thought to fight cancer. And cumin is being studied for potential antioxidant and anticancer effects.

photo, page 183

Each serving provides

Key Nutrients 400 Calories, 150 Calories from Fat, 17g Fat, 3g Saturated Fat, 0g Trans Fat, 29g Protein, 35g Carb, 5g Fiber, 290mg Sodium
Blood Pressure Nutrients 59mg Vitamin C, 98mg Magnesium, 1110mg Potassium, 118mg Calcium

Creamy Turkey Salad with Grapes and Pecans

With its wonderfully contrasting tastes and textures, this salad makes a satisfying main course that is luxurious without containing a lot of saturated fat. It is the perfect recipe for roast turkey leftovers.

Preparation time **25 minutes, plus cooling**   *Serves 4*

8 ounces fusilli pasta

1 cup plain low-fat yogurt

3 tablespoons reduced-fat mayonnaise

1 teaspoon white wine vinegar

2 teaspoons Dijon mustard

3 tablespoons chopped fresh tarragon

9 ounces skinless, boneless roast turkey, cubed

2 celery stalks, cut into thin strips

1 cup seedless black grapes, or a mixture of black and green grapes, halved

1/4 cup toasted and coarsely chopped pecans

Salt and pepper to taste

Sprigs of fresh tarragon
(garnish)

1 Cook the pasta in boiling water according to the package instructions, omitting the salt, until al dente, 10–12 minutes. Drain and rinse with cold water, then drain again and leave to cool.

2 Meanwhile, mix the yogurt with the mayonnaise, white wine vinegar, mustard, and tarragon in a large bowl. Stir until all the ingredients are combined and the dressing is smooth.

3 Add the pasta, turkey, celery, grapes, toasted pecans, and seasoning to taste. Toss until the ingredients are all evenly coated with the dressing.

4 Transfer to a serving dish or plates and garnish with sprigs of tarragon.

(Some More Ideas)

• For a spicy Indian flavor, stir in 2 tablespoons curry paste (or to taste) with the yogurt. Garnish with chopped fresh cilantro instead of the tarragon.

• Use 1/4 cup roasted unsalted cashews instead of the pecans, and 2 cored and chopped apples instead of the grapes. Add 1/4 cup raisins.

• Try 8 ounces firm tofu instead of the turkey to make a vegetarian salad.

Health Points

• Grapes are high in sugar and relatively low in vitamins when compared with other fruits. However, they contain unusually large amounts of bioflavonoids, the antioxidants that help to protect against the damaging effect of free radicals linked with cancer and heart disease. They also have ample amounts of potassium, an important mineral for healthy blood pressure.

• Naturopaths consider grapes to have healing powers.

Each serving provides

Key Nutrients 450 Calories, 110 Calories from Fat, 12g Fat, 2g Saturated Fat, 0g Trans Fat, 27g Protein, 57g Carb, 3g Fiber, 260mg Sodium
Blood Pressure Nutrients 7mg Vitamin C, 73mg Magnesium, 640mg Potassium, 165mg Calcium

Apple and Date Salad

A crunchy salad of fruit, vegetables, and nuts in a creamy yogurt-based dressing, this is attractively presented on chicory leaves, the bitterness of the chicory providing a good contrast to the sweet fruit.

Preparation time **15 minutes**   *Serves 4*

Salad

1/2 cup chopped hazelnuts

2 green-skinned apples, cored and roughly chopped

6 ounces dates, pitted and roughly chopped

1 small red bell pepper, seeded and chopped

2 celery stalks, sliced

1/2 cup halved seedless green grapes

2 heads red or white chicory

2 tablespoons chopped parsley *(optional)*

Dressing

1/2 cup plain low-fat yogurt

4 tablespoons nonfat mayonnaise

1 tablespoon lemon juice

1 teaspoon sugar

Salt and pepper to taste

1 Put the hazelnuts into a small, dry skillet and toast over a moderate heat, stirring, until you can smell the nutty fragrance, about 3 minutes. Add the nuts into a bowl and set aside.

2 To make the dressing, put the yogurt, mayonnaise, lemon juice, and sugar into a large bowl with salt and pepper to taste and mix well.

3 Add the apples to the bowl and stir until the pieces are well coated with the dressing. Add the dates, red pepper, celery, and grapes and stir to mix.

4 Separate the heads of chicory into leaves, trimming off the hard bases. Slice the bottom half of the leaves and add to the salad. Pile the salad on a large plate or in a shallow serving dish and arrange the tops of the chicory leaves around the edge. Sprinkle over the toasted nuts and parsley, if using.

(Some More Ideas)

• Use 1/2 cup raisins in place of the dates.

• You could dress the salad with a vinaigrette instead of the mayonnaise and yogurt mixture. Mix together 3 tablespoons olive oil, 1 tablespoon red wine vinegar or lemon juice, 1/4 teaspoon Dijon mustard, 1/4 teaspoon sugar, and salt and pepper to taste.

Health Points

• This recipe provides plenty of fiber from apples with their skins, celery, chicory, and, of course, dates.

• Radicchio, a member of the chicory family, has deep red-and-white tightly packed leaves. The red pigment means this vegetable is high in beta-carotene.

Each serving provides

Key Nutrients 350 Calories, 130 Calories from Fat, 15g Fat, 2g Saturated Fat, 0g Trans Fat, 6g Protein, 56g Carb, 8g Fiber, 160mg Sodium
Blood Pressure Nutrients 46mg Vitamin C, 55mg Magnesium, 722mg Potassium, 109mg Calcium

Pasta Salad with Cucumber Salsa

Shaped pasta trap an herby yogurt and tomato dressing so that each one is full of flavor. A refreshing vegetable and fruit salsa brings extra nutritional value as well as exciting taste and texture contrast.

Preparation time **40–50 minutes, plus cooling and 1 hour chilling**   *Serves 4*

Salad

8 ounces any shaped pasta

4 tablespoons chopped fresh parsley

4 tablespoons chopped fresh mint

4 tablespoons snipped fresh chives

2 tablespoons fresh tarragon

4 tomatoes, skinned, seeded, and chopped

1 cup plain low-fat yogurt

1 avocado

Salt and pepper to taste

Sprigs of fresh mint *(garnish)*

Salsa

4 celery stalks finely diced

1 green bell pepper, seeded and finely diced or chopped

1/2 cucumber, diced or chopped

4 scallions, finely sliced or chopped

Grated zest of 1 lime *(optional)*

1 cup watercress, coarsely chopped

1 teaspoon olive oil

1 crisp apple, such as Braeburn or Jonagold

1 Cook the pasta in boiling water, according to the package instructions, until al dente, 10–12 minutes.

2 Meanwhile, mix the parsley, mint, chives, and tarragon with the tomatoes in a large bowl (the bowl should be large enough to take the cooked pasta too). Add a little seasoning and then stir in the yogurt.

3 Drain the cooked pasta thoroughly, shaking the shapes in a colander to make sure that there is no cooking water trapped in them. Add the hot pasta to the yogurt dressing and use a large spoon to turn them until they are thoroughly coated. Cover and set aside to cool until just warm. The pasta salad tastes good warm, or it can be served cold, in which case leave to cool completely, then chill for 1 hour. The pasta can be dressed several hours in advance if this is more convenient.

4 Meanwhile, mix together the celery, green pepper, cucumber, and scallions. Stir in the lime zest, if using, and the watercress. Cover and set aside.

5 Shortly before serving, stir the oil into the cucumber mixture with seasoning to taste. Quarter, core, and finely dice the apple, leaving its peel on. Add to the cucumber salsa and stir well so the apple is mixed in.

6 Halve the avocado and remove the pit, then cut it lengthwise into quarters and peel off the skin. Dice the flesh and mix it into the pasta.

7 Serve the cucumber salsa as an accompaniment to the pasta so that it can be added to taste. (The hot pasta absorbs its yogurt dressing, becoming quite dry as it cools, so the cucumber salsa acts as a second dressing.) Garnish with sprigs of mint and serve immediately.

(Some More Ideas)

• Use whole-wheat pasta for a dish that is higher in fiber.

• Add a finely chopped garlic clove to the yogurt dressing.

• Keep the yogurt dressing green by omitting the tomatoes, and make a red salsa using red pepper, instead of green, and a red-skinned apple. Add the tomatoes to the salsa and season it with a little paprika to warm both the flavor and color.

Health Points

• Vitamin C in fruit and vegetables is easily destroyed during cooking, so eating them raw ensures they provide their maximum vitamin content.

• With roughly a dozen fresh fruits, vegetables, and herbs in this recipe, you'll be certain to get a wonderful cross-section of vitamins, minerals, and phytochemicals. While vegetables are always good, getting a mix of them is even better for your health than having a single vegetable per meal.

photo, page 183

Each serving provides

Key Nutrients 380 Calories, 90 Calories from Fat, 10g Fat, 2g Saturated Fat, 0g Trans Fat, 14g Protein, 61g Carb, 7g Fiber, 100mg Sodium
Blood Pressure Nutrients 66mg Vitamin C, 88mg Magnesium, 1077mg Potassium, 177mg Calcium

Warm Kasha and Seafood Salad

Kasha, or toasted buckwheat grains, makes a pleasant change from rice and pasta. Add in seafood and raw vegetables and you have an unusual—and unusually good-tasting—main-dish salad.

Preparation and cooking time **1 1/2 hours** *Serves 4*

Salad

1 cup kasha (toasted buckwheat)

2 cups reduced-sodium chicken or vegetable broth

2 teaspoons canola oil, divided

1 package (1 pound) frozen mixed seafood, thawed

1 cucumber, diced

1/2 pound sugar snap peas, sliced

1 bulb fennel, halved and thinly sliced

4 ounces radishes, thinly sliced

Dressing

1 tablespoon olive oil

1 tablespoon white wine vinegar

1 teaspoon Dijon mustard

2 tablespoons chopped fresh mixed herbs

Salt and pepper to taste

1 Put the kasha in a nonstick saucepan, pour over the broth, and bring to the boil. Cover and simmer until the kasha has absorbed all the broth, about 5 minutes.

2 Stir in half the oil, cover, and cook for 10 minutes. Then remove the lid and fork up the kasha, tossing and turning to separate the grains. Cook over a very low heat, uncovered, for a further 1 hour, tossing the kasha with a fork every 10 minutes to separate the grains.

3 Meanwhile, make the dressing. Put all the ingredients in a bowl and whisk together until thoroughly mixed.

4 Heat the remaining 1 teaspoon oil in a wok or large frying pan. Add the seafood and stir-fry over a moderate heat until hot, 2–3 minutes. Add the hot seafood to the kasha together with the cucumber, sugar snap peas, fennel, and radishes. Drizzle over the dressing and toss gently to mix.

(Some More Ideas)

• Use green beans in place of sugar snap peas.

• Instead of mixed seafood, use 1 pound skinless, boneless chicken or turkey breast, or lean beef or lamb steak, cut into thin strips. Stir-fry until cooked and lightly browned, then toss with the dressed kasha and vegetables.

Health Points

• Sugar snap peas are a good source of vitamin C, and they contain more dietary fiber than ordinary peas. This is because the edible pod contributes to the fiber content.

• Most Americans know of buckwheat flour, but don't cook with buckwheat in whole-grain form. Yet buckwheat is a wonderfully healthy grain, containing lots of plant protein and significant amounts of the important amino acid lysine. Buckwheat is also an excellent source of iron and magnesium.

photo, page 183

Each serving provides

Key Nutrients 390 Calories, 80 Calories from Fat, 9g Fat, 2g Saturated Fat, 0g Trans Fat, 33g Protein, 43g Carb, 8g Fiber, 390mg Sodium
Blood Pressure Nutrients 23mg Vitamin C, 149mg Magnesium, 738mg Potassium, 132mg Calcium

vegetable sides

Asparagus with Confetti Vinaigrette

Fresh asparagus was once just a spring vegetable, but these days it is available year-round. When it's sprinkled with a light and colorful vinaigrette, its uniquely sweet flavor shines through.

Preparation time **10 minutes**   Cooking time **10 minutes**   *Serves 4*

1 1/2 pounds asparagus

Salt to taste

2 large red bell peppers, finely chopped

2 large yellow bell peppers, finely chopped

4 scallions, thinly sliced

2 teaspoons fresh thyme or 1/2 teaspoon dried

1/3 cup reduced-sodium chicken broth

3 tablespoons white wine vinegar

1/2 teaspoon pepper

1 Prepare asparagus. Bring 1/2 inch of water to a simmer in large skillet over medium-high heat. Add asparagus and salt to taste. Simmer until asparagus is tender, 3–4 minutes. Transfer to platter. Keep warm.

2 Wipe skillet dry. Coat with nonstick cooking spray and set over medium-high heat. Sauté red and yellow peppers until tender, about 4 minutes. Stir in scallions and thyme and cook 1 minute longer.

3 Stir in broth and vinegar and bring to a simmer. Sprinkle with pepper and pour over asparagus.

(Some More Ideas)

• Substitute broccoli or cauliflower for the asparagus if your local market is out of spears that look appealing. Asparagus spears should be firm, but tender, with deep green or purplish tips that are closed and compact.

• Use the pepper confetti mixture to top grilled chicken or salmon.

Health Points

• Asparagus is loaded with nutrients such as beta-carotene, vitamin C, folate, and potassium. It is also rich with blood-pressure-friendly fiber. During the 17th and early 18th centuries, King Louis XIV had such a liking for asparagus that it became the rage throughout France, a popularity that continues today.

photo, page 193

Each serving provides

Key Nutrients 100 Calories, 10 Calories from Fat, 1g Fat, 0g Saturated Fat, 0g Trans Fat, 6g Protein, 21g Carb, 7g Fiber, 20mg Sodium
Blood Pressure Nutrients 353mg Vitamin C, 54mg Magnesium, 869mg Potassium, 68mg Calcium

Country-Style Mashed Potatoes

A topping of crumbled, crisp bacon and beautiful brown sautéed onions brings out the personality in these mashed potatoes. This is a side dish that could steal the show.

Preparation time **20 minutes**   Cooking time **20 minutes**   *Serves 6*

Salt to taste
1 1/2 pounds russet or Eastern potatoes
1/3 cup reduced-fat (2%) milk
2 tablespoons margarine, cut into pieces
1/8 teaspoon pepper
2 scallions (green parts only), very thinly sliced
4 slices reduced-sodium turkey bacon, coarsely chopped
1 small red onion, chopped
1 teaspoon chopped fresh thyme

1 Half-fill a medium saucepan with water; add 1/4 teaspoon salt and bring to a boil over high heat. Meanwhile, peel potatoes and cut each into 8 pieces. Add potatoes to boiling water, reduce heat to medium, and simmer until potatoes are tender, about 10 minutes. Drain. Shake potatoes in pan over low heat until dry. Remove from heat, cover, and keep hot.

2 Heat milk and margarine in small saucepan over medium heat until margarine has melted and milk is hot and begins to bubble, about 3 minutes. Pour over potatoes. Add pepper and remaining salt and mash to a chunky puree with a potato masher (not mixer or food processor). Stir in scallions and keep hot.

3 Meanwhile, sauté bacon and onion in medium nonstick skillet over medium-high heat until bacon is crisp and onions are browned, about 7 minutes. Stir in thyme. Spoon on top of potatoes.

(Some More Ideas)

• Here we use reduced-fat milk, but you could also substitute some of the potato cooking water, low-fat buttermilk, reduced-sodium chicken or beef broth, nonfat sour cream, or nonfat plain yogurt.

• Spice up the cooking water by adding cloves of fresh garlic, fresh thyme sprigs, slivers of onion, or a dash of freshly ground black pepper.

Health Points

• Margarine can be a healthy substitute for butter if you choose the right type of margarine—those in tubs and made from canola, safflower, sunflower, olive, or corn oils. In other words, those low in hydrogenated fats or oils. Margarine is comparable to butter in its calories, but supplies much healthier forms of fat to the body.

Each serving provides

Key Nutrients 150 Calories, 45 Calories from Fat, 5g Fat, 1g Saturated Fat, 1g Trans Fat, 4g Protein, 23g Carb, 2g Fiber, 120mg Sodium
Blood Pressure Nutrients 24mg Vitamin C, 30mg Magnesium, 518mg Potassium, 38mg Calcium

VEGETABLE SIDES

Orange-Glazed Carrots

Did Mother Nature color oranges and carrots similarly to tip us off to what a tasty combination they make? Here the carrot-orange combo is divinely enhanced with Moroccan seasonings.

Preparation time **15 minutes**   Cooking time **25 minutes**   *Serves 8*

2 pounds carrots, halved lengthwise and cut into 2-inch lengths

1 can (6 ounces) frozen orange juice concentrate, thawed

2 1/2 teaspoons ground coriander

Salt to taste

3/4 cup water

1 tablespoon margarine

1/3 cup chopped fresh mint

1 Combine carrots, orange juice concentrate, ground coriander, and salt in large skillet. Add water and bring to a boil over medium heat. Reduce to a simmer, cover, and cook until carrots are crisp-tender, about 15 minutes.

2 Uncover, increase heat to high, and cook until carrots are tender, about 7 minutes.

3 Add margarine and cook, swirling pan until carrots are glossy and sauce is creamy, about 1 minute. Stir in mint.

(Some More Ideas)

• To save preparation time, make this dish with peeled baby carrots.

• If you can't find fresh mint, use fresh basil, cilantro, or dill instead.

Health Points

• Carrots contain a unique type of soluble fiber called calcium pectate that is believed to lower LDL ("bad") cholesterol.

• Carrots may not directly help your eyesight as the old truism claims, but they are indeed rich with the important antioxidant beta-carotene. One cup of cooked carrots provides 300% of the recommended daily intake!

Each serving provides

Key Nutrients 100 Calories, 15 Calories from Fat, 2g Fat, 0g Saturated Fat, 0g Trans Fat, 2g Protein, 21g Carb, 4g Fiber, 60mg Sodium
Blood Pressure Nutrients 37mg Vitamin C, 18mg Magnesium, 519mg Potassium, 45mg Calcium

Asparagus with Confetti Vinaigrette *p190*

Orange-Glazed Carrots *p192*

Pan-Roasted New Potatoes with Garlic *p195*

Snow Peas with Apples and Ginger *p194*

Snow Peas with Apples and Ginger

Garlic, ginger…and apples? You bet! Slices of firm apple, briefly stir-fried, have the same crunch as water chestnuts, so they partner well with crisp, fresh snow peas.

Preparation time **10 minutes**   Cooking time **10 minutes**   *Serves 4*

2 teaspoons olive oil

2 tablespoons finely slivered, peeled fresh ginger

3 cloves garlic, minced

1 pound snow peas, strings removed

2 crisp red apples, unpeeled, cut into thin wedges

Salt to taste

1 Heat oil in large nonstick skillet over low heat. Add ginger and garlic, and cook until tender, about 2 minutes.

2 Add snow peas, apples, and salt to skillet and cook, stirring frequently, until peas are crisp-tender, about 7 minutes.

(Some More Ideas)

• For an unusual main-dish salad, fold the cooled snow pea–apple combination into a big bowl of chilled cooked brown rice along with cubes of cooked chicken breast or lean pork loin.

• Use this recipe with sugar snap peas or sliced asparagus in place of the snow peas.

Health Points

• Apples contain anthocyanins, natural pigments in apple skin that may help to improve cardiovascular health. The soluble fiber pectin, abundant in apples, also assists in lowering harmful cholesterol levels. So "an apple a day" *is* good advice.

• Green vegetables such as peas contain chlorophyll, which studies suggest may deter certain chemicals from causing DNA damage to cells.

photo, page 193

Each serving provides

Key Nutrients 110 Calories, 25 Calories from Fat, 3g Fat, 0g Saturated Fat, 0g Trans Fat, 4g Protein, 20g Carb, 5g Fiber, 5mg Sodium
Blood Pressure Nutrients 73mg Vitamin C, 33mg Magnesium, 328mg Potassium, 58mg Calcium

Pan-Roasted New Potatoes with Garlic

The old way to roast potatoes was in a pan with fatty meat. The fresher, tastier way is to roast them separately with olive oil and fragrant spices. Here roasted garlic cloves are a flavorful bonus.

Preparation time **10 minutes**   Cooking time **35 minutes**   *Serves 4*

1 tablespoon olive oil

8 large cloves garlic, unpeeled

3 slices (1/2 inch thick) fresh ginger, unpeeled

1 1/2 teaspoons fennel seeds

1 1/2 teaspoons cumin seeds

1 1/2 teaspoons turmeric

1 1/2 pounds small red-skinned potatoes, cut into 1/2-inch chunks

1/4 cup water

Salt to taste

1 tablespoon fresh lemon juice

1 Heat oil in large nonstick skillet over low heat. Add garlic, ginger, fennel, cumin, and turmeric. Cook 1 minute.

2 Add potatoes, shaking pan to coat potatoes with spice mixture. Cook until potatoes begin to turn golden brown, about 5 minutes. Add water, cover pan, and cook, shaking pan occasionally, until potatoes are tender, about 30 minutes.

3 Sprinkle salt over potatoes and toss. Remove and discard ginger. Sprinkle lemon juice over potatoes. Serve garlic cloves in their skin; each diner can then squeeze the roasted garlic from its skin out onto the potatoes.

(Some More Ideas)

Italian roasted potatoes: Omit the ginger, fennel, cumin, and turmeric. Substitute 1 1/2 teaspoons dried oregano and basil, 1 teaspoon dried thyme, and add 1/2 teaspoon black ground pepper. Add along with the garlic in Step 1.

• Use Yukon Gold or Finnish Yellow Wax potatoes instead of red-skinned potatoes.

Health Points

• It is no coincidence that garlic and ginger are integral to the diet of the world's healthiest cultures. Both are filled with phytochemicals that fight disease and aid the body. Note that among vegetables, herbs, and spices, bold colors and strong flavors are often an indication of their healthy chemistry.

• Don't let all the talk of low-carb diets scare you away from potatoes. Particularly when eaten with their skins, potatoes are filled with vitamin C, potassium, and many phytochemicals.

photo, page 193

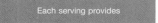
Each serving provides

Key Nutrients 170 Calories, 35 Calories from Fat, 4g Fat, 1g Saturated Fat, 0g Trans Fat, 4g Protein, 30g Carb, 3g Fiber, 15mg Sodium
Blood Pressure Nutrients 37mg Vitamin C, 46mg Magnesium, 836mg Potassium, 45mg Calcium

Sesame Stir-Fried Asparagus and Peas

When asparagus comes into season, run—don't walk—to the nearest greengrocer or farmers' market and buy a big bunch (or two). Toasted sesame seeds add a nutty aroma to this festive dish.

Preparation time **10 minutes**   Cooking time **15 minutes**   *Serves 4*

2 teaspoons hulled sesame seeds
1 1/4 pounds asparagus
1 teaspoon olive oil
1/2 cup minced red onion
1 clove garlic, slivered
1 cup frozen peas
Salt to taste

1 Toast sesame seeds in small, heavy skillet over low heat, stirring frequently until golden brown, about 3 minutes. Transfer to plate to prevent further cooking.

2 Cut asparagus on diagonal into 2-inch lengths. Spray large nonstick skillet with nonstick cooking spray. Add oil and heat over medium heat. Add onion and garlic, and cook, stirring, until onion is tender, about 5 minutes.

3 Add asparagus, peas, and salt to pan and cook, stirring frequently, until asparagus are crisp-tender and peas are heated through, about 5 minutes.

4 Sprinkle sesame seeds over asparagus and peas and toss to combine.

(Some More Ideas)

Sesame vegetable pasta: To serve four, cook 12 ounces pasta (try penne) and toss with the vegetables as prepared above. Add a dollop of fat-free sour cream and serve.

• Serve with roast turkey breast and steamed brown rice and a dessert of nonfat frozen yogurt with slices of crystallized ginger in the mix.

Health Points

• One of the many phyto-chemicals in asparagus is rutin, an antioxidant flavonoid that works hand-in-hand with vitamin C to maintain blood-vessel health.

Each serving provides

Key Nutrients 90 Calories, 20 Calories from Fat, 3g Fat, 0g Saturated Fat, 0g Trans Fat, 6g Protein, 14g Carb, 5g Fiber, 45mg Sodium
Blood Pressure Nutrients 27mg Vitamin C, 37mg Magnesium, 475mg Potassium, 48mg Calcium

Balsamic Baked Tomatoes with Parmesan Crumbs

The complex flavor of balsamic vinegar is the result of its being aged in a succession of barrels, each made from a different kind of wood. This fruity vinegar is the perfect complement to a hearty cheese, like Parmesan, and firm, deep-red tomatoes.

Preparation time **5 minutes**   Cooking time **25 minutes**   *Serves 8*

Tomatoes

4 large tomatoes (8 ounces each)

Salt to taste

2 slices whole-grain bread (2 ounces)

3 tablespoons Parmesan cheese

1 teaspoon olive oil

Glaze

1/3 cup balsamic vinegar

2 tablespoons light brown sugar

2 tablespoons water

1 Preheat the oven to 400°F. Core tomatoes and cut in half horizontally. Place tomatoes, cut-side up, in ceramic or glass baking dish large enough to hold them in a single layer. Sprinkle tomato halves with salt.

2 Place bread in food processor and pulse to fine crumbs. Combine crumbs, Parmesan, and oil in small bowl. Sprinkle tomatoes with crumb mixture.

3 Bake, uncovered, until topping is just beginning to brown and tomatoes are heated through, about 25 minutes.

4 Meanwhile, combine vinegar, brown sugar, and water in small skillet. Bring to a boil over high heat and cook until syrupy, about 3 minutes. Drizzle glaze over baked tomatoes.

(Some More Ideas)

• Use the balsamic vinegar glaze to drizzle over cooked fish such as grilled salmon.

• Parmesan is a flavor-packed cheese that holds up next to other strong flavors. To get the most out of the least amount of cheese, buy a chunk and grate it yourself. Pre-grated cheeses are never as robust.

Health Points

• To keep the saturated-fat levels in this dish low, the proportions of a typical cheese and crumb topping are shifted from mostly cheese to mostly bread crumbs.

photo, page 199

Each serving provides

Key Nutrients 60 Calories, 15 Calories from Fat, 2g Fat, 0g Saturated Fat, 0g Trans Fat, 2g Protein, 12g Carb, 1g Fiber, 60mg Sodium
Blood Pressure Nutrients 17mg Vitamin C, 14mg Magnesium, 237mg Potassium, 28mg Calcium

VEGETABLE SIDES

Lemony Sugar Snap Peas

The very essence of early summer, emerald-green sugar snaps are so tender you can eat them up—pods and all. No fussy sauces or flourishes are needed—just delicate flavorings like these.

Preparation time **10 minutes**   Cooking time **10 minutes**   *Serves 4*

1 1/2 pounds sugar snap peas
2 teaspoons olive oil
3 shallots, thinly sliced
1 clove garlic, minced
1 tablespoon grated lemon zest
Salt to taste

1 Remove strings from both sides of sugar snap peas. Heat oil in large nonstick skillet over medium heat. Add shallots and garlic and cook, stirring, until shallots are softened, about 3 minutes.

2 Add sugar snaps, lemon zest, and salt to skillet and cook, stirring, until peas are just tender, about 4 minutes.

(Some More Ideas)

• You can grate the lemon zest for this recipe on a box grater, but for a more attractive presentation, try making tendrils of lemon zest. To do this, use either a zester or a vegetable peeler. Remove wide strips of lemon zest with the peeler; then, with a paring knife, cut the strips into very fine slivers.

• For a simple, heart-smart meal, serve the sugar snaps with grilled chicken and steamed new potatoes—another early summer delicacy.

Health Points

• Sugar snap peas and other edible podded peas (such as snow peas) supply three times as much vitamin C as shelled peas. To get the most vitamin C, eat the peas raw or cook them briefly, as in this recipe.

Each serving provides

Key Nutrients 130 Calories, 20 Calories from Fat, 3g Fat, 0g Saturated Fat, 0g Trans Fat, 4g Protein, 14g Carb, 4g Fiber, 20mg Sodium
Blood Pressure Nutrients 12mg Vitamin C, 2mg Magnesium, 30mg Potassium, 86mg Calcium

Balsamic Baked Tomatoes with Parmesan Crumbs *p197*

Lemony Sugar Snap Peas *p198*

Roasted Cauliflower with Parmesan and Almonds *p201*

Curried Mushrooms, Peas, and Potatoes *p200*

Curried Mushrooms, Peas, and Potatoes

India's vegetarian cooks turn humble ingredients like potatoes, peas, lentils, and rice into amazingly flavorful, utterly satisfying meals; the secret's in the tantalizing medley of spices.

Preparation time **15 minutes**   Cooking time **30 minutes**   *Serves 4*

1 small onion, cut into chunks

3 cloves garlic, peeled

2 tablespoons sliced fresh ginger

3 tablespoons plus 1 cup water

2 teaspoons olive oil

8 ounces fresh shiitake mushrooms, stems discarded and caps quartered

2 teaspoons curry powder, preferably Madras

12 ounces small red-skinned potatoes, cut into wedges

Salt to taste

1 cup frozen peas

1/2 cup plain low-fat yogurt

1 Combine onion, garlic, ginger, and 3 tablespoons water in blender and puree.

2 Heat oil in large nonstick skillet over medium heat. Add onion puree and cook until liquid has evaporated, about 5 minutes. Add mushrooms to skillet and cook, stirring frequently, until firm-tender, about 3 minutes.

3 Stir in curry powder. Add potatoes and salt to skillet and stir until potatoes are well coated. Add remaining 1 cup water and bring to a boil. Reduce to a simmer, cover, and cook until potatoes are tender, about 15 minutes.

4 Stir in peas and cook until heated through, about 2 minutes. Remove from heat and stir in yogurt.

(Some More Ideas)

• If you cannot find shiitake mushrooms, then white button mushrooms are also fine. Button mushrooms are more mild flavored; shiitake mushrooms have a slightly peppery finish.

• In the summer, use fresh versus frozen peas. Keep peas in the shell in the refrigerator so that their sugar content doesn't turn to starch.

Health Points

• Peas are an excellent source of carbohydrates and nutrients. They are high in fiber, and are a good source of potassium. Make canned peas your last choice, since they are higher in sodium and lower in nutrients than either frozen or fresh.

• Shiitake mushrooms contain an immune-boosting compound called lentinan, which may help to lower blood pressure.

photo, page 199

Each serving provides

Key Nutrients 180 Calories, 30 Calories from Fat, 4g Fat, 1g Saturated Fat, 0g Trans Fat, 7g Protein, 34 Carb, 5g Fiber, 210mg Sodium
Blood Pressure Nutrients 27mg Vitamin C, 49mg Magnesium, 674mg Potassium, 91mg Calcium

Roasted Cauliflower with Parmesan and Almonds

Oven-roasting cauliflower at high heat with a crunchy coating of bread crumbs, almonds, and Parmesan notches up this broccoli cousin's appeal. Raisins add sweetness, color, and surprise.

Preparation time **10 minutes**   Cooking time **30 minutes**   *Serves 4*

1 large head cauliflower (about 1 1/2 pounds), cut into florets

1/2 cup raisins

1/3 cup plain dried bread crumbs

2 tablespoons grated Parmesan cheese

1 tablespoon sliced almonds

2 teaspoons olive oil

2 tablespoons fresh lemon juice

1 Preheat oven to 400°F. Cover large roasting pan with foil and spray foil with nonstick cooking spray. Cook cauliflower in steamer set over pan of boiling water until crisp-tender, about 5 minutes. Transfer cauliflower to roasting pan.

2 Meanwhile, stir together raisins, bread crumbs, Parmesan, almonds, and oil in medium bowl.

3 Sprinkle bread-crumb mixture over cauliflower. Roast cauliflower until crumbs are toasted, about 20 minutes. Drizzle lemon juice on top and roast 5 minutes longer. Serve hot or at room temperature.

(Some More Ideas)

• Store-bought bread crumbs are made from white bread, but you can make a more healthful, fiber-rich version with whole-grain bread. Place slices of bread on a baking sheet and bake them in an oven at 300°F until they are completely dried out, but not browned. Let the toasts cool, then process them to fine crumbs in a food processor or blender.

• Use golden raisins in place of the dark raisins.

• Use the crumb mixture to top cooked carrots.

Health Points

• Cauliflower is an excellent source of folate, vitamin C, and potassium. All three nutrients play a role in the prevention of heart disease and help improve high blood pressure.

• Since cauliflower loses more of its B vitamins (including folate) when cooked in water, we precook the florets by steaming rather than boiling.

photo, page 199

Each serving provides

Key Nutrients 170 Calories, 40 Calories from Fat, 5g Fat, 1g Saturated Fat, 0g Trans Fat, 6g Protein, 32g Carb, 5g Fiber, 130mg Sodium
Blood Pressure Nutrients 117mg Vitamin C, 41mg Magnesium, 581mg Potassium, 91mg Calcium

Tex-Mex Corn Pudding

Something like a soufflé, only easier to make and far more flavorful and colorful, this zesty side dish really jazzes up a simple meal—Texas style!

Preparation time **10 minutes**   Cooking time **50 minutes**   *Serves 6*

1/4 cup fat-free dry milk
2 tablespoons flour
1 cup low-fat (1%) milk
1/2 cup diced red bell pepper
1 tablespoon chili powder
2 teaspoons sugar
Salt to taste
1/2 teaspoon cumin
1 large egg plus 1 large egg white
3 cups frozen corn kernels, thawed
3 scallions, thinly sliced

1 Preheat oven to 375°F. Stir dry milk and flour together in medium saucepan. Whisk in low-fat milk. Bring to a simmer over medium heat. Add bell pepper, chili powder, sugar, salt, and cumin and cook, stirring constantly, until thick enough to coat back of a spoon, about 5 minutes.

2 Lightly beat whole egg and egg white in small bowl. Whisk about 1/2 cup of hot sauce into eggs to warm them.

3 Remove saucepan from heat and stir in warmed egg mixture. Stir in 2 cups of corn and scallions. Puree remaining 1 cup corn in food processor and stir into saucepan.

4 Transfer mixture to shallow 5-cup baking dish. Place baking dish in a larger baking dish or roasting pan and set on oven rack. Pour hot water into larger dish to come halfway up sides of smaller dish. Bake until pudding is set and top is light golden, 35–45 minutes.

(Some More Ideas)

• Make this dish even hotter in flavor by adding 1 diced jalapeño pepper to the batter. Canned jalapeños may be milder than fresh because they're seeded and packed in liquid, but they still have heat to them.

• Serve this dish with grilled turkey burgers and roasted asparagus.

Health Points

• Rather than using several whole eggs, the recipe calls for one egg and one egg white—a trick that knocks out 5 grams fat and 200mg cholesterol.

• Adding fat-free dry milk to low-fat milk adds about 50mg calcium.

Each serving provides

Key Nutrients 130 Calories, 20 Calories from Fat, 2 Fat, 1g Saturated Fat, 0g Trans Fat, 7g Protein, 22g Carb, 3g Fiber, 115mg Sodium
Blood Pressure Nutrients 27mg Vitamin C, 16mg Magnesium, 177mg Potassium, 104mg Calcium

Squash and Eggplant Casserole

This colorful vegetable casserole is transformed into a feast for the eye and palate with a fresh and punchy mixture of parsley, garlic, lemon zest, and toasted almonds, and then simply served with fluffy Parmesan polenta.

Preparation time **about 20 minutes**   Cooking time **about 45 minutes**   *Serves 4*

Vegetables

1 tablespoon olive oil

1 large onion, cut into 8 wedges

12 baby corn

1 small or 1/2 large butternut squash, peeled, quartered lengthwise, seeded, and cut across into 1-inch slices

1 eggplant, halved lengthwise and cut across into 1-inch slices

1 red bell pepper, seeded and cut into 1/2-inch pieces

1/2 cup dry white wine

2 cups reduced-sodium vegetable broth

Salt and pepper

Topping

2 tablespoons slivered almonds

1 garlic clove, finely chopped

Finely shredded or coarsely grated zest of 1 lemon

5 tablespoons chopped parsley

Polenta

1 cup instant polenta

1/4 cup freshly grated Parmesan cheese

2 tablespoons chopped fresh oregano

1 Heat the oil in a flameproof casserole. Add the onion wedges and baby corn and sauté over a medium heat for 5 minutes, stirring occasionally. Preheat the oven to 350°F.

2 Add the slices of butternut squash to the casserole, toss them in the oil, and then stir in the eggplant and red pepper. Cover and leave the vegetables to cook over a low to medium heat, turning them twice, until they are lightly tinged golden brown, about 10 minutes. Pour in the wine, let it sizzle, and then stir in the broth. Bring to a boil and add seasoning to taste. Cover the casserole and cook in the oven for 30 minutes.

3 Meanwhile, make the topping. Preheat the grill to high. Spread the slivered almonds on a baking tray and toast under the grill until they are lightly browned. Watch them closely and shake the tray occasionally to ensure the nuts are evenly toasted. Place in a small bowl and mix in the remaining topping ingredients.

4 To prepare the polenta, bring 3 cups water to a boil in a large saucepan over a high heat. Gradually whisk in the polenta and continue whisking until the polenta absorbs all the liquid. Reduce the heat to medium and cook, stirring, until the polenta is thick, 5–10 minutes. Beat in the Parmesan cheese and oregano with seasoning to taste.

5 To serve, spoon the polenta onto plates or into large individual bowls. Ladle the vegetable casserole on top and sprinkle with the topping.

(Some More Ideas)

• Serve the casserole with potato and carrot puree instead of polenta. Cook 1 pound potatoes with 1/2 pound sliced carrots in boiling water until tender, then drain well and mash with 5 tablespoons fat-free milk. Stir in 1 ounce grated reduced-fat cheddar cheese and 2–4 tablespoons chopped parsley.

• Pearl barley is another delicious alternative to polenta. It can be cooked in the oven with the vegetable casserole. Put 1 cup rinsed pearl barley in a casserole with 1 chopped onion and 1 teaspoon dried sage. Pour in 2 cups hot vegetable broth, cover, and cook in the oven at 350°F until the broth is absorbed and the barley is tender, 45–50 minutes.

Health Points

• Butternut squash is a powerful source of beta-carotene, with one cup providing 96% of the recommended daily allowance. The body converts beta-carotene into vitamin A.

photo, page 205

Each serving provides

Key Nutrients 420 Calories, 80 Calories from Fat, 9g Fat, 2g Saturated Fat, 0g Trans Fat, 12g Protein, 73g Carb, 15g Fiber, 250mg Sodium
Blood Pressure Nutrients 100mg Vitamin C, 87mg Magnesium, 920mg Potassium, 217mg Calcium

Corn Fritters

In this recipe, crisp, juicy corn kernels are added to a thick batter flavored with fresh cilantro, and then pan-sautéed in big spoonfuls. Piled on a bed of watercress and drizzled with a yogurt sauce, the fritters make a delicious quick meal.

Preparation and cooking time **30 minutes**   *Serves 4 (makes 12 fritters)*

Fritters

1/2 cup flour
1/2 teaspoon baking powder
1/2 cup fat-free milk
2 large eggs, lightly beaten
1 package (10 ounces) frozen corn kernels, thawed and drained
3 scallions, finely chopped
1 fresh red chile, seeded and finely chopped
3 heaped tablespoons chopped fresh cilantro
1 tablespoon canola oil
1 cup watercress
Salt and pepper to taste

Sauce

1 cup plain low-fat yogurt
4 scallions, finely chopped
2 tablespoons chopped fresh mint
Grated zest and juice of 1 lime

1 First make the yogurt sauce. Put the yogurt into a serving bowl and stir in the scallions, mint, lime zest, and a pinch of salt. Cover and refrigerate while you make the fritters (keep the lime juice for use later).

2 Sift the flour and baking powder into a bowl. Make a well in the center and add the milk and eggs. Using a wooden spoon, mix together the milk and eggs, then gradually draw in the flour from around the edges. Beat with the spoon to make a smooth, thick batter. Alternatively, the batter can be made in a food processor: Put the milk and egg in the container first, spoon the flour and baking powder on top, and process for a few seconds to blend.

3 Add the corn kernels, scallions, chile, and cilantro to the batter, and season with salt and pepper to taste. Mix well.

4 Heat a griddle or large, heavy skillet then brush with a little of the oil. Drop large spoonfuls of the fritter batter onto the pan—make about 4 fritters at a time—and cook over a moderate heat until golden and firm on the underside, about 2 minutes.

5 Turn the fritters over, using a spatula, and cook on the other side until golden brown, about 2 minutes. Remove the fritters from the pan and drain on kitchen paper. Keep warm while cooking the rest of the fritters in the same way, adding more oil to the pan as necessary.

6 Arrange the watercress on 4 plates and sprinkle with the lime juice. Arrange the corn fritters on top and serve hot, with the yogurt sauce to be drizzled over.

(Some More Ideas)

• Instead of chile and cilantro, flavor the batter with 2 teaspoons green Thai curry paste.

Pea fritters: Replace the corn with frozen peas. Use chopped fresh basil in place of cilantro.

Health Points

• Corn is a good source of fiber as well as vitamins A and C and folate. It is generally a popular food with children, and this recipe makes a healthy dish they are sure to love.

• Watercress, like other dark green, leafy vegetables, contains folate, a B vitamin, which recent research suggests may help to protect the body against heart disease and prevent Alzheimer's disease.

Each serving (3 fritters) provides

Key Nutrients 250 Calories, 70 Calories from Fat, 8g Fat, 2g Saturated Fat, 0g Trans Fat, 12g Protein, 38g Carb, 4g Fiber, 280mg Sodium
Blood Pressure Nutrients 49mg Vitamin C, 48mg Magnesium, 615mg Potassium, 241mg Calcium

Corn Fritters *p204*

Squash and Eggplant Casserole *p203*

Boston Baked Beans *p207*

Sweet-and-Sour Cabbage *p206*

Sweet-and-Sour Cabbage

Cabbage goes from plain-Jane to party-pretty in this four-vegetable toss. Carrots, bell pepper, and red onion—all nutritional superstars in their own right—join in to brighten this variation on a tangy traditional German-style side dish.

Preparation time **15 minutes**   Cooking time **25 minutes**   *Serves 4*

2 teaspoons olive oil

1 large red onion, cut into small chunks

2 carrots, cut into matchsticks

1 red bell pepper, cut into small chunks

6 cups thickly shredded green cabbage (1 small head)

2 tablespoons packed light brown sugar

Salt to taste

1/4 teaspoon rubbed sage

1/4 teaspoon black pepper

1/4 cup cider or rice vinegar

1 Heat oil in large nonstick skillet over medium heat. Add onion and cook until soft, about 5 minutes. Add carrots and bell pepper, and cook, stirring frequently, until crisp-tender, about 5 minutes.

2 Stir in cabbage. Sprinkle brown sugar, salt, sage, and black pepper over cabbage, and cook, stirring frequently, until cabbage is wilted, about 10 minutes.

3 Add vinegar, increase heat to medium-high, and cook until cabbage is well coated, about 3 minutes. Serve warm or at room temperature.

(Some More Ideas)

• Red cabbage can be used as a colorful substitute for green cabbage in this recipe. Add 5 more minutes to the cooking time. The texture of red cabbage may be a little tougher than green, but it has more vitamin C, so it's a wise choice to make.

• In place of rubbed sage, try using dried thyme.

• Serve this cabbage dish over cooked brown rice and add sautéed tofu cubes for a vegetarian meal.

Health Points

• This dish is a bevy of nutrients! Immunity-boosting vitamin C supplied by the pepper and the cabbage, beta-carotene donated by the carrots, and the blood-pressure-lowering benefits of onions make this dish superbly nutritious!

photo, page 205

Each serving provides

Key Nutrients 110 Calories, 25 Calories from Fat, 3g Fat, 0g Saturated Fat, 0g Trans Fat, 3g Protein, 22g Carb, 5g Fiber, 35mg Sodium
Blood Pressure Nutrients 96mg Vitamin C, 33mg Magnesium, 509mg Potassium, 76mg Calcium

Boston Baked Beans

Baked beans aren't just popular in Boston—they're big in Sweden as well! It could be because beans are perfect cold-weather food, or it could be that this rich, sweet contemporary version and others like it are sweeping the globe.

Preparation time **15 minutes plus soaking**   Cooking time **2 hours**   *Serves 8*

1 1/2 cups dried navy beans, rinsed, drained, and picked over

Salt to taste

2 slices reduced-sodium turkey bacon, cut crosswise in half

1 large onion, chopped

1/4 cup packed light brown sugar

1/4 cup reduced-sodium chili sauce or ketchup

1/4 cup light molasses

1 tablespoon dry mustard

1/4 teaspoon black pepper

1 Bring beans and water to cover by 2 inches to a boil in large saucepan; cook 3 minutes. Remove from heat, cover, and let stand 1 hour. Drain beans and rinse with cold water. Return to saucepan.

2 Pour in enough fresh water to cover beans by 2 inches. Add a pinch of salt and bring to a boil over high heat. Reduce heat to medium-low. Cover and cook until beans are tender, about 1 1/2 hours, adding hot water, if necessary, to keep beans covered by 2 inches. Drain beans, reserving 1 1/2 cups cooking liquid. Transfer beans and liquid to 2-quart casserole.

3 Meanwhile, preheat oven to 300°F. Coat medium nonstick skillet with nonstick cooking spray and set over medium-high heat. Cook bacon until crisp. Transfer with slotted spoon to paper towels to drain; crumble. Sauté onion in pan drippings until soft, about 5 minutes. Transfer to casserole.

4 Stir brown sugar, chili sauce, molasses, dry mustard, pepper, and half of bacon into beans. Sprinkle remaining bacon on top. Cover and bake until hot and bubbling, about 30 minutes, stirring once.

(Some More Ideas)

• Serve this side dish with barbecued chicken, mixed vegetables, and a salad with an olive oil vinaigrette.

Health Points

• By flavoring with just a pinch of salt and using low-sodium ketchup or chili sauce, this dish is far lower in sodium than the usual baked beans, making it perfectly appropriate for people with high blood pressure. And by using turkey bacon for the meat instead of salt pork or bacon, you substantially cut the calories.

• All dried beans require soaking—either quick soaking (for an hour) or long soaking (for at least 6 hours). Longer soaking time helps eliminate more of their gas-producing sugars, cutting down on flatulence.

photo, page 205

Each serving provides

Key Nutrients 210 Calories, 10 Calories from Fat, 2g Fat, 0g Saturated Fat, 0g Trans Fat, 10g Protein, 42g Carb, 10g Fiber, 35mg Sodium
Blood Pressure Nutrients 4mg Vitamin C, 73mg Magnesium, 708mg Potassium, 107mg Calcium

Black-Eyed Peas with Sweet Peppers

In the South, black-eyed peas are said to bring their eaters good luck. Turkey bacon adds a smoky meat flavor to this traditional New Year's Day "must have" dish.

Preparation time **15 minutes**   Cooking time **40 minutes**   *Serves 6*

2 teaspoons olive oil

3 strips low-sodium turkey bacon, thinly sliced crosswise

1 medium onion, finely chopped

2 mixed bell peppers (red, yellow, green, or orange), cut into 1/2-inch squares

2 cloves garlic, minced

1 package (10 ounces) frozen black-eyed peas

1/3 cup long-grain white rice

Salt to taste

1/2 teaspoon black pepper

1 cup water

1 1/2 tablespoons red wine vinegar

1 teaspoon hot red pepper sauce

1 Heat oil in nonstick Dutch oven over medium heat. Add bacon and cook until crisp, about 5 minutes.

2 Add onion and cook, stirring frequently, until tender, about 5 minutes. Add bell peppers and garlic, and cook, stirring frequently, until peppers are crisp-tender, about 4 minutes.

3 Stir in black-eyed peas, rice, salt, black pepper, and water, and bring to a boil. Reduce to a simmer, cover, and cook until beans and rice are tender, about 20 minutes. Stir in vinegar and hot sauce.

(Some More Ideas)

• For more fiber, substitute brown rice for the white rice.

• For a fun meal, serve this with lean turkey burgers and a mixed salad, with sliced strawberries for dessert.

Health Points

• Black-eyed peas provide both soluble and insoluble fiber, and are high in potassium, iron, thiamine, folate, and some protein. Even purchasing them frozen does not compromise their outstanding nutritional value.

Key Nutrients 120 Calories, 20 Calories from Fat, 3g Fat, 0g Saturated Fat, 0g Trans Fat, 3g Protein, 21g Carb, 4g Fiber, 65mg Sodium
Blood Pressure Nutrients 59mg Vitamin C, 31mg Magnesium, 317mg Potassium, 71mg Calcium

Vegetable Stir-Fry with Spicy Garlic Sauce

This lively stir-fry will rekindle your love of vegetables. Crisp broccoli, bright red peppers, and tender baby corn are tossed with tantalizing Asian seasonings for a speedy and exotic side dish.

Preparation time **15 minutes**   Cooking time **14 minutes**   *Serves 4*

Sauce

1 1/2 cups reduced-sodium chicken broth

2 tablespoons light soy sauce, or to taste

2 tablespoons cornstarch

1/2 teaspoon Thai chili paste *(optional)*

1 garlic cloves

1 1/2 teaspoons peanut or vegetable oil

3 tablespoons minced peeled fresh ginger

Vegetables

2 cups broccoli florets

1 can (15 ounces) baby corn, drained

1 large red bell pepper, cut into thin strips

1 can (8 ounces) sliced water chestnuts, drained

1 tablespoon sesame seeds, toasted *(garnish)*

1 Combine 1/4 cup broth, soy sauce, cornstarch, and chili paste (if using) in small bowl until smooth. Set aside. Crush garlic cloves by smashing with side of chef's knife and remove peels.

2 Coat large nonstick wok or deep skillet with nonstick cooking spray. Add oil and set wok over high heat until hot but not smoking. Stir-fry ginger and garlic until fragrant, about 1 minute. Remove with slotted spoon and set aside.

3 Add broccoli to wok and stir-fry just until it begins to soften, about 4 minutes. Transfer to bowl. Add corn, red pepper, and water chestnuts; stir-fry just until they begin to soften, about 3 minutes. Return broccoli to wok and add remaining broth.

4 Cover and cook until vegetables are crisp-tender, about 3 minutes. Whisk cornstarch mixture again and add to wok with ginger and garlic. Stir-fry just until sauce thickens and boils, about 1 minute. Sprinkle with sesame seeds.

(Some More Ideas)

• For a full meal, add cubes of extra-firm tofu. Add 1 pound cubed tofu to the beginning of Step 3 before the broccoli. Stir-fry the cubes until lightly browned, about 3–4 minutes, and then remove and set aside. Add the tofu back to the wok after the sauce is added in Step 4 and toss gently to coat the tofu with sauce.

• Use 2-inch pieces of asparagus in place of the broccoli.

Health Points

• Stir-frying remains one of the simplest and healthiest ways to cook. Use a wok whenever you can; its small cooking base and wide sides allow you to conserve on the amount of oil needed. And the fast, high heat helps preserve the food's nutrients, crunch, and color.

• You'll never need table salt to provide flavor in stir-fries. Flavorful ingredients such as garlic, ginger, and light soy sauce will provide the taste without the grams of sodium.

photo, page 211

Each serving provides

Key Nutrients 250 Calories, 45 Calories from Fat, 5g Fat, 1g Saturated Fat, 0g Trans Fat, 8g Protein, 50g Carb, 7g Fiber, 80mg Sodium
Blood Pressure Nutrients 120mg Vitamin C, 62mg Magnesium, 806mg Potassium, 44mg Calcium

Spicy Red Cabbage Dumplings

In this updated version of stuffed cabbage, mellow-flavored red cabbage leaves are filled with a hearty mixture of turkey, lentils, rice, and cashews and baked in a simple tomato sauce.

Preparation time **40 minutes**   Cooking time **30 minutes**   *Serves 4*

1/2 cup long-grain rice
1 cup water
8 large red cabbage leaves
1 tablespoon canola oil
1 onion, finely chopped
1 1/2 teaspoons cumin seeds
1 teaspoon ground coriander
1 teaspoon ground cinnamon
3 tablespoons mango chutney, divided
1/4 cup unsalted cashew nuts, coarsely chopped
1 can (15 ounces) lentils, drained
1/2 pound cooked turkey or chicken, without skin, diced
4 tablespoons chopped parsley
1 cup low-sodium tomato juice
Salt and pepper
Sprigs of fresh parsley *(garnish)*

1 Place the rice in a small saucepan. Pour in water and bring to a boil. Stir once, then reduce the heat to low and cover the pan. Cook for 15 minutes. Remove from the heat and leave the rice to stand, without removing the lid, for 10 minutes.

2 Meanwhile, preheat the oven to 400°F. Trim off the tough stalk from the base of each cabbage leaf. Bring a large saucepan of water to the boil. Add half the leaves, bring back to the boil, and blanch for 30 seconds. Use a draining spoon to remove the leaves from the pan and plunge them into a large bowl of cold water to stop them cooking. Repeat with the remaining leaves. Drain the leaves well and leave to dry, spread out on a clean towel.

3 Heat the oil in a large pan and sauté the onion until softened, about 2–3 minutes. Add the cumin seeds and ground coriander and cinnamon, and cook for a further 2–3 minutes. Remove from the heat.

4 Add 2 tablespoons of the mango chutney to the onion mixture together with the cashews, lentils, turkey or chicken, parsley, and seasoning to taste, and mix well. Stir in the rice until thoroughly combined.

5 Lay a cabbage leaf flat on the work surface, with the stalk end toward you. Place some of the rice mixture on the leaf. Fold the base of the leaf over the filling, then fold in the sides and roll up the leaf to enclose the filling in a neat package. Repeat with the remaining leaves and filling.

6 Mix the remaining 1 tablespoon of mango chutney with the tomato juice and seasoning to taste. Pour about one-quarter of this sauce into a large ovenproof dish. Pack the cabbage dumplings into the dish and pour the rest of the sauce over them. Cover loosely with foil and bake until the leaves are tender, about 30 minutes. Garnish with parsley.

(Some More Ideas)

Chinese-style cabbage dumplings: Use blanched bok choy leaves instead of the red cabbage, and replace the lentils with 1 cup sliced canned baby corn. Add 1 tablespoon finely chopped fresh ginger and 1 large garlic clove, crushed, to the onion. Use plum sauce instead of mango chutney and add 1 ounce toasted sesame seeds to the rice mixture.

• Experiment with different types of rice. Try basmati rice for its delicate flavor, or a mixture of wild rice and white rice. For more fiber, use brown rice, but remember that it requires longer to cook than white rice, so follow the package instructions.

• Cooked lean roast pork or beef can be used instead of the turkey or chicken.

Health Points

• Low in fat and high in protein and fiber, lentils are also particularly rich in folate, with just 1/2 cup providing almost 50% of the recommended daily allowance.

Each serving (2 dumplings) provides

Key Nutrients 410 Calories, 90 Calories from Fat, 10g Fat, 2g Saturated Fat, 0g Trans Fat, 28g Protein, 56g Carb, 12g Fiber, 60mg Sodium
Blood Pressure Nutrients 49mg Vitamin C, 134mg Magnesium, 998mg Potassium, 97mg Calcium

Vegetable Stir-Fry with Spicy Garlic Sauce *p209*

Spicy Red Cabbage Dumplings *p210*

Stuffed Baked Potatoes *p214*

Indian-Style Okra with Potatoes *p212*

VEGETABLE SIDES

Indian-Style Okra with Potatoes

This makes a wonderful accompaniment to a spicy main dish. It is also good as a vegetarian main course for two, especially when served with Indian-style lentil dishes and warm naan bread.

Preparation time **15 minutes**   Cooking time **35–40 minutes**   *Serves 4*

1 large onion, quartered

4 garlic cloves

2-inch piece fresh ginger, peeled

2 tablespoons canola oil

1 fresh red or green chile, seeded and finely chopped

1 teaspoon black mustard seeds

2 teaspoons ground coriander

1 teaspoon ground cumin

1 teaspoon turmeric

2 cups reduced-sodium vegetable broth

1 can (14 ounces) no-salt-added chopped tomatoes

1/2 pound fresh okra, trimmed and sliced

1 pound baking potatoes, peeled and cut into large chunks

1 red, green, or yellow bell pepper, seeded and cut into chunks

4 tablespoons raisins

3 tablespoons chopped fresh cilantro

Salt and pepper to taste

Chopped fresh cilantro *(garnish)*

1 Put the onion, peeled garlic and ginger in a food processor or blender and puree. Alternatively, finely chop the ingredients and mix well together. Heat the oil in a saucepan. Add the onion puree and the chile, and sauté over a low heat until the mixture is beginning to turn golden brown in places, 6–7 minutes.

2 Add the mustard seeds, ground coriander, cumin, and turmeric, and stir to form a paste. Gradually pour in the broth and tomatoes with their juice, stirring well. Bring to a boil, then reduce the heat and cover the pan. Simmer over a low heat for 10 minutes or until the spices are cooked and their flavors blended.

3 Add the okra, potatoes, pepper, raisins, and seasoning to taste. Stir well, then cover again and simmer over a low heat until the potatoes are tender, 15–20 minutes.

4 Stir in the chopped cilantro and serve at once, sprinkled with extra cilantro to garnish.

(Some More Ideas)

• If you are serving this as a vegetarian main dish, plain or spiced basmati rice tossed with chopped almonds or cashews is a tasty pairing.

Health Points

• In addition to the delicious spiciness it brings to the dish, ginger also aids digestion.

• Chile peppers are a good source of vitamin C. Also, red chile peppers contain more beta-carotene than their hot green counterparts.

photo, page 211

Each serving provides

Key Nutrients 300 Calories, 70 Calories from Fat, 8g Fat, 1g Saturated Fat, 0g Trans Fat, 7g Protein, 54g Carb, 9g Fiber, 290mg Sodium
Blood Pressure Nutrients 126mg Vitamin C, 81mg Magnesium, 906mg Potassium, 122mg Calcium

Braised Cabbage, Apple, and Caraway

For versatility, it's hard to beat cabbage. It can be braised, steamed, boiled, or eaten raw in salads. In this recipe, caraway seeds offer pungency, and walnuts add both flavor and crunch.

Preparation time **15 minutes**　　Cooking time **15 minutes**　　*Serves 6*

2 teaspoons vegetable oil
1 small onion, finely chopped
1 teaspoon caraway seeds
1 pound green cabbage, cored and thinly sliced (6 1/2 cups)
1 tablespoon cider vinegar
Salt to taste
2 small crisp red apples such as Gala, Braeburn, or Empire, cored and cut into small cubes
1 teaspoon honey
2 tablespoons chopped walnuts, toasted (optional)

1 Heat oil in large nonstick skillet over medium heat. Add onion and caraway seeds. Sauté until onion is softened, about 5 minutes.

2 Stir in cabbage, vinegar, and salt. Cover. Cook just until cabbage wilts, about 4 minutes. Uncover. Increase heat to high. Add apples and honey. Cook, stirring frequently, until apples are crisp-tender and most of liquid cooks off, 4–6 minutes. Transfer to serving plate. Top with walnuts, if desired, and serve.

(Some More Ideas)

• Substitute red cabbage for the green. It is similar in texture, but sweeter. Generally, red cabbage needs to cook longer than green. Combine red cabbage with acidic ingredients such as orange if you want it to keep its color.

• Pears such as Bosc or Bartlett will also work well in this dish. Use 2 small pears, cored and cut into small cubes, instead of the apples.

Health Points

• Cabbage is nutritionally excellent for battling high blood pressure, given its levels of vitamin C and fiber, but it is even richer in bioflavonoids and other phytochemicals believed to prevent cancer.

• Caraway is part of the carrot family, and contains a phytochemical called limonene that may prevent cancer.

Each serving provides

Key Nutrients 80 Calories, 30 Calories from Fat, 4g Fat, 0g Saturated Fat, 0g Trans Fat, 2g Protein, 12g Carb, 3g Fiber, 15mg Sodium
Blood Pressure Nutrients 27mg Vitamin C, 21mg Magnesium, 266mg Potassium, 45mg Calcium

Stuffed Baked Potatoes

A steaming-hot baked potato makes perfect comfort food. This tasty vegetarian filling combines marinated mushrooms and zucchini, and there are two more satisfying fillings to choose from; tuna and corn, and roasted garlic and tomato.

Preparation time **15–20 minutes**   Cooking time **1 1/4 hours**   *Serves 4*

4 medium baking potatoes
2 tablespoons olive oil
1/2 pound small mushrooms, stems trimmed
1 large zucchini, sliced
1 teaspoon red wine vinegar
1 teaspoon Dijon mustard
4 tablespoons chopped parsley
Salt and pepper to taste

1 Preheat the oven to 400°F. Push a metal skewer through each potato or push the potatoes onto a potato roasting rack. (Pushing a metal skewer into the potatoes helps to conduct heat through to their centers so that they cook more quickly.) Place the potatoes directly on the shelf in the oven and bake until they are tender, about 1 1/4 hours.

2 Make the zucchini and mushroom filling when you first put the potatoes in the oven so that it has time to marinate. Alternatively, it can be made just before the potatoes are cooked, and served hot. Heat a large grill pan or skillet. Drizzle half the oil over the pan and cook the mushrooms and zucchini slices until they are well browned in places, softened, and have released their juices, 10–15 minutes.

3 Transfer the vegetables to a bowl with all their juice and add the remaining oil, the vinegar, and mustard. Season to taste, mix well, and leave to marinate until the potatoes are cooked.

4 Split open the baked potatoes, then press gently to part the halves, keeping them joined at the base. Stir the parsley into the marinated vegetables, then pile them into the potatoes. Serve immediately.

(Some More Ideas)

Roasted garlic and cherry tomatoes–filled baked potatoes: Trim the tough stalk off a whole bulb of garlic and wrap it in foil. Bake in the oven with the potatoes for 45 minutes. Cool the garlic slightly, then squeeze the pulp from each clove into a bowl. Add 1 large bunch fresh basil, tough stalks discarded and leaves torn; 1 tablespoon olive oil; and seasoning to taste. Stir in 1 pound cherry tomatoes, quartered. Preheat the grill to a moderate setting. Scoop some flesh out of the potatoes, leaving a thick layer in the shells, and break the flesh up coarsely with a fork. Stir into the tomato mixture, then spoon the filling back into the potato shells and sprinkle with 1/4 cup freshly grated Parmesan cheese. Brown under the grill and serve.

Health Points

• Potatoes are an excellent source of vitamin C when cooked in their skins, as the vitamin is stored just beneath the skin.

photo, page 211

Each serving provides

Key Nutrients 260 Calories, 70 Calories from Fat, 7g Fat, 1g Saturated Fat, 0g Trans Fat, 7g Protein, 42g Carb, 6g Fiber, 50mg Sodium
Blood Pressure Nutrients 36mg Vitamin C, 77mg Magnesium, 1385mg Potassium, 53mg Calcium

Brussels Sprouts and Potatoes with Caraway-Mustard Sauce

Horseradish adds a bold bite to the warm, creamy dressing that brings this delicious combination of Brussels sprouts, red potatoes, celery, scallions, and apples together.

Preparation time **20 minutes**   Cooking time **15 minutes**   *Serves 4*

Vegetables

1/2 pound small red potatoes, quartered

1 container (10 ounces) Brussels sprouts, quartered

1 red apple, cut into 1/2-inch chunks

2 stalks celery, thinly sliced

3 scallions, thinly sliced

Dressing

1/2 cup apple juice

1/3 cup distilled white vinegar

2 tablespoons flour

1 tablespoon spicy brown mustard

1 tablespoon drained white horseradish

1 teaspoon olive oil

1/2 teaspoon caraway seeds

Salt to taste

1 Cook potatoes in large pot of boiling water for 5 minutes. Add Brussels sprouts and cook until firm-tender, about 5–8 minutes. Drain and place in serving bowl along with apple, celery, and scallions.

2 Whisk together apple juice, vinegar, flour, mustard, horseradish, oil, caraway seeds, and salt in small saucepan. Bring to a simmer over medium heat, whisking constantly. Simmer 2 minutes.

3 Pour hot dressing over vegetables and toss to combine. Serve warm or at room temperature.

(Some More Ideas)

• To substitute frozen sprouts, thaw them first, and reduce the cooking time by a minute or two when they're added to the potatoes.

• Use Yukon Gold potatoes in place of red potatoes. Either purchase very small ones or cut larger ones into small cubes.

• Serve this as a side dish to lean roast meat or as a change of pace from light, leafy salads.

Health Points

• A single serving of Brussels sprouts supplies more than a day's requirement of vitamin C. These tiny members of the cabbage family are also good sources of vitamin B6, folate, and potassium—key ingredients for fighting heart disease.

Each serving provides

Key Nutrients 140 Calories, 15 Calories from Fat, 2g Fat, 0g Saturated Fat, 0g Trans Fat, 4g Protein, 29g Carb, 6g Fiber, 100mg Sodium
Blood Pressure Nutrients 78mg Vitamin C, 38mg Magnesium, 716mg Potassium, 60mg Calcium

Avocado Salad with Raspberries

Avocados do contain a great deal of fat, but it is the good, monounsaturated type. In this salad, the creaminess of avocado is complemented by fresh raspberries and a fruity vinaigrette.

Preparation time **about 10 minutes**   *Serves 4*

Salad

2 avocados

4 cups mixed salad greens

1 1/2 cups raspberries

Sprigs of fresh mint *(garnish)*

Vinaigrette

2 tablespoons olive oil

1 1/2 tablespoons raspberry vinegar

1 tablespoon half-and-half

Finely grated zest of 1/2 orange

1/2 teaspoon orange juice

Pinch sugar

Salt and pepper to taste

1 Put all the ingredients for the raspberry vinaigrette in a large salad bowl, adding salt and pepper to taste, and whisk to mix.

2 Halve the avocados and remove the pit, then peel and dice the flesh. Add immediately to the dressing and turn to coat, to prevent the avocados from turning brown.

3 Add the salad leaves to the bowl and toss gently with the avocados. Scatter over the raspberries and garnish with mint sprigs. Serve at once.

(Some More Ideas)

Tropical avocado and mango salad: Line 4 plates with romaine lettuce leaves. Cut each avocado half horizontally into thin slices and arrange on the plates with 1 thinly sliced, large ripe mango. Scatter 3 chopped scallions over the top. Drizzle each salad with 1 tablespoon olive oil and 1–2 tablespoons orange juice, and dust lightly with cayenne pepper.

Italian-style avocado and mozzarella salad: Thickly slice each avocado half horizontally and arrange on 4 plates with 1 (1 ounce) slice mozzarella cheese per person. Sprinkle with 1/4 cup sliced sun-dried tomatoes, then drizzle 1 tablespoon olive oil. Season with pepper and garnish with fresh basil leaves.

Health Points

• Avocados help to lower levels of LDL ("bad") cholesterol while raising levels of HDL ("good") cholesterol. One avocado provides half the recommended daily intake of vitamin B6.

Each serving provides

Key Nutrients 110 Calories, 70 Calories from Fat, 8g Fat, 1g Saturated Fat, 0g Trans Fat, 1g Protein, 10g Carb, 4g Fiber, 90mg Sodium
Blood Pressure Nutrients 21mg Vitamin C, 22mg Magnesium, 252mg Potassium, 45mg Calcium

Avocado Salad with Raspberries *p216*

Hot Cabbage and Grape Coleslaw *p218*

Oriental Sprouted Salad *p219*

Crunchy Nut Coleslaw *p220*

Hot Cabbage and Grape Coleslaw

Crunchy, lightly cooked white cabbage is perfectly complemented by juicy fruit, walnuts, and herbs in this well-balanced salad. It is a good example of how a combination of familiar ingredients can be elevated into a sophisticated side dish.

Preparation time **about 25 minutes**   Cooking time **7–8 minutes**   *Serves 4*

4 cups mixed salad leaves

3 tablespoons chopped fresh herbs, preferably chives, tarragon, and parsley

1 tablespoon walnut oil

2 teaspoons olive oil, divided

1/2 medium celeriac

1 tablespoon lemon juice

1 Asian pear

5 shallots, chopped

1/2 head medium green cabbage, finely shredded

4 tablespoons red wine vinegar

1/4 pound seedless green grapes, halved

1/4 pound seedless red grapes, halved

1/4 cup walnut pieces

Salt and pepper

1 Combine the salad leaves with the herbs in a bowl. Add the walnut oil and 1 teaspoon of the olive oil and toss well. Arrange the dressed leaves on a serving platter or plates.

2 Peel the celeriac and cut it into matchstick strips. Toss with the lemon juice. Core the Asian pear and cut it into similar-sized strips. Toss with the celeriac and lemon juice, then scatter the celeriac and pear over the salad leaves.

3 Heat the remaining 1 teaspoon of olive oil in a large skillet. Add the shallots and cook, stirring from time to time until lightly browned, about 4–5 minutes. Add the cabbage and toss for 1 minute, then pour in the vinegar and boil until the vinegar has reduced by about half, about 1 minute. Add seasoning to taste and remove from the heat.

4 Add the green and red grapes and walnuts to the hot cabbage salad. Spoon the cabbage salad and its juices onto the dressed leaves, celeriac, and pear, and serve immediately.

(Some More Ideas)

• Use a firm, ripe dessert pear instead of the Asian pear. In the summer, Bartlett are the pears to choose.

• For a main dish, add 1/2 pound cooked cubed chicken breast with the cabbage. Serve with bread or potatoes. For a simple but delicious lunch or supper, serve the salad with baked potatoes.

Health Points

• Cabbage belongs to a family of vegetables that contain a number of different phyto-chemicals that may help to protect against breast cancer. Cabbage is also a good source of vitamin C and is among the richest vegetable sources of folate.

photo, page 217

Each serving provides

Key Nutrients 220 Calories, 100 Calories from Fat, 11g Fat, 1g Saturated Fat, 0g Trans Fat, 6g Protein, 28g Carb, 7g Fiber, 65mg Sodium
Blood Pressure Nutrients 59mg Vitamin C, 61mg Magnesium, 789mg Potassium, 115mg Calcium

VEGETABLE SIDES

Oriental Sprouted Salad

The Chinese-style dressing for this vibrant side salad, with zesty tones of ginger and coriander, complements the fresh flavors of sprouted beans and seeds, apple, and vegetables.

Preparation time **10 minutes**   *Serves 4*

Salad

1 carrot
1 celery stalk
1 large apple
1 cup mung bean sprouts
1 cup sprouted sunflower seeds
1 cup alfalfa sprouts

Dressing

1 tablespoon lime juice
1 tablespoon finely chopped fresh cilantro
2 tablespoons canola oil
1/2 teaspoon toasted sesame oil
1/2 teaspoon light soy sauce
1 teaspoon grated fresh ginger
Salt and pepper to taste

1 Cut the carrot into 1 1/2-inch lengths. Slice thinly lengthwise, then cut into very fine matchsticks. Cut the celery into matchsticks the same size as the carrot. Core the apple and cut into 8 wedges, then thinly slice the wedges crosswise to make fan-shaped pieces.

2 Combine the carrot, celery, apple, mung bean sprouts, sunflower seeds, and alfalfa sprouts in a mixing bowl.

3 To make the dressing, whisk together all the ingredients, seasoning with salt and pepper to taste. Pour the dressing over the salad, toss well to coat evenly, and serve.

(Some More Ideas)

• If you don't have time to sprout your own beans and seeds, you can use sprouts bought from supermarkets and health food stores. Look for bags of mixtures such as sprouted azuki beans, lentils, and chickpeas.

• For a more substantial salad, to serve as a light main dish, replace the mung bean sprouts with sprouted green or brown lentils, and stir in 1/2 pound diced tofu.

Health Points

• Sprouted beans and seeds are a good source of vitamin C and folate, as well as several phytochemicals including lutein, coumarins, and xanthophylls.

photo, page 217

Each serving provides

Key Nutrients 320 Calories, 230 Calories from Fat, 26g Fat, 3g Saturated Fat, 0g Trans Fat, 10g Protein, 19g Carb, 7g Fiber, 55mg Sodium
Blood Pressure Nutrients 12mg Vitamin C, 142mg Magnesium, 44mg Potassium, 61mg Calcium

219

Crunchy Nut Coleslaw

Everyone loves coleslaw. This crowd-pleaser is made with green cabbage, carrot, and radishes, flecked with scallions, sweet raisins, and roasted peanuts, and tossed with a creamy dressing that is tasty, yet low in fat.

Preparation time **15 minutes**   *Serves 4*

1/2 head green cabbage, finely shredded

1 large carrot, coarsely grated

2/3 cup raisins

4 scallions, finely chopped, with the white and green parts kept separate

2 tablespoons reduced-fat mayonnaise

2/3 cup plain low-fat yogurt

6 radishes, sliced

1/3 cup unsalted roasted peanuts

3 tablespoons chopped parsley or snipped fresh chives, or a mixture of the two *(optional)*

Salt and pepper to taste

1 Mix together the cabbage, carrot, raisins, and white parts of the scallions in a large bowl.

2 Stir the mayonnaise and yogurt together and season with salt and pepper to taste. Stir this dressing into the cabbage mixture and toss to coat all the ingredients.

3 Just before serving, stir in the radishes and peanuts, and sprinkle with the chopped green parts of the scallions and the parsley or chives.

(Some More Ideas)

• For a celeriac coleslaw, use 1/2 large peeled celeriac, cut into matchstick strips, instead of cabbage. Flavor the yogurt and mayonnaise dressing with 1 teaspoon Dijon mustard and 1 tablespoon mango chutney.

• Toss 1 cored and diced red-skinned apple with 2 tablespoons lemon juice, then stir into the coleslaw with 1 teaspoon caraway seeds.

• Add 1/2 cup canned or thawed frozen corn.

• Lightly toast 1 tablespoon pumpkin seeds and 2 tablespoons sunflower seeds and use to garnish the coleslaw in place of the herbs.

Health Points

• Roasted peanuts are a nutritious addition to this recipe. New research suggests that a daily intake of peanuts, peanut butter, or peanut oil may help to lower total cholesterol, harmful LDL cholesterol, and triglyceride levels to protect against heart disease.

photo, page 217

Each serving provides

Key Nutrients 250 Calories, 90 Calories from Fat, 10g Fat, 2g Saturated Fat, 0g Trans Fat, 8g Protein, 37g Carb, 6g Fiber, 125mg Sodium
Blood Pressure Nutrients 44mg Vitamin C, 61mg Magnesium, 780mg Potassium, 166mg Calcium

soups and stews

Asparagus and Pea Soup

Served hot or cold, this lovely green soup is ideal for days when the weather is unpredictable. Asparagus and sugar snap peas bring just the right kick to this variation on the classic leek and potato soup.

Preparation time **10 minutes, plus at least 1 hour chilling**   Cooking time **about 20 minutes**   *Serves 4*

1 tablespoon canola oil

1 medium potato, peeled and diced

1 medium leek or onion, coarsely chopped

3/4 pound asparagus, trimmed and chopped

1/2 pound sugar snap peas, chopped

4 cups low-sodium chicken broth

1 tablespoon finely snipped fresh chives or chopped fresh chervil

1/2 cup plain low-fat yogurt

Salt and white pepper to taste

Snipped fresh chives or sprigs of fresh chervil *(garnish)*

1 Heat the oil in a large saucepan, add the potato and leek or onion, and stir well. Cover and cook over a low heat, stirring occasionally, until the leek or onion has softened, but not browned, about 5 minutes.

2 Stir in the asparagus and sugar snap peas, then pour in enough of the broth to cover the vegetables. Bring to a boil. Cover, reduce the heat, and simmer gently until all the vegetables are tender, about 5–7 minutes.

3 Cool for a few minutes, then puree the vegetables with their cooking liquid in a blender or food processor. Pour into a bowl. Stir in the remaining broth, the chives or chervil, and half of the yogurt. Season to taste with salt and white pepper. Leave to cool completely, then chill for at least 1 hour.

4 Taste and adjust the seasoning, if necessary. Ladle the soup into bowls and top each portion with a spoonful of the remaining yogurt. Garnish with chives or chervil and serve immediately, with rolls or crusty bread.

(Some More Ideas)

Chilled cucumber soup: Replace the asparagus and sugar snap peas with 1 cucumber, chopped, and the chives or chervil with 1 tablespoon very finely chopped fresh mint. Cucumber contains a lot of water, so use only 2 cups of broth. Garnish with shreds of fresh mint.

• The soup freezes well, but do not add the yogurt before freezing: Stir in the yogurt when the soup is thawed but still chilled, then season, garnish and serve as usual.

Health Points

• Asparagus is an excellent source of folate, and it provides vitamins C and E as well as beta-carotene. Asparagus also has a mild laxative effect.

photo, page 225

Each serving provides

Key Nutrients 170 Calories, 50 Calories from Fat, 6g Fat, 2g Saturated Fat, 0g Trans Fat, 8g Protein, 20g Carb, 3g Fiber, 140mg Sodium
Blood Pressure Nutrients 14mg Vitamin C, 24mg Magnesium, 420mg Potassium, 114mg Calcium

Cream of Zucchini Soup

This silky-smooth vitamin-rich soup tastes as good as it looks. Top this lively green soup with a pretty swirl of yogurt and you've made a delightful summer luncheon dish or a beautiful beginning to a summer dinner.

Preparation time **20 minutes**   Cooking time **25 minutes**   *Serves 8*

1 tablespoon olive oil

1 large onion, coarsely chopped

2 cloves garlic, finely chopped

2 cans (14 1/2 ounces each) vegetable broth

8 ounces all-purpose potatoes, peeled and diced

1 pound zucchini, trimmed and thinly sliced

1 1/2 cups parsley leaves

1 cup low-fat (1%) milk

Salt to taste

1/8 teaspoon pepper

1 cup nonfat plain yogurt

1 In large saucepan, heat oil over moderate heat. Add onion and garlic, then about 1/4 cup broth. Sauté until softened but not browned. Add potatoes and stir to coat. Pour in remaining broth and bring to boil.

2 Add zucchini and simmer, partially covered, until all vegetables are very tender, about 10 minutes.

3 Remove from heat and stir in parsley. Strain soup into large bowl; puree vegetables in a blender or food processor until very smooth.

4 Stir puree into broth and allow to cool. Stir in milk, salt, and pepper, and chill soup until ready to serve. Before serving, spoon a large spoonful of yogurt into each bowl of soup. With tip of spoon, gently draw yogurt out in circle to make swirl.

(Some More Ideas)

Chilled cream of carrot soup: Substitute 4 large carrots, peeled and diced, for the zucchini.

• For an even richer-tasting soup, use 1 cup evaporated fat-free milk in place of the 1% milk.

Health Points

• Evaporated fat-free milk is a heart-smart pantry staple that's twice as high in calcium as regular fat-free milk. Its thicker consistency makes it a perfect substitute for cream in soups and sauces.

Each serving provides

Key Nutrients 100 Calories, 20 Calories from Fat, 3g Fat, 0g Saturated Fat, 0g Trans Fat, 4g Protein, 16g Carb, 2g Fiber, 240mg Sodium
Blood Pressure Nutrients 27mg Vitamin C, 32mg Magnesium, 394mg Potassium, 114mg Calcium

Cool Blueberry Soup

Start off a light summer supper in Scandinavian style, with a boysenberry-blue colored soup. And you don't even have to wait for summer, because we've used frozen blueberries, full of flavor and ready to use.

Preparation time **5 minutes**   Cooking time **2 minutes**   *Serves 4*

3 tablespoons sugar
1 teaspoon grated lemon zest
1/8 teaspoon allspice
1 cup water
2 bags (12 ounces each) frozen blueberries
1 1/4 cups plain fat-free yogurt
2 tablespoons fresh lemon juice

1 In small skillet, combine sugar, lemon zest, allspice, and water over medium heat. Bring to a boil and boil for 1 minute to dissolve sugar.

2 Place frozen blueberries, 1 cup of yogurt, and lemon juice in food processor or blender. Remove syrup from heat and add to food processor. Puree until smooth.

3 Refrigerate until serving time. Top each serving with 1 tablespoon yogurt.

(Some More Ideas)

Berry sherbet: Freeze the berry puree in an ice cube tray, then briefly process the frozen cubes in a food processor until slushy.

• Follow the blueberry soup with broiled salmon, steamed sugar snap peas, roasted potatoes and biscotti for dessert.

Health Points

• Blueberries supply a type of heart-healthy soluble fiber called pectin. Scientists believe that pectin helps to lower LDL cholesterol levels by binding cholesterol in the intestine and pulling it out of the body before it can be absorbed.

Each serving provides

Key Nutrients 150 Calories, 10 Calories from Fat, 1g Fat, 0g Saturated Fat, 0g Trans Fat, 4g Protein, 36g Carb, 5g Fiber, 40mg Sodium
Blood Pressure Nutrients 12mg Vitamin C, 1mg Magnesium, 10mg Potassium, 120mg Calcium

Cool Blueberry Soup *p224*

Asparagus and Pea Soup *p222*

Peach Soup with Almonds *p226*

Cream of Leek and Potato Soup *p227*

Peach Soup with Almonds

Although this thick, creamy soup tastes like a dessert, it's actually a healthy way to enjoy your daily serving of fruit. Buttermilk and nutmeg combine with the fresh peaches to create a taste sensation that's not too tart and not too sweet.

Preparation time **20 minutes plus chilling**   Cooking time **20 minutes**   *Serves 4*

1 1/2 pounds fresh peaches or 20 ounces, frozen and thawed

Zest of 1 lemon, cut in wide strips

2 tablespoons sugar

2 cups buttermilk or low-fat (1%) milk

Pinch of ground nutmeg

1 cup peach nectar

1/4 cup sliced almonds

1 Bring large saucepan of water to boil. Add a few peaches to pan and return to boil. Transfer the peaches to a bowl of cold water. When cool enough, peel peaches with a small knife and cut into chunks; discard pits. Poach and peel remaining peaches, working in batches.

2 Bring 1 cup water, lemon zest, and sugar to a boil and add peaches. Cover, and simmer, stirring occasionally until very soft, 5–8 minutes. Remove pan from heat; discard lemon zest.

3 Pour 1 cup buttermilk into food processor or blender. Reserving peach syrup, add peaches, and puree. Transfer to a large bowl. Add remaining buttermilk, nutmeg, and peach nectar. Stir in reserved syrup. Cover and refrigerate at least 1 hour.

4 Preheat oven to 350°F. Spread almonds on cookie sheet; toast until golden, about 10 minutes. Cool almonds and sprinkle on soup before serving.

(Some More Ideas)

• Make this soup with many other summer fruits. Nectarines and plums are excellent choices. Try mango nectar instead of peach for a more tropical flavor.

Health Points

• Peaches are an excellent source of vitamin A and a good source of vitamin C. Their moderate amounts of fiber can also help lower cholesterol.

photo, page 225

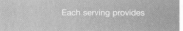
Each serving provides

Key Nutrients 220 Calories, 40 Calories from Fat, 5g Fat, 1g Saturated Fat, 0g Trans Fat, 7g Protein, 40g Carb, 4g Fiber, 65mg Sodium
Blood Pressure Nutrients 24mg Vitamin C, 46mg Magnesium, 611mg Potassium, 199mg Calcium

Cream of Leek and Potato Soup

Leeks are closely related to onions—which accounts for their wonderful similarity in flavor. A pinch of freshly chopped chives and a swirl of creamy white yogurt add just the right contrasting touches to this classic soup.

Preparation time **15 minutes**   Cooking time **45 minutes**   *Serves 6*

1 tablespoon olive oil

8 ounces leeks, white part only, thickly sliced

1 large onion, coarsely chopped

2 cans (14 1/2 ounces each) reduced-sodium chicken broth

1 pound all-purpose potatoes, peeled and diced

Salt to taste

1/8 teaspoon ground white pepper

1/3 cup low-fat sour cream

Chopped chives for garnish *(optional)*

1 In large saucepan, heat oil over moderate heat. Stir in leeks and onion, then 3/4 cup broth. Cover and cook, stirring frequently until soft but not browned, about 10 minutes. Add potatoes and stir to coat with leek and onion mixture.

2 Pour in half of remaining broth and bring to boil. Simmer, partially covered, until potatoes are very soft, 15–20 minutes. Remove from heat. Transfer to blender or food processor and puree until very smooth.

3 Pour remaining broth into pan. Add vegetable puree and bring soup to a simmer, stirring constantly, 2–3 minutes. Season with salt and pepper.

4 Remove from heat and stir in sour cream. Ladle into soup bowls and garnish with chives, if using.

(Some More Ideas)

· Add small cubes of cooked chicken breast to the soup in Step 3 as the soup simmers.

· You could make many "cream" soups in this fashion. Use asparagus, broccoli, or carrots in place of, or in addition to, the potatoes.

Health Points

· Instead of the traditional heavy cream used in potato soups, this equally delicious version is made creamy and thick by pureeing the potatoes and adding low-fat sour cream. This saves many grams of total fat and also many grams of saturated fat.

photo, page 225

Each serving provides

Key Nutrients 160 Calories, 45 Calories from Fat, 5g Fat, 2g Saturated Fat, 0g Trans Fat, 5g Protein, 26g Carb, 2g Fiber, 95mg Sodium
Blood Pressure Nutrients 16mg Vitamin C, 33mg Magnesium, 420mg Potassium, 56mg Calcium

Mediterranean Roasted Vegetable Soup

A Mediterranean sweetness from a bounty of roasted and caramelized vegetables makes each bowl of this soup a treasured memory. Carrot juice in place of broth powers up the nutrition as well as the flavor.

Preparation time **25 minutes**   Cooking time **40 minutes**   *Serves 4*

1 tablespoon olive oil

5 cloves garlic, peeled

12 ounces all-purpose potatoes, unpeeled and cut into 1/2-inch chunks

2 bell peppers (green and yellow), cut into 1/2-inch squares

1/2 teaspoon rosemary, minced

1 yellow squash, halved length-wise and cut crosswise into 1/2-inch pieces

1 large red onion, cut into 1/2-inch chunks

1 1/2 cups carrot juice

12 ounces plum tomatoes, diced

1 teaspoon tarragon

Salt to taste

3/4 cup water

1 Preheat oven to 450°F. Combine oil and garlic in roasting pan and roast until oil begins to sizzle, about 5 minutes. Add potatoes, bell peppers, and rosemary, and toss to coat. Roast until potatoes begin to color and soften, about 15 minutes.

2 Add squash and onion, and roast until squash is tender, about 15 minutes.

3 In medium Dutch oven, combine carrot juice, tomatoes, tarragon, and salt, and bring to a boil over medium heat. Spoon roasted vegetables into Dutch oven.

4 Pour water into roasting pan and scrape up any browned bits that cling to pan. Pour pan juices into Dutch oven. Cook until heated through, about 2 minutes.

(Some More Ideas)

• Try using Yukon Gold potatoes for a rich, buttery flavor. These potatoes have the taste of butter, but it's all potato and none of the fat.

• Use zucchini instead of yellow squash. When picking summer squashes, select ones that seem heavy for their size. Otherwise, they may be dry inside and have less flavor.

Health Points

• Intensely colored vegetable ingredients, like carrots and tomatoes, provide you with potent, disease-fighting carotenoids, such as beta-carotene and lycopene.

photo, page 231

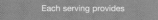
Each serving provides

Key Nutrients 210 Calories, 40 Calories from Fat, 4g Fat, 1g Saturated Fat, 0g Trans Fat, 5g Protein, 41g Carb, 6g Fiber, 40mg Sodium
Blood Pressure Nutrients 99mg Vitamin C, 66mg Magnesium, 1067mg Potassium, 64mg Calcium

Cheddar Cheese and Broccoli Soup

With the creaminess of your favorite comfort food, this recipe delivers a satisfying bowl of goodness—silky-smooth, yet still full of vegetable flavor. The cheddar cheese brings it all together.

Preparation time **15 minutes**   Cooking time **23 minutes**   *Serves 6*

1 pound broccoli

1 tablespoon olive oil

1 onion, chopped

1 celery rib, chopped

2 tablespoons all-purpose flour

1 can (14 1/2 ounces) reduced-sodium chicken broth

1 can (12 ounces) evaporated fat-free milk

1 1/2 cups shredded low-fat cheddar cheese (12 ounces)

1/2 teaspoon pepper

1/4 teaspoon nutmeg

Salt to taste

1 Trim and peel broccoli stems. Cut off 12 small florets. Coarsely chop enough remaining broccoli to equal 2 cups.

2 Blanch chopped broccoli and florets in boiling water just until bright green, about 2 minutes. Drain and set aside.

3 Heat olive oil in medium saucepan over medium heat. Sauté onion and celery until soft, about 5 minutes. Whisk in flour and cook 1 minute. Add broth and milk. Cook, stirring constantly, until mixture simmers and thickens, about 5 minutes.

4 Add chopped broccoli, cheddar, pepper, nutmeg, and salt. Stir until cheese melts and soup is heated through, about 3 minutes. Serve 1 cup per person, garnished with broccoli florets.

(Some More Ideas)

Cheddar cheese and asparagus soup: Trim 1 pound asparagus spears and coarsely chop. The switch from broccoli to asparagus also ups the folate content, which helps protect against heart disease.

• Use low-fat shredded Jack, Muenster or Swiss cheese in place of cheddar to add taste but keep the fat content down.

Health Points

• Calcium plays an important role in keeping your heartbeat strong. It aids in muscle contraction and helps to control high blood pressure.

Each serving provides

Key Nutrients 160 Calories, 45 Calories from Fat, 5g Fat, 2g Saturated Fat, 0g Trans Fat, 14g Protein, 16g Carb, 3g Fiber, 310mg Sodium
Blood Pressure Nutrients 72mg Vitamin C, 27mg Magnesium, 513mg Potassium, 309mg Calcium

Old-Fashioned Chicken Noodle Soup

Anyone can make a wonderful bowl of chicken soup. The trick is to make fresh stock, using good-quality chicken. Add a few vegetables and noodles to the stock, and you'll be in healing heaven.

Preparation time **about 45 minutes**   Cooking time **1 1/4 hours**   *Serves 4*

Stock

1 chicken (about 3 pounds) skinned and seperated, or 4 chicken quarters, skinned

2 onions, halved, the inner layer of skin left on

3 carrots, chopped

3 celery stalks, chopped

1 bouquet garni

4 black peppercorns

1 teaspoon salt

Soup

4 ounces spaghetti or linguine, broken into 2-inch pieces

1 carrot, halved lengthwise and thinly sliced

1 celery stalk, thinly sliced

1/2 cup small broccoli florets

1 cup frozen corn, thawed

2 tablespoons finely chopped fresh parsley

2 teaspoons fresh thyme leaves

1 First make the stock. Put the chicken parts in a large, heavy-based stockpot or saucepan. Add the onions, carrots, and celery, then pour in about 7 cups cold water to cover the ingredients. Bring to the boil, skimming the surface constantly until all gray scum is removed.

2 Reduce the heat to low immediately after the liquid boils. Add the bouquet garni, peppercorns, and 1 teaspoon salt. Partially cover the pan and simmer for 1 hour, skimming as necessary. Test the chicken joints after 30–40 minutes; remove them as soon as the juices run clear when the joints are pierced with the point of a knife. Set aside. Salt and pepper to taste.

3 Line a large colander or sieve with dampened cheesecloth and place it over a large heatproof bowl, then strain the stock through this. Discard the vegetables and flavoring ingredients. Return 5 cups of stock to the cleaned pan. Skim off any excess fat on the surface of the stock. Cool and freeze the leftover stock to use as a chicken stock in other recipes.

4 When the chicken is cool enough to handle, remove and discard all the bones. Cut 1/2 pound meat into bite-size pieces for use in the soup. Reserve the remaining chicken for sandwiches or other recipes.

5 Bring the stock to the boil, then reduce the heat so the stock is simmering. Add the spaghetti or linguine and the carrot, and simmer for 4 minutes. Add the celery, broccoli, and corn, and continue cooking until the pasta and all the vegetables are just tender, about 5 minutes.

6 Stir in the chicken with seasoning to taste and heat through. Sprinkle in the parsley and thyme, and serve the soup at once.

(Some More Ideas)

• Increase the fiber content by using whole-wheat instead of white spaghetti. Alternatively, add 1 (15 ounce) can navy beans, drained and rinsed. Stir in the beans with the chicken and just heat through.

• Vary the vegetables to suit the season. Small cauliflower florets, finely diced celeriac, sliced mushrooms, or diced green, red, and yellow peppers are all ideal. The fresher the better!

Health Points

• Unlike the majority of vegetables, which are most nutritious when eaten raw, carrots are a better source of beta-carotene when they are cooked. Cooking breaks down their cell membranes, making it easier for the body to convert their beta-carotene into vitamin A.

Each serving provides

Key Nutrients 210 Calories, 15 Calories from Fat, 2g Fat, 0g Saturated Fat, 0g Trans Fat, 19g Protein, 31g Carb, 3g Fiber, 95mg Sodium
Blood Pressure Nutrients 16mg Vitamin C, 39mg Magnesium, 366mg Potassium, 36mg Calcium

Old-Fashioned Chicken Noodle Soup *p230*

Mediterranean Roasted Vegetable Soup *p228*

New England Clam Chowder *p232*

Soup of Leafy Greens and Herbs *p233*

New England Clam Chowder

This rich, creamy soup is all that you'd want a chowder to be—hearty with potatoes and chunky with lots of plump, juicy clams. Cherrystone clams work best—adding lots of flavor but without an inky aftertaste.

Preparation time **15 minutes**   Cooking time **30 minutes**   *Serves 4*

24 cherrystone or chowder clams (about 2 pounds), scrubbed

4 slices reduced-sodium turkey bacon, cut into 1/2-inch pieces

1 large onion, chopped

2 tablespoons all-purpose flour

1 pound all-purpose potatoes, peeled and cut into 1/2-inch cubes

2 cups reduced-fat (2%) milk

2 teaspoons fresh thyme leaves

1 bay leaf

Pinch ground red pepper

1/4 cup chopped flat-leaf parsley

1 Bring clams and 2 cups water to a boil in large saucepan over high heat. Reduce heat, cover, and simmer 5 minutes. Uncover and transfer clams with tongs or a slotted spoon to bowl as they open. Strain clam broth, adding enough water to equal 1 1/2 cups; set aside. Wipe out saucepan.

2 Lightly coat saucepan with nonstick cooking spray and set over medium heat. Sauté bacon and onion until onion is golden, about 7 minutes. Sprinkle in flour and cook, stirring constantly, just until bubbling but not browned, about 1 minute.

3 Add potatoes, milk, reserved clam broth, thyme, bay leaf, and pepper. Bring to a simmer and cook, stirring occasionally, until potatoes are tender, about 10 minutes (do not boil).

4 Meanwhile, remove clams from shells and cut into bite-size pieces if necessary. Stir in clams and cook until heated through, about 2 minutes longer. Discard bay leaf. Ladle into bowls and sprinkle with parsley. Serve 2 cups per person.

(Some More Ideas)

Manhattan clam chowder: Omit the milk. Add 2 cups no-salt-added diced tomatoes with liquid to Step 3 with the potatoes. Add 1 cup reduced-sodium chicken broth along with the tomatoes. Continue as directed above.

• To make this recipe with canned clams, use 3 (7 ounce) cans clams, rinse very well, and drain.

Health Points

• This lighter version of clam chowder uses a small amount of lean turkey bacon to add that smoky flavor. It is also made with reduced-fat milk, whisked with a little flour, to make the chowder authentically white, thick, rich, and creamy, but surprisingly healthy.

photo, page 231

Each serving (2 cups) provides

Key Nutrients 390 Calories, 60 Calories from Fat, 6g Fat, 2g Saturated Fat, 0g Trans Fat, 37g Protein, 43g Carb, 3g Fiber, 280mg Sodium
Blood Pressure Nutrients 53mg Vitamin C, 57mg Magnesium, 1256mg Potassium, 253mg Calcium

Soup of Leafy Greens and Herbs

Hearty but not too heavy, this is a wonderful dish for summer and autumn, when so many vegetables are at the peak of flavor. You can use all sorts of greens—simply adjust the cooking time accordingly and get creative!

Preparation time **20–25 minutes**   Cooking time **about 30 minutes**   *Serves 4*

2 tablespoons olive oil

1 leek, white part only, cut into thin strips

1 small onion, chopped

1/2 carrot, thinly sliced

4 garlic cloves, chopped

1/2 teaspoon fennel seeds

2 tablespoons chopped fresh parsley

2 slices reduced-sodium ham (2 ounces), trimmed of fat, then cut into thin strips or chopped

1/4 pound Swiss chard or spinach, very finely shredded

3 small ripe tomatoes or whole no-salt-added canned tomatoes, diced

6 cups reduced-sodium, low-fat chicken or vegetable broth

Pinch of crushed dried red chiles *(optional)*

1/2 pound small pasta shapes, such as conchigliette (shells) or ditalini (small thimbles)

Salt and pepper to taste

2 ounces fresh basil, stalks discarded, then thinly sliced or torn *(garnish)*

2 tablespoons freshly grated Parmesan cheese *(garnish)*

1 Heat the oil in a large saucepan. Add the leek and onion and cook until slightly softened, about 5 minutes. Add the carrot, garlic, fennel seeds, parsley, and ham. Continue cooking for about 5 minutes, stirring occasionally.

2 Stir in the shredded greens and the tomatoes, and cover the pan. Cook until the greens are slightly softened, about 2 minutes, then pour in the broth. Add the crushed dried chiles, if using. Season to taste with salt and pepper. Bring to the boil, then simmer over a medium-high heat until the shredded greens are just tender, about 5 minutes.

3 Meanwhile, cook the pasta in boiling water, according to the package instructions, until al dente, 10–12 minutes. Drain well.

4 Divide the pasta among 4 serving bowls. Ladle the soup into the bowls and sprinkle with the basil and grated Parmesan. Serve immediately.

(Some More Ideas)

Middle Eastern leafy green soup: Omit the ham and use vegetable broth. Stir 1/2 cup plain low-fat yogurt until smooth, then stir into the soup, off the heat. Add 3 tablespoons chopped fresh cilantro and the juice of 1/2 lemon (or to taste). Serve sprinkled with paprika and cayenne pepper to taste.

• For a Chinese-style version, omit the fennel seeds, parsley, ham, basil, and Parmesan, and spice the soup with 1–2 table-spoons peeled, finely chopped fresh ginger, and low-sodium soy sauce. Add 3 ounces firm tofu, cut into small cubes.

• Other greens that are good in this soup include bok choy, napa cabbage, kale, and watercress. Coarser leaves, such as kale, will take a little more time to cook.

Health Points

• Dark green, leafy vegetables provide good amounts of beta-carotene, as well as the B vitamins niacin, folate, and B6.

photo, page 231

Each serving provides

Key Nutrients 390 Calories, 100 Calories from Fat, 12g Fat, 3g Saturated Fat, 0g Trans Fat, 18g Protein, 57g Carb, 5g Fiber, 340mg Sodium
Blood Pressure Nutrients 42mg Vitamin C, 89mg Magnesium, 680mg Potassium, 119mg Calcium

Minestrone with Meatballs

In Italian, a "minestra" is a soup, but a "minestrone" is a BIG soup—a meal in itself. Tender and moist turkey meatballs and a host of seasonal herbs and vegetables enhance the depth of flavor in this one-bowl meal.

Preparation time **15 minutes**   Cooking time **20 minutes**   *Serves 4*

1 teaspoon olive oil
1 small onion, finely chopped
3 cloves garlic, minced
8 ounces skinless, boneless turkey breast, cut into chunks
3 tablespoons old-fashioned rolled oats
1/4 cup low-fat (1%) milk
1/4 cup grated Parmesan
1/2 cup chopped fresh basil
Salt to taste
2 cups reduced-sodium, fat-free chicken broth
1 1/2 cups no-salt-added canned tomatoes, chopped with their juice
2 cups water
2/3 cup small bow-tie pasta (2 1/2 ounces)
4 cups kale, shredded
1 yellow summer squash, quartered lengthwise and thickly sliced

1 In medium nonstick saucepan, heat oil over low heat. Add onion and garlic, and cook, stirring frequently, until onion is tender, about 5 minutes. Transfer to medium bowl and let cool to room temperature.

2 Meanwhile, place turkey in food processor and pulse on and off until finely ground. Transfer turkey to bowl with the onion mixture.

3 Add oats, milk, 2 tablespoons of Parmesan, 2 tablespoons of basil, and 1/4 teaspoon of salt to bowl and mix to combine. Gently shape mixture into 24 small meatballs.

4 In Dutch oven, combine remaining 1/2 teaspoon salt, broth, tomatoes, and water and bring to a boil over high heat. Add pasta and kale, and cook 5 minutes.

5 Reduce to a simmer, add remaining basil and meatballs, and cook for 1 minute. Add yellow squash, cover, and simmer until meatballs are cooked through and kale is tender, about 5 minutes. Serve sprinkled with remaining 2 tablespoons Parmesan.

(Some More Ideas)

• Make this soup using chicken breast instead of turkey. Or combine 4 ounces ground beef and the turkey or chicken for richer-tasting meatballs.

• Omit the kale and use 4 cups spinach leaves instead. Kale has more vitamin C, but spinach has a higher amount of beta-carotene.

Health Points

• Kale is an often forgotten leafy green. It is mild enough to be acceptable to most palates. It is rich in fiber and calcium and can nicely substitute for spinach in many recipes.

Each serving provides

Key Nutrients 210 Calories, 35 Calories from Fat, 4g Fat, 2g Saturated Fat, 0g Trans Fat, 22g Protein, 24g Carb, 5g Fiber, 200mg Sodium
Blood Pressure Nutrients 97mg Vitamin C, 60mg Magnesium, 665mg Potassium, 194mg Calcium

Minestrone with Meatballs *p234*   Beefy Mushroom Barley Soup *p236*

Speedy Two-Bean Chili *p240*

Moroccan Vegetable Stew *p239*

Beefy Mushroom Barley Soup

Visions of Grandma's kitchen and potbellied stoves come to mind with each ladleful of this robust beefy-flavored soup. Big-bowl meals are all the rage now, but it's easy to see how this one-dish meal has satisfied generations.

Preparation time **20 minutes**   Cooking time **1 hour**   *Serves 6*

12 ounces lean beef chuck, cut into 1-inch cubes
3 medium onions, coarsely chopped
10 ounces mushrooms, sliced
3 large carrots, sliced
1/2 cup pearl barley
7 cups reduced-sodium beef broth
1 cup dry red wine or no-salt-added tomato juice
Salt to taste
1/2 teaspoon pepper
1 cup frozen green peas
2 teaspoons fresh lemon juice

1 Coat soup pot or large, heavy saucepan with nonstick cooking spray and set over medium-high heat until hot but not smoking. Sauté beef until brown, about 5 minutes. Transfer with slotted spoon to double layer of paper towels to drain.

2 Sauté onions and mushrooms in pan drippings until onions are golden, about 7 minutes. Return beef to pot. Stir in carrots, barley, broth, wine, salt, and pepper, and bring to a boil.

3 Reduce heat to medium-low. Simmer, partially covered, until beef and barley are tender, about 45 minutes. Stir in peas and cook, uncovered, until tender, about 5 minutes. Remove from heat; stir in lemon juice.

(Some More Ideas)

Beefy mushroom and brown rice soup: Instead of barley, add 1 cup rinsed brown rice along with the carrots in Step 2. Simmer for 45 minutes as in Step 3.

• Use 12 ounces cubed boneless, skinless chicken thigh meat for the lean beef.

Health Points

• The barley and vegetables, full of nutritious complex carbohydrates, balance out the beef in just the right proportions. Barley is a fair source of the B vitamins necessary for energy production.

photo, page 235

Each serving provides

Key Nutrients 270 Calories, 30 Calories from Fat, 4g Fat, 1g Saturated Fat, 0g Trans Fat, 26g Protein, 28g Carb, 7g Fiber, 170mg Sodium
Blood Pressure Nutrients 11mg Vitamin C, 55mg Magnesium, 912mg Potassium, 42mg Calcium

Tomato and Lentil Soup

Lentils bring a robust, earthy flavor to this soul-soothing lunch or light supper fare. Pungent ginger and sweet tarragon perk up these tender legumes and already-tasty tomatoes.

Preparation time **10 minutes**   Cooking time **55 minutes**   *Serves 4*

1/4 cup dried porcini or shiitake mushrooms

1 cup hot water

1 tablespoon olive oil

1 large onion, finely chopped

3 cloves garlic, minced

1 can (15 ounces) no-salt-added diced tomatoes

1 teaspoon ground ginger

1 teaspoon tarragon

Salt to taste

2 cups water

1/2 cup lentils, picked over and rinsed

1 Combine mushrooms and hot water in small bowl. Let stand 20 minutes until softened. With slotted spoon or fingers, scoop mushrooms from soaking liquid. Strain liquid through fine-meshed sieve and set aside. Coarsely chop mushrooms.

2 Meanwhile, heat oil in large saucepan over medium heat. Add onion and garlic, and cook, stirring frequently, until onion is golden, about 7 minutes.

3 Stir in mushrooms, mushroom soaking liquid, tomatoes and their juice, ginger, tarragon, salt, and water. Add lentils and bring to a boil. Reduce to a simmer, cover, and cook until lentils are tender, about 30 minutes. (Recipe can be made ahead to this point. Reheat gently, adding a tablespoon or so of water if soup is too thick.)

(Some More Ideas)

Tomato and yellow split pea soup: Use yellow split peas instead of lentils. Use the same amount and cook in the same amount of time. Serve the soup with whole-grain bread, with fresh fruit for dessert.

• For an even heartier-tasting soup, use reduced-sodium chicken broth in place of the water.

Health Points

• Another way to work dried mushrooms, loaded with blood-pressure-lowering potassium, into your food is to pulverize them into a powder and then use the powder to flavor and thicken sauces and stews.

Each serving provides

Key Nutrients 180 Calories, 35 Calories from Fat, 4g Fat, 1g Saturated Fat, 0g Trans Fat, 11g Protein, 28g Carb, 11g Fiber, 50mg Sodium
Blood Pressure Nutrients 12mg Vitamin C, 32mg Magnesium, 303mg Potassium, 48mg Calcium

Chickpea Soup with Asparagus

Adding orzo, a rice-shaped pasta, instantly ups the interest of this tasty and filling soup. For a main meal, serve with a little strong-flavored cheese and a slice or two of warm, crusty bread.

Preparation time **15 minutes**   Cooking time **about 40 minutes**   *Serves 4*

1 can (15 ounces) chickpeas, drained

1 onion, coarsely chopped

2 garlic cloves, chopped

3 cups reduced-sodium, low-fat chicken or vegetable broth

2/3 pound asparagus, trimmed and cut into bite-size pieces

1 cup orzo or other soup pasta

Salt and pepper to taste

Fine strips of zest from 1 lemon *(garnish)*

2 tablespoons chopped fresh parsley *(garnish)*

1 lemon, cut into wedges *(to serve)*

1 Put chickpeas, onion, garlic, and broth in a saucepan and bring to boil. Reduce heat and simmer until onion is very tender and the chickpeas are falling apart, about 20 minutes.

2 Ladle about one-third of the soup into a blender or food processor and puree it until it is smooth. Return the pureed soup to the pan and bring back to simmering point. Add the asparagus, cover the pan, and cook gently until the asparagus is just tender, about 5–6 minutes.

3 Meanwhile, cook the orzo or other pasta shapes in boiling water, according to the package instructions, until al dente, about 10–12 minutes. Drain the pasta and add it to the soup with seasoning to taste.

4 Mix together the lemon zest and parsley for the garnish. Top each bowl of soup with a small spoonful of the lemon and parsley garnish, and serve immediately, offering lemon wedges so that the juice can be added to the soup to taste.

(Some More Ideas)

• Use small broccoli florets instead of asparagus. Broccoli is an excellent source of vitamin C, and the quantity in this soup will provide about one-quarter of the recommended daily intake of that vital vitamin.

• There are many tiny pasta shapes for soup (called *pastina* in Italy). Orzo is rice-shaped; other shapes are stelline (stars), ditalini (tubes), conchigliette (shells) and farfallini (bow ties). You can also use larger pasta shapes (penne or rigatoni, for example), if you prefer.

Health Points

• Asparagus is a rich source of many of the B vitamins, especially folate. New research suggests that folate may also have a role in helping to prevent Alzheimer's disease.

Each serving provides

Key Nutrients 460 Calories, 35 Calories from Fat, 4g Fat, 1g Saturated Fat, 0g Trans Fat, 22g Protein, 87g Carb, 9g Fiber, 90mg Sodium
Blood Pressure Nutrients 17mg Vitamin C, 113mg Magnesium, 257mg Potassium, 105mg Calcium

Moroccan Vegetable Stew

Even meat eaters will love this flavor-packed vegetable stew, also known as tagine. Despite the long list of ingredients, the stew is simple to prepare for a hearty family meal.

Preparation time **25 minutes**   Cooking time **30 minutes**   *Serves 4*

Stew

1 tablespoon olive oil
1 large red onion
4 garlic cloves, sliced
1 tablespoon fresh ginger
1 medium butternut squash
1 teaspoon ground cinnamon
1 teaspoon ground cumin
1 teaspoon ground coriander
6 green cardamom pods, split open and seeds lightly crushed
3 bay leaves
2 cans (14 ounces each) no-salt-added chopped tomatoes
3 large carrots, thickly sliced
1 1/4 cups low-sodium chicken or vegetable broth
1/2 cup raisins
1/3 cup dried cherries
1/2 cup sliced okra
1 large red bell pepper, chopped
1 can (15 ounces) chickpeas
1/4 cup toasted sliced almonds
3 tablespoons chopped parsley

Couscous

1 cup couscous
2 cups vegetable broth
2 teaspoons olive oil
1 teaspoon chile sauce
1/2 teaspoon ground coriander
1/2 teaspoon ground cumin

1 Peel, seed, and cube the squash. Heat the oil in a very large pan and stir-fry the roughly chopped onion over a high heat until beginning to soften and color, 2–3 minutes. Toss in the garlic and minced ginger and cook for a few more seconds. Add the squash and stir-fry for about 1 minute.

2 Turn down the heat to medium. Add the spices, the bay leaves, tomatoes, and carrots. Pour in the broth and bring to a boil. Stir in the raisins and cherries, then cover and simmer for 10 minutes.

3 Meanwhile, prepare the couscous. Put the couscous in a large bowl and pour in the boiling broth. Add the oil, chile sauce, and spices. Leave until the liquid has been completely absorbed, then fork the mixture through to separate the grains. Pour into a colander lined with greaseproof paper.

4 Stir the okra and red pepper into the stew, then cover and leave to simmer for 5 minutes. Add the drained chickpeas and stir. Set the colander containing the couscous over the pan and simmer until all the vegetables are tender, but still retain their shape and texture, and the couscous is hot, 5–10 minutes.

5 Add the couscous to a platter. Pile the vegetable stew on top of the couscous and scatter over the toasted almonds and chopped fresh parsley.

(Some More Ideas)

Apricot and coriander tagine: Replace the cherries and raisins with dried apricots, use halved French beans instead of the okra, and substitute fresh cilantro for the parsley. Add 2 tablespoons chopped fresh cilantro to the tagine at the end of the cooking time as well as scattering some over the finished dish.

• Whole new potatoes can replace the carrots. Red kidney beans can be used as an alternative to the chickpeas, or instead of adding them to the tagine, toss them into the couscous for added texture.

Health Points

• Beans and chickpeas are an excellent source of protein, even better when they are eaten with grains such as wheat (couscous) and rice. Canned versions are a convenient way of including them in the diet with the minimum of effort.

photo, page 235

Each serving provides

Key Nutrients 600 Calories, 100 Calories from Fat, 11g Fat, 2g Saturated Fat, 0g Trans Fat, 19g Protein, 109g Carb, 19g Fiber, 190mg Sodium
Blood Pressure Nutrients 123mg Vitamin C, 142mg Magnesium, 1107mg Potassium, 227mg Calcium

Speedy Two-Bean Chili

Here's a hearty and satisfying chili—without the meat but with all the flavor. This version combines two varieties of beans with sweet corn in a rich tomato sauce seasoned with herbs, fresh chile, and chili sauce.

Preparation time **5 minutes**   Cooking time **25 minutes**   *Serves 4*

2 tablespoons olive oil
1 large onion, halved and sliced
1 fresh red chile, seeded and chopped
1 can (14 ounces) no-salt-added chopped tomatoes
1 tablespoon chili sauce
2 tablespoons low-sodium tomato ketchup
2 cups low-sodium chicken or vegetable broth
1 tablespoon chopped parsley
1 tablespoon chopped fresh oregano
1 can (15 ounces) red kidney beans, drained and rinsed
1 can (15 ounces) cannellini beans, drained and rinsed
1 cup frozen corn, thawed
Salt and pepper to taste
1/2 cup light sour cream
2 tablespoons snipped fresh chives
Fresh oregano leaves *(garnish)*

1 Heat the oil in a large skillet. Add the onion and chile, and cook over medium heat, stirring occasionally, until the onion is lightly browned, about 5 minutes.

2 Stir in the tomatoes with their juice, the chili sauce, ketchup, broth, parsley, and oregano, with seasoning to taste. Bring to the boil, then reduce the heat and simmer for 10 minutes, stirring occasionally.

3 Add the kidney and cannellini beans and the corn. Simmer for 10 minutes.

4 Meanwhile, mix the sour cream with the snipped chives. Taste the chili for seasoning and adjust if necessary. Serve the chili sprinkled with the oregano leaves and offer the sour-cream mixture separately.

(Some More Ideas)

Vegetarian chili burgers: Cook the onion and chile as in the main recipe, then place in a food processor. Omit the tomatoes and broth, but add all the remaining ingredients to the processor. Add 1 egg yolk and 1 cup fresh bread crumbs. Process until smooth, then divide into 8 portions. Shape into burgers and chill for at least 1 hour. Coat the burgers with more fresh bread crumbs, pressing them on neatly; you will need 2 1/2 ounces. Brush each burger with a little olive oil and cook on a grill pan or in a nonstick skillet for 10 minutes on each side.

Health Points

• Beans have a lot going for them. They are a cheap source of protein, a good source of B-group vitamins and, when sprouted, are an excellent source of vitamin C. Kidney beans and cannellini beans provide more than 3 times the amount of fiber found in many vegetables.

photo, page 235

Each serving provides

Key Nutrients 360 Calories, 90 Calories from Fat, 10g Fat, 3g Saturated Fat 0g Trans Fat, 16g Protein, 53g Carb, 16g Fiber, 430mg Sodium
Blood Pressure Nutrients 41mg Vitamin C, 42mg Magnesium, 503mg Potassium, 159mg Calcium

desserts

Frozen Pineapple and Berry Slush

A cross between a breakfast sorbet and a thick drink, this refreshing, virtually fat-free start to the day takes just seconds to whip up. The secret of preparing it quickly is to keep a selection of chopped fruit in the freezer.

Preparation time **5–15 minutes, plus about 1 1/2 hours**   *Serves 4*

8 ice cubes
1/2 pound hulled strawberries, frozen
1 cup fresh pineapple chunks, frozen
1/2 cup pineapple juice
2 tablespoons skim milk powder
1 tablespoon sugar, or to taste
Sprigs of fresh mint *(garnish)*

1 Put the ice cubes in a food processor or heavy-duty blender and process until they are finely crushed. Alternatively, crush the ice cubes in a freezerproof bag, using a rolling pin, and then put them in the processor or blender.

2 Add the strawberries, pineapple chunks, pineapple juice, and milk powder and process again until blended but still with small pieces of fruit and ice visible.

3 Taste and sweeten with sugar if necessary. (The amount of sugar required will depend on the sweetness of the fruit.) Process briefly, using the pulse button.

4 Spoon into tall glasses, decorate each with a sprig of mint, and serve with long spoons.

(Some More Ideas)

• If the recipe makes more than you need, freeze it in ice cube trays. On another morning, you can just puree the cubes in a food processor or blender for an instant slush. Add fruit juice to dilute, if necessary.

Summer fruit slush: Use a 1/2-pound bag of frozen mixed summer fruit, including blackberries, blueberries, cherries, red currants, raspberries, and strawberries. Add 4 tablespoons unsweetened orange juice and 2 tablespoons skim milk powder and process. Sweeten with a little sugar to taste, if necessary.

Tropical slush: Use 2 mangoes, pitted, chopped, and frozen, and 1 fresh banana. Add 4 tablespoons light coconut milk and 4 tablespoons unsweetened orange juice.

Health Points

• Dry skim milk powder, used here to give the slush some body, provides calcium, essential for healthy bones and teeth, as well as protein, zinc, and vitamins B2 and B12.

Each serving provides

Key Nutrients 60 Calories, 5 Calories from Fat, 0g Fat, 0g Saturated Fat, 0g Trans Fat, 1g Protein, 14g Carb, 2g Fiber, 15mg Sodium
Blood Pressure Nutrients 46mg Vitamin C, 18mg Magnesium, 216mg Potassium, 42mg Calcium

Frozen Pineapple and Berry Slush *p242*

Fruit Boats with Orange Glaze *p246*

Far Eastern Fruit Salad *p247*

Mango, Peach, and Apricot Fizz *p244*

Mango, Peach, and Apricot Fizz

Fruit pureed with a little fizzy ginger ale makes a wonderfully refreshing drink that also offers a healthy serving of fruit. Choose perfectly ripe, fragrant fruit for the smoothest fizz.

Preparation time **5–10 minutes**   *Serves 4*

1 ripe mango
1 ripe peach
2 large ripe apricots
2 cups ginger ale
Fresh mint leaves *(garnish)*

1 Peel the mango and cut the flesh away from the pit. Roughly chop the flesh and put it into a blender or food processor.

2 Cover the peach and apricots with boiling water and leave for about 30 seconds, then drain and cool under cold running water. Slip off the skins. Roughly chop the flesh, discarding the pits, and add to the mango in the blender or food processor.

3 Pour just enough ginger ale to cover the fruit, then process until completely smooth. Pour in the remaining ginger ale and process again.

4 Quickly pour into tall glasses, preferably over crushed ice. Decorate with fresh mint. Serve immediately with wide straws or swizzle sticks.

(Some More Ideas)

• Use low-calorie ginger ale to reduce the calorie content.

• So many different fruit and fizz combinations are possible. Using about 1 pound fruit in total, try: raspberry, peach, and melon with no-sodium club soda; or strawberry, banana, and orange segments with tonic water.

• When soft fruit are not in season, use fruit canned in juice as a substitute. A delicious combination is fresh melon, banana, and canned apricots with sparkling mineral water.

Health Points

• Peaches are full of vitamin C; apricots are a good source of the B vitamins (B1, B6, and niacin); and mangoes are an excellent source of vitamin A.

• A wide variety of fruit is now available frozen. This may be a better source of vitamins than some "fresh" fruit that has been badly handled or has languished on the shelf. It is particularly useful for blended drinks.

photo, page 243

Each serving provides

Key Nutrients 90 Calories, 0 Calories from Fat, 0g Fat, 0g Saturated Fat, 0g Trans Fat, 1g Protein, 24g Carb, 2g Fiber, 10mg Sodium
Blood Pressure Nutrients 18mg Vitamin C, 9mg Magnesium, 182mg Potassium, 13mg Calcium

Tomato and Citrus Blush

This wonderfully tangy drink makes an excellent alcohol-free alternative to a cocktail before lunch or dinner. It is best made with sweet, full-flavored tomatoes, preferably vine-ripened, and a perfectly ripe mango.

Preparation time **10 minutes**   *Serves 4*

Drink

1 ripe mango

1 pound tomatoes, peeled, halved, and seeded

1 cup watermelon chunks

Grated zest and juice of 1 orange

Grated zest and juice of 1 lime

To Serve

Ice

Orange and lime slices

1 Peel the skin off the mango, then cut the flesh away from the pit. Coarsely chop the flesh.

2 Put the chopped mango, tomatoes, watermelon, and orange and lime zest and juice in a food processor or blender and puree until smooth. Depending on the capacity of your blender, you may have to do this in 2 batches.

3 Half-fill 4 large tumblers with ice and pour over the tomato and citrus blush. Garnish with orange and lime slices. Serve immediately.

(Some More Ideas)

• For a summer starter, serve as a cold soup. Omit the ice cubes, orange and lemon slices, and swirl in a little plain low-fat yogurt.

Gazpacho quencher: Skin, seed, and roughly chop 1/2 pound tomatoes, a 2-inch piece of cucumber, 1 celery stick, 2 scallions, and 1 garlic clove. Puree the ingredients with 1 cup tomato juice. Stir in 2 teaspoons balsamic vinegar and 1 cup water. Half-fill 4 tall tumblers with ice and pour in the drink. Serve with long celery sticks for stirring, and top with a sprinkling of chopped scallions and diced tomato.

Health Points

• Tomatoes, mangoes, and watermelon all provide vitamin C, an important nutrient for healthy blood pressure, maintaining immunity, and promoting healthy skin.

• Mango also provides beta-carotene, which the body converts to vitamin A, essential for good vision, especially in dim light.

Each serving provides

Key Nutrients 80 Calories, 5 Calories from Fat, 1g Fat, 0g Saturated Fat, 0g Trans Fat, 2g Protein, 20g Carb, 3g Fiber, 10mg Sodium
Blood Pressure Nutrients 65mg Vitamin C, 25mg Magnesium, 435mg Potassium, 22mg Calcium

Fruit Boats with Orange Glaze

Fresh melon boats, carved in only minutes and overflowing with tart kiwis, ripe berries, and juicy melon balls, are the perfect refresher. A sweet-and-sour glaze gives the fruits unexpected zest for a summery lunch.

Preparation time **20 minutes**   Cooking time **5 minutes**   *Serves 4*

Fruit

1 large cantaloupe

1 pint strawberries, hulled and quartered

1/2 pint blueberries

1/2 pint raspberries

2 kiwifruits, peeled, halved, and cut into thin wedges

Orange Glaze

1/4 cup balsamic vinegar

1/4 teaspoon grated orange zest

2 tablespoons fresh orange juice

2 teaspoons brown sugar

1 Make the glaze: Combine vinegar, orange zest and juice, and brown sugar in microwavable dish. Microwave on High until syrupy, 2–3 minutes. Or cook over medium-high heat in a small saucepan, 4–5 minutes. Set glaze aside.

2 Cut the cantaloupe in half and remove the seeds and pulp. Using a melon-ball scoop or a small spoon, scoop out as many melon balls as you can from the cantaloupe. Put cantaloupe balls, strawberries, blueberries, raspberries, and kiwis in large bowl. Cut the cantaloupe rinds again, leaving you with 4 "boats."

3 Drizzle fruit with glaze. Toss to coat evenly. Spoon into cantaloupe boats and serve immediately.

(Some More Ideas)

• Top the fruit boats with a scoop of fruit sorbet.

• Use the orange glaze to drizzle on cooked salmon.

• Omit the cantaloupe and use pineapple chunks instead. Spoon the fruit salad into pineapple shells instead of the cantaloupe boats.

Health Points

• Raspberries are one of the highest-fiber berries. It is the little drupelets, the individual sections of fruit that contain their own seed, that make raspberries such a good source of fiber.

• Balsamic vinegar has a naturally sweet taste, giving food sweetness without having to add excess sugar.

photo, page 243

Each serving provides

Key Nutrients 180 Calories, 10 Calories from Fat, 2g Fat, 0g Saturated Fat, 0g Trans Fat, 3g Protein, 43g Carb, 8g Fiber, 30mg Sodium
Blood Pressure Nutrients 183mg Vitamin C, 50mg Magnesium, 992mg Potassium, 60mg Calcium

Far Eastern Fruit Salad

A can of fruit can be transformed into a special-tasting salad with the minimum of effort. Here canned lychees are enhanced with ginger and lime for an Oriental flavor, then tossed with apple, oranges, and grapes from the fruit bowl.

Preparation time **15–20 minutes**   *Serves 4*

1 can (15 ounces) lychees in syrup

3 pieces crystallized ginger, cut into thin strips

Grated zest and juice of 1 lime

2 oranges

1 cup seeded purple grapes, halved

1 red-skinned apple, cored and chopped

Fine shreds of lime zest *(garnish)*

1 Drain the lychees in a sieve set over a bowl. Discard half of the syrup that has drained into the bowl, then add the lychees. Stir in the ginger and the lime zest and juice.

2 Cut the peel and pith away from the oranges with a sharp knife. Holding the oranges over the bowl so that all the juice will drip into the salad, carefully cut between the membrane to release the segments. Add the segments to the bowl. Squeeze the membrane and add the juice to the bowl.

3 Stir in the grapes and apple and toss to mix. Pile the salad into small bowls to serve, decorated with shreds of lime zest.

(Some More Ideas)

• If you usually serve ice cream with a fruit salad as a dessert, you might instead try topping with a scoop of sorbet, which is deliciously fruity and fat-free. A sorbet such as lemon or mango would be particularly good with this fruit salad.

Health Points

• Purple grapes provide useful amounts of bioflavonoids and antioxidants, which help to protect the body against the damaging effect of free radicals.

• Oranges provide useful amounts of the B vitamin folate. They also provide pectin, which is a type of soluble fiber that may help stabilize blood sugar and lower cholesterol levels.

photo, page 243

Each serving provides

Key Nutrients 200 Calories, 5 Calories from Fat, 1g Fat, 0g Saturated Fat, 0g Trans Fat, 2g Protein, 51g Carb, 5g Fiber, 0mg Sodium
Blood Pressure Nutrients 92mg Vitamin C, 21mg Magnesium, 391mg Potassium, 54mg Calcium

Raspberry Frozen Yogurt

This frozen yogurt, exotically flavored with rose water, is much lower in sugar than store-bought frozen yogurt.
Serve scoops on their own, or pile into sundae glasses with fresh fruit and mint.

Preparation time **15–20 minutes, plus freezing**   *Serves 8*

1 pound raspberries
4 tablespoons seedless raspberry jam
2 tablespoons rose water *(optional)*
1 pound plain nonfat yogurt
3 tablespoons confectioners' sugar, or to taste
Raspberries *(garnish)*
Fresh mint leaves *(garnish)*

1 Put the raspberries into a saucepan and add the raspberry jam. Warm over a low heat until the raspberries are pulpy, stirring occasionally, about 5 minutes.

2 Press the raspberries and their juice through a sieve into a bowl; discard the seeds in the sieve. Stir in the rose water, if using. Whisk in the yogurt until smoothly blended. Taste the mixture and sweeten with the sugar.

3 Pour into an ice-cream machine and freeze according to the manufacturer's instructions. When you have a smooth and creamy frozen mixture, spoon it into a rigid freezerproof container. Freeze for at least 1 hour. If you do not have an ice-cream machine, pour the mixture straight into a large freezer-proof container and freeze until set around the edges, about 1 hour. Beat until the mixture is smooth, then return to the freezer. Freeze for 30 minutes, then beat again. Repeat the freezing and beating several times more until the frozen yogurt has a smooth consistency, then leave it to freeze for at least 1 hour.

4 If storing in the freezer for longer than 1 hour, transfer the frozen yogurt to the fridge 20 minutes before serving, to soften slightly. Decorate with raspberries and mint, if desired.

(Some More Ideas)

• Use frozen raspberries instead of fresh.

Mango frozen yogurt: Replace the raspberries and jam with 2 cans mangoes, drained and pureed. There should be no need to sweeten the mixture.

Health Points

• Raspberries are an excellent source of vitamin C, whether fresh or frozen. If freshly picked, there may be more C, but it is not always easy to tell how long fruit has been sitting on the shelf, and vitamin C content will be going down steadily following picking. Frozen fruits are usually processed immediately after picking and may therefore be a richer source of this vital vitamin.

Each serving provides

Key Nutrients 80 Calories, 5 Calories from Fat, 0g Fat, 0g Saturated Fat, 0g Trans Fat, 3g Protein, 18g Carb, 4g Fiber, 35mg Sodium
Blood Pressure Nutrients 17mg Vitamin C, 10mg Magnesium, 86mg Potassium, 87mg Calcium

Raspberry Frozen Yogurt *p248*

Ambrosia *p250*

Pineapple Foster *p251*

All-Time Favorite Apple Crisp *p252*

Ambrosia

'Tis Christmas Day and the table is laden with roasted turkey and all the trimmings—plus a fresh fruit dessert so good that it's called ambrosia (which in Greek mythology was the food of the gods).

Preparation time **30 minutes plus chilling**   *Serves 6*

3 navel oranges
1 small pineapple
2 large bananas
3/4 cup miniature marshmallows
1/3 cup sweetened flaked coconut
Fresh mint sprigs *(garnish)*

1 Cut thin slice off top and bottom of each orange. Remove peel and white pith with paring knife. Holding orange over large bowl, cut between membranes and lift out sections with knife, letting them fall into bowl with the orange juice.

2 Using long serrated knife, cut top and bottom off pineapple. Stand up pineapple and cut off peel in sections, from top to bottom. Halve pineapple lengthwise. Place one half, cut-side down, on cutting board and slice lengthwise into 3 equal sections. Slice off hard core, about 1 inch wide from each section, then cut sections crosswise into chunks, about 1 inch thick. Add to oranges in bowl and toss. Repeat with second half of pineapple.

3 Slice bananas 1/4 inch thick and add immediately to fruit and juice in bowl; toss to coat. Gently fold in marshmallows and coconut. Cover with plastic wrap and refrigerate at least 2 hours or overnight to blend flavors. Garnish with mint sprigs.

(Some More Ideas)

• Use chopped apples instead of the oranges.

• Add 1 tablespoon dark rum for an "adult" flavor.

• Purple grapes add more color. Halve 1 cup seeded grapes and toss in with the oranges, pineapple, and banana.

Health Points

• The fruits in this dish are high in bioflavonoids, substances with antioxidant properties that prevent tumor growth and help keep arteries healthy. Plus, there's as much fiber per serving as in a bowl of whole-grain breakfast cereal.

photo, page 249

Each serving provides

Key Nutrients 160 Calories, 20 Calories from Fat, 2g Fat, 2g Saturated Fat, 0g Trans Fat, 2g Protein, 38g Carb, 4g Fiber, 5mg Sodium
Blood Pressure Nutrients 65mg Vitamin C, 36mg Magnesium, 449mg Potassium, 46mg Calcium

Pineapple Foster

Bananas Foster is a beloved New Orleans dessert, created in the 1950s at Brennan's Restaurant. This healthy, low-fat pineapple variation, in which the fruit is sautéed in butter, rum, and brown sugar and then flambéed, will bring raves.

Preparation time **15 minutes**   Cooking time **10 minutes**   *Serves 4*

1 large ripe pineapple
1 tablespoon unsalted butter
3 tablespoons packed light brown sugar
1/4 teaspoon ground nutmeg
3 tablespoons dark rum
2 tablespoons Grand Marnier or other orange liqueur
1 1/3 cups vanilla nonfat frozen yogurt

1 Cut off leaves and stem end from pineapple. Remove skin and "eyes." Slice pineapple into rings 3/4 inch thick. Cut each slice into thirds and remove hard core.

2 In large skillet, melt butter over moderate heat. When butter begins to foam, add brown sugar and nutmeg, and heat until sugar melts. Stir in rum and bring to a simmer. Add pineapple and cook, turning often, until the pineapple is warmed through, about 4 minutes.

3 Leaving skillet on heat, drizzle Grand Marnier over pineapple. Standing back, ignite liqueur with long match. Shake pan gently until alcohol burns off. Spoon pineapple slices and sauce over frozen yogurt.

(Some More Ideas)

• Make this dish as the original; use 4 bananas instead of pineapple.

• This dish is even delicious served cold.

Health Points

• Pineapple is the only major food source of bromelain, an enzyme so strong that workers in canning plants need to wear protective clothing to prevent skin damage. More than 400 research papers have been written on the healing powers of bromelain. Its most important health function is as an anti-inflammatory, making it useful for everything from infections to arthritis to healthier arteries.

photo, page 249

Each serving provides

Key Nutrients 250 Calories, 30 Calories from Fat, 4g Fat, 2g Saturated Fat, 0g Trans Fat, 4g Protein, 43g Carb, 1g Fiber, 55mg Sodium
Blood Pressure Nutrients 18mg Vitamin C, 20mg Magnesium, 320mg Potassium, 118mg Calcium

All-Time Favorite Apple Crisp

Why not enjoy your proverbial "apple a day" in a satisfyingly sweet dessert? An abundance of apples, a crunchy oatmeal topping, and a spoonful of yogurt add up to a crisp that's full of flavor and nutrition.

Preparation time **25 minutes**   Cooking time **40 minutes**   *Serves 12*

2 tablespoons plus 1/2 cup packed light brown sugar

2 tablespoons plus 1/3 cup all-purpose flour

1 teaspoon cinnamon

Salt to taste

1 vanilla bean (about 5 inches long) or 1 teaspoon vanilla extract

3 tablespoons fresh lemon juice

3 pounds baking apples

1/2 cup old-fashioned oats

6 tablespoons cold margarine, cut into pieces

1 quart frozen nonfat vanilla yogurt

1 Preheat oven to 350°F. Lightly coat 13 x 9-inch baking dish with nonstick cooking spray. Mix 2 tablespoons brown sugar, 2 tablespoons flour, 1/2 teaspoon cinnamon, and salt to taste in food processor bowl. Cut vanilla bean in half lengthwise with paring knife. Scrape out seeds with the back of knife. Add to food processor and pulse to combine, about 10 seconds. Or put in medium bowl and work with hands until well mixed.

2 Put lemon juice in large bowl. Peel apples and cut into 1/4-inch slices (you need about 7 cups). Add to bowl, tossing with juice frequently. Sprinkle with brown sugar mixture and toss until evenly coated. Spread in baking dish.

3 Combine oats, remaining brown sugar, remaining flour, and remaining cinnamon in a medium bowl. Using your fingers, work margarine into flour mixture until coarse crumbs appear. Sprinkle over apples. Bake until topping is golden and apples are tender, about 40 minutes. Serve with scoops of frozen yogurt.

(Some More Ideas)

• Make a pear crisp. Substitute 3 pounds Bartlett or Comice pears for the apples.

• Increase the fiber in this dessert by using whole-wheat flour in place of the white.

Health Points

• Both apples and oats are great for helping reduce heart disease. The soluble fiber they contain aids in withdrawing cholesterol from the blood.

photo, page 249

Each serving provides

Key Nutrients 270 Calories, 60 Calories from Fat, 6g Fat, 1g Saturated Fat, 1g Trans Fat, 5g Protein, 50g Carb, 4g Fiber, 130mg Sodium
Blood Pressure Nutrients 8mg Vitamin C, 20mg Magnesium, 342mg Potassium, 125mg Calcium

Fruit with Cannoli Cream

Italian cannoli pastries, with their fried exteriors and ricotta cheese filling, are full of fat and cholesterol. Save your heart: Skip the fried dough and dip fresh fruit into chocolate-flecked cannoli "cream" made in a light way.

Preparation time **15 minutes**   *Serves 4*

Cream

1 cup low-fat (1%) cottage cheese

2 tablespoons fat-free half-and-half

2 tablespoons sugar

1/2 teaspoon vanilla

1/4 cup dried apricots, coarsely chopped

2 tablespoons mini chocolate chips

Fruit

2 Bartlett pears, cut into 1/2-inch wedges

2 large apples, cut into 1/2-inch wedges

1 Combine cottage cheese, half-and-half, sugar, and vanilla in a food processor and puree until smooth.

2 Transfer to bowl and stir in apricots and chocolate chips. (Recipe can be prepared to this point a day ahead. Cover and refrigerate until serving time.)

3 Arrange pears and apples on a platter and serve the cannoli cream in the center.

(Some More Ideas)

• Add strawberries or blue-berries to the cannoli cream.

• For a different twist, add butterscotch-flavored chips instead of chocolate chips.

Health Points

• Fat-free half-and-half works well in a variety of dishes calling for cream. Its rich taste is a boon for adding flavor to recipes, but with none of the fat.

• Be sure to use 1% cottage cheese. Using a 4% milkfat cottage cheese, you double the fat content.

• With 5 grams of fiber and 8 grams of protein per serving, this is one amazingly healthy dessert!

Each serving provides

Key Nutrients 220 Calories, 35 Calories from Fat, 4g Fat, 2g Saturated Fat, 0g Trans Fat, 8g Protein, 41g Carb, 5g Fiber, 230mg Sodium
Blood Pressure Nutrients 9mg Vitamin C, 18mg Magnesium, 392mg Potassium, 63mg Calcium

Fresh Plum Tartlets

These scrumptious tartlets, with their crisp, cookie-like crust, are topped with both prune butter and sliced fresh plums for a treat as delicious as it is heart-healthy.

Preparation time **25 minutes**   Cooking time **20 minutes**   *Serves 6*

1 cup old-fashioned rolled oats
1/2 cup walnuts
1 cup corn flakes
1/2 cup sugar
2 large egg whites
2 tablespoons fresh lime juice
1 teaspoon grated lime zest, plus extra for garnish
1/2 cup prune butter
1 pound fresh plums, halved, pitted, and sliced into thin wedges

1 Preheat oven to 350°F. Combine oats and walnuts in baking pan and bake until oats are toasted, about 7 minutes.

2 Transfer oats and walnuts to food processor along with corn flakes and sugar and process to fine crumbs. Add egg whites and 1 tablespoon of lime juice and pulse until evenly moistened.

3 Line large baking sheet with parchment paper. Divide dough into 6 pieces. With moistened hands, pat each piece out to a 4-inch round. Use tips of fingers to give each round a raised edge. Bake until crisp, about 10 minutes. Cool 2 minutes on baking sheet, then transfer to wire rack to cool completely.

4 Combine remaining 1 tablespoon lime juice, lime zest, and prune butter in small bowl. Spread mixture inside each cooled round. Arrange plums over prune butter mixture. Garnish with lime zest, if desired. (Recipe can be made ahead and refrigerated. Cover tarts loosely to keep plums from drying out.)

(Some More Ideas)

• Use pecans or almonds in place of the walnuts.

• Peach tarts are equally delicious. Use 1 pound fresh peaches, halved, pitted, and sliced into thin wedges.

• These tartlets are meant to be handheld and eaten like a giant cookie. But let them sit overnight and they soften enough to be eaten with a knife and fork.

Health Points

• Plums and prunes are rich in potassium and soluble fiber, both key nutrients for battling high blood pressure. But they also contain phytochemicals, such as chlorogenic acid, that are thought to detoxify carcinogenic chemicals that enter your body from the environment, such as smoke.

Each serving provides

Key Nutrients 300 Calories, 70 Calories from Fat, 8g Fat, 1g Saturated Fat, 0g Trans Fat, 7g Protein, 54g Carb, 4g Fiber, 55mg Sodium
Blood Pressure Nutrients 10mg Vitamin C, 30mg Magnesium, 294mg Potassium, 15mg Calcium

Fresh Plum Tartlets *p254*

Daffodil Cake *p258*

Checkerboard Cherry Pie *p256*

Banana Cream Pie with Honey-Wafer crust *p257*

Checkerboard Cherry Pie

Life is a bowl of cherries when you dig into a wedge of this juicy pie. Enjoy—without feeling guilty! The crust bakes up delectably flaky from a combination of reduced-fat sour cream and a little margarine.

Preparation time **25 minutes**   Cooking time **45 minutes**   *Serves 8*

2 cups all-purpose flour

1 cup sugar

Salt to taste

2 tablespoons cold margarine, cut up

1/2 cup reduced-fat sour cream

3 to 4 tablespoons ice water

2 cans (14 1/2 ounces each) sour cherries packed in water, drained

2 tablespoons cornstarch

1/4 teaspoon almond extract

1 egg white beaten with 1 teaspoon water

1 Pulse flour, 2 tablespoons sugar, and 1/4 teaspoon salt in food processor to mix. Add margarine and pulse until coarse crumbs form. With motor running, add sour cream, then water, 1 tablespoon at a time, and process until pastry holds together. Shape into two 8-inch disks, wrap in plastic, and refrigerate 30 minutes. Meanwhile, combine cherries, 3/4 cup sugar, cornstarch, almond extract, and remaining salt in large bowl. Set aside.

2 Coat 9-inch pie plate with nonstick cooking spray. Lightly flour work surface and roll out pastry disk into 15-inch round. Gently roll pastry onto rolling pin and ease into pie plate. Trim edge, leaving 1-inch overhang. Brush pastry with about 2 teaspoons egg-white mixture. Spoon in cherry filling.

3 Preheat oven to 425°F and arrange oven rack in center. Roll out remaining disk of pastry into 12-inch round. Cut pastry into 3/4-inch-wide strips with fluted pastry or pizza wheel. Weave strips on top of pie filling to make lattice pattern. Trim strips, leaving 1-inch overhang. Make 1-inch stand-up edge, folding in the ends of lattice strips as you go. Flute edge.

4 Brush top of pie with remaining egg-white mixture, and sprinkle with remaining sugar. Place pie on foil-lined baking sheet to catch any overflow. Bake 10 minutes. Reduce temperature to 350°F and bake until crust is lightly browned and juices are bubbling in center, 35 to 40 minutes.

(Some More Ideas)

• Use 4 cups pitted frozen cherries instead of canned cherries.

• Make this a blueberry pie using canned or frozen blueberries.

Health Points

• The pastry gets its flaky texture from a combination of reduced-fat sour cream and just a little margarine. This combination makes quite a difference fat-wise as compared to the traditional lard laden crusts.

• While the vitamin C in cherries get diminished from cooking, cherries are particularly rich in phytochemicals that battle free radicals, inhibit inflammation, and help keep arteries healthy. This combination makes them a particularly fine food for improving blood pressure.

photo, page 255

Each serving provides

Key Nutrients 300 Calories, 45 Calories from Fat, 5g Fat, 2g Saturated Fat, 0g Trans Fat, 5g Protein, 61g Carb, 2g Fiber, 60mg Sodium
Blood Pressure Nutrients 2mg Vitamin C, 15mg Magnesium, 161mg Potassium, 33mg Calcium

Banana Cream Pie with Honey-Wafer Crust

A cream pie on a lower-blood-pressure diet? Absolutely! This one has all of the flavor of the traditional homemade custard pies, but with less fat and cholesterol. And there are plenty of luscious, healthful bananas in every bite!

Preparation time **30 minutes plus chilling**   Cooking time **15 minutes**   *Serves 8*

48 reduced-fat vanilla wafers (about 8 ounces)
2 tablespoons honey
1/2 cup sugar
1/3 cup all-purpose flour
Salt to taste
3 cups reduced-fat (2%) milk
1/2 cup fat-free egg substitute
1 tablespoon margarine
1 tablespoon vanilla extract
6 large bananas
1/4 cup orange juice
3 tablespoons apricot preserves, melted

1 Preheat oven to 350°F. Lightly coat 9-inch pie plate with nonstick cooking spray. Pulse vanilla wafers, honey, and 2 tablespoons water in food processor until fine crumbs form. Press into pie plate to shape crust. Bake until set, about 10 minutes. Cool on wire rack.

2 Meanwhile, whisk sugar, flour, and salt in medium saucepan until blended. Slowly whisk in milk and bring to a simmer over medium heat. Measure egg substitute in 2-cup measure and whisk in about 1 cup hot-milk mixture, then return mixture to pan (this avoids curdling). Cook, whisking, until mixture comes to a full boil and thickens. Remove from heat. Whisk in margarine and vanilla. Let cool 15 minutes.

3 Slice bananas; toss with orange juice. Line crust with one-third of bananas and top with one-half of filling. Repeat, then arrange remaining bananas on top in spiral design, with slices overlapping. Brush apricot preserves over bananas. Cool 30 minutes at room temperature, and then chill at least 4 hours, or overnight.

(Some More Ideas)

• Make a chocolate crust by using reduced-fat chocolate wafers instead of the vanilla ones.

• Use strawberries and straw-berry jam to top the pie instead of bananas.

Health Points

• When 2% milk is used instead of cream, this pie is significantly reduced in fat. You can even use 1% milk, but skim milk will produce a filling that is too thin and not as rich tasting.

photo, page 255

Each serving provides

Key Nutrients 380 Calories, 70 Calories from Fat, 8g Fat, 3g Saturated Fat, 1g Trans Fat, 8g Protein, 73g Carb, 3g Fiber, 170mg Sodium
Blood Pressure Nutrients 10mg Vitamin C, 36mg Magnesium, 491mg Potassium, 122mg Calcium

Daffodil Cake

Usher in spring the traditional way, by baking a daffodil cake—a fragrant, delicate sponge cake with swirls of yellow and white in every slice. This festive, healthy treat is lightly flavored with orange.

Preparation time **20 minutes**   Cooking time **35 minutes**   *Serves 16*

10 large eggs, separated
1 1/2 cups granulated sugar
2 teaspoons grated orange zest
1 tablespoon vanilla
Salt to taste
1/2 teaspoon cream of tartar
1 1/3 cups sifted cake flour
1/3 cup sifted confectioners' sugar

1 Preheat oven to 375°F. Beat 4 egg yolks (reserve remaining 6 yolks for another recipe), 1/4 cup granulated sugar, and orange zest in large bowl with electric mixer at high speed until batter is thick and lemon-colored, about 10 minutes. Scrape down bowl occasionally with spatula. Beat in vanilla.

2 Beat all 10 egg whites and salt in separate large bowl with clean beaters at high speed until foamy. Add cream of tartar and beat until soft peaks form. Add remaining granulated sugar, 2 tablespoons at a time, beating at high speed until sugar has dissolved and stiff, glossy peaks form.

3 Sift flour over egg whites, 1/3 cup at a time, gently folding in each addition with a wire whisk just until flour is no longer visible. Fold one-third of egg white mixture into yolk mixture.

4 Alternately spoon heaping tablespoons of yellow and white batters into a 9- or 10-inch tube pan. Swirl thin spatula or knife through batter to marbleize. Lightly swirl top of cake. Bake until cake springs back when lightly touched, about 35 minutes. Invert cake in pan onto bottle and cool completely. Run knife around pan to loosen cake. Remove cake from pan, place on serving plate, and sprinkle cake with confectioners' sugar.

(Some More Ideas)

• Make a lemon-flavored daffodil cake. Use 2 teaspoons lemon zest instead of orange zest.

• Present the daffodil cake whole and fill the center with fresh chunks of mixed fruit.

Health Points

• The original recipe for daffodil cake dates back to 1930. This version increases the egg whites and leaves out the yolks, contributing to a wonderfully low level of fat—just 1 gram per slice!

photo, page 255

Each serving provides

Key Nutrients 170 Calories, 30 Calories from Fat, 3g Fat, 1g Saturated Fat, 0g Trans Fat, 5g Protein, 31g Carb, 0g Fiber, 40mg Sodium
Blood Pressure Nutrients 0mg Vitamin C, 5mg Magnesium, 67mg Potassium, 18mg Calcium

Cappuccino Chiffon Cake

When chiffon cakes first appeared in the 1940s, the focus was on how easy they were to mix. Today we still value that they are easy to make, even in healthier variations such as this one.

Preparation time **15 minutes**   Cooking time **45 minutes**   *Serves 16*

2 1/4 cups cake flour

1 1/2 cups granulated sugar

1 tablespoon baking powder

3/4 teaspoon cinnamon

1/2 teaspoon salt

1/2 cup walnut oil or extra-light olive oil

2 large eggs, separated, plus 4 large egg whites

3/4 cup brewed espresso or other dark-roast coffee, at room temperature

2 tablespoons unsweetened cocoa powder

1 teaspoon vanilla

1/2 teaspoon cream of tartar

2 tablespoons confectioners' sugar

1 Preheat oven to 325°F. Stir together cake flour, granulated sugar, baking powder, cinnamon, and salt in medium bowl. Whisk the walnut oil, egg yolks, espresso, cocoa powder, and vanilla together in large bowl until smooth. Fold flour mixture into egg mixture until well combined.

2 Beat 6 egg whites until frothy in separate bowl. Beat in cream of tartar and continue beating until stiff peaks form. Gently fold egg whites into batter.

3 Spoon batter into ungreased 10-inch tube pan. Bake until cake tester inserted in center comes out clean, about 45 minutes.

4 Invert pan to cool. Once cooled, run a metal spatula around the inner and outer edges of the cake and invert onto a serving plate. Dust cake with confectioners' sugar.

(Some More Ideas)

Vanilla chiffon cake: Eliminate the espresso and cocoa, and increase the vanilla to 1 tablespoon.

• Add 1/4 cup very finely chopped walnuts to complement the flavor of walnut oil.

Health Points

• Walnut oil is a rich source of heart-healthy monounsaturated fat. A little goes a long way, as walnut oil is intensely flavored.

Each serving provides

Key Nutrients 220 Calories, 70 Calories from Fat, 8g Fat, 1g Saturated Fat, 0g Trans Fat, 3g Protein, 36g Carb, 1g Fiber, 80mg Sodium
Blood Pressure Nutrients 0mg Vitamin C, 9mg Magnesium, 167mg Potassium, 50mg Calcium

Chocolate Chip Oatmeal Cookies

Look what has happened to the traditional chocolate chip cookie! This one has only half the fat of the original, plus old-fashioned oats give it a fiber boost. Yet all of the changes have not slimmed down the flavor.

Preparation time **15 minutes**   Cooking time **20 minutes**   *Makes 36*

1 cup all-purpose flour
1/2 teaspoon baking soda
Salt to taste
1 cup old-fashioned oats
4 tablespoons margarine
2/3 cup packed light brown sugar
1/2 cup granulated sugar
1 large egg
1 1/2 teaspoons vanilla
1/3 cup reduced-fat sour cream
3/4 cup semisweet chocolate chips

1 Preheat oven to 375°F. Line two large baking sheets with parchment paper. Whisk flour, baking soda, and salt in medium bowl. Stir in oats.

2 Cream margarine, brown sugar, and granulated sugar in large bowl with electric mixer at high speed until well blended. Add egg and vanilla and beat until light yellow and creamy, about 3 minutes. Blend in sour cream with wooden spoon, then flour mixture all at once, just until combined (don't overmix or the cookies may become tough). Stir in chocolate chips.

3 Drop dough by heaping teaspoonfuls 2 inches apart onto baking sheets. Bake cookies until golden, about 10 minutes. Cool on baking sheets 2 minutes, then transfer to wire racks and cool completely. Store in airtight container for up to 2 weeks or freeze for up to 3 months.

(Some More Ideas)

• Add 1/2 cup dried cherries to the batter. Cherries and chocolate are a great flavor combination.

• Make these cookies more fiber-rich by using whole-wheat flour in place of the all-purpose flour.

Health Points

• Low-fat dairy products like the sour cream in this recipe are particularly good sources of nutrients, including calcium and potassium, the minerals best linked to improved blood pressure.

• Oats are a great source of vitamins B1, B2, and E, as well as a long list of phytochemicals that fight cancer, cardiovascular disease, and diabetes.

Each serving (1 cookie) provides

Key Nutrients 80 Calories, 25 Calories from Fat, 3g Fat, 1g Saturated Fat, 0g Trans Fat, 1g Protein, 13g Carb, 1g Fiber, 40mg Sodium
Blood Pressure Nutrients 0mg Vitamin C, 12mg Magnesium, 44mg Potassium, 10mg Calcium

Chocolate Chip Oatmeal Cookies *p260*

Pecan Icebox Cookies *p262*

Lemon Angel Food Cake with Strawberries *p264*

Ginger-Pear Upside-Down Cake *p265*

Pecan Icebox Cookies

These are traditional icebox cookies—the type Grandma made—in which the dough is made ahead and kept in the refrigerator or freezer until it's time to bake them. Freshly baked cookies are always only 10 minutes away.

Preparation time **15 minutes plus chilling**   Cooking time **10 minutes**   *Serves 72*

1 3/4 cups all-purpose flour
1/2 teaspoon cinnamon
Salt to taste
1/4 teaspoon baking soda
1/4 cup (1/2 stick) margarine, softened
2/3 cup granulated sugar
1/3 cup packed light brown sugar
1 large egg
1 tablespoon vanilla
1/3 cup nonfat sour cream
1/3 cup chopped pecans, toasted

1 Whisk flour, cinnamon, salt, and baking soda in medium bowl. Cream margarine, granulated sugar, and brown sugar in large bowl with electric mixer at high speed until light and fluffy, about 4 minutes. Add egg and vanilla and beat until well blended. Using a wooden spoon, stir in flour mixture, and then sour cream and pecans.

2 Tear off 20-inch sheet of plastic wrap and sprinkle lightly with flour. Transfer dough to plastic wrap and shape into 15-inch log. Tightly roll in plastic and refrigerate until firm, about 2 hours. (Or wrap dough in heavy-duty foil and freeze up to 1 month.)

3 Preheat oven to 375°F. Cut dough into rounds 3/16-inch thick, making 72 cookies. Working in batches, place 1/2 inch apart on ungreased baking sheets. Bake just until crisp and golden brown around edges, about 8 minutes (do not overbake). If using frozen dough, bake 10 minutes. Transfer cookies to wire racks to cool completely before storing in airtight container.

(Some More Ideas)

Chocolate icebox cookies: At the beginning of Step 1, whisk 1/3 cup unsweetened cocoa into the flour mixture. Increase the margarine to 1/3 cup and sour cream to 1/2 cup.

• Toasting nuts doubles their flavor. You can get away with using less simply by placing nuts in a dry skillet, then toss the nuts for a few minutes until lightly browned over a medium flame.

• Use almonds instead of pecans.

Health Points

• Cinnamon may have anti-bacterial and antimicrobial properties, and it may also reduce discomfort from heartburn. In addition, cinnamaldehyde, a phyto-chemical in the spice, may ward off bacteria such as *H. pylori,* the bacteria linked to ulcers.

photo, page 261

Each serving (1 cookie) provides

Key Nutrients 35 Calories, 10 Calories from Fat, 2g Fat, 0g Saturated Fat, 0g Trans Fat, 0g Protein, 5g Carb, 0g Fiber, 15mg Sodium
Blood Pressure Nutrients 0mg Vitamin C, 2mg Magnesium, 12mg Potassium, 4mg Calcium

Chocolate Snacking Cake

Craving some chocolate? Each of these luscious little gems has only 70 calories and 1 gram of fat.
Go ahead and indulge yourself!

Preparation time **15 minutes**   Cooking time **35 minutes plus cooling**   *Serves 36*

1 1/3 cups sifted self-rising flour

1 cup plus 2 teaspoons unsweetened cocoa powder

1/4 cup nonfat buttermilk

1 tablespoon instant espresso powder

1 cup granulated sugar

1/2 cup packed light brown sugar

1/2 cup unsweetened applesauce

2 teaspoons vanilla

2 large egg whites

1/2 cup mini chocolate chips

1 tablespoon confectioners' sugar

1 Preheat oven to 325°F. Line 8-inch square baking pan with foil, leaving 1-inch overhang. Sift flour and 1 cup cocoa together into small bowl. Heat buttermilk and espresso in small saucepan over low heat until espresso is dissolved.

2 Mix granulated and brown sugars, applesauce, buttermilk mixture, and vanilla in medium bowl. Stir in flour mixture just until blended. Beat egg whites in large bowl with electric mixer at high speed just until soft peaks form. Fold egg whites into batter. Stir in chocolate chips.

3 Scrape batter into pan. Bake just until set, about 35 minutes (do not overbake). Cool in pan on wire rack 15 minutes. Lift out cake and set on rack to cool completely. Sift confectioners' sugar and remaining cocoa over cake. Cut into thirty-six 1 1/2-inch squares.

(Some More Ideas)

• Add 1 tablespoon coffee liqueur to the batter for a more "grown-up" taste.

• Substitute mini white chocolate chips for the regular chocolate ones.

Health Points

• By using applesauce, this recipe needs no oils or butter. The slight apple flavor it imparts complements the coffee-chocolate taste combination.

Each serving (1 square) provides

Key Nutrients 70 Calories, 10 Calories from Fat, 1g Fat, 1g Saturated Fat, 0g Trans Fat, 1g Protein, 16g Carb, 1g Fiber, 65mg Sodium
Blood Pressure Nutrients 1mg Vitamin C, 18mg Magnesium, 74mg Potassium, 24mg Calcium

Lemon Angel Food Cake with Strawberries

Angel food cake is a dream dessert for cholesterol-conscious eaters. Whipped up from egg whites but no yolks, this lofty delight doesn't even require shortening. The vividly colorful fruit sauce makes the cake worthy of a festive occasion.

Preparation time **20 minutes**   Cooking time **50 minutes**   *Serves 12*

Fruit

1 bag (20 ounces) frozen strawberries, thawed

1/2 cup orange juice

Cake

12 large egg whites, at room
temperature

1 1/4 teaspoons cream of tartar

1/2 teaspoon salt

1 1/4 cups sugar

3 tablespoons grated lemon
zest

1 teaspoon vanilla

1 cup flour

1 Combine strawberries and orange juice in large bowl. Refrigerate.

2 Preheat oven to 325°F. Beat egg whites, cream of tartar, and salt in large bowl with electric mixer until foamy. Gradually beat in sugar, 2 tablespoons at a time, until thick, soft peaks form. Beat in lemon zest and vanilla.

3 Gently fold flour into egg-white mixture, 1/4 cup at a time, until incorporated. Spoon into ungreased 10-inch angel food or tube pan. Bake until top springs back when lightly pressed, about 50 minutes.

4 Invert cake pan to cool. If pan does not have legs, hang pan over the neck of a bottle. Cool cake completely. Run metal spatula around edges and center of pan, then invert onto cake platter. Serve with strawberries and juice.

(Some More Ideas)

• Make this cake with any other berries; raspberries and blueberries are both good choices.

• Add 1/3 cup mini chocolate chips to the batter. You get plenty of chocolate flavor, but with less overall fat than a chocolate cake.

Health Points

• When you just have to have a cake, angel food is a great choice. It's low in sodium and has no fat or cholesterol; its only vice is its relatively plentiful sugar content. However, since it uses a fresh fruit topping rather than a fatty, sugary frosting, you have the almost perfect healthy dessert.

photo, page 261

Each serving provides

Key Nutrients 160 Calories, 0 Calories from Fat, 0g Fat, 0g Saturated Fat, 0g Trans Fat, 5g Protein, 35g Carb, 1g Fiber, 135mg Sodium
Blood Pressure Nutrients 21mg Vitamin C, 11mg Magnesium, 184mg Potassium, 13mg Calcium

Ginger-Pear Upside-Down Cake

Greet the first chilly day of fall with a tender yellow cake topped with caramelized pears. Although very little fat goes into the batter—just 3 tablespoons of heart-smart olive oil—the cake has a warm, spicy richness.

Preparation time **15 minutes**   Cooking time **35 minutes**   *Serves 10*

2 tablespoons dark brown sugar

3 firm ripe Bartlett pears

1 1/4 cups cake flour

1 teaspoon ground ginger

3/4 teaspoon baking powder

1/4 teaspoon baking soda

Salt to taste

3 tablespooons extra-light olive oil

3/4 cup granulated sugar

1 1/2 teaspoons grated lime zest

1 teaspoon coconut extract

1 large egg plus 1 large egg white

3/4 cup buttermilk

1 Preheat oven to 350°F. Spray bottom of 9-inch round non-stick cake pan with nonstick cooking spray. Sprinkle brown sugar over bottom, shaking pan to coat evenly.

2 Peel, core, and halve pears. Slice pears crosswise into 1/3-inch-thick slices. Evenly spread pears in pan, making sure bottom of pan is covered.

3 Mix together flour, ginger, baking powder, baking soda, and salt on a sheet of wax paper. With electric mixer, beat together oil, granulated sugar, lime zest, and coconut extract in large bowl. Beat in whole egg and egg white until thick.

4 With a spatula, alternately fold flour mixture and buttermilk into egg mixture, beginning and ending with flour mixture, until just blended.

5 Pour batter over pears, smoothing top to cover pears completely. Bake until a toothpick inserted in center comes out clean, about 35 minutes. Transfer to a wire rack. Let cake cool in pan on rack for 10 minutes, then invert onto a platter. Let cool slightly before slicing.

(Some More Ideas)

Apple upside-down cake: Slice 3 Granny Smith apples in place of the pears.

• For a really fresh ginger taste, grate 1 teaspoon fresh ginger and add in Step 3 with the oil and sugar.

• Make the cake more fiber-rich by substituting 1/2 cup whole-wheat flour for 1/2 cup cake flour.

Health Points

• Pears contain ample amounts of potassium to help relieve high blood pressure.

• Pears also contain high amounts of pectin, a particular type of fiber that is very useful in preventing cholesterol from being absorbed in the body.

• Interestingly, pears are considered among the least allergenic foods in the food kingdom!

photo, page 261

Each serving provides

Key Nutrients 220 Calories, 50 Calories from Fat, 6g Fat, 1g Saturated Fat, 0g Trans Fat, 3g Protein, 40g Carb, 2g Fiber, 35mg Sodium
Blood Pressure Nutrients 2mg Vitamin C, 8mg Magnesium, 139mg Potassium, 48mg Calcium

Lemon Mousse with Strawberries

Sampling this mousse, which sparkles with fresh lemon flavor, is like spooning up sunshine. We've lightened it up by substituting gelatin and yogurt for the usual quantities of eggs and cream.

Preparation time **15 minutes**   Cooking time **5 minutes plus chilling**   *Serves 8*

1 pint strawberries
1 packet unflavored gelatin
1/2 cup cold water
3/4 cup sugar
2 teaspoons grated lemon zest
1/2 cup fresh lemon juice
1 tablespoon extra-light olive oil
1 large egg
1 1/3 cups plain fat-free yogurt

1 Hull strawberries and thickly slice. Sprinkle gelatin over 1/4 cup cold water in small bowl. Let stand 5 minutes to soften.

2 Whisk together remaining 1/4 cup water, sugar, lemon zest, lemon juice, oil, and egg in medium saucepan until well combined. Cook over low heat, whisking constantly, until mixture is hot, about 5 minutes. Whisk in softened gelatin and cook, whisking constantly, until gelatin has dissolved, about 1 minute.

3 Remove from heat, transfer to medium bowl, and cool to room temperature, whisking occasionally. Whisk in yogurt. Alternately layer strawberries and lemon mousse in 8 dessert bowls and chill until set, about 3 hours.

(Some More Ideas)

Orange mousse: Substitute grated orange zest and orange juice for the lemon zest and juice.

• Top the mousse with any other sliced fruit instead of strawberries. Blueberries, raspberries, or sliced bananas are good choices.

Health Points

• By using the protein gelatin, you can create so many low-fat mousselike desserts. The gelatin helps to stabilize dairy products that do not contain enough fat to stabilize on their own.

• One serving of the mousse provides healthy portions of vitamin C and calcium, both important nutrients for controlling hypertension.

Each serving provides

Key Nutrients 140 Calories, 20 Calories from Fat, 3g Fat, 0g Saturated Fat, 0g Trans Fat, 6g Protein, 26g Carb, 1g Fiber, 40mg Sodium
Blood Pressure Nutrients 33mg Vitamin C, 7mg Magnesium, 97mg Potassium, 63mg Calcium

Blueberry Bavarian *p268*

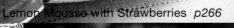
Lemon Mousse with Strawberries *p266*

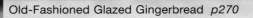
Old-Fashioned Glazed Gingerbread *p270*

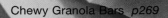
Chewy Granola Bars *p269*

Blueberry Bavarian

Spoon up a tangy-sweet mouthful of our custardy berry blend and discover how sublime a heart-friendly dessert can be. Instead of heavy cream and whole eggs, we use low-fat milk, dry milk, sour cream, and gelatin.

Preparation time **10 minutes**   Cooking time **15 minutes plus chilling**   *Serves 6*

1 cup low-fat (1%) milk
1/4 cup fat-free dry milk
2 packages (12 ounces each) frozen blueberries, thawed
1/2 cup plus 1 tablespoon sugar
Salt to taste
1 cup fat-free sour cream
1 packet unflavored gelatin
1/4 cup cold water
1/2 cup fresh blueberries

1 Combine milk and dry milk in small bowl and whisk until well blended. Place in freezer for up to 30 minutes.

2 Combine frozen blueberries, 1/2 cup sugar, and salt in medium saucepan over low heat. Bring to a simmer and cook until sugar has dissolved, berries have broken up, and mixture has reduced to 2 1/4 cups, about 10 minutes. Let cool to room temperature. Stir in 2/3 cup sour cream.

3 Sprinkle gelatin over 1/4 cup cold water in heatproof measuring cup. Let stand 5 minutes to soften. Set measuring cup in small saucepan of simmering water and heat until gelatin has melted, about 2 minutes. Let cool to room temperature.

4 With a hand mixer, beat chilled milk until thick, soft peaks form. Beat in remaining 1 tablespoon sugar until stiff peaks form. Beat in gelatin mixture. Fold milk mixture into blueberry mixture.

5 Spoon into 6 dessert bowls or glasses. Chill until set, about 2 hours. At serving time, top each with a dollop of remaining sour cream and fresh blueberries.

(Some More Ideas)

Strawberry/peach Bavarian: Use 2 packages of either frozen strawberries or peaches for the filling and top with fresh blueberries and diced fresh peaches.

Health Points

• By adding dry milk to low-fat milk, you get a thick milk when chilled that can be whipped and used like heavy cream. The mixture is stabilized with gelatin to keep it firm.

• Blueberries are brimming with heart-protective nutrients, including potassium, folate, magnesium, fiber, and vitamin C.

photo, page 267

Each serving provides

Key Nutrients 270 Calories, 50 Calories from Fat, 6g Fat, 4g Saturated Fat, 0g Trans Fat, 4g Protein, 38g Carb, 3g Fiber, 45mg Sodium
Blood Pressure Nutrients 5mg Vitamin C, 17mg Magnesium, 205mg Potassium, 115mg Calcium

Chewy Granola Bars

Start with a double dose of oats and you're on your way to a heart-healthy snack. For a gift, wrap the bars in wax paper or plastic wrap, then in colorful wrapping paper, and then tuck them into a pretty basket. They'll keep about 1 week.

Preparation time **15 minutes**   Cooking time **40 minutes**   *Makes 12 bars*

1 1/2 cups old-fashioned or quick-cooking oats

1/2 cup oat bran

1/3 cup flour

2/3 cup dried apricots, coarsely chopped

1/3 cup walnuts, coarsely chopped

2 tablespoons toasted wheat germ

Salt to taste

1/4 cup frozen pineapple juice concentrate

2 tablespoons packed light brown sugar

2 tablespoons honey

1 teaspoon vanilla

1 Preheat the oven to 350°. Line an 11 x 7-inch metal baking pan with foil, leaving 1 or 2 inches hanging over ends. Spray with nonstick cooking spray; set aside.

2 Place oats and oat bran on jelly-roll pan and toast until oats are lightly browned and fragrant, about 10 minutes. Transfer to large mixing bowl and add flour, apricots, walnuts, wheat germ, and salt.

3 Combine pineapple juice concentrate, brown sugar, and honey in small skillet. Cook over medium heat until brown sugar has dissolved, about 4 minutes. Remove from heat and stir in vanilla. Pour honey mixture over oat mixture, stirring to coat.

4 Spoon oat mixture into baking pan. With moistened hands, press mixture into even layer in pan. Bake until firm, about 20 minutes. Using foil, carefully lift out mixture and cool on wire rack. On work surface, cut into 12 bars.

(Some More Ideas)

• Substitute dried raisins, cherries, or chopped dried apples for the apricots.

• Use peanuts, almonds, or pecans instead of the walnuts.

• Try a stronger honey such as buckwheat, or if you prefer a milder one, use clover.

Health Points

• These bars are significantly lower in fat and total carbohydrate than commercially boxed granola bars. They are also light in sodium, which is important for healthy blood pressure.

• Using fruit juice concentrate eliminates the need for oil in this recipe. The concentrate gives the bars moistness and provides some extra flavor as well.

photo, page 267

Each serving (1 bar) provides

Key Nutrients 140 Calories, 30 Calories from Fat, 4g Fat, 0g Saturated Fat, 0g Trans Fat, 4g Protein, 26g Carb, 3g Fiber, 0mg Sodium
Blood Pressure Nutrients 4mg Vitamin C, 50mg Magnesium, 245mg Potassium, 19mg Calcium

Old-Fashioned Glazed Gingerbread

This is not your mother's—or your grandma's—gingerbread! Sure, it has that same memorable flavor and moistness. But in this blood-pressure-friendly makeover, applesauce stands in for some of the fat.

Preparation time **30 minutes**   Cooking time **45 minutes**   *Serves 12*

Bread

1 1/3 cups all-purpose flour

1 1/2 teaspoons pumpkin pie spice

3/4 teaspoon baking soda

1/2 teaspoon salt

1/2 cup unsweetened applesauce

1/4 cup light molasses

1 large egg, lightly beaten

4 tablespoons margarine

1/2 cup packed dark brown sugar

2 teaspoons grated peeled fresh ginger

Topping

3 tablespoons finely chopped crystallized ginger

3/4 cup sifted confectioners' sugar

1 1/2 tablespoons water

1 Preheat oven to 350°F. Generously coat 8-inch square cake pan with nonstick cooking spray. Place cooling rack on wax paper. Whisk flour, pumpkin pie spice, baking soda, and salt in medium bowl. Blend applesauce, molasses, and egg in separate bowl.

2 Cream margarine and brown sugar in medium bowl with electric mixer at high speed until light, 3–4 minutes. Reduce speed to low and beat in applesauce mixture. Stir in flour mixture with wooden spoon just until combined. Blend in fresh ginger.

3 Scrape batter into cake pan. Bake until cake tester inserted in center comes out with moist crumbs clinging, about 45 minutes. Cool in pan on wire rack 10 minutes. Remove from pan and set, right side up, on rack. Cool completely.

4 Scatter crystallized ginger on top of gingerbread. Blend confectioners' sugar with enough water (about 1 1/2 tablespoons) to make spreadable glaze. Drizzle glaze over crystallized ginger with fork, letting some glaze drizzle down sides.

(Some More Ideas)

• Add finely diced peeled pears or apples to the batter for extra flavor and fiber.

• If you want even more distinctive flavors, substitute 1/4 teaspoon cinnamon, 1/4 teaspoon nutmeg, and 1/4 teaspoon ground cloves for the pumpkin pie spice.

Health Points

• Using three types of ginger— ground (in pumpkin pie spice), fresh, and crystallized— instead of fat and sugar really punches up the flavor of this cake. In addition to its extraordinary flavor, ginger is considered one of the most healthful spices available. Substances in ginger— including gingerol, shogaol, and zingiberene—have antioxidant capabilities, which may help to prevent heart disease. Ginger also has antiinflammatory properties, and its soothing effect for digestion is well heralded.

photo, page 267

Each serving provides

Key Nutrients 180 Calories, 40 Calories from Fat, 5g Fat, 1g Saturated Fat, 1g Trans Fat, 2g Protein, 34g Carb, 1g Fiber, 220mg Sodium
Blood Pressure Nutrients 2mg Vitamin C, 7mg Magnesium, 177mg Potassium, 35mg Calcium

Chocolate-Nut Meringue Cookies

Here's an astounding achievement: chocolate-nut cookies with less than half a gram of fat apiece! The secret is meringue, that versatile blend of whipped egg whites and sugar. Using cocoa, rather than solid chocolate, is also a major fat-cutter.

Preparation time **10 minutes**   Cooking time **30 minutes plus cooling**   *Makes 36*

1/3 cup walnuts
1/2 cup plus 2 tablespoons confectioners' sugar
4 teaspoons unsweetened cocoa powder
1/4 teaspoon cinnamon
2 large egg whites
1/8 teaspoon salt

1 Preheat oven to 300°F. Line 2 baking sheets with parchment paper. Toast walnuts in small skillet, stirring frequently until crisp and fragrant, about 7 minutes. When cool enough to handle, coarsely chop.

2 Sift together 1/2 cup confectioners' sugar, cocoa powder, and cinnamon on sheet of wax paper.

3 With electric mixer, beat egg whites and salt in large bowl until stiff peaks form. With rubber spatula, gently fold cocoa mixture into egg whites. Gently fold in nuts.

4 Drop batter by generous teaspoonfuls onto baking sheets, spacing them 1 inch apart. Bake until set, about 20 minutes. Remove and cool on wire rack. Dust with remaining 2 tablespoons confectioners' sugar just before serving.

(Some More Ideas)

• Eliminate the cocoa and add 1 teaspoon vanilla extract with the egg whites to prepare vanilla meringue cookies.

• Use pecans or almonds instead of walnuts.

Health Points

• Using parchment paper eliminates the need for greasing baking sheets. The small amount of fat in each cookie comes from the nuts, which contain healthy omega-3 fatty acids.

• It's the yolk of the egg that provides the nutrients to a chick embryo, so it's the part with all the fat and cholesterol. Egg whites have zero of both, but still contain lots of protein as well as vitamins and minerals.

Each serving (1 cookie) provides

Key Nutrients 15 Calories, 5 Calories from Fat, 1g Fat, 0g Saturated Fat, 0g Trans Fat, 1g Protein, 2g Carb, 0g Fiber, 10mg Sodium
Blood Pressure Nutrients 0mg Vitamin C, 4mg Magnesium, 12mg Potassium, 1mg Calcium

eat to beat high blood pressure featuring the
DASH-Plus Plan

On the surface, blood pressure is easy to understand: It's a measure of how easily blood flows through your body. What could be simpler?

In truth, many things are simpler. Blood pressure—and more specifically, high blood pressure—can be a confusing, sometimes complex subject.

For example, take the seemingly simple task of measuring blood pressure. Not only is there more than one measurement (the well-known "top number" and "bottom number"), but they change all the time, based on activity, time of day, and state of mind. More challenging is that there are so many things that can affect blood pressure, in both good ways and bad. Add to that the many different effects high blood pressure can have on your body and the fact that the condition itself has almost no symptoms but a potentially deadly outcome, and you start to understand that blood pressure is worthy of learning a little more about.

Here's a good question to start with: What is perhaps the most important lifestyle factor that influences your blood pressure? (Hint: Reader's Digest has put its first-ever program for reducing blood pressure inside a cookbook!)

The answer, of course, is food. Doctors and scientists have long known that food has an enormous influence on the health of your circulatory system. DASH—which stands for Dietary Approaches to Stop Hypertension—is a set of eating guidelines established in 1997 and based on an extensive study of how wholesome food choices can best reduce blood pressure. It remains a "gold standard" program for eating for healthy blood pressure. But we weren't satisfied with that, so we have added even more simple, natural ways to battle blood pressure to DASH to create what we believe is the best plan of attack possible for this escalating health problem. We call it the DASH-Plus Plan, and you'll learn all about it in the pages ahead.

But to start, let's explore the truths and myths of high blood pressure. Once you're armed with this knowledge, applying the DASH-Plus Plan becomes even easier.

Defining Blood Pressure

It's 5 p.m. on a Friday in the height of summer. You're heading—along with what seems like 300,000 others—from your home in the city to a secluded weekend escape. Two miles out from the city, traffic slows to a crawl. There's no accident, no construction—simply too many cars trying to move on a highway that just can't accommodate that much traffic. So the pressure builds as you sit in your steaming car, waiting and waiting and waiting.

Much the same thing happens when you have high blood pressure. With every beat of your heart, oxygen-rich blood is pumped throughout the 60,000 miles of blood vessels in your body. *Blood pressure* describes the force of that blood as it wends its way through your arteries. As long as the walls of your arteries are clean, smooth, and flexible, the blood flows smoothly and your pressure remains low.

Sometimes, though, artery walls become stiff, so they're unable to contract and expand easily. Or they get clogged with sticky plaque, clots, and other gunk, thus narrowing the space through which blood can flow. Or too much fluid enters them. When any one of these happens, pressure builds inside your blood vessels, and the next thing you know, you're listening to some white-coated professional reading you the riot act about your diet, exercise, weight, and health.

Like the unexpected traffic jam, there are no warning signs of high blood pressure. If you don't have regular checkups with your doctor that include blood pressure monitoring, you could walk around for years with dangerously high levels without a clue. No wonder they call hypertension the silent killer.

> High Blood Pressure vs. Hypertension

When it comes to weight, there are three main categories: **healthy, overweight,** and **obese.** While many of us are overweight, we are not technically obese. The government officially considers obesity, as determined objectively based on a person's body mass index, a disease that warrants regular medical care.

Similar ratings apply to blood pressure. A reading of 120/80 mmHg or less is considered **healthy.** A higher reading signals **high blood pressure,** and you should be addressing it, just as you would if you were overweight. If your reading is above 140/90, you have **hypertension,** which needs a doctor's ongoing monitoring and treatment.

Make no mistake: Blood pressure can kill. Just as the growing rush-hour tension on the expressway increases the likelihood of an accident, so the growing pressure of blood against arterial muscles increases the risk of serious damage. It could be a clot breaking loose from an artery wall and traveling to your brain, causing a stroke. It could be microscopic damage to the artery walls themselves that eventually leads to plaque buildup and a heart attack. Or it could be long-term damage to the heart itself as it's forced to pump harder and harder to get blood through narrowed arteries.

Overall, a diagnosis of hypertension means that your risk of heart attack, heart failure, stroke, and kidney disease has just skyrocketed. Consider this: If you're between 40 and 70, each 20-point increase in systolic blood pressure (the top number) or 10-point rise in diastolic pressure (the bottom number) *doubles* your risk of *any* cardiovascular disease.

If you lower those readings to normal levels, you reduce your risk of stroke by 35 to 40 percent, cut your risk of heart attack by 20 to 25 percent, and lower your risk of heart failure by more than 50 percent. Obviously, then, the benefits of following the DASH-Plus Plan and making the recipes in this book the centerpiece of your diet are enormous. Even better—it doesn't take long to make a difference, as you'll see.

What Causes High Blood Pressure

There are two types of high blood pressure. Primary, or "essential," high blood pressure is by far the most common, affecting an estimated 90 to 95 percent of those with high blood pressure. Most likely, this is the form you have. This is also the type for which no specific cause is known, although researchers do have some theories.

One of the main theories is that primary high blood pressure is the result of a hyperactive sympathetic nervous system, which controls involuntary actions, such as breathing, blinking, and pushing blood through the body. Other theories blame hormonal imbalances and damage to the endothelium, the inner layer of blood vessels, which prevents them from dilating. In addition, mutations in the genes that control blood volume and sodium; low intake of micronutrients such as potassium, magnesium, and calcium; and high sodium intake (the one you're probably most familiar with), may play a role.

The other form of high blood pressure, called secondary, is a by-product of having a specific medical condition. These include kidney disease, Cushing's syndrome (which is a rare hormonal condition), pregnancy, an overactive thyroid gland, and neurological disorders. In addition, certain medicines can cause secondary high blood pressure, such as high doses of estrogen, corticosteroids, and nonsteroidal anti-inflammatory drugs.

High blood pressure is actually a fairly modern illness; 100 years ago, it, like most chronic heart conditions, barely existed. That's because few people were overweight, and most got plenty of physical activity and ate diets that were relatively healthy, with few processed foods.

You see, you don't get high blood pressure from viruses or bacteria. You get it from the way you live. Although researchers aren't sure of the exact physiological mechanism that increases blood pressure, they certainly know the triggers. Stated simply, the way you live is the greatest contributor to your risk of developing high blood pressure. Among the things that increase your risk of hypertension:

- **Being overweight**
- **Heavy alcohol consumption**
- **A high-sodium diet**
- **Use of oral contraceptives**
- **A sedentary lifestyle**
- **High levels of anxiety and stress**

What's noteworthy is that all of these factors are within your control. While medications exist to deal with the physiology of high blood pressure, the way you eat, move, and deal with the day-to-day stresses of life has the greatest impact on achieving healthy blood pressure.

FYI *You're not alone. One out of every four American adults has high blood pressure.*

Demystifying Blood Pressure

You probably know the blood pressure drill. A nurse wraps the cuff of a sphyg-momanometer (pronounced *sfig'-mo-ma-nom'-e-ter*) around your arm and squeezes on a hand-held pump to inflate the cuff, cutting off the blood flow in your artery for a few seconds. Then, just when you're sure your arm is going to burst, she releases a valve that lets some of the air out of the cuff and enables your blood to flow again. She listens with a stethoscope placed on your arm so she knows when blood flow has resumed. A numbered dial or column of mercury on the blood pressure apparatus shows the blood pressure reading, which the nurse marks in your chart. Fancier versions work automatically, and if you've ever been hospitalized, no doubt you've been hooked up to a device that automatically inflates and deflates every few minutes to monitor your pressure.

The nurse then recites some numbers— 160 over 90, 120 over 80, etc.—before telling you the doctor will be right with you. But she almost never says just what those numbers mean (and you can rarely tell by the look on her face). So we'll tell you.

First, the numbers you hear are not set in stone. They change a fair amount from one doctor's visit to the next, and even from one hour to the next. Your blood pressure is not static. It's generally highest in the morning and lowest at night when you're sleeping. Thus, one reading of "high" blood pressure is nothing to worry about. It's when you have several high readings over a relatively short period of time that you should be concerned.

Blood pressure is measured in mmHg, or millimeters of mercury. The systolic reading indicates the pressure when the left ventricle of your heart contracts. That means it's a measurement of how high your pressure is when your heart has just pushed fresh blood into the arteries. The diastolic reading indicates the pressure when the ventricle relaxes, or when blood is flowing on its own. The higher either of those numbers, the harder your heart is working to pump blood through your arteries.

When it comes to cardiovascular disease, systolic pressure is the one to worry about: In people older than 50, pressure higher than 140 mmHg contributes more to cardiovascular disease than high diastolic pressure. Work closely with your doctor to bring your systolic pressure down, since studies have found that this is most effective at reducing blood vessel damage from hypertension.

That doesn't mean you should ignore the diastolic pressure, though. If it is significantly elevated (above 120 mmHg), it's an emergency, and you may need to be hospitalized to lower it and avoid organ damage.

Here's what your numbers mean:

Normal blood pressure. A systolic reading of less than 120 and a diastolic pressure of less than 80. If you're in this category, give yourself a congratulatory pat on the back—but don't rest on your laurels. Your lifetime risk of developing hypertension is still 90 percent. Follow the guidelines in this book to ensure that your blood pressure remains normal.

> Getting an Accurate Reading

No doubt you've heard of "white-coat hypertension." Basically, this occurs when your blood pressure is high in the doctor's office but normal otherwise, because the stress of seeing the doctor acts on its own to increase it. Some studies find the "white-coat" effect in 20 to 35 percent of patients.

Other things can cause a high reading, including a too-small blood pressure cuff, tight sleeves, or an artery that is too stiff to be compressed, a problem sometimes seen in the elderly. For your regular doctor's visit, however, you can ensure a more accurate reading by:

> Not smoking or eating or drinking anything with caffeine for at least 30 minutes before the visit.

> Sitting quietly in a chair for at least 5 minutes before the pressure is taken, with your arm at heart level.

> Asking the health professional to take a second reading 2 minutes after the first and average the two results. If the two measurements differ by more than 5 points, additional measurements need to be taken and averaged.

Prehypertension. Systolic blood pressure of 120 to 139 or diastolic pressure of 80 to 89. This is a new category, introduced in May 2003 in the seventh report of the Joint National Committee on Prevention, Detection, Evaluation, and Treatment of High Blood Pressure. Think of it as a warning sign that you need to get your act together before it's too late. If you fall into this category, you are at increased risk of progressing to full-blown hypertension. So yes, you should be afraid. Those in the 130/80 to 139/89 mmHg range are twice as likely to develop hypertension as those with lower readings.

Stage 1 hypertension. Systolic blood pressure of 140 to 159 mmHg or diastolic pressure of 90 to 99 mmHg. In this stage, you may require medication, although aggressive lifestyle changes (in diet and fitness) may help you avoid having to take prescription drugs.

Stage 2 hypertension. A systolic reading of 160 mmHg or higher or a diastolic reading of 100 mmHg or higher. In this stage, you can expect to be placed on medication, as well as be counseled to make significant lifestyle adjustments.

Naturally, there are other considerations when contemplating your blood pressure readings. Here are but a few:

- **If you have diabetes or kidney disease.** The American Diabetes Association and the National Kidney Foundation say you should maintain a blood pressure below 130/80 mmHg for optimal health. In other words, their threshold for taking action against high blood pressure is lower than for people without diabetes or kidney disease.
- **If you are in your late 60s or older.** You may have what's called isolated systolic hypertension (ISH), in which your systolic blood pressure remains high while your diastolic pressure is normal. In the old days (pre-1991), doctors didn't even treat this condition, believing it was a normal part of aging.

Contraception, Pregnancy, and High Blood Pressure

Yes, it seems unfair. But women of childbearing age face unique issues when it comes to high blood pressure.

Contraception. High blood pressure is two to three times more common in women taking oral contraceptives—especially in obese and older women—than in women not taking them. Also, the longer women take them, the greater the risk of hypertension. That's why your doctor will question you closely about your blood pressure history before prescribing birth control pills, and will want to keep a close watch on your blood pressure when you're taking them. Interestingly, there is no evidence that hormone replacement therapy, which contains significantly less estrogen than oral contraceptives, increases blood pressure.

Pregnancy. Obstetrical visits usually include a blood pressure check. This is to monitor for gestational hypertension, in which your blood pressure rises during pregnancy. High blood pressure problems occur in 6 to 8 percent of all pregnancies in the U.S., about 70 percent of which are first-time pregnancies. In such cases, high blood pressure can harm the mother's kidneys and other organs, and cause low birth weight and early delivery of the baby. Several blood pressure medications are considered safe to use during pregnancy. And, of course, the DASH diet and regular exercise, as well as the other components of the DASH-Plus Plan described here, can also help women maintain a healthy blood pressure during pregnancy.

Now we know differently. Treating ISH with low-dose (and inexpensive) diuretic drugs reduces the incidence of stroke by 36 percent and nonfatal heart attack by 27 percent in those over 60.

- **If your diastolic and systolic numbers are unusually wide apart.** Pulse pressure is the difference between systolic and diastolic blood pressure. A 1999 article in the journal *Circulation* asserted that it is a better predictor of overall heart disease risk than either blood pressure reading. A normal pulse pressure is 30-40 mmHg. More or less than that is considered problematic.

An important note: If your systolic and diastolic pressures fall into different categories, your doctor will rate your blood pressure by the highest category. For example, 150/85 mmHg is classified as stage 1 hypertension, not prehypertension.

- **If your blood pressure measurements vary over time.** As mentioned earlier, a single blood pressure reading is just a snapshot in time that reflects as much on the previous few days' diet and stresses as on your broader health. Some people's pressure increases merely because they are at the doctor's office, getting a blood pressure reading (see Getting an Accurate Reading on page 276). If you and your doctor believe that better monitoring is important, consider ambulatory blood pressure monitoring, in which you wear a monitor for 24 hours. During that time, the monitor takes periodic readings, collecting them for your doctor to evaluate.

With the plethora of easy-to-use home blood pressure monitors on the market, people with high blood pressure should consider having one under their bathroom sink and should use it frequently to monitor their pressure. A good time to check your blood pressure is about an hour after you wake up. Although blood pressure is typically highest in the morning, one major study published in the journal *Circulation*, March 2003, found that those with highest morning "surge" (the difference between the systolic pressure's lowest value at night and the highest one during the two hours after getting out of bed) were most likely to have a stroke.

Researchers identified a "high" morning surge as at least a 55-point difference, finding that those with such a high surge were three times as likely to have a stroke as those with lower surges. For you, this means that if you have systolic values in the morning that are much higher than what you measure at other times in the day, give your doctor a call. Your blood pressure medication may need to be adjusted for better control.

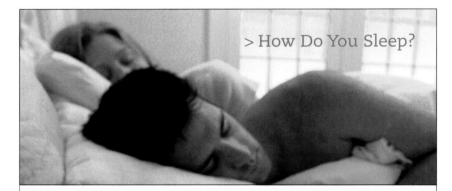

> How Do You Sleep?

Your answer may provide a clue to the health of your blood pressure. If you often wake up still tired and with a headache, if you've been told you snore heavily, and/or you find yourself nodding off during the day, you may have obstructive sleep apnea. With this condition, your breathing is frequently interrupted during the night as your throat keeps closing. Studies have found that half of those with obstructive sleep apnea also have hypertension.

Apnea can be treated with surgery or continuous positive airway pressure, in which you wear a mask at night to constantly deliver air that keeps your airway open. If you suspect sleep apnea is your problem, ask your doctor for a referral to a sleep study center for the necessary tests. Treating apnea will also reduce hypertension and could save your life.

The Dangers of High Blood Pressure

The threat to your health isn't from the high pressure itself but from the damage such pressure eventually causes to arteries and smaller blood vessels. This damage is particularly devastating to the small blood vessels in organs such as your eyes, kidneys, brain, and heart. These vessels are simply not designed to consistently withstand high levels of pressure. They cope with it by becoming more muscular, a process called hypertrophy, or enlargement of tissue. This harms the organ that contains the vessels because even though the vessels get bigger overall to handle the increased pressure, the space (or lumen) within them narrows. This narrowing makes it harder for blood to flow through the vessels, prompting the heart to work harder to push blood through. All of this further increases blood pressure, creating a dangerous cycle that continues until blood flow to the organ is compromised or the blood vessels are damaged, leading, most commonly, to kidney failure, heart attack, or stroke. Here's a short primer on the conditions strongly linked to hypertension.

Atherosclerosis. This is hardening and narrowing of the arteries caused by the slow buildup of plaque on the inside of artery walls. It can lead to several serious medical conditions, including coronary artery disease, angina, heart attack, sudden death, stroke, and transient ischemic attacks (TIA), or mini-strokes.

Cardiovascular disease (CVD). This is a catchall term for all diseases affecting the heart and blood vessels.

Coronary artery disease (CAD) or coronary heart disease (CHD). Coronary artery disease, the most common heart condition in Americans, occurs when the arteries that supply blood to the heart muscle (coronary arteries) become hardened and narrowed due to the buildup of plaque on their inner walls or lining (atherosclerosis). This in turn reduces blood flow to the heart, decreasing oxygen supply to the heart muscle. Over time, this lack of oxygen decreases the ability of the heart muscle to pump at full capacity when you're doing more than basic activities. Symptoms of CAD can include chest pain (angina) and shortness of breath with exertion.

Heart attack. Also referred to as a coronary occlusion, a heart attack occurs when the supply of blood and oxygen to an area of heart muscle is blocked, usually by a clot in a coronary artery. Unless the blockage is treated within a few hours, the affected heart muscle dies and is replaced by scar tissue.

Heart failure. This condition develops over time as the heart has increasing trouble pumping blood throughout the body. It's also known as congestive heart failure (CHF).

Stroke. There are two main types of stroke. The most common is ischemic stroke, which occurs when something

> 911 Signs

Call 911 immediately if you have high blood pressure and begin experiencing any of the following symptoms.

> **Numbness**
   and tingling in your hands and feet

> **Coughing up blood**
   or severe nosebleeds

> **Shortness of breath**

> **Chest pain**

> **Sudden, severe headache**
   with no known cause

> **Sudden weakness or numbness**
   in your face, arm, and/or leg on one side of the body

> **Sudden dimming**
   or loss of vision

> **Trouble speaking**
   or understanding speech

> **Shakiness**
   or a sudden fall

suddenly blocks the blood supply to an area of the brain. The other form is hemorrhagic stroke, which occurs when a blood vessel in the brain bursts, spilling blood into the spaces surrounding the brain cells. Both lead to the death of brain cells as oxygen is cut off and result in temporary or permanent neurological damage or death.

A transient ischemic attack, or ministroke, is technically not a stroke but rather a neurological deficit that lasts less than 24 hours. It's caused by a temporary interruption of the blood supply to an area of the brain and should serve as a warning sign, since about one-third of those who have a TIA will have an acute stroke some time in the future.

Dementia. People with hypertension are more likely than those with normal blood pressure to experience dementia and other cognitive problems as they age. There's also some evidence that uncontrolled hypertension may increase the risk of Alzheimer's disease. Although we don't know all the reasons for the connection, one theory is that over years, hypertension

decreases the elasticity of blood vessels in the brain, increasing resistance and reducing their responsiveness.

Kidney disease. Uncontrolled hypertension is the second leading cause of chronic kidney disease (diabetes is the first). It speeds the deterioration of kidney function to the point where lifesaving measures, such as dialysis or kidney transplant, are needed.

Blood vessel damage. Constant high blood pressure can damage the lining of the blood vessels. This can increase the rate at which plaque accumulates on blood vessel walls (atherosclerosis), narrowing the blood vessels and reducing the amount of blood flowing to the body's organs.

Retinopathy (eye damage). High blood pressure affects the blood vessels on the inner surface of the eye in much the same way that it affects blood vessels in the heart or kidneys. Over time, uncontrolled high blood pressure can cause a blood vessel in the eye to burst, bleed, or occlude, leading to blurred vision or even blindness.

FYI *Of those with high blood pressure:*

31.6% don't know they have it

27.4 % control it with medication

26.2% take medication but don't control it

14.6% handle it without medication

A growing number of clinical studies attest to the role of lifestyle changes in controlling and reducing blood pressure. From what you eat and how much you eat to how you cope with a traffic jam and how much exercise you get, lifestyle modifications can do as much if not more than medication to lower blood pressure.

Here are seven major studies that provide proof that a healthy lifestyle lowers blood pressure:

Framingham Heart Study. The grandfather of all population-based studies, this research began in 1948 when scientists from the U.S. Public Health Service chose the town of Framingham, Massachusetts, and its residents to help them learn more about the growing epidemic of heart disease. Results from Framingham have proven the connection between hypertension and heart disease, exercise and hypertension, diet and heart disease, and diabetes and heart disease, among others.

Dietary Approaches to Stop Hypertension (DASH). This study, published in the *New England Journal of Medicine* in 1997, evaluated 459 middle-aged Americans with and without high blood pressure as they followed one of three diets: the typical American diet, one that included more fruits and vegetables than the typical American diet, or the DASH diet, an eating program specifically designed to be high in those nutrients found to positively affect blood pressure and low in those found to negatively affect it. A later

> Leading Studies on Reducing Blood Pressure without Drugs

study, the DASH-sodium study, coupled the DASH diet with reduced sodium intake and found an even greater drop in blood pressure.

Nurses' Health Study. This long-term, ongoing study evaluates the health and lifestyle habits of 82,473 U.S. nurses. A major finding of the study was that each 2.2 pounds of weight gain after age 18 increased a woman's risk of hypertension by 5 percent. This risk increase occurred even if a woman's weight remained in the so-called normal range, generally defined as a body mass index (BMI) of less than 25. Conversely, a group of studies finds that losing 4 to 8 percent of body weight results in at least a 3/3 mmHg drop in blood pressure and less need for medication.

TOMHS. The best currently available data on combined dietary intervention comes from the Treatment of Mild Hypertension Study (TOMHS), in which 902 patients with mild diastolic hypertension (90 to 100 mmHg) followed a program to lose weight, restrict sodium and alcohol, and increase physical activity. Then they received either placebos (dummy pills) or one of five different antihypertensive drugs. All improved their blood pressure, with the group on placebos maintaining an average 8.6/8.6 mmHg blood pressure reduction four years after the trial ended. Plus, their levels of "bad" cholesterol dropped, and their levels of "good" cholesterol rose, reducing their overall cardiovascular risk.

Trials of Hypertension Prevention, Phase II. This study focused on 2,382 men and women, ages 30 to 54, who had blood pressures less than 140/83-89 mmHg and who were 110 to 165 percent of their ideal body weight. All were given the same medical treatment, and then were split into four groups. The first received no extra guidance, the second reduced their salt intake, the third began a weight-loss program, and the fourth both cut back on salt and lost weight. Compared with those receiving just typical care, those who reduced sodium intake saw their blood pressures fall an average of 2.9/1.6 mmHg, those who lost weight saw average reductions of 3.7/2.7 mmHg, and those on the combined therapy had the greatest reduction: 4.0/2.0 mmHg. Four years after the study ended, those who received the interventions were less likely to have progressed to true hypertension than those who received only medication.

TONE Study. The Trial of Nonpharmacologic Interventions in the Elderly (TONE), was the first multicenter clinical trial of sufficient size and duration (30 months) to show that lifestyle modifications can be used to control high blood pressure in older people. The first results from this trial, published in the *Journal of the American Medical Association* in March 1998, found that losing weight and cutting down on salt could lessen and even eliminate the need for blood pressure-lowering medications in the elderly.

PREMIER Clinical Trial. This was the first clinical trial to put together everything we know about lifestyle changes and blood pressure to see how the different changes interacted with one another to reduce blood pressure. Supported by the National Heart, Lung, and Blood Institute, this study compared the effects of two behavioral interventions on blood pressure in 810 adults who had high blood pressure but were not taking antihypertensive medications.

At the start of the trial, 38 percent of participants were diagnosed as hypertensive, and most were overweight and got little physical activity. Participants either received advice only (typically from a dietitian), implemented established recommendations (quitting smoking, losing weight, increasing exercise) for lowering blood pressure, or combined established recommendations with the DASH diet. After six months, participants in both interventional groups lost weight, improved their fitness, lowered their sodium intake, and reduced their blood pressure. The group following established guidelines reduced their systolic blood pressure by an average of 3.7 mmHg, while those who also followed the DASH diet had reductions of 4.3 mmHg.

By the end of the study, 26 percent of those in the advice-only group still had hypertension, compared with just 17 percent who followed the established guidelines and 12 percent who also used the DASH diet.

Eat to Beat High Blood Pressure

Wouldn't it be reassuring to know that by eating delicious, interesting, healthy foods, you could almost certainly prevent a deadly major disease like hypertension? Well, there is compelling evidence that this is indeed the case.

First, consider the general trends. Hypertension rates are much higher in modern, fast-moving cultures like ours than in less industrialized parts of the world. The main difference? Diet. In the United States, we eat huge portions of highly processed foods and minimal amounts of fruits, vegetables, and unprocessed grains. People in less industrialized cultures have simpler, healthier diets. To help illustrate the point, note that hypertension is much more prevalent in Asians living in the United States than in those living in Asian countries.

Then there is the fact that people who maintain a healthy weight are less likely to have hypertension than people who are overweight or obese. Also, vegetarians and those who follow the so-called Mediterranean diet (high in vegetables, fruits, whole grains, and unsaturated fats) generally have lower than average blood pressure levels.

There is also emerging evidence that individual foods and nutrients play an important role in either lowering or raising blood pressure. As it turns out, the greatest effects of healing foods come not from changing one or two aspects of your diet but from changing its overall makeup, as you'll see when we talk about the DASH diet.

The bottom line: Before you turn to medication, you need to take a good, hard look at what you're eating. In the following pages, we'll review the foods and nutrients that best help in the battle against high blood pressure, as well as the foods that cause the most damage. We'll detail the most proven eating plan for healthy blood pressure—the DASH plan. Finally, we'll turn our attention to the role of weight loss in managing high blood pressure and give you our top 10 tips for launching a successful weight-loss effort.

The Sodium/Salt Connection

Here's where everyone starts when it comes to blood pressure and diet. For years, the common thinking was that salt was the primary culprit in high blood pressure, but the reality is more complicated than that.

Sodium (one-half of the sodium chloride that is table salt) is one of the most studied nutrients when it comes to blood pressure. Today we know that excess sodium in the body causes arterioles—thin-walled arteries that end in capillaries—to contract, which raises blood pressure. Sodium also draws more fluid into the bloodstream and holds it there. The more fluid, the more pressure. Think of a garden hose. If you turn the water on as a trickle, there's little pressure. Turn it on full blast, and it gushes out with such force that the hose may jump out of your hands.

But the issue of whether sodium has an ongoing effect on blood pressure is still unresolved. The research designed to answer that question once and for all, the INTERSALT study, only confused things more. This massive study, begun in 1984, included 10,000 participants from 52 communities around the world. The results, first published in 1988, appeared to prove that sodium intake increased blood pressure. When researchers removed four communities with unusually low blood pressure from the statistical analysis, however, they found little correlation between salt and blood pressure in the remaining 48.

Fast-forward a decade. In 1999, another major, government-sponsored study was published. This one, which used the national record of what Americans ate to evaluate the effect of sodium on heart health, went much further than simply looking at blood pressure. After all, what is blood pressure but a signal of a far deeper problem?

The study, published in the *Journal of the American Medical Association* in December 1999, found that for people who ate the most salt and were overweight, the risk of having a stroke increased by 32 percent. They were also 89 percent more likely to die from stroke, 44 percent more likely to die from coronary heart disease, 61 percent more likely to die from all cardiovascular disease, and 39 percent more likely to die from all causes than those who got 2,300 milligrams or less of sodium a day. On the other hand, though, the study also showed that those who were *not* overweight had no higher risk of dying from these conditions even if they consumed the extra salt.

To further muddy the salt water, an analysis of 11 clinical trials on the issue published in the *British Medical Journal* in September 2002 concluded that while manipulating dietary sodium intake may help maintain blood pressure control in people with hypertension and may even enable them to stop taking medication, it also may have adverse effects on overall health. Some larger studies have found that lower salt intake in people with hypertension may be associated with a higher risk of cardiovascular events.

Flip the coin (or the medical journal), and you get the DASH-sodium study, on which our DASH-Plus Plan is based, which found that the less sodium participants consumed, the lower their blood pressures dropped.

How could the studies yield such confusing results?

Well, researchers suspect a strong genetic component, meaning that some people have certain genes that make them particularly sensitive to the effects of sodium. Of course, there's no simple test to see which category you fall into, and everyone agrees that the typical American diet, which includes 3,600 to 4,000 milligrams of sodium a day, is simply too high in the mineral. So our DASH-Plus recipes focus on natural foods with a minimum of added sodium and use fresh herbs, garlic, and onions to kick up the flavor.

All of which brings us to the cornerstone of the DASH-Plus Plan, the DASH diet itself.

> Painless Ways to Lose the Salt

You don't *have* to count milligrams of sodium as if they were diamonds. Nor do you have to stay away from the salt-shaker on your table—if you stick with "real" foods. What do we mean by real?

Foods that are close to their natural state, such as fresh vegetables and fruits; unadorned meats, poultry, and fish; and unaltered grains and cereals. It's when foods are processed that the

sodium gets poured on—the manufacturer's way of assuring we'll like the taste. Just compare the differences:

Natural Food	Sodium (mg)		Processed Food	Sodium (mg)
Cooked cereal, rice, pasta, unsalted, 1/2 cup	0–5	vs	Ready-to-eat cereal, 1 cup	100–360
Fresh or frozen vegetables, 1/2 cup	1–70	vs	Canned or frozen vegetables with sauce, 1/2 cup	140–460
Canned diced tomatoes, no salt added, 1/2 cup	20	vs	Canned diced tomatoes, 1/2 cup	200
		or	Canned tomato juice, 3/4 cup	820
Low-fat milk, 1 cup	120	vs	Natural cheeses, 1 1/2 oz	110–450
		or	Processed cheeses (American, etc.), 1 1/2 oz	600
Unsalted peanuts, 1/3 cup	0–5	vs	Salted peanuts, 1/3 cup	120
Cooked dried or frozen beans, 1/2 cup	0–5	vs	Canned beans, 1/2 cup	400
Fresh meat, poultry, or fish, 3 oz	30–90	vs	Canned water-packed tuna, 3 oz	250–350
		or	Lean roasted ham, 3 oz	1,020

Source: National Heart, Lung, and Blood Institute

> Learning the Language of Salt

One of the best ways to reduce your sodium consumption is to read labels. But before you snatch up that can of low-sodium beans, convinced it fits on your low-sodium diet, you need to know what the phrases really mean. Also, keep in mind the relatively small size of a "serving" as listed on most labels, since few of us really stick to those servings. If a 1/2-cup serving contains 150 milligrams of sodium, but *your* typical serving is closer to 2 cups, you're really getting 600 milligrams.

Phrase	What It Means
Sodium free or salt free	Less than 5 mg of sodium per serving
Very low sodium	35 mg or less per serving
Low sodium	140 mg or less per serving
Low-sodium meal	140 mg or less per 3.5 oz
Reduced or less sodium	At least 25 percent less than the regular version
Light in sodium	50 percent less than the regular version
Unsalted or no salt added	No salt added to the product during processing

The DASH Diet

Think how easy it would be to eat healthy and lose weight if someone else shopped for and prepared every morsel of food that entered your mouth. Well, that's exactly the advantage the participants in the Dietary Approaches to Stop Hypertension (DASH) study got when they joined the government-sponsored trial in the early 1990s.

The diet isn't a weight-loss diet per se, since it's based on 2,000 calories a day. If you're overweight, though, you'll probably find yourself losing weight anyway, with the bonus of watching your blood pressure drop along with your weight. Another plus? Studies have found that the DASH diet helps lower levels of cholesterol and homocysteine, both major risk factors for heart disease.

Before we get into the specifics of what you're going to eat, let's talk about the DASH study.

Even before beginning the study, researchers knew that certain diets, primarily vegetarian diets and those with moderate amounts of lean protein, lowered blood pressure. They also knew that meatless meals had limited appeal, so they wanted to find a program that would satisfy the largest number of Americans.

The 459 people who joined the DASH study were 44.6 years old on average and had blood pressures lower than 160/95 mmHg. Nearly half were women, and 6 out of 10 were African-American, which was important because hypertension is particularly prevalent among blacks in this country. Also important was the fact that 62 percent of the women and half of the men were obese, with a body mass index (BMI) of 30 or higher.

The volunteers spent three weeks eating their "regular" diets before their blood pressures were measured. Then they were assigned to one of three groups. The first group continued eating the average American diet, high in fat and limited in fruits, vegetables, and fiber. The second group increased the amounts of fruits and vegetables they ate but made no other changes. The third group followed what eventually became known as the DASH diet.

All three groups consumed the same amount of salt (about 3,000 milligrams per day, slightly less than the average American intake), limited the amount of alcohol they drank to one or two drinks a day, and had no more than three servings a day of caffeinated beverages (soda, coffee, or tea). In addition, the participants' calorie intakes were closely monitored to prevent any changes in their weight for the duration of the study.

After eight weeks, all of those on the DASH diet saw their blood pressures drop an average of 5.5/3.0 mmHg, or about as much as might be expected if they were taking antihypertensive medications. Those who were already hypertensive, however, had the greatest reductions: an average of 11.4 mmHg in systolic pressure and 5.5 mmHg in diastolic pressure. The news was even better for the African-Americans, in whom blood pressure dropped an average of 13.2/6.1 mmHg. Researchers estimated that even the smaller reductions could reduce the overall incidence of coronary artery disease by 15 percent and of stroke by 27 percent.

Then, to see if reducing salt would improve the results, researchers launched a second trial, this time putting DASH diet participants on either a high-sodium (3,300 milligrams), intermediate-sodium (2,400 milligrams), or low-sodium (1,500 milligrams) diet for one month. Those on the low-sodium DASH plan saw their

FYI. *Beware. Foods such as olives, bacon, pickles, ketchup, barbecue sauce, smoked salmon and seasoning blends can be high in sodium.*

blood pressures drop the greatest amount, an average of 9.0/4.5 mmHg. They even had fewer headaches.

And the best news? The results happened fast—in just about *two weeks!*

So what does the DASH diet look like? Well, if you bundled up all the basic nutritional advice we've received over the past 20 years and put it into one yummy program, you'd get DASH. In fact, this is a program your entire family should follow, regardless of their blood pressure. It might help them avoid the nearly inevitable rise in blood pressure that comes with age (although there are no studies as yet that prove this), and it will certainly reduce their risk of various cancers, heart disease, diabetes, and other chronic health conditions.

In a nutshell, the DASH diet reduces the overall amount of fat, saturated fat, and cholesterol in the typical American diet; increases the number of fruits, vegetables, and low-fat dairy foods; increases fiber with whole grain products; and reduces the number of sweets and sugary drinks. The low-sodium version reduces the amount of sodium to 1,500 milligrams a day. It provides about 27 percent of calories from fat and 18 percent from protein, with the remainder (55 percent) from carbohydrates. Compare that with the "typical" American diet, in which 40 percent of calories come from fat, 43 percent from carbohydrates, and 17 percent from protein. It's not rocket science, and it's not magic. It's just good, commonsense eating.

More specifically, the DASH diet calls for:

> **Seven to eight servings a day of whole grains or grain products,** including bread, cereal, and pasta. We're not talking Cocoa Puffs here, but high-fiber, low-sugar cereals such as Raisin Bran, real oatmeal, or Grape-Nuts. Wonder Bread won't cut it either. Reach instead for a loaf of bread on which "whole grain" tops the ingredient list.

> **Four to five servings of vegetables each day.** Don't be afraid of this; one 7-ounce bag of washed lettuce equals a bit more than one serving. Add a sliced tomato, half a red pepper, and a quarter-cup of raw broccoli, and you've just eaten four servings. This category is particularly important because, as you'll see later, vegetables are good sources of potassium and magnesium, minerals that are important when it comes to controlling blood pressure.

> **Four to five servings of fruit daily.** You can eat them fresh, canned, juiced, and even dried.

> **Two to three daily servings of low-fat or fat-free dairy products.** We're talking cheese, milk, yogurt—even ice cream!

> **No more than two servings a day of meat, poultry, or fish.** This includes nonmeat protein, such as eggs and tofu, and all types of seafood.

> **Four to five servings a week of nuts, seeds, and legumes.** Think of it as a handful of peanuts every weekday. Nuts are great sources of magnesium, potassium, protein, and fiber.

> **No more than three servings a day of fats.** This includes all oils, butter, regular salad dressings, and mayonnaise.

> **No more than five servings a week of sweets.** That's basically anything with added sugar.

Put it all together, and here's what it looks like. We've provided portion sizes for three different daily caloric targets:

• 1,600 calories, for healthy men or women seeking to lose weight, or small-framed women with sedentary lifestyles.

• 2,000 calories, for regular-framed women seeking a stable weight, or men with sedentary lifestyles.

• 2,400 calories, for moderately active men, or highly active women.

THE DASH EATING PLAN

Food Group	Daily Servings			Serving Sizes	Examples	Blood Pressure–Related Nutrient
	1,600 calories per day	**2,000** calories per day	**2,400** calories per day			
Grains and grain products	6	7–8	9–10	• 1 slice bread • 1 oz dry cereal (1/2–1 1/4 cups) • 1/2 cup cooked rice, pasta, or cereal	Whole-wheat bread, English muffin, pita, bagel, cereals, grits, oatmeal, crackers, unsalted pretzels and popcorn	Major source of energy and fiber
Vegetables	3–4	4–5	5	• 1 cup raw leafy vegetable like lettuce or spinach • 1/3 cup cooked vegetable • 6 oz vegetable juice	You know your veggies!	Rich sources of potassium, magnesium, and fiber
Fruits	4	4–5	5	• 6 oz fruit juice • 1 medium fruit • 1/4 cup dried fruit • 1/2 cup fresh, frozen, or canned fruit	You know your fruits!	Important sources of potassium, magnesium, and fiber
Low-fat or fat-free dairy foods	2–3	2–3	3	• 8 oz milk • 1 cup yogurt • 1 1/2 oz cheese	Fat-free or low-fat (1%) milk, buttermilk, regular or frozen yogurt, or cheese	Major sources of calcium and protein
Meats, poultry, and fish	2 or fewer	2 or fewer	2	• 3 oz cooked meat, poultry, or fish	Select only lean cuts. Trim away visible fat. Broil, roast, or boil instead of frying. Remove skin from poultry.	Rich sources of protein and magnesium
Nuts, seeds, and dried beans	3 a week	4–5 a week	1 a day	• 1/3 cup or 1 1/2 oz nuts • 2 Tbsp or 1/2 oz seeds • 1/2 cup cooked dried beans or peas	Almonds, filberts, mixed nuts, peanuts, walnuts, sunflower seeds, kidney beans, lentils	Rich sources of energy, magnesium, potassium, protein, and fiber
Fats and oils	2	2–3	3	• 1 tsp soft margarine • 1 Tbsp low-fat mayonnaise • 2 Tbsp light salad dressing • 1 tsp vegetable oil	Soft margarine, low-fat mayonnaise, light salad dressing, vegetable oil (olive, corn, canola, or safflower)	
Sweets	0	5 a week	1 a day	• 1 Tbsp sugar • 1 Tbsp jelly or jam • 1/3 oz jelly beans • 8 oz lemonade	Maple syrup, sugar, jelly, jam, fruit-flavored gelatin, jelly beans, hard candy, fruit punch, sorbet, ices	Make sure your sweet tooth is assuaged by low-fat sweets

Source: National Heart, Lung, and Blood Institute

EAT TO BEAT HIGH BLOOD PRESSURE

The Blood Pressure Super Nutrients

Whether or not you follow the DASH diet to the letter, there are certain foods and nutrients you should be sure to keep in— or kick out of—your diet. The recipes in this book are heavy on these good nutrients, such as magnesium, potassium, and calcium, and light on the bad, such as sodium and saturated fats. Simply choosing dishes from this book will give you a tremendous boost up (or down, if we're talking about blood pressure), even if you don't follow DASH strictly. And, because no one heads out for a romantic dinner hoping for a great dish of magnesium and potassium, we've listed super sources of these important nutrients.

Potassium. Potassium is the yin to sodium's yang. Not only does supplementing with potassium lower blood pressure, but diets high in this mineral tend to be lower in sodium. Potassium is thought to act by increasing sodium excretion in the urine, which helps blood vessels dilate, and changing the interactions of hormones that affect blood pressure. In one analysis of several studies that looked at the ability of supplemental potassium to lower blood pressure, participants taking 2.3 to 4.7 grams a day of supplemental potassium had an average blood pressure reduction of 4.4/2.5 mmHg.

In the INTERSALT study, described on page 283, all populations that consumed more salt than potassium saw their blood pressures rise, while those consuming more potassium than salt had no increase. And when Harvard researchers followed 43,738 men for eight years, they found a 38 percent reduced risk of stroke in those who got the most potassium. If you follow the DASH-Plus Plan, you're going to get plenty of potassium in your diet. If you find it difficult to stick to the eating plan, you might consider taking a potassium supplement or a multivitamin with extra potassium.

• **SUPER FOODS: Bananas, orange juice, spinach, chard, mustard greens, zucchini, and button mushrooms.**

Magnesium. If sodium and potassium are yin and yang, then potassium and magnesium are fraternal twins. If your diet is rich in potassium, chances are it's also rich in magnesium, since the two are often found together in food. It's clear that a diet high in magnesium benefits those with hypertension, most likely by contributing to the relaxation of the smooth muscles of the blood vessels. Again, if you follow the DASH-Plus Plan, you're going to get plenty of magnesium. However, if vegetables and fruits grace your plate about as often as calf brains, you might want to consider taking a magnesium supplement. One study found that taking magnesium in

amounts as low as 365 milligrams per day with beta-blockers significantly reduced blood pressure compared with taking the medication alone.

• **SUPER FOODS: Whole grains, chard, spinach, sea vegetables, basil, dill, and squash. Avoid overcooking to minimize mineral loss.**

Calcium. Got milk? It could be the ticket to reducing your blood pressure. Numerous studies suggest that high intake of dietary calcium (whether from milk, cheese, yogurt, or ice cream) contributes to lower blood pressure. Because calcium is needed for smooth muscle relaxation and contraction, increased consumption can have a direct effect on blood vessels. It's best to get your calcium from your diet; studies have found that compared with supplements, dietary calcium has twice the benefits for blood pressure.

• **SUPER FOODS: Low-fat or fat-free milk, cheese, and yogurt.**

Vitamin C. This powerful antioxidant has a significant effect on blood pressure. In one study, researchers found that people taking 500 milligrams of supplemental vitamin C a day for one month saw their systolic, diastolic, and mean blood pressures drop by about 9 percent, a pretty significant decline. One possible explanation: Vitamin C helps support the body's production of nitric oxide, which is critical to normal functioning of blood vessels.

FYI *Age matters. One out of every two Americans over 60 have high blood pressure.*

The better your blood vessels work, the lower your risk of hypertension.

• **SUPER FOODS: Chile peppers, parsley, broccoli, bell peppers, strawberries, oranges, lemon juice, papayas, cauliflower, kale, mustard greens, and Brussels sprouts.**

Fiber. Fiber—the indigestible part of plants—has long been the butt of late-night comedy routines. Now it's time to give it a little respect. Fiber is a powerhouse when it comes to health, reducing your risk of everything from colon cancer and heart disease to hypertension, and even helping you maintain or lose weight. When it comes to fiber, keep in mind that there are two kinds. Soluble fiber forms a kind of jelly in your stomach that helps slow the digestion of food, letting you feel full longer and consequently helping to slow the passage of food through the intestines, thus maintaining steadier blood sugar and insulin levels. Insoluble fiber acts as a giant vacuum cleaner, sweeping away toxins as it passes through the digestive system.

What does this have to do with blood pressure? Well, researchers suspect that fiber works its magic by improving your body's ability to use insulin and thus process glucose, both of which have a direct impact on blood pressure. Also, high amounts of fiber in your diet generally suggest an overall healthy diet, including more fruits and vegetables—which, as we've seen, makes a big difference when it comes to blood pressure control. There are also phytochemicals and antioxidants in whole grains (a great source of fiber) that may be partially responsible for some of fiber's beneficial effect on blood pressure.

Those benefits can be big. When researchers had 41 study participants double their soluble fiber intake and increase their protein intake with soy, their systolic blood pressures dropped by about 10.5 mmHg, and their diastolic readings declined by 3.5 mmHg. Even just increasing the fiber resulted in a drop of 2.4/1.9 mmHg.

Fiber can also help prevent the initial development of high blood pressure, which is particularly important if you fall into the prehypertension category. Harvard researchers found that volunteers who consumed more than 24 grams of fiber a day were 50 percent less likely to develop high blood pressure than those who consumed less than 12 grams a day. For the record, the average American consumes less than 15 grams a day.

• **SUPER FOODS: Whole grains, fruits, and vegetables. For a major wallop, try oat cereal for breakfast. A small study at the University of Minnesota found that 73 percent of participants who ate oats every day were able to reduce the amount of blood pressure medication they took after 12 weeks.**

Protein. You'd expect to see low blood pressures in people who follow vegetarian diets, but researchers were really surprised when they found that adding lean meat to a vegetarian regimen maintained the lower blood pressure. As it turns out, protein is critically important in maintaining healthy blood pressure. It contains two amino acids important to blood vessel health: l-arginine, a precursor of nitric oxide, which dilates blood vessels and lowers blood pressure, and taurine.

Several studies have found that restricting animals' ability to make nitric oxide

results in hypertension. And when six healthy participants were randomly assigned to one of three diets for a week—a control diet, a natural-foods diet enriched with l-arginine, or a diet identical to the control diet but with the addition of l-arginine supplements—both groups receiving l-arginine saw their blood pressures drop.

The other amino acid, taurine, also has antihypertensive effects. When 19 study participants with borderline hypertension supplemented their diets with 6 grams of taurine daily for seven days, systolic blood pressure dropped an average of 9 mmHg, compared with a 2 mmHg decrease in patients treated with placebos, while diastolic pressure dropped an

289

average of 4 mmHg, compared with 1 mmHg drop in the placebo group. Taurine seems to control levels of the stress hormone epinephrine, which have been found to be higher in people with hypertension. It also relaxes blood vessels by improving production of "feel good" hormones called endorphins, resulting in lower blood pressure.

• **SUPER FOODS: Eggs, poultry, tofu, fish, and lean pork, beef, and lamb.**

Omega-3 fatty acids. Found primarily in cold-water fish, this form of fat (yes, the "f" word), is like a winning lottery ticket for your heart, improving electrical activity and reducing risk of heart disease, stroke, and heart attack. In one well-designed study, participants who received 3 grams of an omega-3 fatty acid supplement a day showed significant improvement in something called systemic arterial compliance, which is really a fancy way of saying how well your larger artery works. The stiffer the artery, the higher your systolic

---

> ### > Helpful Hint: Keep Your Oil Fresh

If you tend to reuse your cooking oil, consider changing your ways. A Spanish study found that people who reused cooking oil several times were more likely to have high blood pressure than those who used fresh oil. The researchers also found higher blood pressure levels in those using sunflower oil, while those who used mainly olive oil had a lower risk of hypertension.

---

and pulse pressure. But after seven weeks on this regimen, the participants' arterial compliance rose 36 percent with one form of omega-3 fatty acid (EPA) and 27 percent with another (DHA). The best source of omega-3 fatty acids is fish, which would explain why an Australian study found that people who ate diets both high in fish and low in fat had significantly lower blood pressures than those who followed one or the other.

• **SUPER FOODS: Mackerel, anchovies, salmon, tuna, and herring.**

Celery. This crisp vegetable has traditionally been used as a blood pressure treatment in Asian medicine. More recent studies in rats have found that animals injected with celery extract (the equivalent of four stalks of the green roughage) had blood pressure reductions of 12 to 14 percent within a week. The key celery nutrient believed to fight hypertension is 3-n-butyl phthalide, which helps artery muscles dilate and reduces stress hormones in the blood. A bonus: Celery packs a whopping 8 grams of fiber in each large stalk.

Garlic. If you're looking for a savory substitute for salt, try some minced garlic mixed into your food. Not only does it pack a seasoning punch with no sodium, but several clinical trials attest to its blood pressure–lowering properties. In fact, as little as one clove a day can significantly reduce your overall blood pressure. You can expect to see improvement in as little as three months.

Coenzyme Q10. There's a great deal of evidence that oxidative stress may be a

contributing factor in hypertension. Oxidative stress occurs as a basic side effect of living—it's wear and tear on cells that in turn produces wear and tear on your body as a whole. Normally, we have defenses in place to arrest this damage in the form of antioxidants, which do just what their name implies—reverse or prevent oxidative damage.

Much of that antioxidant power comes from nutrients in food, including antioxidant vitamins E, C, and beta-carotene. Another important antioxidant is coenzyme Q10 (CoQ10). It's long been known to be critical for overall heart health, and several recent studies suggest that part of its benefit may stem from its effects on hypertension. An eight-week trial completed in 1999 on 59 men with hypertension found that those who received 120 milligrams per day of CoQ10 saw their blood pressures drop an average of 16/9 mmHg, while a group taking placebos had no change. A 2001 study of 46 men and 37 women with systolic hypertension found that taking 60 milligrams of CoQ10 twice a day resulted in an average reduction in systolic blood pressure of nearly 18 mmHg, with 55 percent of the patients showing a drop. Although we can get CoQ10 from food (see below), people taking cholesterol-lowering statin drugs and those with diabetes may benefit from supplementing with this antioxidant.

• **SUPER FOODS: Fresh sardines, mackerel, beef, pork, and eggs. Vegetable sources include spinach, broccoli, peanuts, wheat germ, and whole grains.**

Blood Pressure Danger Foods

Just as there are certain foods shown to improve blood pressure and reduce your risk of hypertension, there also some that are known to make things worse. You already know about sodium, so here are others to avoid or, at the very least, enjoy in moderation.

Alcohol. More than 50 studies attest to the blood pressure–raising effects of alcohol consumption, suggesting that the more you drink, the greater the effect. Overall, for every alcoholic drink you *cut out* a day, you can expect your blood pressure to fall about 1 to 2 mmHg, a result that translates directly into a reduction in long-term risk for hypertension. For instance, a 1999 analysis of three major studies found that people who drank less than an ounce of alcohol a day (0.88 ounce) had a 40 percent increase in their risk of hypertension, while those drinking 3.5 ounces a day (the amount found in a typical drink) increased their risk by 300 percent. Drinking is so strongly linked with hypertension that there's some talk about establishing a separate blood pressure category called alcohol-related hypertension.

If you enjoy wine occasionally, you don't have to go overboard and become a teetotaler. But as we recommend in the DASH-Plus Plan, you need to limit your alcohol intake to one or two drinks a day at most. And skip the New Year's Eve blowout; studies have found that binge drinking and heavy drinking put you at significantly high risk for hemorrhagic stroke.

Caffeine. The data on caffeine and blood pressure is about as mixed as that on sodium. Researchers don't even know for sure what chemicals in coffee affect blood pressure. It could be caffeine, but recent studies suggest that some unknown ingredient or ingredients may actually be to blame. And while we're pretty clear on the fact that a cup of coffee temporarily raises your blood pressure, we're less clear on the long-term effects of coffee drinking. For instance, studies on young people with normal blood pressure find little effect, but studies on older people with high blood pressure find that coffee drinkers have even higher blood pressure—about 5/3 mmHg higher than those who abstain. The effects are much worse if they smoke.

We're not going to tell you to give up your morning java. If you have high blood pressure, though, don't couple coffee with a cigarette or drink it when you're stressed or just before you exercise. These combinations may exacerbate its effects.

Saturated fats. Until the DASH study, there was no sense that changing levels of dietary fat affected blood pressure. Given the significant results of DASH, which calls for reduced levels of overall fat and saturated fat in particular, that understanding has been called into question. Regardless of blood pressure research, there is clear evidence of the heart-damaging effects of high intake of saturated fat, the kind found primarily in full-fat animal products such as dairy foods and meats. Our recipes were developed to contain low amounts of saturated fat, both to provide the heart health benefits and to assist you in your efforts to lose weight or maintain a healthy weight.

Licorice. If you love the strongly flavored chewy candy and have high blood pressure, there could be a connection. A study by researchers in Iceland found that eating even small amounts of licorice (comparable to a handful of jelly beans) raised blood pressure an average of 3.5 mmHg. Try assuaging your sweet tooth with a piece of dark chocolate instead. Loaded with antioxidants, chocolate (in small doses) is actually good for your heart.

> ## > Forget Weight-Loss Supplements

If you're considering finding your weight-loss solution in a tablet, beware. Certain ingredients in over-the-counter supplements, such as ephedra, or ma huang (banned by the FDA in late 2003), and bitter orange, may significantly increase blood pressure, as can the use of cocaine, amphetamines, and other illegal drugs. Also be careful when using decongestants and cold and flu remedies. Most contain adrenergic compounds such as pseudoephedrine, phenylephrine, or phenylpropanolamine (also known as PPA). They work on your stuffy nose by constricting blood vessels, thus reducing swelling in nasal passages, but this action also makes your blood pressure rise.

Lose Weight, Lower Blood Pressure

Just as research associates lung cancer and emphysema with smoking, it shows a similarly strong correlation between hypertension and obesity. It turns out that a body mass index (BMI) of 27 or more and significant fat deposits around the abdomen are directly linked to high blood pressure. In fact, it's estimated that the growing obesity epidemic in the United States is responsible for 2 percent of the 3.6 percent increase in the prevalence of hypertension between 1991 and 2000.

Body weight affects blood pressure in three ways. With increased weight, you have increased blood volume, which can lead to higher blood pressure. Also, people who are overweight are more likely to be salt sensitive. Finally, overweight people are more insulin resistant, meaning that their cells bar access to insulin so they can't accept energy-providing glucose. The resulting excess of glucose and insulin contributes to high blood pressure.

The good news is that losing as few as 10 pounds of body weight can significantly improve your blood pressure readings. Although the DASH diet was not designed for weight loss, that doesn't mean you can't lose weight while following it. In fact, one of the main complaints of participants in the DASH study was that they had to eat *too much* food! For instance, a sample dinner might include 3 ounces of baked cod, 1 cup of rice, 1/2 cup of broccoli, 1/2 cup of stewed tomatoes, a small spinach salad, one whole wheat dinner roll with a teaspoon of margarine, and 1/2 cup of melon balls.

Thus, it's quite likely you'll lose a few pounds on DASH without even trying. But if you are trying, some simple substitutions can make a big difference in your overall calorie intake. Couple that with an increase in your physical activity as called for in the DASH-Plus Plan, and you should see the pounds drop.

> Easy DASH Diet Substitutions

if you usually have	try instead	calories saved
orange juice	mandarin-flavored seltzer water	104
popcorn with 2 tablespoons butter	unbuttered, air-popped popcorn	200
canned fruit cocktail in heavy syrup	canned fruit cocktail in extra-light syrup	65
eggs	egg substitute	50
2 tablespoons ranch dressing on salad	lemon juice and tarragon	148
chocolate ice cream	low-fat, low-sugar chocolate frozen yogurt	87
mocha frappaccino	regular coffee	420
vegetables with sauce	vegetables with herbs	105

10 Essential Steps to Losing Weight

Follow the steps below—all proven to help you lose weight and keep it off—and watch the pounds, along with your blood pressure, drop.

1 Stick to real foods. If you make fruits, vegetables, fish, poultry, and even meat the mainstays of your diet and eschew processed foods, including cakes, chips, candy, and stripped-of-nutrients grains, you'll find the pounds dropping with little or no effort.

2 Forget about the fat. It's not the fat that makes you fat, but the calories. And some fat, particularly omega-3 fatty acids and the monounsaturated fats found in olive oil and many nuts, provide significant health benefits. Plus, if you compare the calorie content of regular and low-fat versions of the same foods, you'll find there's often little or no difference. Ultimately, as you know, losing weight is all about calories.

3 Pay attention to portions. American portions have morphed from normal to super-size in the past 20 years, yet we've kept right on cleaning our plates as if our mothers were still standing over us. And it's not just Big Gulps and Biggie fries; consider that identical recipes in old and new editions of classic cookbooks such as *The Joy of Cooking* or those for tollhouse cookies yield fewer servings today than in the past. If you train yourself to eat half or even three-quarters of what's put in front of you, and eat it slowly so your brain gets the message that you're full, you'll find the pounds slipping off effortlessly.

4 Eat breakfast every day. Studies find it's a sure step to weight loss. The best breakfast includes some kind of high-fiber food, such as whole-grain toast or cereal; a protein food, such as peanut butter or low-fat cheese; and a piece of fruit.

5 Never let yourself get hungry. If you're starving, you're going to eat whatever is available as quickly as you can get it. If you keep packets of peanuts, small cartons of yogurt, cubes of cheese, and other healthy snacks at home or in the office (or even in the car) and have a snack midway between meals, you'll take the edge off your hunger and be able to wait until you have a healthier meal option instead of scarfing down that bag of pork rinds.

6 Go for low energy density. One of the newest buzzwords in weight-loss circles is energy density, or how much water a food contains. The higher the water content, the lower the energy density. The lower the energy density, the more you can eat and the fuller you'll feel, while consuming far fewer calories than if you chose a food with higher energy density. For example, you can have a bowl of condensed chicken soup for the same number of calories found in an ounce of pretzels. We guarantee the soup will stick with you longer.

7 Monitor your liquids. The average American consumes an extra 245 calories a day from soft drinks. That's nearly 90,000 calories a year. Divide that by the 3,500 calories it takes to gain or lose a pound of fat, and you could lose 25 pounds a year just by switching from Coke to water or fat-free milk.

8 Think about why you're eating. Too often, we reach for food as a way to assuage a hunger that has nothing to do with our stomachs. Food soothes hurt feelings, comforts us when we're sad, and releases frustration when we're having a bad day at work. But this emotional eating, or unconscious eating, packs on the pounds with almost hideous efficiency. The next time you find yourself reaching for the Ben & Jerry's, stop and think about why you want to eat it. Maybe taking a bath, writing in your journal, or even going for a walk would help you cope with those feelings better than the butterfat.

9 Write it down. That means every bite you put into your mouth. People who are successful at weight loss keep an accurate food diary even after they've reached their goals. They write down every morsel that enters their mouths, from a can of soda to a bag of pretzels.

10 Up your movement. The formula for weight loss is simple: Calories in must be fewer than calories out. Other than starving yourself (proven time and time again to fail as a weight-loss approach), your best bet is to move more. Look for hidden opportunities for activity, such as going to the bathroom upstairs instead of the one down the hall, buying a push mower and ditching the riding one, and using a snow shovel rather than a snow blower.

Six Steps Beyond Food

What you eat—and how much you eat of it—are not the only contributors to high blood pressure, nor is changing them the only way to control it. How you live your life, the way you handle stress, and even what supplements you take all have roles to play. Additionally, for most people with hypertension, medication is a factor.

In the next several pages, we will show you how your day-to-day habits, routines, and reactions can affect your blood pressure, as well as easy ways to tweak them for better health. These will play a role in the DASH-Plus Plan, so read on!

1. Lifestyle and Habits

In a moment, we'll get to the most important lifestyle issues affecting blood pressure—exercise and stress. But first, let's talk about the even more basic topics of sleep, emotions, and habits; the roles they play in your risk of hypertension; and their ability to help you control it.

It should come as no surprise that the most vilified bad habit—smoking—has a deleterious effect on your blood pressure; after all, it's pretty bad for everything else connected with your health. While it does not *cause* high blood pressure, nicotine constricts blood vessels and temporarily raises blood pressure. Smoking also damages arteries, increasing the buildup of plaque and making them less flexible. Even chewing tobacco can make it harder to control your blood pressure.

Other consumption-oriented habits—including drinking alcohol and overindulging in sweets or salty snacks—are also uniformly bad for blood pressure health. As we noted in the last chapter, alcohol is particularly troublesome for blood pressure, as are being overweight and binging on high-salt or high-sugar foods.

FYI *90% of older Americans have a lifetime risk of developing high blood pressure.*

Your emotions also affect your blood pressure. For instance, studies have found that depressed people with high blood pressure have a more difficult time controlling it than those who are not depressed. There are many possible reasons, including the fact that people who are depressed may lose interest in taking their medication and may be less likely to follow the kind of healthy lifestyle necessary to control blood pressure. But researchers suspect there may also be hormonal changes in the brains of people with depression that may affect blood pressure. You don't have to suffer with depression, however. It is eminently treatable with medication and/or therapy.

How well you sleep also makes a difference when it comes to blood pressure control. When researchers deprived 36 people with mild to moderate hypertension of sleep for one night, then compared blood pressure levels after the sleepless night with those following a good night's sleep, they found that both blood pressure and heart rate levels were higher after the sleepless night than after a good snooze. The results, researchers note, suggest that sleepless nights may represent increased risk for both organ damage and acute cardiovascular disease.

We could continue, but the point is simple: A healthy, happy lifestyle contributes to healthy blood pressure. Unlike viral infections or allergies, which have clear external triggers and causes that are out of your control, high blood pressure is almost entirely linked to the daily choices you make.

2. Exercise

It's well established that regular physical activity reduces your risk of all forms of cardiovascular disease. It's less clear whether physical activity on its own lowers blood pressure. But since physical activity is critical to maintaining a healthy weight, and a healthy weight is critical to controlling your blood pressure, we (and all experts) consider exercise and other physical activity to be vital components of any lifestyle program designed to control high blood pressure. Thus, we've made it an important part of the DASH-Plus Plan.

It doesn't take intense physical activity to benefit your health or your weight. Studies have found that moderate-intensity activity is just as beneficial as high-intensity activity when it comes to blood pressure control, a plus for those of us who prefer a brisk walk to a jog. In fact, a review of 16 studies on walking concluded that a moderate walking program (about 30 minutes three to five times a week) reduced systolic and diastolic blood pressure by 2 percent. Even just increasing the amount of physical activity in everyday life—parking at the far end of the parking lot, for example, taking the stairs instead of the elevator, or walking to the store instead of driving—was as effective for reducing blood pressure as a structured aerobic exercise program.

It doesn't take a lot of effort to become physically active. All you need is 30 minutes of moderate activity on most days of the week. In fact, benefits on blood pressure have been noted for those who exercised as few as three times a week, as little as 20 minutes a time. Need some ideas? Check out the chart below.

> ### > Easy Exercise Ideas
>
> *Common Chores*
>
> **Washing and waxing a car for 45–60 minutes**
>
> **Washing windows or floors for 45–60 minutes**
>
> **Gardening for 30–45 minutes**
>
> **Wheeling self in wheelchair for 30–40 minutes**
>
> **Pushing a stroller 1 1/2 miles in 30 minutes**
>
> **Raking leaves for 30 minutes**
>
> **Shoveling snow for 15 minutes**
>
> **Stair walking for 15 minutes**
>
> **Walking 2 miles in 30 minutes (1 mile in 15 minutes)**
>
> *Sporting Activities*
>
> **Playing volleyball for 45–60 minutes**
>
> **Playing touch football for 45 minutes**
>
> **Shooting baskets (basketball) for 30 minutes**
>
> **Dancing fast (social) for 30 minutes**
>
> **Performing water aerobics for 30 minutes**
>
> **Swimming laps for 20 minutes**
>
> **Playing basketball for 15–20 minutes**
>
> **Jumping rope for 15 minutes**
>
> **Running 1 1/2 miles in 15 minutes (1 mile in 10 minutes)**

Source: National Institutes of Health

Also try some popular activities such as yoga and tai chi. Growing evidence suggests these low-intensity exercises may be just as effective as high-intensity workouts for lowering blood pressure. For instance, one study comparing the blood pressure–lowering effects of tai chi with moderate aerobic activity found that both significantly decreased overall blood pressure. Tai chi, of course, is better suited for older, sedentary people, since it doesn't require the same heart rate elevation as aerobic exercises. Several studies have found similar benefits from yoga.

And don't forget resistance training, whether with weights and special equipment or simply with certain floor exercises that work against your body weight. While studies to date don't show any significant improvement in blood pressure from resistance training alone, these muscle-building exercises play an important role in any program to lose weight or maintain a healthy weight.

3. Stress

Are you a Type A or a Type B? A person whose patience is tried by every salesclerk with a room temperature IQ, or a laid-back, take-whatever-comes kind of person? The answer is important when it comes to your blood pressure. A pretty solid body of research supports the commonsense theory that stress, anxiety, and hostility play substantive roles in the development and progression of cardiovascular disease, particularly hypertension.

Researchers have always suspected that stress and anxiety contribute to hypertension, but they're coming to realize more clearly that the effect is due not to the events that cause the stress per se, but rather to the way you react to them.

For instance, researchers involved with the landmark Framingham Heart Study, which has been following residents of Framingham, Massachusetts, for more than 50 years to evaluate their heart health, found that participants who had high levels of anxiety in middle age were twice as likely as those with low anxiety levels to develop hypertension over the following 20 years.

Another study found that young adults who had a strong sense of time urgency and impatience (the kind who blow their horns when they're stuck in a traffic jam), also had a significantly increased risk of developing hypertension later in life. And those who ranked high on hostility tests were 84 percent more likely to develop hypertension 15 years after they were studied than those who ranked lowest.

Physiologically, the stress/personality/blood pressure triumvirate works something like this: When you're stressed, you have the classic "fight or flight" reaction, a throwback to the days when stress meant something life-threatening, not a missed deadline at work. The human body, however, reacts to modern stresses in the same ways it did to long-ago dangers. That means that you breathe faster (to bring in more oxygen), and your heart pumps harder (to send extra oxygen to the rest of your body). This combination results in a narrowing of blood vessels and an increase in blood pressure.

In the short term, this reaction won't kill you or even necessarily cause lasting harm. But if you're constantly stressed, anxious, or impatient, a different mechanism kicks in, and you begin breathing more shallowly and quickly. This changes your blood chemistry as more carbon dioxide builds up and you begin retaining more sodium. Combined with the high amounts of sodium most of us get in our daily diets, that sounds like a recipe for high blood pressure—and indeed, studies with animals have found that the combination is enough to generate progressive hypertension in a matter of days.

Now, we know there's no way you can change your personality overnight (although there is evidence that your personality changes as you age). Instead, what seems to work is implementing stress-reducing, mind-body exercises such as meditation and yoga over time to reduce your anxiety levels and curb your impatience. In one study, researchers found that nearly 70 percent of participants with mild to moderate hypertension who used techniques to reduce stress were able to reduce their medication after six weeks; after one year, 55 percent required no medication.

The best place to start is with a phone call to your local hospital. Many hospitals today offer stress-management programs, sometimes at no charge. And they really do work. One analysis of 37 studies that examined the effects of health education and stress management found a 34 percent reduction in deaths from cardiovascular events, a 29 percent reduction in heart attacks, and significant positive effects on dietary and exercise habits, weight, smoking, cholesterol, and blood pressure. Another study found that when people who already had coronary artery disease received stress-management training, they had fewer recurrent coronary events (heart attacks and angina) after five years than those who received only basic care.

> Beat Blood Pressure with Fido

How's this for a fun way to lower your blood pressure? Get a pet. In one study published in 2001, 48 people with hypertension were given either lisinopril (Zestril), a popular prescription medicine for hypertension, or a dog. After six months, their responses to mental stress were measured. The group that had the pets had significantly lower blood pressure changes in reaction to stress than those who received only the drug. Don't try this with a goldfish, however; the researchers speculate that the increased social support that pet ownership provides was responsible for the reaction, which is something you probably won't get with a fish.

The same social support theory also comes into play with studies linking active religious faith with healthy blood pressure levels—but you have to go to church or synagogue. Just listening to religious services on the radio or watching them on television has no apparent effect.

4. Breathing

Along the same lines as managing stress is the idea that proper breathing is critical to blood pressure control. Slower breathing reflexively leads to a lower heart rate due to a complex set of involuntary nervous connections between the lungs, brain, and heart. Blood pressure, among other things, is a function of heart rate, so when your heart rate decreases, so does your blood pressure. In addition, taking longer, deeper breaths allows more blood to

return to the heart because of changes in the pressure in the chest. This means that your heart doesn't have to work as hard to move blood from the arteries to the veins and back again.

The focus on breathing in many stress-reduction exercises may be one reason that numerous studies find a correlation between calming practices such as meditation and blood pressure reductions.

Now there's actually an FDA-approved, over-the-counter device to help you breathe properly. It's called RESPeRATE, and clinical trials have found that it reduces blood pressure solely through breathing exercises. The battery-operated device, about the size of a paperback book, costs about $299 and is available in various retail outlets as well as from the company's website, www.resperate.com.

In several small studies, people who used the device for 15 minutes a day had sustained blood pressure reductions within eight weeks, with no side effects. It works like this: You slip an elastic belt attached to a respiration sensor around your stomach over your clothes, then put on headphones. The device automatically analyzes your individual breathing pattern and creates a personalized guiding "melody" composed of two distinct tones: one for inhaling and one for exhaling. As you listen to the melody, you synchronize your breathing with the tones until you are breathing in the "therapeutic zone."

Now, we're not suggesting that buying and using RESPeRATE will solve your blood pressure problems. We are suggesting that you consider incorporating the device into your weekly routine as part of the DASH-Plus Plan, particularly if you're unable to integrate other relaxation/breathing techniques such as meditation into your week.

5. Supplements

We talked quite a bit in the previous chapter about the role of individual nutrients in maintaining healthy blood pressure. Ideally, you'll get these nutrients—vitamin C, calcium, magnesium, potassium, and CoQ10—from the foods you eat. As we noted, though, depending on your diet, you may want to talk to your doctor about taking them in supplement form. At a minimum, consider taking a good-quality multivitamin with minerals each day as a low-cost, no-risk insurance policy to make sure you get all the nutrients you need.

In addition to supplemental nutrients, certain herbs have been used throughout history to control blood pressure. We list several below. A word of warning: Don't try any of these or other herbs or supplements without first talking to your health care provider. Some may interact with prescription medications you're already taking.

In addition to garlic, which we discussed on page 290, some of the more common herbal preparations believed to lower blood pressure include:

Black cumin seeds. Extracts of this herb have a long history of use in folk medicine as diuretic and blood pressure–lowering agents, and animal studies have found that cumin has actions comparable to those of common diuretics, such as furosemide (Lasix) and nifedipine (Adalat).

Coleus. The active ingredient in this herb is forskolin, a substance that relaxes muscles, thus providing a relaxing effect for arteries. However, it may interact with blood thinning medications such as warfarin (Coumadin).

Hawthorn. This herb contains combinations of chemicals that improve the heart's pumping action and dilate coronary blood vessels. Give it time, though; it may take up to four weeks before you see any effect. Also be careful with the dosage; too much could cause a dangerous drop in blood pressure.

FYI. Among Americans ages 20 to 74, the following have high blood pressure:

25.2% of Caucasian men and 20.5% of Caucasian women
36.7% of African-American men and 36.6% of African-American women
24.2% of Hispanic men and 22.4% of Hispanic women.

Indian snakeroot. Forget the common perception of snakeroot as a hoax. This herb is cultivated especially for the medicinal use of its 30 phytochemicals, many of which have antihypertensive properties. They are believed to work by controlling nerve impulses along certain pathways that affect heart and blood vessels, thus lowering blood pressure. Several clinical studies have shown significant reductions in blood pressure when various extracts were used.

Olive leaf extract. This herb contains several phytochemicals, including oleuropein, a complex structure of flavonoids, and other chemicals that act as vasodilators, opening blood vessels and thus lowering blood pressure and preventing angina attacks. In one study of 30 people with hypertension who received the extract for three months, all had a statistically significant decrease in blood pressure, with no side effects.

Stevia. This perennial South American shrub has leaves that are naturally sweet. While stevia has been widely used as a sweetener and flavor enhancer for centuries, its legal status in the United States is confused and controversial: allowed as a dietary supplement, but banned as a sweetener. Animal studies have shown that stevia may lower blood pressure, and tests on people have generally been positive as well. Stevia appears to have three positive effects. First, it contains several chemicals that cause blood vessels to widen. Second, it may improve the muscle tone of the heart. Third, it promotes the loss of water from the body.

6. Medication

One of the greatest success stories in the history of health care has been the dramatic decline in deaths from heart disease in this country over the past 30 years. Some of that is due to healthier living—the number of people who smoke, for instance, has dropped from 42 percent in 1965 to 22 percent in 2001—but much of it is a result of discovering better treatments for heart disease and the precursor conditions that contribute to it, such as high cholesterol and high blood pressure.

Nowhere has this been more successful than in the treatment for hypertension. Today, more Americans take prescription medications for hypertension than for any other medical condition.

If you fall into the category of Stage 1 hypertension—with systolic blood pressure of 140 to 159 mmHg or diastolic pressure of 90 to 99 mmHg—talk to your doctor about trying the DASH-Plus Plan first, before starting on any medication. Chances are, he will be happy to let you go ahead. If, after six months, you still exhibit consistently high blood pressure, or if you have Stage 2 hypertension (a systolic reading of 160 or higher or a diastolic reading of 100 or higher), you're likely to need a bit more help in the form of medication. In fact, most patients with hypertension eventually require two or more drugs to control it.

This doesn't mean that you or the DASH-Plus Plan have failed. It just means that given your genetic history and your individual health status, altering your lifestyle and diet alone isn't enough to get you into the safe zone. For instance, if you have diabetes, organ damage, or other cardiovascular risk factors, your doctor is going to be much more aggressive in treating you than if your only health problem were hypertension. Also, if you're African-American, chances are you'll need to take at least two blood pressure medications, since studies find that blacks don't respond as well to single-agent pharmaceutical therapy as other ethnic groups.

An important note: This doesn't mean you should stop following the DASH-Plus Plan. Every study ever conducted shows additional benefits from the kind of lifestyle changes included in the plan compared with simply taking medication alone. Taking blood pressure medication without implementing a healthier lifestyle is like being treated for lung cancer without quitting smoking. It just makes no sense.

Keep making the recipes in this book, maintain your activity levels, and look for ways to moderate your reaction to stress. At the same time, adhere strictly to the medication schedule that your doctor prescribes. Here's what you need to know about current and future treatments for hypertension.

Making Sense of the Medication Maze

A word about control: In the world of hypertension, the idea is to "get to goal." That means a fairly stable blood pressure of less than 140/90 mmHg, or less than 130/80 mmHg if you have diabetes or kidney disease. Because most people will automatically reach the diastolic goal if they can meet the systolic goal, the focus is usually on that first number.

Today, doctors have a plethora of pharmaceuticals to get you there, most divided among four main categories, plus two emerging categories.

Diuretics. Long considered the first step in any medical management of hypertension, diuretics, which help your body get rid of excess fluid and sodium, fell out of favor in the 1990s as newer drugs were introduced. But the medical community got a major wakeup call in the spring of 2000 with publication of the results of the Antihypertensive and Lipid-Lowering Treatment to Prevent Heart Attack Trial (ALLHAT), designed to evaluate the possible superiority of three newer classes of drugs—alpha-blockers, calcium channel blockers, and angiotensin-converting enzyme (ACE) inhibitors—over diuretics in lowering blood pressure and preventing coronary heart disease in high-risk hypertensive people 55 and older.

The results were so astounding that researchers halted one part of the trial early after finding that the risk of combined cardiovascular events was more than 25 percent greater in people treated with the alpha-blocker doxazosin (Cardura) than in those treated with a "thiazide" type of diuretic. It's no wonder then, that between 1999 and 2002, annual new alpha-blocker prescription orders dropped by 26 percent, dispensed prescriptions declined by 22 percent, and physician-reported drug use fell by 54 percent.

Then, in December 2002, another study from the same trial, which was published in the *Journal of the American Medical Association,* showed that diuretics were more likely than calcium channel blockers and ACE inhibitors to prevent heart failure and strokes, especially among African-Americans.

What does this mean to you? Well, if you're taking blood pressure medication but aren't taking a thiazide-type diuretic, talk to your doctor about adding such a drug to your regimen.

Although ALLHAT evaluated only thiazide diuretics, other classes of diuretics include loop diuretics, such as Lasix, and potassium-sparing diuretics, such as amiloride (Midamor).

Beta-blockers. This class of drugs, which includes such popular prescription drugs as atenolol (Tenormin), metoprolol (Lopressor), and propranolol (Inderal), work by slowing your heartbeat, thus relaxing blood vessels.

ACE inhibitors. Angiotensin-converting enzyme inhibitors work by blocking the action of a chemical called angiotensin II, which is responsible for narrowing blood vessels and raising blood pressure.

Calcium channel blockers. Although these drugs are prescribed for hypertension, there is no clear evidence that they reduce either death or complications from cardiovascular disease. They work by relaxing the tone of the muscles in blood vessels so they dilate better. Generally, you shouldn't be taking a calcium channel blocker for hypertension unless all other classes of medication—diuretics, ACE inhibitors, and beta-blockers—have failed to control your pressure.

Angiotensin-II receptor blockers (ARBs). The drugs in this newer class of antihypertensives work somewhat like ACE inhibitors but don't lead to the accumulation of the enzyme bradykinin, which can cause coughing. Expect your doctor to consider an ARB if you are unable to tolerate an ACE inhibitor.

Selective aldosterone receptor antagonists. The first approved drug in this new class is named eplerenone (Inspra). It is used primarily in people with heart failure or as an additional medication to treat hypertension that doesn't improve with other medications. One study found that Inspra was as effective as a popular calcium channel blocker in treating systolic hypertension.

The DASH-Plus Plan

And now, without further ado, the star of our show, the program that can save lives, the meals that will thrill, the hardest-working health advice in show biz…ladies and gentlemen, the DASH-Plus Plan!

Seriously now. In the next several pages, we'll show you exactly how to use the recipes in this book, as well as the knowledge you gained in the previous chapters, to lower your blood pressure safely, substantially, and permanently—without drugs. Do that, and *you* are worthy of a Hollywood spectacular!

Getting Ready

Our plan goes several steps beyond the clinically proven DASH diet to incorporate physical activity, breathing exercises, and stress reduction into one comprehensive program that should enable you to lower your blood pressure by at least 10 percent in as soon as two weeks, if you implement the entire plan at once.

That said, though, we recommend that you take a more measured approach to the DASH-Plus Plan. Your first goal might be to lower your blood pressure quickly, but your real aim should be to keep it down for the rest of your life. By slowly and incrementally introducing the skills and practices of the plan, you make it that much more likely that it will be the last health program you'll ever have to use.

In fact, to help make your efforts even more successful, we offer the following suggestions for preparing for the plan.

- **Sorry, but if you smoke, don't start the plan until you've quit**. Use whatever works for you—cold turkey; the patch, lozenges, nasal spray, or gum; medication; or support groups or talk therapy. We didn't include this as an official part of the DASH-Plus Plan because without quitting, much of it would be wasted. Need a motivation beyond improving your health? A pack-a-day smoker who pays $3 a pack can expect to save more than $1,000 per year. If you're paying $7 a pack, as some do, your savings shoot up to $2,500.

If you're in the process of quitting, don't worry too much about your weight while doing the DASH-Plus Plan. You may actually find yourself gaining some weight as you stop smoking. That's okay. Quitting smoking is the most important thing you can do right now for your blood pressure; it's even more important than losing weight. Later, once you've successfully kicked the habit, you can focus your attention on weight loss.

- Another item we didn't include in the DASH-Plus Plan, but one we recommend, is **an appointment with your doctor**. Let the doctor know you are launching a serious effort to get your blood pressure into a healthy range, now and forever. You'll want some benchmark measurements as well as your physician's best advice and perspective, particularly when it comes to any medications you're taking.

  Talk to your doctor about whether an ambulatory blood pressure test, which tracks your blood pressure over a 24-hour period instead of just one or two isolated times at the medical office, is a good idea. Depending on your age, you may also want to ask for an electrocardiogram to test your current heart health, or, if you're a woman, an exercise stress test, which has been shown to be the most effective noninvasive test for identifying nonsymptomatic heart disease in women.

Other tests to consider include urinalysis; blood glucose levels; and hematocrit, serum potassium, creatinine, and calcium blood tests. You probably also need a lipid profile after a 9- to 12-hour fast to measure your cholesterol and triglyceride levels. Together, these will provide a good overview of your health, including your heart and kidney health and your risk of diabetes.

Tell your doctor what you're planning to do to control your blood pressure; you may even want to take this book to your appointment. Ask if you can have a try at lowering your blood pressure with lifestyle changes first, without medication. If you're already taking medication, let your doctor know your plans so he can track your progress and reduce your dosages as necessary.

- On your way home from the doctor's office, stop at a drugstore and **pick up a home blood pressure monitoring device**. Just as a scale can help you keep tabs on your weight and make minor adjustments, regular blood pressure monitoring can send you a signal that it's time to exercise more or cut down on salt or stress.

- Next, it's time to **clean out the kitchen**. Pack a box with all the high-sodium, prepared, and canned foods in your pantry and donate them to a food bank. Ditto with bags of chips and boxes of cookies, cakes, Pop Tarts, and other nutritionally empty—yet calorie dense—foods. Rid your freezer of the same types of food, but throw them away. This may seem wasteful at first,

but if the food's not in your house, it won't tempt you.

- Then **make your shopping list**. The two-week daily food plan below will give you a good start with your new eating pattern and help you stock the essentials of a healthy pantry. Fill your list with lots of fruits and vegetables (pick up at least two of each that you've never tried before), and be sure that any starches you buy—bread, pasta, or rice—are whole grain. While you're at the store, hit the spice aisle. Buy five kinds that don't already live in your spice cabinet. How about Spanish paprika? Or turmeric? Or cumin? What about coriander, star anise, or lemongrass? Also pick up three different kinds of onions and two types of garlic for seasoning. Try a jar of minced garlic for quick meals when you don't feel like lugging out the cutting board.

- If you have the money to spare, we strongly recommend that you **buy a RESPeRATE device** (discussed on page 303). You can order it online at www.resperate.com, or you may be able to find it at a major retail outlet. Research has proven that it can greatly help reduce your blood pressure and overall heart health.

- The only other equipment you'll need is a pair of **well-fitting walking shoes** and some **comfortable workout clothes**. Oh, and a few sharp pencils, a notebook, and lots of copies of the logs that appear on page 310, so you can track your progress and remember the different components of the plan.

> ## > Surprising Sources of Salt

Watch out for cured foods, such as olives, bacon, and lunchmeats; pickled vegetables, including pickles and sauerkraut; condiments, including mustard, ketchup, horseradish, and barbecue sauce; smoked seafood, such as smoked oysters, clams, or salmon; and seasoning blends. All can be high in sodium.

> The Plan

And here we are: the 10-step DASH-Plus Plan. Here are the actions you should take to maximize your fight against high blood pressure, now and forever:

1 Follow the DASH diet program. Specifically, make sure your daily diet is made up of the following:

- Seven to eight servings of whole grains or grain products
- Four to five servings of vegetables
- Four to five servings of fruit
- Two to three servings of low-fat or fat-free dairy products
- No more than two servings of meat, poultry, or fish
- No more than three servings of fat (butter, oil, or mayonnaise)
- Eight or more glasses of water

In addition, your weekly diet can include:

- Four to five servings of nuts, seeds, and legumes
- No more than five servings of sweets (cookies, brownies, cakes, candy, and soda)

2 Make 90 percent of your diet fresh foods that have no added sodium or salt. That means foods that are as close as possible to their natural state. Packaged foods, such as potato chips, frozen dinners, breaded chicken nuggets, processed breakfast cereals, and boxed macaroni and cheese, should make up 10 percent of your diet at most. Thus, instead of using Hamburger Helper to doctor up ground turkey, use your own ingredients, such as whole-wheat pasta, diced fresh tomatoes, and reduced-fat cheddar cheese.

3 Reduce your reliance on the salt-shaker. Use lemon juice, salt substitutes, dried garlic, or other savory seasonings in place of salt.

4 Limit alcohol. Women should have no more than one drink a day, and men two a day.

5 Get 30 minutes or more of aerobic activity at least five days a week. That means exercising hard enough to increase your heart rate but not so hard that it affects your ability to talk. Ideally, taking a 30-minute walk or two 15-minute walks daily is the easiest, most uncompli-cated way to reach this goal.

6 Do at least two 15-minute sessions of strength training a week. If you don't belong to a gym, purchase an exer-cise video that includes resistance exercises or buy a set of hand weights at Wal-Mart and spent 15 minutes every other day using them. Also, sometime within the next three months, take a class in a new activity, such as yoga or tai chi, both of which have been shown to reduce blood pressure.

7 Each morning and evening, spend 5 minutes in a quiet room alone, with no distractions. The goal is to relax, purge any anxiety about the day ahead or day behind, recharge your energy, and clear your mind. You can meditate or just focus on your breathing. A good way to stay focused is to light a candle and stare into its flame, letting your thoughts wash through your mind without agitating you.

8 Do a daily breathing exercise. If you purchased a RESPeRATE, use it for 15 minutes a day for the next eight weeks, then just three times a week. If you start to see your blood pressure rise, begin using it daily again. If you didn't get one, do 15 minutes of focused breathing each day. Concentrate on lengthening the exhale, not the inhale. Exhale slowly until you are at the point of tensing up to force out the last bit of air. Let your lungs reinflate natu-rally, then repeat the lengthy exhale. Do this anywhere, anytime. Over the coming weeks, see if you detect a slowing in your breathing as a result of these exercises.

9 Each day, take three conscious actions to reduce stress and anxiety. These could include:

THE DASH-PLUS PLAN

- Taking a short walk
- Doing a calming exercise, be it yoga or golf
- Stepping outdoors for a few minutes and stretching
- Putting on soothing, personal music in the morning or at night rather than watching TV
- Driving calmly in the right lane rather than weaving your way to work
- Giving extra hugs and kisses to your spouse or children
- Phoning a friend for a short chat
- Responding to hostility, anger, or provocation with calm and humor
- Making yourself a cup of tea and taking 15 slow minutes to drink it to reward yourself for completing a tough task
- Turning off the car radio and driving in silence

Small steps like these add up to a healthier, calmer attitude far more quickly than you would expect. By consciously saying a few times a day, "I'll take the calm choice here," you can greatly improve your blood pressure and overall health.

10 **Track your efforts every day for the next six weeks.** Make copies of the DASH-Plus Daily Tracker on page 310 and check off your daily food portions, as well as your exercise and lifestyle efforts. At the end of each week, take your blood pressure, then pour yourself a glass of wine (if you drink) or sparkling cider and go over your week. Where did you succeed? Where do you need to put more effort? How did your blood pressure change? Use the information to plan the coming week.

Tips for the Plan

Now that you've seen the plan, it seems so easy, doesn't it? You can do it all, starting immediately, right? Wrong. Changing your diet takes time and commitment. So does exercising. So does relaxing. Here is advice for making the plan work its very best for you.

> **Introduce the steps into your life one at a time.** Unlike many other health programs, this isn't a "12 weeks and you're done" plan. Each of the 10 steps in the DASH-Plus Plan presents a task that is worthy of doing for a lifetime. Relax. You're in no rush. What matters is that you learn to practice good eating, healthy movement, and a healthy lifestyle the right way, so you never have to learn it again.

> **Start with the most important part:** Steps one and two, which focus on healthy eating. Learn the DASH diet. Figure out how to make it a reality for you. Practice the recipes and cooking techniques in this book. Learn how to order a healthy restaurant meal or choose a snack that's good for you.

> **Begin implementing some of the next steps.** We recommend that you start the aerobic exercise step, which calls for you to walk for 30 minutes a day five days a week. Perhaps you can also work in some breathing exercises. Stay with it until they have become a routine, natural part of your day.

> **Start making the anti-stress choices we recommend.** If everything's progressing well, then perhaps it's a good time to work on issues of stress and anxiety. Take your time. Make a habit out of having a positive, peaceful attitude.

> **Strength training may be the last big step.** While it's far more fun and rewarding than many nonexercisers think, it's also the DASH-Plus step that's hardest to make a habit.

> **Along the way, write, write, write.** Make enough copies of the logs we've provided for six weeks of writing and put them in a notebook. Each evening before bed, fill one out. We're talking about 30 seconds of work. Merely thinking each day about your desire to lower your blood pressure will help you succeed.

> **Look for encouragement.** It's helpful to follow this program with someone else, such as your spouse or a friend. The two of you can compare progress, hold little contests (who ate the most vegetables this week, for example), and, best of all, walk together. If you can't find a DASH-Plus partner at home or in your neighborhood, how about inviting a long-distance friend or relative to follow the plan with you? Send your buddy a copy of this book to get started, then follow each other's progress via e-mail and phone.

> **It gets easier.** Understand that the longer you do this and the lower you see your blood pressure go, the easier it will be for you to continue. Nothing feeds success like success.

The Rest of Your Life

Just as we'll never again live in a world without terrorism, you will never again live in a world without high blood pressure. There is no cure for hypertension. Nevertheless, just as we've learned to live with the threat of terrorism through stepped-up security measures and increased surveillance, you can learn to live with your blood pressure, all the while controlling it so it does no real damage to your body.

Don't take this analogy too far, though. Unlike the constant vigilance needed by those who watch for terrorists, eating and living for healthy blood pressure should provide loads of pleasure. Healthy meals should and can be utterly delicious, as the recipes in this book prove! Exercising and achieving calm make you feel young and vibrant. Follow the DASH-Plus Plan, and the benefits won't be merely statistical. You will feel healthier, more upbeat, and more alive than ever!

There's more good news: Researchers are becoming even more aggressive in their hunt for the causes and effects of, as well as treatments for, high blood pressure. You can expect announcements of better drugs and other treatments for years to come. If you work in close conjunction with your doctor, you'll realize that there has never been so much hope for managing high blood pressure easily and effectively.

So continue the DASH-Plus Plan. Eat healthfully and pleasurably. Visit your doctor regularly for checkups, and monitor

your blood pressure carefully (get a home monitor if you can).Your health—and your life—are worth it.

Two Weeks of Great Eating

To help you understand the DASH approach to eating, we've prepared sample menus for two weeks, using several of the recipes in this book but also including several grab-bag meals. The meals for each day in this sample plan provide roughly 1,800 to 2,000 calories—a level appropriate for a woman to maintain or slowly lose weight.

If you actually want to eat according to this plan, terrific! We're sure you will be delighted by the mix of flavors. If you want to try it for just one day, that's great, too. But even if you have no interest in following such a meal plan, read through it. Having good intuition about how much food to eat in a day is crucial to mastering the DASH diet and to using food to best effect for lowering blood pressure.

In addition to the meals listed below, plan on having two snacks a day. Try to choose snacks that combine complex carbohydrates with protein and add up to roughly 100 calories. Some choices:

- A handful of peanuts with a sliced pear
- A cube of reduced-fat cheese with a cut-up apple
- 1 cup fat-free vanilla yogurt with cut-up grapes and cherries added
- 1 cup low-fat, low-sugar frozen yogurt with 1 tablespoon chocolate sauce and 1 banana
- 1 package low-sodium, low-fat microwave popcorn
- Pecan Icebox Cookies (page 262) and 1 orange

WEEK ONE >

Day 1

Breakfast

High-Vitality Milk Shake (page 10)

1 slice **whole-wheat toast** spread with 1 teaspoon trans-fat-free, unsalted soft **margarine**

Lunch

Fresh Artichoke and Crab Salad (page 176)

1 cup sliced **strawberries** sprinkled lightly with **confectioners' sugar**

Dinner

4 ounces broiled **pork chop** brushed with **Dijon mustard**

Noodles with Roasted Vegetables (page 176)

1 piece (1 ounce) high-quality **dark chocolate**

Day 2

Breakfast

2/3 cup **bran cereal** with 1/2 cup fat-free **milk**

1 slice **whole-wheat toast** spread with 2 teaspoons **jelly**

1 medium **banana**

Lunch

Chicken Salad Sandwich made with:

- 2 slices toasted **whole-wheat bread**
- 3/4 cup **chicken salad** (homemade without salt)
- 2 tablespoons **mustard**

1 cup mixed sliced **cucumbers** and **tomatoes** with fat-free **ranch dressing**

1/2 cup canned **fruit cocktail** (no added sugar)

Dinner

3 ounces **lean roast beef**

2 tablespoons low-fat **gravy**

Sesame Stir-Fried Asparagus and Peas (page 196)

1 small **baked potato** with:

- 2 tablespoons fat-free **sour cream**
- 1 tablespoon chopped **scallions**
- 1 small **whole-wheat roll**

1 small **apple**

1 cup fat-free **milk**

Day 3

Breakfast

Sweet Couscous (page 16)

1/2 cup mixed **fruit salad**

1 scrambled **egg**

Lunch

Roast beef sandwich made with:

- 2 slices **whole-wheat bread**
- 1 teaspoon Dijon mustard
- 2 ounces roast beef
- 1 slice reduced-fat **provolone cheese**
  Lettuce
  Sliced **tomato**

1 cut-up **apple**

Dinner

Spaghettini with Seafood (page 108)

Spinach salad (spinach, grated carrots, and sliced mushrooms) with low-fat dressing

Sliced **tomato** sprinkled with 1 tablespoon crumbled **feta cheese**

1 cup canned **pears**

Day 4

Breakfast

1/2 cup instant or regular **oat-meal** made with 1/3–1/2 cup fat-free **milk** and a sprinkling of **cinnamon**

1 small **whole-wheat bagel** spread with 1 tablespoon fat-free **cream cheese**

1 **banana**

1 cup fat-free **milk**

Lunch

Chicken sandwich made with:

2 slices **whole-wheat bread**

1 tablespoon low-fat **mayonnaise**

3 ounces **chicken breast**

1 slice reduced-fat American **cheese**

Lettuce

Sliced **tomato**

1 **peach**

1 cup **apple juice**

Dinner

Crispy Tuna Steaks in Citrus Sauce (page 107)

Pan-Roasted New Potatoes with Garlic (page 195)

Steamed **carrots** sprinkled with **thyme** and **rosemary**

Garden salad (romaine lettuce and **assorted vegetables** with **low-fat dressing**)

Day 5

Breakfast

Pecan Waffles with Maple, Pear, and Blackberry Sauce (page 24)

1 **orange**

1 cup fat-free **milk**

Lunch

Greek Chicken Pitas (page 83)

Carrot sticks with fat-free **ranch dressing** for dipping

1 cup fat-free **milk**

Dinner

Speedy Two-Bean Chili (page 240)

1 cup **pear and walnut salad** (**lettuce, sliced pear,** and **toasted walnuts**) sprinkled with 2 tablespoons grated reduced-fat cheddar cheese and 1 tablespoon low-fat vinaigrette

1 small **whole-wheat roll**

Day 6

Breakfast

1 low-fat, whole-grain **granola bar**

1 **banana**

1 cup fat-free fruit **yogurt** (no sugar added)

1 cup fat-free **milk**

Lunch

Turkey sandwich made with:

2 slices **whole-wheat bread**

2 teaspoons low-fat mayon-naise mixed with 1 tablespoon Dijon mustard

3 ounces **turkey breast**

2 slices reduced-fat cheddar cheese

1 large leaf **romaine lettuce**

2 slices **tomato**

1 cup steamed **broccoli**

1 medium **orange**

Dinner

Seared Sirloin with Garden Vegetables (page 66)

1 cup **brown rice**

1 cup steamed **carrots** sprin-kled with **dill**

1 small **whole-wheat roll** spread with 1 teaspoon trans-fat-free, unsalted soft **margarine**

1 cup fat-free **milk**

Day 7

Breakfast

1 **hard-boiled egg** mashed with 1 tablespoon reduced-fat **mayonnaise**

2 slices **whole-wheat bread**

1 cup **fruit salad**, fresh or canned in its own juices

1 cup fat-free **milk**

Lunch

Cream of Leek and Potato Soup (page 227)

1 **whole-wheat roll** with 1 teaspoon trans-fat-free, unsalted soft **margarine**

Spinach salad with sliced **tomatoes** sprinkled with 1 ounce toasted **pine nuts**

1 cup fat-free **milk**

Dinner

Classic Grilled Dover Sole (page 110)

Steamed **green beans** sprinkled with **almonds**

1 cup **rice pilaf**

Sautéed **squash** with **lemon juice**

1/2 cup sliced **strawberries**

WEEK TWO >

Day 8

Breakfast

1 cup fat-free **yogurt** (no sugar added) blended with 1 **banana,** 1/2 cup **strawberries,** and 1 teaspoon **honey**

1 slice **whole-wheat bread** spread with 1 tablespoon **peanut butter**

1 **orange**

Lunch

Tuna sandwich made with:

Water-packed **tuna**

2 tablespoons fat-free **mayonnaise**

2 stalks chopped **celery**

2 slices **whole-wheat bread**

1 leaf **lettuce**

2 slices **tomato**

1 ounce baked low-salt **chips**

1/2 cup **grapes**

1 cup fat-free **milk**

Dinner

Chicken with Apples and Calvados (page 80)

Steamed **broccoli** drizzled with 2 tablespoons fat-free **ranch dressing**

1 cup whole-grain **pasta** with 1 teaspoon trans-fat-free, unsalted soft **margarine,** if desired

Dark **green lettuce salad**

1 cup fat-free **milk**

Day 9

Breakfast

Potato, Corn, and Pepper Frittata (page 20)

1 **orange**

1 cup fat-free **milk**

Lunch

Grilled chicken salad made with:

3 ounces sliced **chicken**

1 chopped **tomato**

1 chopped **apple**

1 bag **salad greens**

2 tablespoons fat-free **dressing**

10 **whole-wheat crackers**

1 cup fat-free **milk**

1 **banana**

Dinner

Shrimp Scampi (page 112)

1 cup **brown rice**

Diced yellow **squash** and **eggplant** sautéed with **garlic** in **olive oil**

Day 10

Breakfast

1 cup **grape juice**

1 cup instant or regular **oatmeal** made with 1/3-1/2 cup fat-free **milk** and 1/4 cup **raisins**

1/4 wedge **cantaloupe**

Lunch

Roast beef sandwich made with:

Whole-wheat **pita**

1 tablespoon Dijon **mustard**

3 ounces **roast beef**

1/2 sliced **tomato**

Lettuce

1 cup fat-free **yogurt** (no sugar added) with 1 cup **mixed fruit,** fresh or canned in its own juices

Dinner

1 cup **whole-wheat pasta** with 1/2 cup low-sodium **marinara sauce**

Salad made with:

1 cup chopped **romaine lettuce**

1/2 cup shredded **carrots**

1/2 cup shredded **red cabbage**

Homemade **vinaigrette** made with **olive oil**

2 slices toasted **Italian bread** brushed with **olive oil** and rubbed with **garlic**

Day 11

Breakfast

2/3 cup high-fiber **cereal** with 1/2 cup fat-free **milk**

1 sliced **banana**

2 slices toasted **whole-grain bread** spread with 1 table-spoon **jam**

Lunch

2 ounces reduced-fat **cheese** with 3 slices **tomato** placed on 1 slice (1 ounce) **whole-wheat bread**, melted open-face under broiler. Add second half of bread to form a sandwich.

Garden salad with **low-fat dressing**

1 cup fat-free **milk**

Dinner

Turkey Cutlets with Pineapple-Cranberry Sauce (page 98)

Nutted Lemon Barley (page 132)

Steamed **broccoli** with **lemon juice**

1 cup fat-free **milk**

Day 12

Breakfast

1 **whole-wheat burrito** sprin-kled with grated reduced-fat **Cheddar cheese** and chopped **tomato**, toasted or microwaved until cheese melts

1/4 wedge **cantaloupe**

1 cup fat-free **milk**

Lunch

Turkey Salad with Red Cabbage (page 175)

Cooked **carrots**

1 sliced **pear**

1 cup fat-free **milk**

Dinner

Linguine with No-Cook Sauce (page 154)

Salad made with:
 1 cup **spinach**
 1 chopped **tomato**
 1 chopped hard-boiled **egg**
 1/2 chopped small **cucumber**
 2 tablespoons fat-free **vinai-grette**

1 cup **fruit salad**, fresh or canned in its own juices

Day 13

Breakfast

Whole-Grain Pancakes with Fresh Fruit and Yogurt (page 23)

1 cup fat-free **milk**

Lunch

Tuna sandwich made with:
 Whole-wheat **pita**
 Water-packed **tuna**
 2 tablespoons fat-free may-onnaise
 2 stalks **celery**, chopped

Spinach salad sprinkled with 2 tablespoons crumbled **feta cheese**

1/2 cup sliced **strawberries**

1 cup fat-free **milk**

Dinner

3 ounces lean **steak**

1 medium **baked potato** with 2 tablespoons fat-free **sour cream**

Lemony Sugar Snap Peas (page 198)

Steamed **broccoli**

Day 14

Breakfast

1 cup **orange juice**

1 cup **oatmeal** made with 1/3–1/2 cup fat-free **milk**

1 **banana**

1 slice **whole-wheat bread** spread with 1 tablespoon **jelly** and trans-fat-free, unsalted soft **margarine**

Lunch

Falafel Pitas (page 140)

2 cups cut-up **fruit** mixed with 1 cup fat-free **yogurt** (no sugar added)

Dinner

Grilled Salmon with Pepper-Corn Relish (page 114)

Steamed **green beans** sprin-kled with **almonds**

Wild Rice with Walnuts (page 131)

Celery spread with low-fat **cream cheese** and sprinkled with **dill**

1 cup fat-free **milk**

Portion Tracker

Whole-grain foods
1 2 3 4 5 6 **7** **8** 9 10

Vegetables
1 2 3 **4** **5** 6 7 8

Fruit
1 2 3 **4** **5** 6 7 8

Low-fat dairy foods
1 **2** **3** 4 5

Meat/poultry/fish
1 **2** 3 4 5

Fats
1 **2** **3** 4 5

Nuts/seeds/legumes
0 **1** 2

Sweets
0 **1** 2

Water
1 2 3 4 5 6 **7** **8** 9 10

Alcohol
0 **1** **2** 3

Today's Progress

Eating

Did I meet the DASH diet portion targets?	Y N
Did I keep my overall food intake at a healthy level?	Y N
Did I do a good job of avoiding packaged foods?	Y N
Did I do a good job of avoiding salty foods?	Y N
Did I enjoy my food?	Y N

Lifestyle

Aerobic exercise?	Y N
Time:_____ Type: _____	
Strength exercise?	Y N
Time:_____	
5-minute morning break?	Y N
5-minute evening break?	Y N
Breathing exercises?	Y N

Anti-stress actions?
1. Y N Action:_____
2. Y N Action:_____
3. Y N Action:_____

My energy rating for today:
1 2 3 4 5

My attitude rating for today:
1 2 3 4 5

My health rating for today:
1 2 3 4 5

Notes

Healthiest thing I did today:
_____
_____
_____

Happiest thing I did today:
_____
_____
_____

For tomorrow:
_____
_____
_____
_____
_____
_____

Health Glossary

Words and terms related to high blood pressure and its treatment

Allicin The chemical responsible for garlic's odor and health effects.

Angina Pain that occurs when insufficient oxygen-carrying blood reaches the heart.

Angiotensin converting enzyme (ACE) inhibitors Drugs that stop production of ACE, a chemical that makes blood vessels narrow.

Anthocyanins Antioxidant flavonoids found in many plant pigments.

Antioxidant A substance that protects cells from the damaging effects of free radicals. Some are made by the body; others, such as vitamins C and E, can be obtained only from food or supplements.

Atherosclerosis A process in which fatty substances build up inside the walls of blood vessels and/or blood components stick to the insides of vessel walls. The vessels narrow and "harden," becoming less flexible (atherosclerosis literally means "hardening of the artery").

Beta-blockers Drugs that lower adrenaline levels.

Beta-carotene One of a group of nutrients known as carotenoids.

Beta-glucan The soluble fiber component of barley and oat bran.

Bromelain An enzyme found in the pineapple plant.

Calcium The most plentiful mineral in the body and a major component of bones, teeth and soft tissues. It is needed for nerve and muscle function, blood clotting, and metabolism, and it plays a role in moderating blood pressure.

Calcium channel blockers Drugs that relax blood vessels and are prescribed for high blood pressure and chest pain.

Calorie The basic unit of measurement for the energy value of food and the energy needs of the body.

Carbohydrates Simple carbohydrates, such as table sugar, bleached flour, and white rice, are foods that are easily digested and converted into glucose. Complex carbohydrates, which make up the bulk of whole grains and vegetables, are starches composed of complex sugars, fiber, and other nutrients. They take longer to digest and have more beneficial components.

Carotenes Yellow and red pigments that color yellow-orange fruits and vegetables and most dark green vegetables. They are among the antioxidants that protect against the effects of aging and disease.

Chlorogenic acid A phytonutrient found in high levels in coffee and shown to increase levels of homocysteine, a marker for heart disease.

Coronary heart disease A disease of the blood vessels of the heart that, if untreated, can cause heart attacks.

Daily Value (DV) The percentages listed on food labels that refer to the recommended daily amounts of vitamins, minerals, and other major nutrients.

Diabetes A disorder of carbohydrate metabolism, characterized by inadequate production or utilization of insulin and resulting in excessive amounts of glucose in the blood and urine. Also known as diabetes mellitus.

Diastolic blood pressure The measurement of the pressure when the left ventricle of the heart relaxes; expressed as the bottom number in a blood pressure reading.

Dietary fiber Indigestible material in food that stimulates peristalsis in the intestine.

Diuretic A substance that causes the body to excrete excess fluid in the form of urine.

Ellagic acid A phytochemical found in 46 different fruits and nuts, such as pomegranates, red raspberries, strawberries, blueberries, and walnuts, that has very strong antioxidant properties.

Essential fatty acids The building blocks that the body uses to make fats.

Estrogen A female sex hormone produced in both sexes, but found in much greater quantities in women.

Fats A class of organic chemicals, also called fatty acids or lipids. When digested, they create nearly double the energy of the same amount of carbohydrates or protein.

Flavonoids Plant pigments that are potent antioxidants.

Forskolin The active ingredient in the herb coleus, it relaxes muscles, thus providing a relaxing effect for arteries.

Free radicals Waste products of oxygen metabolism that can damage cell components.

Glucose A simple sugar that the body converts directly into energy. Blood levels of glucose are regulated by several hormones, including insulin.

Glycemic index A scale of numbers that rates carbohydrate foods according to their effect on blood sugar. There are two scales. In one, 100 represents a glucose tablet, having the most rapid effect on blood sugar. In the other, 100 represents white bread.

Heart attack An injury to the heart that occurs when blood flow to a part of the heart is suddenly cut off, causing permanent damage to the heart muscle.

Hypertension A medical condition in which a person has abnormally high blood pressure, typically defined as 140/90 or higher.

Insulin A hormone that regulates carbohydrate metabolism.

Lignans Phytonutrients found in whole grains and other plant-based foods that may be responsible for some of the health benefits attributed to fiber.

Lutein A phytochemical found in spinach and other dark green leaves.

Lycopene The main pigment in certain fruits, such as tomatoes.

Lysine An amino acid basic to human nutrition.

Macronutrients Nutrients the body requires in large amounts for energy—specifically, carbohydrates, proteins, and fats.

Magnesium A trace mineral needed for healthy bones, the transmission of nerve signals, protein and DNA synthesis, and the conversion of glycogen stores into energy.

Metabolism The body's physical and chemical processes, including conversion of food into energy, that are needed to maintain life.

Micronutrients Essential nutrients that the body needs in only very small amounts.

Monounsaturated fats Fats that are liquid at room temperature and semisolid or solid under refrigeration. They are believed to help protect against heart disease.

Omega-3 fatty acids Polyunsaturated fatty acids essential for normal kidney function that influence various metabolic pathways, resulting in lowered cholesterol and triglyceride levels, inhibited platelet clotting, and reduced inflammatory and immune reactions, as well as lowered blood pressure.

Pectin A type of soluble fiber that regulates intestinal function and can help lower blood cholesterol levels and blood pressure.

Peristalsis Wavelike muscle contracts that help propel food and fluids through the digestive tract.

Phosphorus A mineral needed for healthy bones, teeth, nerves, and muscles and for many bodily functions.

Phthalide A component of celery, 3-n-butyl phthalide, gives this plant its characteristic smell and taste and has blood pressure–lowering properties.

Phytochemicals Compounds found in plants that have various health benefits.

Polyphenols Organic compounds, including tannins, that combine with iron and can hinder its absorption. Found in a number of foods, tea, and red wines.

Polyunsaturated fats Fats containing a high percentage of fatty acids that lack hydrogen atoms and have extra carbon bonds. They are liquid at room temperature.

Potassium A trace mineral needed to regulate fluid balance and many other functions.

Preeclampsia A condition that may occur in women during the second half of pregnancy. Symptoms include high blood pressure, swelling that doesn't subside, and higher-than-normal amounts of protein in the urine. Also known as toxemia.

Protein Part of a large class of chemicals called amino acids. The body uses proteins to build and repair muscles and tissues. They occur in plant foods and are the main component of animal foods such as beef, poultry, seafood, and dairy products.

Quercetin A phytonutrient found in apples and onions that has been linked to healthy heart function.

Renin. A hormone that kidney cells release into the blood as a result of sodium depletion or low blood volume. It converts a particular liver protein into angiotensin, which ultimately helps the body decrease its sodium loss. Angiotensin also causes small blood vessels to constrict, increasing blood pressure.

Resveratrol A phytochemical derived from grape skins.

Saturated fats Lipids with a high hydrogen content; the predominant fat in animal products and other fats that remain solid at room temperature. A high intake of saturated fat is linked to an increased risk of heart disease, certain cancers, and other diseases.

Sodium A trace mineral essential for maintaining fluid balance. It combines with chloride to form table salt.

Soluble fiber Dietary fiber that becomes sticky when wet and dissolves in water.

Sphygmomanometer A machine commonly used by doctors and nurses to measure blood pressure involving an inflatable arm cuff.

Stenosis Narrowing of an artery due to the buildup of plaque on the inside wall of the artery.

Systolic blood pressure A measurement of the pressure when the left ventricle of the heart contracts; expressed as the top number in a blood pressure reading.

Tannins Astringent substance derived from plants that can cause contraction of blood vessels and body tissues.

Triglycerides The most common form of dietary and body fat; high blood levels have been linked to heart disease.

Uric acid The end product of protein when it is metabolized by the body. High uric acid levels contribute to high blood pressure because they can damage the kidneys.

Vitamin C A water-soluble antioxidant vitamin found in citrus fruits and green vegetables.

Vitamin E An important antioxidant found in vegetable oils, whole grain cereals, butter, and eggs.

Zeaxanthin A phytonutrient found in collards, kale, mustard greens, and spinach.

Index

Note: Page references in italics indicate photographs.

About the Authors

Robyn Webb, M.S., (recipe editor) is founder and head of Pinch of Thyme, a healthy-cooking business that offers lessons, catering, and tours, as well as providing nutritional counseling and consulting to corporations and government agencies. She is the author or editor of many health cookbooks, has appeared widely on national television, and has written articles for major newspapers and magazines. Webb received her master's degree in nutrition from Florida State University and has been in the healthy-cooking field for fifteen years.

Jamy D. Ard, M.D., (medical advisor) is an assistant professor in the departments of Nutrition Sciences and Medicine at the University of Alabama at Birmingham, where he conducts research on the dietary management of blood pressure and obesity. He is the co-author of several research papers on nutritional science. He received his medical degree from Duke University Medical Center.

Debra L. Gordon (writer) has contributed to several Reader's Digest health books, including *Allergy & Asthma Relief* and *Cut Your Cholesterol.* She has been a professional health writer and editor for more than fifteen years, eight of them as a reporter for such newspapers as the *Virginian-Pilot* and the *Orange County Register.* She has written or contributed to more than twenty books, and her articles have appeared in dozens of magazines, including *Family Circle, Good Housekeeping, Prevention,* and *BusinessWeek.*

Books of related interest from Reader's Digest

Eat to Beat Diabetes

Vegetables for Vitality

Eat Well, Stay Well

Taking Charge of High Blood Pressure

Cut Your Cholesterol